WHY SCHOOLS MATTER

WHY SCHOOLS MATTER

*A Cross-National Comparison
of Curriculum and Learning*

William H. Schmidt

Curtis C. McKnight

Richard T. Houang

HsingChi Wang

David E. Wiley

Leland S. Cogan

Richard G. Wolfe

JOSSEY-BASS
A Wiley Company
www.josseybass.com

Published by

JOSSEY-BASS
A Wiley Company
350 Sansome St.
San Francisco, CA 94104

www.josseybass.com

Copyright © 2001 by John Wiley & Sons, Inc.

Jossey-Bass is a registered trademark of John Wiley & Sons, Inc.

Jossey-Bass books and products are available through most bookstores. To contact Jossey-Bass directly, call (888) 378-2537, fax to (800) 605-2665, or visit our website at www.josseybass.com.

Substantial discounts on bulk quantities of Jossey-Bass books are available to corporations, professional associations, and other organizations. For details and discount information, contact the special sales department at Jossey-Bass.

We at Jossey-Bass strive to use the most environmentally sensitive paper stocks available to us. Our publications are printed on acid-free recycled stock whenever possible, and our paper always meets or exceeds minimum GPO and EPA requirements.

Library of Congress Cataloging-in-Publication Data

Why schools matter : a cross-national comparison of curriculum and learning / William H. Schmidt . . . [et al., editors].
    p. cm. — (The Jossey-Bass education series)
Includes bibliographical references and index.
    ISBN 0-7879-5684-8 (alk. paper)
    1. Mathematics—Study and teaching. 2. Science—Study and teaching. 3. Education—Curricula. I. Schmidt, William H. II. Series.

QA11.2 .W538 2001
510'.71—dc21   2001004860

HB Printing   10 9 8 7 6 5 4 3 2

The Jossey-Bass Education Series

For
Keara
Maegan
Chip
Ruth
Alex
Emily
Brent
Alexis
Bradley
QiChen
QiWen

We wrote this book with you and all of
America's children in our thoughts,
knowing that schools do matter.

CONTENTS

LIST OF FIGURES

LIST OF TABLES

PREFACE

CURRENTLY THERE SEEMS to be no lack of material critical of the state of education in the United States, particularly regarding science and mathematics education. We know from many sources that U.S. performance in mathematics and science has not been particularly strong by international standards. Many in the United States have not been pleased with this relatively undistinguished position. Numerous reform efforts have arisen to address various perceived vulnerabilities in our education system. Although some of our previous work has documented the unsatisfying relative performance of U.S. students in mathematics and science, our goal has not been to demean U.S. education, teachers, or students but rather to identify weaknesses in such a way that meaningful and effectual policy could be crafted. What is not needed is yet another book chronicling yet another way that our education system is failing the students it serves. Even less needed is another book that decries the inadequacies of our system without clear and reasonable suggestions for remedial policy direction.

In this book we seek to offer fresh hope and direction to reform efforts by focusing on a fundamental aspect of education accessible and amenable to education policy and change—the curriculum. We document in detail aspects of the mathematics and science curriculum in the United States and other Third International Mathematics and Science Study (TIMSS) countries. In the course of this examination, we've been able to demonstrate very dramatic results on the strength of the relationship of curriculum to learning. The idea that curriculum—that aspect of education specifying what students are expected to study and learn—plays a critical role on the education stage may seem almost laughably obvious to some but has been all but dismissed in much research and many education reform movements. Curriculum is at the very center of intentional learning in schools, specifying content and directing students in their efforts to understand mathematics and science. This, we argue, is *why* schools matter: schools matter because the curriculum-learning opportunities they provide students have a profound impact on the mathematics and science students actually learn.

In this book we examine how curriculum affects student learning through in-depth analyses of information from TIMSS. Certainly in the popular media in particular, the main message communicated concerning TIMSS has related to the horse-race aspect of the ranking of countries' students on the TIMSS mathematics and science assessments. Here we use this information on students to explore more fully the role that curriculum plays in their learning. We begin by presenting and discussing a conceptual model of how curriculum may affect what students learn. We then detail the various ways in which curriculum was measured in TIMSS and how these various curriculum measures differed from one country to another. One of the surprising discoveries documented here was the degree to which different curriculum measures for a single country presented contrasting curriculum portraits. This may well be a reflection of the education system in a country and the way in which the system disseminates curricular policy. Finally we move to formal analyses documenting relationships among curriculum measures and how these are related to what students have learned. The major conclusion to all this work is that even controlling for many student background differences, these curriculum measures are strongly related to what students learn. This is why we believe schools matter and why an important reform effort needs to be directed to detailing a challenging and coherent curriculum across all the years of schooling for all students.

ACKNOWLEDGMENTS

WE GRATEFULLY ACKNOWLEDGE the International Association for the Evaluation of Educational Achievement (IEA), under whose auspices the Third International Mathematics and Science Study (TIMSS) was conducted. We would not have been able to write such a book without the dedication of the people within each of the countries that were responsible for collecting the data. We also express our appreciation to the International Study Center at Boston College for its role in the collection of the data and ensuring its quality. The work presented in this work was funded by the National Science Foundation (NSF) through a grant (REC-9550107), and we gratefully acknowledge this support. However, the authors alone assume responsibility for the results and interpretation presented in *Why Schools Matter*.

Two individuals who were instrumental in funding our project are Kenneth Travers (now back at the University of Illinois) and Larry Suter (both NSF officers) who were willing to take a risk in funding a new idea and corresponding methodology for the measurement of curriculum on an international scale—something that had never been done before. Without their courage in terms of providing NSF support, this book and its substance would never have been possible.

Over the last ten years, many people have contributed to different parts of the work presented here. We acknowledge their intellectual contribution and express an appreciation for their involvement. These include Christine DeMars, Gilbert Valverde, Leonard Bianchi, Pamela Jakwerth, Senta Raizen, Ted Britton, and Leigh Burstein.

We also appreciate the supportive work provided by Jacqueline Babcock, Marlene Green, and our cadre of undergraduate and graduate students who helped in the preparation of tables and graphs. These include Christine DeMars, Shelly Naud, Wen-Ling Yang, Maribel Sevilla, Vilma Mesa, Meng-Jia Wu, and Sarah Kuper. We are also grateful to Larry Suter, NSF project director, and Richard Shavelson of Stanford University, who read an earlier draft and made helpful comments. Finally, we express our deep appreciation to Torsten Husen, whom we consider to be the father of the fundamental idea that opportunity to learn is an important component of international educational research.

THE AUTHORS

LELAND S. COGAN is a senior researcher with the U.S. National Research Center for the Third International Mathematics and Science Study (TIMSS) at Michigan State University. He has undergraduate degrees in psychology and microbiology and a doctorate in educational psychology from Michigan State University. He coordinated data collection and analyses for the Survey of Mathematics and Science Opportunities (SMSO), a multinational project that researched and developed the TIMSS's questionnaires. He has collaborated in observational and quantitative studies of educational practices and policy and coauthored several technical reports and articles on TIMSS. He is also one of the authors of a recent book, *Facing the Consequences*, that presents a comprehensive evaluation of U.S. mathematics and science education. Dr. Cogan's research interests include parents' and teachers' beliefs; students' learning and motivation; and instructional practices, particularly as these relate to the learning of mathematics and the sciences.

RICHARD T. HOUANG earned his Ph.D. in psychometrics from the Graduate School of Education, University of California–Santa Barbara. He has been with Michigan State University since 1979. Specializing in educational statistics and psychometrics, he has also taught graduate courses in research methods. He also has spent a lot of time with computing technology at Michigan State University, especially networking and network applications on campus.

Richard joined the U.S. TIMSS National Research Center in 1994. He was heavily involved with a major component of TIMSS, the collection and analysis of more than fourteen hundred documents from fifty countries. Richard has coauthored books, articles, and reports from the U.S. TIMSS Research Center, the most recent of which is *Facing the Consequences: Using TIMSS for a Closer Look at U. S. Mathematics and Science Education*.

Richard is married and has one daughter who is finishing eighth grade. She serves as his motivation for improving our understanding of the educational process.

CURTIS C. MCKNIGHT is currently professor of mathematics at the University of Oklahoma, where he has been since 1981, serving as associate chairman of the mathematics department from 1987 to 1994. He received his Ph.D. from the University of Illinois. He served as national research coordinator and executive director of the U.S. National Center for the Second International Mathematics Study (SIMS). He currently serves as the senior mathematics consultant to the U.S. Research Center for TIMSS and is the author of more than one hundred publications and papers. His specialties include cross-national comparative studies; cognitive studies of mathematics learning and performance; and curriculum policy studies, such as those involved currently in U.S. calculus reform curricula. He has received over twenty research grants and served as consultant on many other projects.

WILLIAM H. SCHMIDT received his undergraduate degree in mathematics from Concordia College in River Forest, Illinois, and his Ph.D. from the University of Chicago in psychometrics and applied statistics. He carries the title of *university distinguished professor* at Michigan State University and the national research coordinator and executive director of the U.S. National Center which oversees U.S. participation in TIMSS. He was also a member of the senior executive staff and head of the office of Policy Studies and Program Assessment for the National Science Foundation in Washington, D.C. from 1986 to 1988. His work has been widely published in numerous journals, including the *Journal of the American Statistical Association, Journal of Educational Statistics, Multivariate Behavioral Research, Journal of Education Psychology, Journal of Educational Measurement, Educational and Psychological Measurement Journal, American Educational Research Journal*, and the *Journal of Curriculum Studies*, and has delivered numerous papers at conferences including those of the American Educational Research Association, Psychometric Society, American Sociological Association, International Reading Association, and National Council of Teachers of Mathematics. He has also coauthored seven books related to the TIMSS. He was awarded an honorary doctoral degree at Concordia University in 1997 and received the 1998 Willard Jacobson Lectureship from The New York Academy of Sciences.

HSINGCHI WANG is a senior researcher at the U.S.-National Center. Dr. Wang also has been involved at the University of Southern California, where she has worked with the Los Angeles Systemic Initiative on designing and evaluating science education reform projects. She received her undergraduate degree in physics from Tunghai University in Taiwan, a master's degree in science education from the University of Southern California, and a Ph.D. in the curriculum and instruction at the University of Southern California School of Education. Her major research areas include historical perspectives in science education reform, curriculum ideology versus science education standards, science instructional materials studies, science education program evaluation, and the relationship between mathematics and science learning. She is also active in research on problem-based learning (PBL) as it applies to various educational sectors. Since 1997, she has been actively engaging in the design of in-service workshops to bridge the gap between educational researchers and school educators using the PBL approach.

DAVID E. WILEY is professor at the School of Education and Social Policy, Northwestern University, and senior technical advisor for the New Standards Project. A statistician and psychometrician by training and early work, much of his recent research and writing has focused on public policy and program evaluation as related to educational testing, teaching-learning processes, and legislative initiatives affecting these aspects of education. He has been involved in international comparative studies of education since 1971 and recently completed (with T.N. Postlethwaite) a volume reporting findings of the second science study of the International Association for the Evaluation of Educational Achievement (IEA). More recently, he has coauthored a volume reporting the findings of the TIMSS international curriculum analysis study in mathematics and the first volume reporting the findings of the TIMSS Survey of Mathematics and Science Opportunity. He has also served on the IEA International Technical Committee, and has been working with the California Assessment System, the states of Delaware and Kentucky, and the New Standards Proj-ect to design and implement new systems based on student performance of extended-response (as opposed to multiple-choice) test tasks. His current research is focused on (1) the implementation of curricular control policies, (2) the determinants and distribution of learning opportunities, (3) the role of standards in large-scale assessment, and on (4) the integration of frameworks for the assessment of learning, ability, and performance. He received an A.B. degree from San Diego State College and an M.S. and a Ph.D. from the University of Wisconsin.

RICHARD G. WOLFE is an associate professor at the Ontario Institute for Studies in Education of the University of Toronto's Department of Curriculum, Teaching, and Learning (Measurement and Evaluation Program). He was the consultant on methodology to the international mathematics committee for SIMS, prepared the databank for the IEA Second International Study of Science (SISS), and contributed to the analysis and reporting for both studies. He was the chair of the sampling and methodology committee for the TIMSS during its initial design stages. He has worked with a number of state assessment programs and with national and international assessment projects in Latin America. His specialties are assessment survey design, sampling, and data analysis.

WHY SCHOOLS MATTER

HOW DOES CURRICULUM AFFECT LEARNING?

SCHOOLS MATTER. This statement is a truism to most. However, it must be followed by a statement of why schools matter, especially in light of the current debate surrounding the quality of American public education. Working from the seemingly simple belief that schools matter, assumptions will be made and policies will follow them on how to improve the quality of public schools. If there is no statement of why schools matter based on empirical data, the assumptions may be wrong and the policies may hinder rather than help improve the quality of public education.

Some have argued that the key to quality education lies with policies concerning students and their characteristics. These policies lead to practices such as grouping students into tracks so the "right" students get the "right" opportunities. This type of practice is based on the belief that socioeconomic status, parents' education, student aptitude, and other background factors are more important to students' achievement than what happens in schools.[1] In short, according to this belief schools matter only if the right students are in the right classes at the right time, and this is true no matter how effective those classes may be.

We believe that schools do matter; we have written this book to try to show why they matter using data on curriculum and achievement from a cross-national study—the Third International Mathematics and Science Study (TIMSS). Schools matter in many ways—they distribute resources, they create learning climates, they provide opportunities for learning experiences, and so on. This book focuses on one aspect of schooling: curriculum. Curriculum represents the intended courses of study and sequences of learning opportunities in formal schooling. We believe the TIMSS data clearly show that curriculum affects learning.

How does curriculum affect learning? Surely the answers to this question are essential to meaningful educational changes, yet the question is far from simple. To even grasp the question we need an understanding of curriculum, of learning, and of ways in which the two may interact. This question helps provide a raison d'être for large-scale cross-national comparative studies of achievement. Without such serious questions, those studies become nothing more than exercises in politics. The authors believe that the most important purpose for these studies, and for the TIMSS in particular, is to answer such questions. It is to those answers that this book is devoted.

The Question of Curriculum

Taking the question of how curriculum affects learning as our starting point, we need to investigate what we mean by curriculum and by learning, and how these interact. We begin first with the question of what we mean by curriculum.

The term *curriculum* comes from words meaning to "run a (race) course" and refers to a sequence of steps or stages in teaching and learning specific content. If we think of curriculum as a sequence of learning experiences, we immediately run into the difficulty that no one—teacher or otherwise—can consistently control the experiences of individual students. All that can be done is to provide students with opportunities to learn specific content. Thus, a good definition for curriculum is a sequence of learning opportunities provided to students in their study of specific content.

There is one obvious difficulty with curriculum being defined as sequences of learning opportunities. Such curriculum is invisible. We cannot see "sequences of learning opportunities." We can see the plans for such sequences. We can see classroom activities meant to serve as opportunities to learn specific content in the sequence. We can see textbook pages that help provide those learning opportunities. However, we cannot see curriculum directly. We can see the artifacts and effects of curriculum, but not curriculum itself.

As a sequence of learning opportunities, curriculum has several aspects. It exists as plans and intentions—the sequence of learning opportunities that one wishes students to experience. It exists as patterns of classroom activities that are meant to implement those plans and provide the desired learning opportunities. It exists in textbooks as pages intended to support or present those classroom learning opportunities. It leaves marks on what time is devoted to specific contents by teachers or textbooks. It impacts what students obtain as a result of opportunities to learn. Curriculum has these many different aspects and indications.

When we wished to study curriculum as a part of TIMSS, one of our first tasks was to choose artifacts and effects of curriculum we thought would reflect the various aspects of curriculum—intentions, implementations, and attainments. The latter was represented by student achievement on the TIMSS tests designed to measure student attainments at particular ages or grades in specific aspects of mathematics and the sciences. Assessing intentions and implementations was more problematic.

What artifacts (documents, books, lesson plans, etc.) should be taken as indicators of the intentions and implementations of curriculum? What aspects of classroom activities should be taken as indicators of curriculum by its effects? Although several artifacts were examined, we focus on four: content standards, textbooks, teachers' content goals, and duration of content coverage.

First, official documents often provide direct statements of the content and performance levels desired for students. Let us call these content standards. We systematically collected content standard documents from the countries participating in TIMSS. We then analyzed the specific science and mathematics content specified in the documents and the kinds of performance abilities expected from students. These content standards documents were taken as indications of curriculum as intention—as plans and goals.

Second, student textbooks are used in virtually all countries to support or more directly guide the learning opportunities of children. Textbooks represent ways in which curriculum can be implemented as opportunities to learn. We systematically collected representative samples of student textbooks in all participating countries for TIMSS Populations 1 and 2 (essentially fourth and eighth grade) and for the specialized content (e.g., calculus and advanced mathematics, and physics) of Population 3 (the end of secondary school). We have analyzed many aspects of those textbooks and continue to analyze others. For the purposes of this book, we focus primarily on the proportion of textbook space devoted to specific content areas in mathematics and the sciences. We consider this indicator of curriculum to be a bridge, expressing both curriculum as intention and, potentially, curriculum as implementation, depending on how and if specific parts of the analyzed textbooks are actually used in classroom instruction.

Finally, we wished to have some indicator of curriculum as it is actually implemented by teachers in attempting to provide learning opportunities for their students. Of the range of possibilities explored, two such indicators are used in this book. We consider teachers' indicated learning goals and time coverage as our third and fourth indicators of curriculum. We consider these effects to be indicators of curriculum as implemented. They can be analyzed for the proportion of time or emphasis devoted to various contents.

Thus, we use these four aspects of curriculum—content standards, textbook space, teacher content goals, and duration of content coverage—to make visible the invisible. We use data on these four factors to search for answers to how curriculum affects learning. These were not the only choices possible or the only that we explored. They are, however, sufficient to reveal some important things about how curriculum matters, as will be seen later in this book.

The Question of Learning

To answer the question of how curriculum affects learning, we must not only have some understanding of curriculum; we must also have some understanding of learning.

When we talk about learning we are not talking about understanding the cognitive mechanisms of individual learning, which vary among children and among cultures. We are talking about gains in competencies and knowledge, about growth in attainment, and about what happens in schools. We are interested in what affects gains in the achievements of children. The empirical data with which we work are the results of the TIMSS achievement tests.

We put safeguards in place in our collection of TIMSS data to ensure that the samples are representative of each country's children at a particular age or grade.[2] We also made every reasonable effort to find high-quality test items that measure relevant mathematics and science contents and student competencies so that the resulting performances are typical of what those children can do repeatedly, and accurately reflect the nature and level of those children's learning.[3] Neither process was perfect but both were reasonably successful.[4] Now that the data have been collected, equally careful efforts are needed for scale development, analysis, interpretation, and reporting.

In official international reports of TIMSS achievement data, most scores were reported for large collections of items. Aggregate scores were reported for mathematics and for science at each sampled population. These scores were based on the entire collection of mathematics and science items, respectively, at each test level. Slightly more specific scores were reported for broad categories within mathematics and within the sciences (algebra, earth sciences, etc.). Attention was focused on the comparative status of the achievement of each participating country's students.

Does comparative achievement status using such broad categories reflect learning? It does so only in a broad, cumulative sense—what has been learned in broad content areas over many years of schooling. Such broad measures are unlikely to be sensitive to the specifics of curriculum coverage in mathematics and the sciences, especially at any single grade level. Learning consists of change and gain in educational attainments. Curriculum specifics are most relevant to such gains.

TIMSS focused on three populations. Population 1 consisted of the two adjacent grades containing the majority of nine-year-olds in each country. Population 2 consisted of the two adjacent grades containing the majority of thirteen-year-olds in each country. Population 3 consisted of all students in the last year of secondary school with subpopulations for those still studying advanced mathematics or physics or both. The first two populations allowed for a focus on students of a specific age or in a specific grade.

Tests were given toward the end of the school year in each case. By drawing samples carefully from two adjacent grades, it was possible to measure achievements in both grades and to construct an indication of gain from one grade's school experience at the national level. This was not a truly longitudinal study because the same students were not followed throughout a period of time. No gain data could be reported for individual students. However, the TIMSS data might be considered "quasi-longitudinal." By measuring similar students in each country at two close periods of time separated mainly by one year's instruction, gains seen in the higher grade could be interpreted as an indication of what was learned in mathematics and the sciences during that year's instruction. Although these gain data could be estimated only in the aggregate such as at the national level, they still served as a better indicator of learning in a specific grade than comparative achievement status. The latter at best indicated something about cumulative learning.

Measuring learning in ways that are sensitive to curriculum factors is enhanced not only by using gain rather than status scores, but also by using measures created by combining only those items more specific to particular topic areas. Common practice is to combine the items into a total score or some other scale value related to total score (usually using item response theory such as Rasch scaling). A common feature of this approach is an attempt to measure a single trait or competency that lies behind success in all of the items combined. Answering more items correctly in a set to be scaled is taken to imply possession of more of the trait or a greater amount of the underlying competency. Unfortunately, a set of items measuring diverse topic areas yields only a measure of whatever common competency lies behind all those items. If the topics represented by the items are very diverse, the underlying competency must be more general.

This practice of combining items into a total score (or a similarly broad category score such as physics or algebra) creates a crucial trade-off. More items permit a more accurate estimate of an underlying competency. However, in cross-national comparative studies of student achievement, there is always a desire to cover a broad range of content with as few items as possible given limited testing time. As a result, even when mathematics or science items are grouped into broad categories (algebra, earth science, etc.), the content of these categories is very diverse. When scales are for all of mathematics or all of science at a specific grade level, the sets of items are diverse indeed and the competencies measured correspondingly are even more general.

Why is this a problem in studying the relationship between curriculum and learning? Put simply, the more general the competency measured, the more likely it is to be influenced by factors outside of schooling such as motivation, social class, and general aptitude. An achievement measure that is sensitive to curriculum differences must draw on one or more specific competencies that are affected by learning opportunities provided by those curricula. Differences among curricula should show differences in patterns of achievement for large samples of students—for example, in national estimates. Diverse sets of items measuring only very general competencies are far less likely to yield measures that are specific enough to be affected by curriculum differences in a given year. For the purposes of studying the effect of curriculum on learning, greater diversity and the resulting measures of more general competencies are less desirable. Use of more specific, closely related sets of test items yield measurements of more specific skills relevant to those items.

Thus, closely related item sets are more likely to be sensitive to differences among curricula in how content needed for correct responses to those closely related items are treated in providing students with an opportunity to learn. Unfortunately, limitations on testing time and the need for broad content coverage make it virtually impossible to include enough sets of closely related items to provide scale scores that measure all the things one would like to compare among students of similar ages or grades from different countries. In studying curriculum and learning, however, a focus on smaller, more closely related item sets may yield measures of learning that are more sensitive to curriculum differences.

Curriculum, Learning, and Culture

In first addressing the question of how curriculum affects learning, we said we needed to know not only something about learning and curriculum, but also about how the two are related. Much of that relationship is discussed in the subsequent chapters of this book. First, there is one aspect of the link between learning and curriculum that we wish to discuss briefly here.

We believe that there is a close relationship between curriculum, learning, and culture. The term *culture* can have many different meanings—everything from "high" culture ("the best that has been thought and felt" in a country or civilization, according to Matthew Arnold) to the ideology of a particular subgroup within a society (their conceptual and political way of interpreting their world). We want to focus on "lived culture"—how everyday life for children in school is experienced and shaped through the social institutions in their country. We wish to examine the relationship between curriculum and learning for each country that participated in TIMSS, so we focus on "lived culture" at a national level.

Explorations of culture are not easily approached through quantitative data. True understanding requires a wealth of qualitative data and investigation. That is beyond the scope of the TIMSS data on curriculum and achievement. Thus, what we offer here is not what can be proved about the relation of curriculum, learning, and culture, but rather a hypothesis that seems revealing and appropriate given the relationships we have seen in the quantitative data on curriculum and achievement.

We will offer a variety of cultural hypotheses throughout this report, but each is a variation of a more general one we might call *the* cultural hypothesis: how curriculum matters to learning is affected by how curriculum is shaped by the lived culture that affects schooling and school experiences.

Although it is an oversimplification, we may say that the past shapes our schools and our schools shape the future. A nation's culture or cultures shape its history and self-image, including values, institutions, goals, and the events that unfold from these. A nation's educational system is shaped by these same factors—even the very idea of what schools are and should accomplish. Curricula and other policies express cultural values, goals, and commonly accepted ways to reach those goals. The same forces give particular form to educational systems.

The most fundamental question is not *whether* culture has an impact on learning, but rather *how* culture has an impact on learning. Culture acts in both direct and indirect ways. Culture shapes what we value and thus enters our judgments in everyday living. Culture also acts less directly by shaping the social institutions we encounter, which in turn help create our everyday experiences. In this context, institutions such as school, grade level, subject area, and others emerge. They are shaped by the socialization through which education's institutions are formed and change.

Children encounter formal schooling primarily through education's social institutions. The organization of education within a culture is shaped to determine who receives which opportunities and when they receive them. This does not imply that the informal learning of socialization stops when formal schooling begins, but rather that the informal and the formal proceed side by side throughout the years of schooling.

The more diffuse impacts of culture are left for ethnographic study and cultural analysis—we do not attempt to address them here. They are certainly real, but they are beyond the scope of even the complex TIMSS data. On the other hand, insights into how social institutions function and, in particular, how education's social institutions function are accessible through quantitative data. The TIMSS data seems to offer strong possibilities here. We want to view how culture functions indirectly through education's social institutions.

Within a country, socioeconomic status, race, gender, and subculture memberships can have the same sort of impacts as those of differing countries in cross-national comparisons. These factors have indirect as well as direct effects. In the United States and some other countries, they make an impact through local control. Local control sets up local school subcultures that have differing impacts on curriculum, which, in turn, impacts achievement. The lack of an institutional center for curriculum in the United States (see Chapter Four) allows for greater differences in curriculum and different impacts on learning. For the most part this book focuses on differences between countries, although there are some ventures into intra-country analyses in Chapter Ten.

We will focus on selected aspects of educational institutions—educational decision making, subject matter content, and so forth—and how these vary among national education systems formed through different cultural and institutional histories. *Institution* here refers not to formal organizations or buildings but rather to ways of conducting and organizing aspects of education, to what sociologists mean when they talk about social institutions and institutionalized aspects of society. We hope to demonstrate the clear impact of those differences in educational institutions (in the sociological sense). We hope the understanding of these differences will make clear relationships in the data of curriculum and achievement that would remain unclear if these data were approached without cultural awareness or with more simplistic views of culture and social institutions.

For the present analyses, we will focus on four key aspects of social educational institutions. First, we recognize the goals and purposes of education in society as an institution not because we study it but because of its centrality from a conceptual point of view. Education's goals and purposes reflect cultural beliefs and values. These goals and purposes are institutionalized in different ways in different nations and education systems. This affects many aspects of how goals and intentions shape education practically. For example, in some cultures and countries, official goals remain at very global levels, while in others they are specific and myriad. This "grain size" of curricular goals seems likely to have an impact on how formal education is conducted. We need to explore the differences among these national methods of articulating educational goals and purposes because they both affect and are affected by that which comes afterward in education. For the most part, however, this is a study that must be left to others. It was not what TIMSS was designed to investigate.

Two key aspects of schooling affected by educational goals and purposes are authority within educational institutions and how authority is exercised in practical decision making. Surveying the arena of goals and authority cross-nationally makes it clear that specific goals are not wedded to specific arrangements for the distribution of authority and decision making. The centers of decision-making authority vary greatly among countries whether at the national, local, or school levels. For example, Switzerland has no school principals at certain grade levels, so does not even have school-level authorities for making educational decisions. Data that we present below examines the kinds of authorities with responsibilities for making educational decisions and the kinds of decisions for which each has responsibilities. These data make clear considerable differences in how nations organize educational decision making. The locus of authority and how authority is exercised in decision making are related but show considerable variety. Thus, authority and educational decision making are a second kind of societal institutionalization examined here.

Curricular areas and topics are affected by goals and purposes and by authority and decision making as they are made real in the social institutions of various countries. For example, in mathematics in some countries proportionality is a separate content area treated directly in documents and textbooks and by teachers. In other countries, this content exists only as a part of the topic of algebra rather than as a separate topic. Thus curricular area or content topic is a third social institution of education that will be examined. Some reserve the term *topic* for a segment of subject matter content, while *curricular area* is used for how a topic is represented in specific curricula. We will not maintain that fine a distinction here. We will use *curricular areas* and *topics* to refer to the content and expected performances, for contents of teaching units whether stated in official curriculum documents or in textbooks or as recognized by teachers. In this sense, a topic may not correspond from country to country because they are conceptualized, sequenced, and delivered differently. However, the commonalities are most often sufficient to recognize a core similarity for these curriculum areas and topics. When necessary, essential dissimilarities will also be emphasized.

Fourth and finally, achievement (or learning as change in achievement) is a social institution that is defined in varying ways in various societies. It is a reflection of what is learned and what capabilities are developed through the educative process. It is measured in different ways. In some countries, teachers' judgments without the use of formal assessment techniques are used to evaluate student attainments, especially prior to formal, national tests at the end of schooling. In other countries (for example, the United States), formal evaluation techniques such as teacher-made and standardized tests are used intensively as part of the common educational experience. For the sake of using TIMSS data, "achievement" is defined as a common core of what is measurable through tests related to curricula. These tests demand the display of learned capabilities under timed conditions and may or may not be perceived by those taking the tests as the more familiar, higher-stakes tests that are institutionalized in their country.

There is variation in curriculum among countries, regardless of the indicator used to reflect curriculum. There is variation in achievement and learning (gains in achievement) regardless of how this is limited by the way in which achievement is measured. However, our hypothesis is that national culture has an impact on curriculum. We believe it also has an impact on learning. Apart from how culture has an impact on curriculum and learning separately, culture also has an impact on the relationship between the two. This remains a hypothesis but we believe that it is true because we consistently find differences between countries. The way in which curriculum is related to learning varies among national cultures. For example, how directly textbooks reflect the content standards or curricular intentions and how directly they are related to achievement varies among countries. More detail on this and other examples are reported in various chapters throughout this book.

Figure 1.1. Four Social Institutions of Education Model.

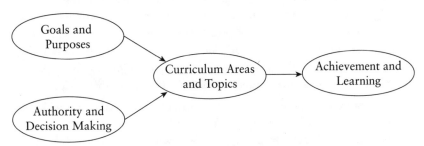

The interactions of these institutions are complex, as are their conceptualizations. For the purposes of investigation here, we will assume a simple model that links these institutionalized components of education (see Figure 1.1). We believe it is reasonable to assume that the way a society institutionalizes goals and purposes relates to the way it institutionalizes authority and decision making. We believe further that these two typically interact and that together they help to shape curriculum areas and topics as they are institutionalized in national and subnational curricula of various forms. Further, we believe that curriculum areas and topics affect how achievement is realized. For simplicity, we assume that goals and decision making work through curriculum to affect achievement. Recall that this is an attempt to indicate key aspects of culture's impact on education indirectly through educational social institutions. Direct, diffuse culture impact is presumed informally to maintain its continuous impact on students at the same time.

The question as it is posed in general form here is not, "Does culture affect learning?" That is assumed. Instead we ask, "Specifically, how does culture, through educational social institutions shaped by culture, affect educational practice and outcomes?" We believe this to vary among countries and education systems. In this book we set ourselves the task of exploring this variation and answering the specific question as part of an answer to the question of how curriculum affects learning. More detailed models flowing from Figure 1.1 come in later chapters.

NOTES

1. The popular interpretation of the Coleman report (Coleman et al., 1966) was that schools don't make a difference, a perception that continues to

persist despite challenges to this interpretation (Hanushek, 1997) and other analyses that contradict it (Wenglinsky, 1997). A similar conclusion regarding schools appears to be supported by the argument set forth in *The Bell Curve* by Herrnstein and Murray (1994). A recent review argues that international studies provide critical evidence of the importance of schools in students' learning and cites the recantation Coleman made of his earlier work upon a re-analysis of international data (Suter, forthcoming).

2. Statistics Canada, Canada's national statistical agency, consulted with researchers in each country to draft national sampling plans according to the published TIMSS documents (Wolfe & Wiley, 1992; Foy & Schleicher, 1994). In addition, they reviewed and approved each country's sampling plan and all stages of the data sampling. See Foy, Rust, and Schleicher (1996) for a detailed account.

3. In the design and implementation of data gathering on comparative achievement, consensus political methods and multiple viewpoints affected the actual form, choice, and placement of items.

4. See relevant chapters in the three technical volumes edited by Michael O. Martin and Dana L. Kelly (1996, 1997, and 1998). These are available online at http://times.bc.edu.

2

A MODEL OF CURRICULUM
AND LEARNING

IN THE PREVIOUS CHAPTER we identified four social institutions of education of which three are focuses of our investigation in this book—decision-making authority, curriculum topics, and student attainment. These are fundamental aspects of formal education in any educational system in any country. They are almost certainly affected by the social, political, and cultural context of the educational systems that they help to characterize. They are so central to the educational enterprise that studying them can be complex, messy, and far from simplistic. However, portraying these aspects of education realistically is likely to give insight into the educational opportunities for students in various countries. More specifically, these phenomena explored realistically should capture the variety that is only possible in cross-national comparisons. There is no point in conducting cross-national comparative educational research unless researchers are willing to go beyond the simplistic portrayal of educational phenomena in the particularity of national and cultural contexts.[1]

The investigations here are tightly focused around issues of schooling and curriculum. This does not mean the investigators are not aware of the important contributions of informal, out-of-school experiences to students' conceptual and cognitive development. We do not simplistically equate schooling and learning. Informal learning is an important way in which parents and cultural institutions contribute to what is "taught" to children.[2]

The TIMSS has been recognized as the most comprehensive educational research project ever undertaken. Students at three different points in the education system—approximating fourth, eighth, and twelfth grade students in the United States—were tested in areas of mathematics and science. Students completed surveys concerning their interests, study habits, motivation, and classroom experiences as did their teachers and school administrators. An extensive document analysis examined official curriculum content standards and commonly used textbooks. Nearly fifty countries participated in one or more aspects of the TIMSS, allowing for the collection of a large amount of information about education, schooling, the curriculum, and student attainments.

Conceptions of Curriculum

For the purposes of our investigations we conceive of curriculum as a sequence of opportunities to learn specific disciplinary content, in our case in science and mathematics. Even this limited concept of curriculum considered holistically involves issues of topic selection, topic emphasis, and the sequencing of topics, whether within a given year's schooling or across all the years of students' schooling experiences. Such a conception of curriculum leads to a focus on the specific topics selected for instruction, the amount of time spent on these topics, and the company topics keep in the course of the instructional sequence. Those aspects of educational systems and schooling become the objects for study.

The perspective on curriculum used for our investigations here is not meant to exclude or diminish other conceptions of curriculum. Indeed, there is a "bewildering" array of definitions for curriculum.[3] One conception of curriculum focuses on it as a cultural artifact.[4] Others take a more investigative approach to curriculum, using a variety of concepts of curriculum for that purpose.[5] Still others take a public policy approach to curriculum that leads to a focus on issues of public education and school organization and reform.[6] Still others take a more political or philosophical approach, seeing curriculum as an issue of power and access.[7]

In short, any investigation that focuses on curriculum focuses only on certain aspects and conceptions of this multifaceted centerpiece of schooling. We have chosen a formal approach to curriculum as learning opportunities focused around specific topics in school mathematics and science because this is appropriate to our investigation of actual learning as achievement change for science and mathematics.

Models Relating Curriculum and Achievement

The present TIMSS study is firmly rooted in the tradition of comparative education studies carried out by the International Association for the Evaluation of Educational Achievement (IEA). Historically, the IEA has explored issues of schooling's organization and structure, along with investigations of specific subject matter pedagogy and achievement. At least since the IEA's Second International Mathematics Study (SIMS), an informal model identifying three faces of curriculum has informed its studies. These faces are the intended, implemented, and attained curriculum.[8] Figure 2.1 embeds the tripartite IEA curriculum model into our model of the four education institutions.

The TIMSS benefited from previous IEA studies and drew upon that work to inform and guide the clarification of issues to be studied and the development of research instruments. The National Science Foundation and the U.S. Department of Education supported a research and

Figure 2.1. Conceptual Model Relating Curriculum and Achievement.

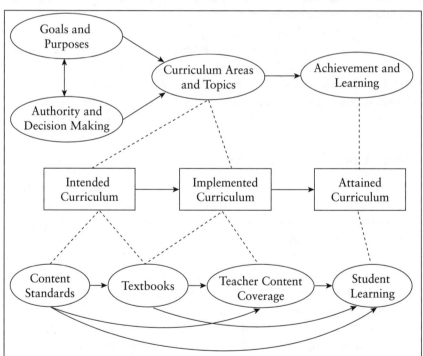

Note: *Solid lines with arrows represent possible empirical links between model constructs; dashed lines identify definitional links between models.*

development project to investigate and develop the methodologies for studying the many concepts of interest.[9]

Figure 2.1 shows how some of these concepts were operationalized. The intended curriculum was represented by official content standards documents produced by education systems to inform and guide instruction. Textbooks were considered another aspect of the intended curriculum, but in our developmental work we came to view these documents differently. From the traditional IEA perspective, textbooks are a part of the intended curriculum because they embody specific academic goals for specific sets of students. From a practical perspective, textbooks represent the implemented curriculum because they are most often employed in classrooms to organize, structure, and inform students' learning experiences. However, the extent to which textbooks actually represent the curriculum as implemented in the classroom is very much dependent on both the nature of the textbook and how the teacher chooses to make use of it. These considerations led us to add the *potentially implemented* curriculum to the IEA's three curriculum faces inasmuch as textbooks begin to bridge the gap between official intentions and concrete lessons that may be implemented in classrooms.[10]

The implemented curriculum is represented by teachers' indication of the topics to which they devoted instructional time and the relative amounts of instructional time devoted to various topics. The attained curriculum, for purposes of this book, is represented by the results of the TIMSS achievement tests aggregated to national levels to obtain representative scores on specific content topics for each country.

Some Concluding Remarks

The full model portrayed in Figure 2.1 and used to guide our investigations is simple and comprehensive but certainly not exhaustive of all factors influencing curriculum and achievement, let alone schooling or student development. The subject matter and pedagogical knowledge of teachers, the role of systemwide testing, and the nature of classroom instructional practices are some of the more salient of these influential factors. The latter is included in some of the models we discuss but the other two are not since the TIMSS did not provide measurements for either of them. Other models are possible (for example, economic models of education) as was suggested by the variety of conceptions of curriculum to which we alluded earlier.

Our model focuses on subject matter since our interest was primarily in using cross-national comparisons to illuminate the relationship between curriculum and learning in school science and mathematics. We regard subject matter as a fundamental aspect of schools, schooling, and student learning. We have tried to portray subject matter as an aspect of education with sufficient complexity so as not to be misleading and to make effective use of the cross-national educational comparisons. It is likely that relationships we uncover represent conditions necessary for effective schooling, but not necessarily sufficient to guarantee it by themselves. The organization of schooling and instruction is also important, as we have explored elsewhere.[11] Certainly, views of schooling and curriculum that do not focus on subject matter are important, as are richer views of student learning and development.

We hope our discussion of the relationship between curriculum topics and student learning is enlightening rather than misleading. We hope it will affect future science and mathematics education goals in U.S. schools. Clearly change is needed; it seems so much a part of the public debate as to be inevitable. What is not inevitable is whether this change will be informed either by empirical studies or by sufficiently realistic analyses of educational efforts and outcomes. We hope to help make this more certain.

A model to guide research is not useful unless its concepts can be measured with reliable and valid data. The model presented in this book includes concepts from three different levels in the education system—students, teachers and classrooms, and educational systems. In the next chapter we detail how each of the model concepts were measured for the investigations reported in this book.

NOTES

1. National systems will have developed in varied social, historical, and cultural contexts. Their educational systems, as portrayed through the four social institutions previously identified (goals, decision-making authority, curriculum topics, and student attainment), should reflect this variety. This variety, then, should allow comparisons to provide a laboratory in which a range of alternatives becomes clear. A variety of goals should be seen. Differing patterns of decision making should appear, as well as contrasting conceptions of curriculum and providing students with learning opportunities. Examining this variety may provide new insights into how curriculum and schooling are linked to student learning and achievement. This chance to gain new insight into one's own educational system through the laboratory of cross-national comparisons was one of the primary motivations behind the TIMSS and its predecessor cross-national comparative studies.

2. Martin, 1996.

3. Jackson, 1992, p. 11.

4. Anthropology and cognitive psychology recognize that there is a difference between school subjects and the less formal concepts embedded in practical cultural activity. Examples abound from studies of ethnomathematics, mathematics as it exists in other cultural contexts. For example, Saxe (1985) documented the number system of the Oksapmin of Papua, New Guinea that was based on twenty-seven locations on the body rather than the Arabic base-ten number system. Similarly, Bockarie (1993) studied the Mende culture of Sierra Leone, whose number system is base-twenty. In contrast to the mathematical activity most students encounter in school, the Mende never engage in nonsituated, abstract calculations in their mathematics program. In another study, Saxe (1988, 1990), contrasts the flexible arithmetic reasoning of young Brazilian candy sellers to the formal algorithms taught in school. He found that the sort of categories that were problematic in school (e.g., single- vs. double-digit subtraction) were not relevant in describing how the candy sellers functioned mathematically. However, he found that their flexibility in adding and subtracting was limited to practical situations involving currency and did not transfer to identical calculations performed on paper. Lave (1988, 1990) draws upon this type of research to conclude that the cognitive processes associated with education and learning are fundamentally social and cultural in nature, since both problems and solutions are identified within specific cultural settings.

5. Evaluation studies of various curricula or curriculum models may include detailed descriptions but typically focus on results from the employment of specific curricula. Examples are the comparison of preschool curricula (Schweinhart, Weikart & Larner, 1986) and the federally mandated evaluation of Chapter One/Title One enrichment programs (Puma et al., 1997). Others have studied how curriculum materials may be used—for example, how teachers plan their instruction (Floden, Porter, Schmidt, Freeman & Schwille, 1981)—or the effect that particular curricular goals or instructional approaches have on student motivation and learning (Eccles & Midgley, 1989; Resnick & Klopfer, 1989; McCaslin & Good, 1993).

6. Typically this approach weighs the effects various social policy practices have on the curriculum students study in schools. Little specification is given to the curriculum save the broad labels commonly applied to the disciplines studied in schools. Ravitch (1985, 1995a, 1995b), for example, has written extensively on the importance of standards toward the goal of improving the quality of the curriculum. Others have identified the various social and political constituencies that influence the school curriculum (see

Sears and Carper, 1998). Porter, Archbald, and Tyree (1991) examined policies regarding teachers' professional development, school organization, and other leadership policies relating to curricular change and reform. The distinctive characteristic here is the identification and evaluation of various policies governing some aspect of the education enterprise, together with their potential or actual effect on the school curriculum.

7. Questions such as what counts as knowledge, and whose knowledge will count, as well as who has access to this knowledge and by what means characterize this approach. The new sociology of education identified these and other questions as legitimate lines of curriculum inquiry fostering the view of curriculum as a "form of domination" (Young, 1998). Apple and his colleagues have written extensively from this perspective exploring both the intentional and unintentional marginalization experienced by members of one or more groups considered to have minority status by the society at large (Apple, 1990, 1996; Beyer & Apple, 1998).

8. The *intended* curriculum encompasses all those aims and goals that an education system has for students. Such aims and goals may find expression in formal documents such as content standards and official textbooks, or they may be deduced from common practices. The *implemented* curriculum encompasses all that is done in schools to further the aims and goals of schooling. Teachers are in a pivotal position to provide and structure students' opportunities to accomplish the various goals and aims articulated by the system. Thus, opportunity-to-learn measures have found prominence in virtually every IEA-sponsored study. For these measures, teachers provide some indication of students' exposure to the specific subject matter assessed (McKnight et al., 1987). The *attained* curriculum refers to that portion of the curriculum actually attained by students. Certainly this includes achievement measures related to specific subject matter concepts, but it also includes attitudes, perspectives, and values students may have acquired during their schooling.

9. Schmidt et al., 1996.

10. Schmidt et al., 1996; Valverde, Bianchi, Houang, Schmidt, & Wolfe, forthcoming.

11. Schmidt, McKnight, Cogan, Jakwerth, & Houang, 1999.

3

MEASURING CURRICULUM
AND ACHIEVEMENT

IN CHAPTER ONE we discussed the conceptual framework of the investigations in this book. In Chapter Two we discussed the model behind our research and the aspects of curriculum with which it dealt. Neither the concepts nor the model would be meaningful if we could not measure the elements involved in a practical way that provided empirical data for investigation. This chapter discusses such issues of measurement. The measurement of achievement has a long and varied history. We discuss only certain features that are important to the investigations that follow. In contrast, measuring aspects of curriculum quantitatively is essentially a new field. We describe in broad terms the procedures that we developed to do just this. Further, we discuss in general terms how we intend to study the relationship of curriculum and achievement and how this relates to cultural context.

Measuring Curriculum

We want to study the relationship of aspects of curriculum to changes in student achievement. We wish to do this quantitatively. To do this we must first find ways to measure aspects of curriculum quantitatively so that, using standard statistical analyses, they can be related to quantitative measures of achievement. Curriculum is a well-developed field that has proceeded almost exclusively by means of qualitative studies. Rich verbal descriptions and categorizations of aspects of curriculum have been used to characterize curriculum and its functions in numerous contexts. We believe that we have successfully developed tools for the quantitative study of selected aspects of curriculum and that this provides new methods for the study of curriculum.

Operationalizing Curriculum Measurement

How do we operationalize the quantitative measurement of at least some important aspects of curriculum? Our methods began by collecting important documents. For TIMSS these included content standards documents (241 in mathematics and 251 in science) and student textbooks (318 in mathematics and 312 in science). We then developed methods for partitioning these curriculum documents into "building blocks" through which content and activities were presented. We developed a category system that would characterize certain aspects of each block, including the content topics involved and what students were expected to perform with that content. This allowed us to build up aggregate characterizations of documents and to characterize curriculum for a particular country by aggregating documents. This same category system allowed us to characterize aspects of teacher implementation of the curriculum and aspects of the TIMSS achievement tests. We begin our more detailed overview of methods by describing this category system.

THE TIMSS MATHEMATICS AND SCIENCE FRAMEWORKS The TIMSS frameworks were captured in two sets of nested categories with varying degrees of detail that described possible contents in school mathematics and science and the performances that might be expected of students in learning those contents. These category systems—the TIMSS mathematics and science frameworks—served as a measurement tool because they provided qualitative descriptive categories, which could be identified and then quantified.

The TIMSS frameworks for mathematics and science were developed to provide a common language for describing and examining what students in many different countries study in their schools. Although the frameworks were developed and published in English, they needed to be sufficiently broad to include any topic found in any of the participating countries' curricula, yet sufficiently precise so as to provide accurate portraits that could be compared and analyzed.[1] A major focus of the TIMSS was on the two grades containing the majority of a country's thirteen-year-old students[2] and the two grades containing the majority of a country's nine-year-old students.[3] Consequently, the curriculum frameworks were developed with the curriculum for the first eight years of schooling particularly in mind.[4]

Given this set of goals that informed the development of the TIMSS curriculum frameworks, it is not surprising to discover that not every topic represents a comparably sized slice of the mathematics or science studied in schools.[5] For example, the final version contains fifteen arithmetic topics, eight geometry topics, and only two algebra-related topics. This concentration on arithmetic topics reflects much more the eighth-grade focus on arithmetic in the United States than the eighth-grade focus elsewhere, which is typically geometry and algebra.[6] Nonetheless, this issue of "grain size" does not threaten the validity of any of the curriculum portraits created or the analyses conducted. It does, however, point out one of the limitations. The more finely detailed framework areas allow more finely detailed descriptions and analyses than the other less detailed areas.

Each framework aspect is arranged in a hierarchical manner with nested subcategories of increasing specificity.[7] At any given level, topic arrangement does not necessarily reflect any canonical ordering. The mathematics framework contains ten major categories, each of which has from one to twenty subcategories for a total of forty-four content-specific topics altogether (see Table 3.1). The science framework, also illustrated in Table 3.1, has eight main categories—one of which has twenty-nine subcategories—and a total of seventy-nine content-specific topics altogether. The performance expectation aspect is similarly arranged. The mathematics framework details twenty-one performance expectations while the science framework details twenty performance expectations. (See Appendix A for a complete listing of the mathematics and science frameworks.)

DOCUMENT ANALYSIS These frameworks were used to analyze two types of curriculum documents: content standards and textbooks. These two types of documents represent different manifestations or aspects of curriculum as explained in the previous chapters. Content standards (curriculum frameworks, guides, national curricula, etc.) are documents that present and articulate an education system's curricular intentions and are intended to guide and direct the educational process in schools and classrooms.

Textbooks embody a different sort of curricular intention. Through the presentation of specific pedagogical approaches and resources, textbooks represent a powerful resource that may guide what teachers do in their classrooms. They move beyond the mere statement of intentions by presenting selected curriculum topics in a specific sequence and by making use of particular pedagogical approaches. In this way, textbooks represent the potentially implemented curriculum, recognizing that the actual impact any text has on what is done in the classroom depends on how teachers choose to utilize textbooks as a resource to inform and guide their teaching.

Table 3.1. Number of Subareas in Each Major Category of the TIMSS Mathematics and Science Frameworks.

Mathematics

Content Category

	Content Category	Number of Subareas
1.1	Numbers	20
1.2	Measurement	3
1.3	Geometry: position, visualization, and shape	5
1.4	Geometry: symmetry, congruence, and similarity	3
1.5	Proportionality	4
1.6	Functions, relations, and equations	2
1.7	Data representation, probability, and statistics	2
1.8	Elementary analysis	2
1.9	Validation and structure	2
1.10	Other content	1

Performance Expectation Category

	Performance Expectation Category	Number of Subareas
2.1	Knowing	3
2.2	Using routine procedures	3
2.3	Investigating and problem solving	5
2.4	Mathematical reasoning	6
2.5	Communicating	4

Science

Content Category

	Content Category	Number of Subareas
1.1	Earth sciences	14
1.2	Life sciences	20
1.3	Physical sciences	29
1.4	Science, technology, and mathematics	5
1.5	History of science and technology	1
1.6	Environmental and resource issues related to science	6
1.7	Nature of science	2
1.8	Science and other disciplines	2

Performance Expectation Category

	Performance Expectation Category	Number of Subareas
2.1	Understanding	3
2.2	Theorizing, analyzing, and solving problems	
2.3	Using tools, routine procedures, and science processes	5
2.4	Investigating the natural world	5
2.5	Communicating	2

Identifying the curriculum element to be coded for each type of document involved several steps. First, curriculum documents—a representative sample of content standards and student textbooks—were identified and collected in each participating country. Documents were then divided into smaller portions reflecting some functional organization. Each of these was subsequently divided into homogeneous building blocks.[8]

Each block was then coded by assigning as many content, performance expectation, and perspective categories to it as were needed to characterize its content. This "vector" of content, performance expectation, and perspective codes was called the "signature" of that block. Thus a signature was a qualitative description in the language of the framework's three aspects.[9]

In making judgments and selecting from among the many framework categories to code curricular elements, the assignment of performance expectations was always made relevant to a specific content or topic. Thus performance expectation information was always collected in a conditional manner. Expectations for students were evaluated with respect to a specific content that students were expected to learn. In this way, the performance expectation information collected does not represent disconnected intentions for the development of isolated skills, but explicitly expressed intentions embedded in specific content.[10]

Those who are familiar with a country's curriculum as reflected in the curriculum documents analyzed are best suited to appropriately characterize key elements of the curriculum. Internationally trained coders partitioned documents into blocks and assigned the codes to make up the signature of a block from each participating country.[11]

FROM THE QUALITATIVE TO THE QUANTITATIVE Blocking and coding provided systematic qualitative characterizations of curriculum elements from curriculum documents. However, once aspects of curriculum documents had been "parsed" into these small units and each had been characterized, it was possible to build up aggregate portraits of documents—and of countries by aggregating a sample of documents. Thus national curriculum portraits were methodically developed through careful quantification of the qualitative descriptions found in the coded blocks for each curricular element. The selection criteria for the documents that would be coded—standards and textbooks—required that national samples include sufficient documents that pertained to at least 50 percent of the students in the TIMSS focal grades. In addition, a country's document sample was required to cover all major regions and all types of schools and educational tracks (e.g., public, private; vocational, technical, academic).

Most of the country level curriculum portraits discussed here and in other reports that have analyzed the TIMSS curriculum data have all been developed on the basis of the systematic and detailed analyses of countries' standards and textbook documents. Some comparative discussions have drawn upon country portraits developed through another technique called General Topic Trace Methodology (GTTM). These data were collected from curriculum experts in each country who were asked to indicate for each framework topic and for each grade/year of schooling whether instruction was intended to begin, to continue, to be emphasized, or to complete students' consideration of the topic. These judgments were to be made based on the country's standards documents and, therefore, may be considered as another indicator of the country's education system's curricular intentions. These data were gathered to provide a description of intentions across all the years of schooling since analysis of curriculum documents at every year of schooling was beyond the resources of the TIMSS curriculum analysis. Obviously these data do not represent as rigorous a curriculum measure as the detailed analyses of focal grade documents but do provide an important context for them.

Characterizations of each country's curriculum provide the appropriate measures to compare with other countries and to relate to achievement measures reported at the country level. In instances in which a single document—either for standards or textbooks—was relevant for all students within a country, generation of the country's portrait was quite straightforward. A number of countries, however, had more than one document that needed to be considered. In each case, appropriate methods were used to combine these documents to represent the country as a whole.[12] Thus it is clear that the country level curriculum portraits developed are appropriate for comparisons across countries and for relating to country level achievement measures. However, the curriculum described may not—and in the case of Switzerland certainly does not—represent the educational experience of any one student in the country.

Measuring Curriculum Implementation

The TIMSS frameworks were also used to measure the curriculum implemented in the classroom. This was accomplished in a section of the TIMSS Teacher Questionnaire that asked teachers to indicate in how many lessons they had covered specific topics in their instruction. Most topics listed in this section combined two or more topics from the relevant TIMSS framework to reduce the burden of responding to an overly long topic list. However, the listed topics were exhaustive of the entire content aspect of the frameworks and were tightly related to the full set of content topics. Consequently, seventh and eighth grade mathematics teachers responded to a list of twenty-one math topics while science teachers responded to a list of twenty-two science topics.[13] (See Appendix B for a listing of the framework topics contained in each teacher topic.)

For each listed topic, teachers were asked to indicate their coverage according to four categories: one to five periods/lessons, six to ten periods/lessons, eleven to fifteen periods/lessons, or more than fifteen periods/lessons. These options approximate one, two, three, or more than three weeks of instruction. Three additional options allowed teachers to indicate whether the topic had been taught a previous year, was not taught this year, or would be taught yet later in the year. Since all the TIMSS surveys were completed very near the end of the year, these options were not included in the analyses reported here.

In measuring curriculum documents, "blocks" were the fundamental units that were coded, counted, and analyzed for specific topics. In this instance, "lessons" or "instructional periods" were the fundamental unit that was coded, counted, and analyzed with respect to specific topics. Consequently, the measurement of the curriculum as found in textbooks and what teachers reported doing in their classrooms share the topic content categories defined by the TIMSS curriculum frameworks. The indicators formed for textbooks and classroom instruction also share a common metric. Both are analyzed as percentages: textbooks as a percent of space (blocks) addressing a topic and classroom instruction as both the percent of teachers within a country addressing a topic as well as the mean percent of instructional time teachers gave to teaching the topic. Ideally, it would have been desirable to measure teachers' performance expectations as well as their content coverage. However, this proved infeasible given the long list of desired things to be surveyed and the required tradeoffs necessary in creating instruments that were considered by a number of countries to be of acceptable length.[14]

Measuring Achievement

Unlike the quantitative characterization of aspects of curriculum, the quantitative measurement of achievement has a long and complex history. Certainly it seems unnecessary to recapitulate that history here. However, there are a few specific issues of measuring achievement that are relevant for discussion here so that they will be clear in later chapters.

Learning versus Achievement

MEASURING ACHIEVEMENT AT SPECIFIC GRADES The curriculum measures that we have described above—both those from analyzing documents and those from teacher responses—focus on creating accurate indications of what students studied in a particular school year (grade). Detailed measurements of standards and textbooks were for a specific year of schooling—that is, fourth grade or eighth grade. What was actually taught in classrooms was measured by having teachers respond for a particular class during the year in which the TIMSS achievement tests were taken.

To detect any effect of curriculum on achievement, it is necessary that achievement measure not just the status of what students have attained in mathematics or science at a single point in time. Instead, student achievement measures must be sensitive to what students have attained at the end of the year of study that they did not know before this year of study for those curriculum aspects that were measured. That is, the achievement measures used must be sensitive to the effects of curriculum during a particular year or grade's study. We need to measure students' grade-specific learning—that is, the learning they have acquired during that specific grade.

LEARNING AS CHANGE IN ACHIEVEMENT Any representation of what students have learned in a specific grade would have to distinguish what they have learned during that specific grade from what they have learned more generally. That is, we can best represent learning by a change in achievement from beginning to end of a grade rather than from a measure of the status of achievement at the end of that grade.

The distinction is important given what we wish to learn from measuring achievement. We can measure achievement at any point during schooling and obtain a valid and reliable indication of the status of student achievement to that point in schooling for the content of the achievement test. Assessments of student *learning*, however, refer to what students have acquired in some specified period of time—a measure of what students have gained in the kinds of achievement measured.

SPECIFICITY OF ACHIEVEMENT MEASUREMENT The TIMSS frameworks applied to achievement test items make it possible to identify very specifically the contents that are measured by particular test items. The use of this common framework both to analyze test items and elements of curriculum content allow careful matching of test content to curriculum manifestations.

Previous investigations examining the relationship between what students study and their achievement—particularly those making cross-national comparisons—have often seemed to reveal few achievement differences attributable to specific aspects of curriculum. This may have been, in part, because different systems of measurement were used for curriculum and achievement and because the studies sought only to relate global characterizations of curriculum to fairly global measures of achievement. Most studies have relied on traditional achievement measures that employ global or scaled scores combining many different areas of subject matter content.

However, aggregating achievement scores in this fashion serves to obscure rather than reveal relationships between curriculum specifics and achievement specifics (see Chapter One). Only specificity has a reasonable chance to reveal relationships of curriculum to achievement and then only when achievement change for a specific period on specific content is related to curriculum efforts in that specific period related to that same specific content.[15]

ALL TESTS ARE NOT THE SAME If student knowledge is measured using more detailed topic categories, student performance may demonstrate variation more likely to reflect underlying curricular differences.[16] For example, analyzing countries' mean student performance in TIMSS employing more detailed framework topic categories yielded considerable variation in countries' ranks. When specifically similar items were combined there were fifteen to twenty-one different topic areas for which achievement measures could be obtained. The actual number of topic areas differed by the subject matter—mathematics or science—and by the grade involved. Each country's students' performances were not uniform across all of those different topics. Students' performances were not monolithic either with reference to their own performance on each of the tested topics or with reference to the performance of other countries' students.[17]

Clearly, the specific topics on which students were tested mattered in creating indicators of students' learning. Countries demonstrated profiles of contents on which they did relatively better and relatively worse. Within any one country, students' performance varied across topics. No country's students performed equally well across all topics. In addition, countries' performances relative to other countries' also varied with the particular topic measured by the various topic-specific subtests. A few countries fairly consistently occupied relatively higher or relatively lower rankings across the various topic subtests in mathematics or science. The vast majority had performance that differed considerably from that depicted by the single scaled score performances.[18]

Psychometric Concerns

Traditional psychometric concerns have focused on making global achievement estimates that were both valid and reliable—that is, measuring what they purported to measure and doing so with as little error as possible. In this context we concern ourselves primarily with content validity—the extent to which a particular content or topic is adequately represented by and measured by a particular set of items. This is essentially a conceptual issue. Some degree of subjectivity always remains in forming a conclusion about *adequate* representation, but the goal is to obtain representative items that truly measure what one desires to measure. Several different panels of U.S. mathematicians and scientists have judged the TIMSS tests as having done an adequate job in this respect (although not without some criticism).

Reliability, on the other hand, estimates the amount of measurement error in the tests.[19] The published median reliability estimates across the eight TIMSS test booklets for eighth grade mathematics and science were .89 and .78 respectively.[20]

The TIMSS curriculum frameworks provided definitions for forming more precise content-specific tests that contained anywhere from five to twenty-seven items for areas in mathematics and from three to twenty-seven items for areas in science.[21] (See Appendix C for the definitions of each of the content-specific tests including the number of items and a listing of the framework topics included in each test.)

Measuring Gain at Specific Grades in TIMSS

Measurement of achievement at two points in time is needed if one is to estimate change in achievement during the period between those two points. The most valuable measurement of this sort is to measure the achievement of every student at both of those two points in time. If that is done, one is able to determine the change in achievement over the period for each individual student. Unfortunately, the resources for TIMSS were too limited to allow such measures of every student.

A more practical, cost-effective design that allows national estimates of achievement change is called a "synthetic cohort" method.[22] Two of the student populations defined for TIMSS embraced two adjacent grades. One could measure the achievement of the cohort of students at the end of the lower grade and gather a similar measure of the achievement of a corresponding cohort of students at the end of the higher grade (for most analyses here, seventh and eighth grades). These data could be used to make estimates of the achievements of the two cohorts one grade apart.

One might assume that there was sufficient homogeneity in the abilities and educational experiences of the two cohorts other than the educational experiences of the grade in question (for example, eighth grade) to allow them to be considered equivalent. This is not an unreasonable assumption if one is careful to identify the cohort at the higher grade and then draw an appropriate sample from the lower grade that proportionately represents all the "feeder schools" that go into creating a cohort at the upper grade. One can then treat these two measurements as if they were measures giving national estimates of the same cohort's achievement at two points in time.

If this is reasonable, then the gains in achievement on content-specific tests from the lower grade compared to the next adjacent grade may be directly related to the upper grade's curriculum and instruction. In this way we can obtain national estimates of curriculum sensitive measures of learning (achievement change) that can be related to the particular qualities of the year's curriculum. [23]

Additional Issues Related to Analyses

We have discussed how to operationalize the quantitative measurement of aspects of curriculum in school science and mathematics. We have also discussed some of the issues of measuring achievement—and, especially, achievement change—to obtain quantitative estimates of what was learned in a single grade.

The Model

In Chapter Two we proposed a model of how curriculum and achievement are related. That model serves as the basis for quantitatively relating curriculum and achievement. In Figure 3.1 a structural model is proposed like that of Figure 2.1 but one that includes structural coefficients (α, β, η, ξ, γ, δ) to indicate the strength of the relationships between the different aspects of curriculum and achievement.

Each "path" in the model stands for a complex social relationship between the two aspects of curriculum and/or achievement that are

Figure 3.1. Structural Model Relating Curriculum and Achievement.

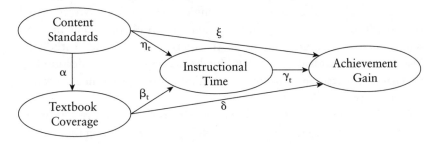

(a) Percent of Teachers in a Country (p) Teaching the Topic

(b) Percent of the Instructional Time (t) Spent by a Teacher
on the Topic Averaged over Teachers in a Country

involved. For example, the path between "content standards" and "textbook coverage" (the magnitude of the relationship of which is represented by α) stands for the social institutions and pressures that operate so that officially articulated goals (captured in content standards) affect the shape and selection of textbooks. In one country this may be through a national curriculum (set out in content standards) shaping the content of a national textbook. In another country this may be through the influence of content standards documents of one type or another on the market forces that lead to the development, adoption, and sustaining of one or more textbooks.

Similarly content standards could affect teacher topic coverage (η_p) or amount of instructional time (η_t) through the role they play in the preparation of teachers or in the continued professional development of teachers. Textbook coverage of content has obvious links to teacher coverage of that content (β_p) and instructional time (β_t) devoted to it by teachers using the textbooks involved to provide instruction.

Teacher content coverage (γ_p) and instructional time (γ_t) have obvious linkages to how student achievement changes for the content involved. The quality of textbooks as reflected in textbook content coverage and its nature seems likely, in many cases, to have an impact on student achievement gains (δ) for the relevant topic—especially in those countries in which each student has a book to use at his or her discretion. Content standards may have effects on student achievement gains in some countries that operate outside of their impacts on teachers and textbooks (ξ). For example, they might affect parents' understanding of what is expected of their children or they might affect the general social climate motivating a country's children to master certain contents nationally recognized as important. It is also likely that the standards would determine the content that is tested on examinations that play a critical role in students' lives. In some countries, this would further affect parents' understanding of what is expected and students' motivation to learn given the high stakes associated with such tests.

It is these kinds of relationships that we attempt to represent in the structural model. We now turn to discussing issues of relating these quantitative measurements of curriculum and achievement gain—toward estimating the coefficients of the model.

Levels of Description

The TIMSS frameworks are hierarchical. Lower (more nested) levels of the framework are more specific descriptions of the same content described more globally and less precisely by the higher levels that subsume those lower levels. This permits descriptions and comparisons at different levels of specificity. Content standards and textbooks were measured using the most content-specific, "lowest level" framework topics, forty-four for mathematics and seventy-nine for science. The frameworks' hierarchical arrangement was used to group all framework topics into a smaller number of categories for teachers' responses. Finally, the TIMSS test included items assessing a subset of topics from both the mathematics and science frameworks. Consequently, relationships exist between every topic measured in standards and textbooks and those that measured teachers' instruction. It is only possible to relate these curricular elements to those topics represented by a sufficient number of items on the TIMSS tests to allow a separate topic-specific subtest (achievement estimate).[24]

Performance Expectations

Complete measurements of student expected performances were only conducted for content standards and textbooks.[25] The hierarchical arrangement of performance expectations allowed analyses to be conducted at the most finely defined level as well as for more inclusive and broadly defined levels. Characterizations of documents have also made use of the five major performance expectation divisions.[26]

Analyses in this book involve contrasts of performance expectations that may be considered to require more advanced or complex, "higher order," demanding considerations. These involve two major performance expectation categories each for mathematics and science. They involve "investigating the natural world" and "theorizing, analyzing, and solving problems" for science. They involve "mathematical reasoning" and "investigating and problem solving" for mathematics. These analyses are always linked to the topic(s) under consideration—that is, only the portion of a document that involves both the relevant topic(s) and the relevant performance expectation are included. The curriculum indicators then are the percent of textbook space allocated to higher order considerations but only considering the blocks associated with the specific topic.

Country-level Estimates

All descriptions, analyses, and relations use indicators that are aggregated to the country or national level (with the exception of Chapter Ten). These accurately represent the variation from one country to another in the various indicators, whether these indicators are describing curriculum documents, teachers' instructional emphases, or students' test performance. This is, in part, necessary because of the reliance on "synthetic cohorts" in measuring achievement change. The inferences drawn from these analyses are appropriate to observed *cross-national* variation. Applying conclusions that have been developed from cross-national variation to what occurs within any one country or within a school or a classroom is a logical fallacy (the ecological fallacy). These measures say what they say about nations and cannot be used to infer what happens in any smaller unit considered (school, classroom, teacher, and student).

What may best explain observed differences across countries may not necessarily explain any variation found within one country or may have a completely different relationship to achievement within a country. For example, the high performing Asian countries such as Hong Kong, Korea, and Japan had more than 90 percent of their students in classes with more

than thirty students. The majority of students in most of the lower performing countries were in classes with fewer than thirty students. Internationally, then, the relationship between class size and achievement
would appear to favor larger classes.[27] Nonetheless, this international
trend does not necessarily negate the conclusions of those who have found
a significant relationship between achievement and smaller class size in
the United States.[28] Inferences drawn on the basis of cross-national comparisons thus do not *automatically* suggest how reform in any one country should proceed.

Examining Variation Two Ways

We have discussed how we are going to characterize curriculum aspects
from content standards, textbooks, and teachers. We have also characterized how we will estimate changes in achievement as a surrogate for
measuring learning that takes place in connection to curriculum activities.
There is still one important feature of our analyses to make clear. We
examine the relationship of curriculum to achievement change for specific
topics in specific countries. We do this for sets of topics and sets of countries. We can use these results either to say something about topics or
about countries.

TOPICS AS A FOCUS OF THE ANALYSES If we focus on topics, we can
discover how emphasis on a particular topic varies from one country to
another. Focusing on topics also permits a "world-wide" or "global" view
(at least according to the "world of TIMSS") of what constitutes eighth
grade mathematics or eighth grade science. With respect to each curricular aspect, it is possible to construct a "world core" curriculum that
reflects the intersection of most of the TIMSS "world."

One way of establishing this curriculum is to find those topics that a
majority of countries include in their eighth grade curriculum. Previously, using 70 percent of countries as the criterion, we have reported
the eighth grade mathematics and science world core for both content
standards and textbooks.[29] For example, from the forty-four possible
mathematics topics, the eighth grade world core included eighteen topics for content standards, nineteen topics for textbooks, with an overlapping world core of thirteen topics across the two curricular aspects.
This method of establishing a core curriculum identifies which topics
constitute the focus of the year's study but does not provide any differentiation among the topics.

A second way of looking at the "world core" curriculum indicates emphasis. Identifying the five most emphasized topics across all countries yields a sort of cross-national consensus about which topics are most important to include and emphasize.[30] Variation among topics is more thoroughly reviewed in Chapter Five.

Establishing a "world core" of topics for each curricular aspect raises the question of how these aspects relate to one another. For instance, what is the effect of including a topic in curriculum content standards? Does the amount of textbook space devoted to this topic increase, decrease, or is there no discernable effect of including it in content standards? Do teachers appear more likely to teach a topic if it is included in their content standards or if the textbook devotes a large proportion of its space to that topic? The relationships among these various curricular aspects for each mathematics and science topic are explored in Chapter Six.

COUNTRIES AS A FOCUS OF THE ANALYSES If specific countries are the focus of analysis then the relative emphases between topics become evident.[31] The most emphasized topics within a country reveal what may be considered the "heart" or core of mathematics or science for that country in a way analogous to the "world core" curriculum. For example, Flemish Belgium eighth-grade science teachers spend more time, on average, teaching a single science topic—human biology and health—than teachers in any other country. Furthermore, the four most emphasized science topics according to the amount of time these teachers devote to them, on average, are all in the area of life science and consume nearly two-thirds of the year's teaching. In contrast, the five topics most emphasized by Czech Republic eighth grade science teachers command about 50 percent of the year's instruction and include two earth science topics and three physical science topics. The country-specific descriptions and relationships are also explored in Chapters Five and Six.

NOTES

1. A 1989 project funded by the British Columbia Ministry of Education to analyze mathematics textbooks was the seminal basis for the curriculum frameworks. Development continued in 1990 as a part of the Survey of Mathematics and Science Opportunities (SMSO) project at Michigan State University which was funded by the U.S. National Center for Education Statistics (NCES) in conjunction with the U.S. National Science Foundation (NSF). One of the fundamental goals for TIMSS was to provide a

cross-national benchmark for all of the participating countries and educational systems. The desire to provide important and relevant information for each participating country's ongoing education and curriculum reform efforts motivated this goal. To achieve this end it was essential that the frameworks reflect an international consensus appropriately created through collaborative development of the measurement procedures—the TIMSS curriculum frameworks. In the context of a conference sponsored by NCES in May 1991, educators from a number of countries besides the United States spent two days analyzing and commenting on a seminal draft of the frameworks. Later that year, a revised draft was circulated for comments to all participating TIMSS representatives (SMSO, 1991a, 1991b). In this manner, three drafts of the frameworks were reviewed and revised through a negotiated and consensus-seeking process to produce the final published version (Robitaille, Schmidt, Raizen, McKnight, Britton, Nicol, 1993).

2. Eighth grade or its equivalent in the U.S. and most other TIMSS countries.

3. Fourth grade or its equivalent in the U.S. and most other TIMSS countries.

4. Consequently the frameworks only minimally represent the subjects that were the focus of the end-of-secondary "specialists" survey, e.g., calculus for mathematics and physics for science. Investigations of the many curricular issues surrounding these specialists topics have needed to expand the relevant portions of the TIMSS curriculum frameworks (e.g., see Britton & Raizen, 1996).

5. This issue of the "grain size" of various curriculum framework topics is, in part, a reflection of the necessary compromise struck between exhaustive and sufficient description. This is dramatically illustrated through a comparison between the first circulated draft of the mathematics framework and the final published version. The latter has less than one fourth the number of topics of the former, which contained twenty-seven arithmetic topics, twenty-four geometry topics, and twenty-six algebra topics.

6. Schmidt, W. H., McKnight, C., & Raizen, S. (1997). *A splintered vision: An investigation of U.S. science and mathematics education.* Dordrecht/Boston/London: Kluwer. Schmidt, W. H., McKnight, C., Cogan, L. S., Jakwerth, P. M., & Houang, R. T. (1999). *Facing the consequences: Using TIMSS for a closer look at U.S. mathematics and science education.* Dordrecht/Boston/London: Kluwer.

7. The TIMSS frameworks provide for a multifaceted specification of any curricular element using three different aspects: content, performance expectation, and perspective. *Content* specifies the topics addressed by the school subjects of mathematics or science. *Performance expectations* identify what students may be asked to do with any particular topic. *Perspective* identifies

a range of orientations students may be encouraged to adopt or develop toward the subject matter, its place among the disciplines, and its role in everyday life. The perspective categories were not used in the work reported in this book. Any curricular element may thus be characterized using as many categories as may be required from each of the three aspects to fully and accurately represent it. Each element may have a unique and, as we often found, complex set of content, performance expectation, and perspective categories. This flexible multidimensionality allows elements' descriptive portraits to be as simple or complex as needed.

8. Content standards were first divided into their smallest functional segment or "unit." Textbooks were divided into "lessons," e.g., the amount of material likely to be covered in one to three days of instruction. These segments were further divided into smaller segments, or "blocks," according to specified guidelines for identification and coding with the TIMSS curriculum frameworks (see Schmidt, McKnight, Valverde, Houang & Wiley, 1997; Schmidt, Raizen, Britton, Bianchi & Wolfe, 1997; and McKnight, Britton, Valverde & Schmidt, 1992 for more detail on curriculum analysis and coding). Six unit types were identified for standards: introduction, policy, objective, content, pedagogy, and other. Units specifying content or objectives were the most prevalent types identified. Five types of lessons were identified in textbooks: introduction, lesson, multiple lesson pages, instructional appendix, and other. Lesson units were, by far, the most commonly occurring (see Schmidt, McKnight, Valverde, Houang & Wiley, 1997, page 199; Schmidt, Raizen, Britton, Bianchi & Wolfe, 1997, page 209). Reflecting the differences in the two document types, seven block types were specified for standards and ten for textbooks. Block types for standards included official policies, objectives, content element, pedagogical suggestion, examples, assessment suggestions, and other. The type of blocks identified in textbooks included narrative, related narrative, unrelated instructional narrative, related graphic, unrelated graphic, exercise or question set, unrelated exercise or question set, activity, worked example, and other. Content element, objectives, and pedagogical examples were the predominate block types in standards. Exercise/question set blocks dominated mathematics textbooks while science textbooks demonstrated less emphasis on a single block type with an almost equal preponderance of narrative and related graphic blocks (see Schmidt, McKnight, Valverde, Houang & Wiley, 1997, page 202; Schmidt, Raizen, Britton, Bianchi & Wolfe, 1997, page 213).

9. Curriculum elements as described here were blocks from curriculum documents. A similar approach was later used on questions from teacher

questionnaires and on achievement test items. This allowed a common characterization of the content that cut across various aspects of the curriculum to be studied and the tests used to measure achievement.

10. A possible exception to this would be the abstract intention statements that may be found in the "objective" blocks of standards.

11. This raised the question of the trade-off between familiarity with the curriculum and reliability and standardization of blocking and coding. We took the approach that familiarity was important and thus that blocking and coding should be done by persons from the country supplying the documents. We also believed that translation would only introduce other sources of error into the process. To achieve reliability and standardization, training materials for face-to-face international training of coders were written and the same trainers provided that face-to-face training in a series of regional international training workshops. Initial samples were coded by the trained coders and then also coded by international coding referees to allow assessment of the reliability of blocking and coding and how well the rules provided in training were being followed. Careful international monitoring and other measures were used to maintain quality assurance of national coders' work. Estimated inter-rater reliabilities were .7 and higher depending on the aspect and the hierarchical level of the coding.

12. Sometimes this was because no single document addressed the totality of the focal grade's curriculum. For example, two eighth grade textbooks were analyzed for Japan, Germany, Romania, and the Russian Federation since each textbook covered only half the subject matter students were expected to learn in that school year. Typically this meant that one textbook covered the geometry topics and another textbook covered the algebra topics. In this instance, the union of these textbooks appropriately represents the eighth grade curriculum for these countries.

In other instances, countries had multiple documents that represented various regional or other types of subsystems. Given that the entire collection of documents was necessary to characterize a country's curriculum for at least 50 percent of their students, the appropriate country level curriculum characterization was, again, generated from the union of all documents, i.e., all region-specific and/or track-specific documents were analytically combined into a single country document. As an example, fourteen states' standards were analyzed together as a single document to characterize the intended curriculum for students in the USA. Another example is provided by Switzerland, which analyzed three sets of documents. Although Switzerland is divided into a number of cantons these are typically grouped according to the three main languages spoken in Switzerland: German, French, and

Italian. Considering all the appropriate documents from each of these language groups generated characterizations of the Swiss curriculum.

13. Teachers completed the topic list section of the TIMSS questionnaire with respect to a specific class they taught. TIMSS sampling for the two younger student populations identified entire classrooms for participation in the assessment. The mathematics and science teachers of these students were then asked to complete teacher surveys. Accordingly, teachers were asked to complete the topic list section with respect to what they had taught the class that had been assessed for TIMSS. The goal of this sampling strategy was to obtain an indication of what teachers actually did in teaching the tested classes rather than a generalized indication of what might be considered typically taught in a particular type of course. In addition, teachers had the advantage of stimulating their recall of their instructional history with respect to a specific class.

14. Schmidt et al., 1996.

15. See Schmidt, McKnight, Cogan, Jakwerth, and Houang, 1999, pages 115–162.

16. Jakwerth, 1996; Jakwerth, 1997; Jakwerth & Wolfe, 1997; Schmidt, Jakwerth, & McKnight, 1998.

17. Schmidt, McKnight, Cogan, Jakwerth, and Houang, 1999.

18. Performance on the eighth grade TIMSS mathematics assessment provides a more specific illustration. On the total score, U.S. performance was no different than the international mean with the scores of twenty countries significantly higher, seven countries significantly lower, and thirteen countries no different than that of the US. Greater variation was apparent in the six topic areas included in the international report. In these six areas, the number of countries who had scores significantly greater than that of the U.S. ranged from nine (in data representation and analysis) to thirty (in measurement) (National Center for Education Statistics, 1996; Schmidt, Jakwerth & McKnight, 1998). The greatest difference in rank for the U.S. across these six areas was fourteen. Across all countries, the mean difference in a country's highest and lowest rank was ten. For the Slovak Republic, Switzerland, and the Netherlands, three countries that significantly outperformed the US on the scaled score, the greatest difference in ranks were twenty-one, sixteen, and sixteen respectively.

Even greater variation was evident on the twenty topic tests that are used in the analyses reported here. Differences between countries' lowest and highest scores—expressed as a percent of the items correct—ranged from twenty to fifty-five percentage points. This means that in one country the difference between the percent correct in students' best topic and worst topic was twenty percentage points while this difference was as great as fifty-five percentage points in another country. This yielded large differences in countries' relative ranks on the twenty topic tests. The greatest rank difference for the U.S. was twenty-seven with the mean across all countries about eighteen. The greatest differences for the Slovak Republic, Switzerland, and the Netherlands were twenty-six, nineteen, and twenty-four respectively.

19. See Chapter Eight for more discussion of tested topic reliabilities.

20. The KR-20 reliability estimates are given in Beaton, Mullis, Martin, Gonzalez, Kelly, & Smith, 1996, page A-26 and Beaton, Martin, Mullis, Gonzalez, Smith, & Kelly, 1996, page A-26.

21. Appendix C presents the number of items and the TIMSS Framework content codes for each of these content specific tests which were based on the codes for each item. If an item had two content codes, the item was included in both of the content-specific tests defined by those codes. In mathematics, there were 150 items on the TIMSS test. Six items had two parts; one item had three parts. Forty-two of these had double codes yielding a total of 199 items distributed across the twenty content-specific tests. In science, there were 135 items, four of which had two parts and one of which had three parts. Twenty-five were double coded for a total of 165 items that were distributed across seventeen content-specific tests. Reliabilities of these content-specific tests are explained and discussed in further detail in Chapter Eight. Here we merely note the importance of these more precisely defined content-specific tests as a precondition to drawing relevant curricular conclusions.

22. Wiley, D. E., & Wolfe, R. G. (1992). Major survey design issues for the IEA Third International Mathematics and Science Study. *Prospects, 22*(3), 297–304.

23. Wiley & Wolfe, 1992.

24. The blueprints for the TIMSS tests were developed from early results of the TIMSS curriculum analysis. They were subsequently reviewed and approved by all the participating countries (SMSO, 1993; McKnight, Schmidt, & Raizen, 1993). Presumably, therefore, the tested topics represent those on which countries intended to focus on or emphasize in their focal grade's curriculum—for example, eighth grade. Thus content can be characterized at the lowest level of the framework, the level of the teacher questionnaires, and the level of the reporting categories or "tested topic areas" for which a sufficient number of items exist to provide a separate achievement score. The relationships between the three different topic measurements are specified in Appendix B.1 (mathematics) and B.2 (science).

25. Schmidt, McKnight, Valverde, Houang, & Wiley, 1997; Schmidt, Raizen, Britton, Bianchi & Wolfe, 1997.

26. Schmidt et al, 1996; Schmidt, McKnight, Valverde, Houang, & Wiley, 1997; Schmidt, Raizen, Britton, Bianchi, & Wolfe, 1997.

27. Schmidt & Kifer, 1989; Beaton, Mullis, Martin, Gonzalez, Kelly, and Smith, 1996, page 152.

28. See, for example, Pate-Bain, Boyd-Zaharias, Cain, Word, & Binkley 1997; Wenglinsky, 1997; and Achilles, 1998 for studies in U.S. classrooms that support the positive effect of small class size on student achievement.

29. Schmidt, McKnight, Valverde, Houang, & Wiley, 1997, page 97; Schmidt, Raizen, Britton, Bianchi, & Wolfe, 1997, pages 105–106.

30. The manner in which this is determined differs for standards and the other instantiations. For standards, the most emphasized topics are those intended by the most countries. For the other instantiations, e.g., textbooks and teachers, the most emphasized topics are those with the highest percentage of coverage.

31. The number of countries involved in any of these analyses varies. Not all countries collected all types of data. For example, Latvia was included in the science analyses but not in the mathematics analyses since they did not collect mathematics textbook data. Similarly, Israel is not included in any analyses involving student learning (gain) since they administered the student assessment only to eighth grade students. Although forty-nine countries submitted at least one type of data such as for content standards, textbooks, student assessments, or teacher surveys, only thirty-seven countries submitted data from most of these different sources. Analyses for mathematics involving all data sources involved thirty-one countries, as did the analyses for science. The full set of data from all sources for both mathematics and science was available for thirty countries. This was the full data set employed in all the two-way analyses reported in Chapter Six.

4

THE ARTICULATION
OF CURRICULUM

CURRICULUM IS a multifaceted structure that shapes learning opportunities. In this chapter we examine the means by which curricula are articulated in different countries. Curricular goals are set forth and decisions are made in relation to the social institutions of a country and its culture. Those goals, decisions, and choices constitute curricular policy, and that curricular policy has a context. Who makes the decisions? Which kinds of decisions do they make? How do the various participants in the educational system see their role in such decisions? We need to understand the context of curricular policy to properly understand the relationship between curriculum and learning.

Perhaps the most fundamental educational question for any country is that of what students are expected to learn. Education, formal as well as informal, has as one of its tasks transmitting key elements of appropriate national or other cultures to new generations. The content of the culture or cultures to be shared helps provide answers to what students are expected to learn in formal schooling. Certainly schools alone are not responsible for cultural transmission. It is a shared (often implicit) mission of many other institutions in society—familial, political, religious, peer group, ethnic, racial, regional, gender, and so on. Further, not all learning expectations are set by cultural demands. Educational institutions develop their own life and momentum, often resulting in decisions based on the internal life of those institutions that are only later and eventually changed by cultural impacts.

However, formal educational institutions formally articulate learning expectations for a country's students. They manipulate and carry out public policies that shape the goals and implementations of curricular decisions. To understand more fully the relationship of curriculum to learning, we must have a clear understanding of that policy context. The purpose of the present chapter is to seek such an understanding.

Looking Through the Lens of Educational Goals

We can pursue that understanding through a series of questions about learning goals. What goals are pursued at a national or regional level? What goals are pursued at the level of individual schools or for various types of schools? What goals are pursued in individual classrooms or for various types of classrooms or streams of students? How are these learning goals for the classroom and school related to the national or regional goals? How are the goals aligned to grades and sequenced? Who decides which goals are pursued, and how are these decisions made? How and on what basis are pupils differentiated with respect to the goals that are viewed as appropriate for them to pursue? Clearly these are among the most fundamental educational and societal questions that must be answered by the curricular policy of any country.

We focused on four key elements of curriculum and educational practice to explore curriculum policy further. Those four elements were goals for students, the content of instruction, the methods of instruction, and examinations. By exploring decision making around these four elements, we believe we can picture fairly clearly the flow of curricular policy and its implementation. By studying who makes decisions about each of these four elements, we believe we can map the way educational systems articulate curricular policy.

We operationalized each of these four elements in more detail to make our investigation more fine grained. The subelements for each of the four elements are listed as follows.

GOALS FOR STUDENTS

The goals for students to be obtained by completing the course of learning in the overall educational system

The goals for students to be obtained by completing intermediate stages of the educational system

The goals for students in differentiated program types

The goals to be reached at a given grade

The goals that apply for a specific school

THE CONTENT OF INSTRUCTION

The courses of study that are offered

The rules that determine which students are assigned to specific courses of study

The content of the syllabi for the courses of study

The auxiliary content, if any, that would give students an opportunity to learn outside the syllabi through instruction

The textbook selection

METHODS OF INSTRUCTION

Planning individual lessons

Instructional methods and techniques

EXAMINATIONS

The content of examinations

The standards of successful student performance on examinations

The Ambiguity of Centralization

Can policy alone create coherence in educational practice? Traditionally it has been held that this was true and that coherence could be examined by considering educational and curricular policies. More recently some have held that there must be a "living" institutional center to maintain coherence in the curriculum.[1] They argue that policy levers alone are not enough to create this coherence. A responsive institution must serve as a center to provide the coordination and glue to hold the curriculum together and to make adequately responsible curricular decisions. They hold that in fragmented rather than coherent systems, it is "quite difficult to locate authority and responsibility. What is missing is an institutional center that coalesces disparate interests and provides coherence to the educational system."[2]

Even if, as suggested, an institutional center is necessary to provide coherence to curriculum policy, there is still the question of how that institutional center is located within the elements—centralized or otherwise—of an educational system. Before addressing the question of what institutional centers were involved in the articulation of curricular policy, we felt it necessary to first address the question of what an educational system was and how many existed within a country.

For this part of our investigation, thirty-seven countries responded. The data they supplied involved 102 educational systems. An *educational system* was defined as a set of schools that operate with a particular sponsor or under a particular authority or control. From this information alone it can clearly be seen that the typical pattern was not that of one country, one educational system. We explicitly recognized five categories of educational systems in this sense. These included

1. National public schools—a single system or several corresponding to different branches of government or to separate linguistic or cultural groups

2. Regional or provincial public school systems

3. Locally operated public school systems—for example, school districts, city school systems, and so on

4. Nonpublic school systems of national, regional, or local scope

5. Nonpublic schools or systems that operate essentially as independent enterprises

Data for the analyses here came from a national-level participant questionnaire (PQII) that was designed for completion by ministry-level personnel. Nineteen of thirty-seven TIMSS countries (51 percent) reported having only one system, that is, national public schools. Only two of these nineteen indicated that the single system that they described was an aggregation of many systems of a similar kind (such aggregations were permitted when authority was centralized).

Other countries had far larger numbers of systems. These included Spain, Switzerland, Australia, Germany, and the United States, which, with over fifteen thousand local educational systems, had by far the largest number of systems among the countries that supplied data. The other countries with more than one system typically had around thirty or less. In some countries with multiple systems, the systems were differentiated by sponsorship—government, religious, private, and the like. In others, the differentiation stemmed from different government authorities, and in still others, the differentiation came from both of these two sources.

With this context of system multiplicity, we can now more reasonably address the question, "What was the institutional center in most countries for curriculum decision making?" To answer this question, we looked at the 102 systems for which data were provided. We asked how many of these had a national institution (most often a national ministry) as their central authority for curricular decision making. Almost 70 percent of systems (70 of 102) systems were reported to have this structure. This was, of course, true in all nineteen of the countries reporting only 1 system.

This was even true for two-thirds of the countries that indicated that they had multiple systems (twelve of eighteen). This means that in those twelve countries, each of the multiple systems—for example, private schools, religious schools, and so on—had the same national institutional center for curriculum even though control and authority sponsorship resided with multiple entities such as the national government and the church. In one of the six countries that reported not having a national center for all systems, a center was the same for many but not all of its educational systems.

Policy analysts and those who do research in educational policy often speak of centralized systems as a monolith according to a simple prototype—a single national system headed by a national ministry. In fact, based on the sample of TIMSS countries that supplied data, this was true for only about one-half of the countries. Other versions of centralization existed. For example, one country had 12 different systems headed by different institutions and government agencies but all of which had the same institutional center for matters related to curriculum.

Essentially then, the idea of educational centralization is far more subtle and ambiguous than is typically envisioned. Any cross-national investigation or report of educational practice that divides countries into two or three categories—for example, centralized or not—should be considered immediately suspect. They should be suspect as not having a clear picture of the true range of organizational diversity and as making distinctions that are too superficial to have much valid explanatory potential. It would merely be reification for such a study to find that centralization seemed not to be linked to any meaningful distinction in education practice or achievements.

It is not necessarily the uniformity of systems—a form of centralization—that produces coherence in curriculum. Rather, we hold with Timar, Kirp, and Kirst (1998) that it is the provision of an effective institutional center. The characteristics of that center and its policies regarding decision making and enforcement of those decisions are all part of characterizing an institutional center that can provide coherence in curriculum. Simplistic characterizations of centralization are a pale substitute.

The other six countries not yet discussed had systems where the institutional center was typically regional and for which there was a separate one for each distinct system. This was true for five of the six—that is, distinct systems were simply for different regions of Australia, Germany, Switzerland, Canada, and Belgium.

All of this suggests that a new image might emerge when speaking of centralization. This is an image of religious or ethnic school systems, of several public and private school systems, each sponsored and run by its own sponsoring agency—for example, the Catholic church or the national or regional government. However, within that context of multiple sponsorship, in matters of curriculum all systems still turn to one institutional center for their coherence. Is such a system the same as one with a single public school system headed by a national ministry? That hardly seems likely in any effective sense. A more refined conceptual framework seems essential to describe such variation and thus to find something more than the traditionally ambiguous use of the term *centralization.*

The key question would seem to become "centralization with respect to what?" That is, what specific role does the institutional center play? Is it advisory, or does it have final authority? For which of the elements and facets of curriculum and educational practice previously described does it have which type of authority? Exploring these questions should yield a far more refined, effectual concept of centralization.

This is further complicated by the fact that even in countries with an institutional center defined at the national level, other institutional centers at regional or local levels have some form of involvement in curriculum. Thus, the answer to what specific role an institutional center plays becomes more complex: "Who is responsible for what?" Who plays what role in shaping, articulating, and implementing curriculum?

In those systems with an institutional center that is the national ministry or its equivalent, 75 percent (52 of 70) also have regional or provincial government agencies involved, and about 60 percent (40 of 70) also have local government centers as well. All of the systems without such a national center have some form of subsystem. Obviously the curriculum policy context is complex in most countries. Simplistic labels must be avoided. Perhaps it is time to call a moratorium on the use of the term *centralization* until it could be used to call forth more subtle forms of institutional arrangements.

Who Makes What Decisions?

Clearly from the previous discussion, most countries have multiple governmental agencies involved in making decisions about curriculum. However, just as there are a range of agencies, there is also a range of decisions. This context makes pressing a different sort of question: Who makes what decisions? The dominant pattern in most countries is to have an institutional center at the national level. However, there may be considerable variety even then in how decision-making roles are distributed among multiple authorities.

For analysis, four roles were defined as possible for an institutional center or potential decision-making authority:

1. No formal role in curricular decision making
2. Giving advice and making recommendations about curricular decisions
3. Constraining, vetoing, or modifying recommendations about curricular decisions
4. Having final authority or approval of curricular decisions

Curricular decisions in this context may mean any from the range outlined earlier. An agency may play one role with one type of decision and a different role with a different type. It is this variety and possible distribution of decision making that makes "Who decides what?" an interesting question. We consider five possible sources of authority in terms of the "who." Each of the next five tables gives the results for national centers, subnational centers, schools, departments within schools, and teachers.

The Role of National Centers

What decision-making role is typical for national institutional centers? They play a strong role in decisions about curricular goals, as can be seen in Table 4.1. In our survey of educational systems, at least 75 percent of the national institutional centers had the final authority or approval of decisions about curricular goals. The exception to this was school-specific goals, in which only about 55 percent of the national centers had final authority or approval. Almost 30 percent of national institutional centers had no formal role in setting school-specific goals.

National institutional centers played a similarly strong role in decisions about the content of instruction. However, this was not equally true for all the aspects of determining content. The national center had the final authority in over 70 percent of the systems for course offerings and the content specification of syllabi for courses. They even had such an approval role in about 60 percent of the systems in determining rules for assigning students to courses. However, for specifying content outside the course syllabi and for selecting textbooks, national centers had final authority and approval in only about 50 percent of the systems. In fact, national centers had final authority for decisions about content outside of

Table 4.1. Percent of Educational Systems with Specific Roles Taken by the National Center for Each Decision Area.

	No Formal Role (0)	Advice and Recommendations (1)	Constrain, Veto, or Modify Recommendations (2)	Final Authority or Approval (3)	Total
Goals					
Overall for system completion	6	4	3	87	100
Intermediate-stage specific	7	3	3	87	100
Program-type specific	20	1	4	75	100
Grade-level specific	4	10	4	82	100
School-specific	28	15	2	55	100
Content of Instruction					
Course offerings	17	1	3	79	100
Course assignment roles	27	10	4	59	100
Syllabi for courses	20	7	1	72	100
Content outside syllabi	51	23	7	19	100
Textbook selection	31	16	3	50	100
Methods of Instruction					
Lesson planning	66	31	0	3	100
Instructional methods	51	49	0	0	100
Examinations					
Content	50	22	2	26	100
Performance standards	17	9	2	72	100

the syllabi in only about 20 percent of the systems and had no formal role at all in about 50 percent of the systems.

In contrast, the national institutional center had no formal role in decisions about methods of instruction in over 50 percent of the systems. For those systems where national centers did have a role, that role was only advisory.

The role of national centers differed for decisions about examinations depending on whether the decisions were about content or about performance standards. The national centers had final authority for content decisions in examinations in only about 30 percent of the systems (and no formal role in about 50 percent). In contrast, national centers had final authority for performance standards for examinations in about 70 percent of the systems.

Subnational and Regional Centers

A much smaller set of countries (five) had an institutional center that was defined at a subnational or regional level that had final authority for important curricular decisions but had no national centers. Others had both national and subnational or regional institutional centers involved, but these are discussed later in this chapter.

What role did subnational and regional centers play in curricular decision making when there was no national center behind them? The answer generally, as found in Table 4.2, was that they played a very different role from that of a national institutional center. In the area of goals, these institutional centers had final authority or approval for goals of the overall system in about 85 percent of the cases. In all other areas pertaining to goals, less than 40 percent of these centers had final authority.

Almost 90 percent of the systems with regional or subnational centers as the most centralized level of decision making gave them final authority for the specification of content in course syllabi. These centers had only an advisory role or no formal role for textbook selection in about 80 percent of the cases. These regional and subnational institutional centers thus had a strong role in determining the content of instruction as reflected in system goals and course syllabi, but this contrasted with the systems that had national centers. National centers had final authority over much more, even over textbook selection, in approximately half of the systems.

Regional and subnational centers had no formal role in determining methods of instruction in about 65 to 70 percent of the cases. For examinations, another interesting contrast emerged. These centers, too, had final authority (when they were not backed by a national center) for performance stan-

Table 4.2. Percent of Educational Systems with Specific Roles Taken by the Regional Center for Each Decision Area.

	No Formal Role (0)	Advice and Recommendations (1)	Constrain, Veto, or Modify Recommendations (2)	Final Authority or Approval (3)	Total
Goals					
Overall for system completion	0	8	8	84	100
Intermediate-stage specific	31	19	11	39	100
Program-type specific	27	31	4	39	101
Grade-level specific	46	23	4	27	100
School-specific	62	8	3	27	100
Content of Instruction					
Course offerings	35	23	3	39	100
Course assignment roles	50	23	8	19	100
Syllabi for courses	8	5	0	87	100
Content outside syllabi	46	50	0	4	100
Textbook selection	42	39	4	15	100
Methods of Instruction					
Lesson planning	69	19	0	12	100
Instructional methods	64	24	0	12	100
Examinations					
Content	24	16	4	56	100
Performance standards	23	15	4	58	100

Note: *This table applies only for those systems in countries that have no national center.*

dards in a large percentage of the systems, just as national centers did. However, they also had final authority over the content of examinations in over 50 percent of the systems. This was about twice the percentage for national centers in this area of decision making. National centers had tighter control than regional or subnational centers over textbook selection (50 percent versus 15 percent), whereas the regional centers had a tighter control over the content of examinations (56 percent versus 26 percent). Thus, subnational centers, when they were the most powerful institutional center for curricular decision making, had final authority over the content of instruction mainly through the specification of system goals and the content of course syllabi and examinations. This differed markedly from systems in which national institutional centers were the most centralized level of authority.

Multiple Decision-Making Agencies

Multiple government agencies were at least partially involved in curricular decision making, both in the systems that had national institutional centers and in those that had regional or subnational institutional centers. For the systems with national centers, there were two other levels—regional and local decision-making centers. For those with only regional or subnational centers as the most centralized agency in curricular decision making, there was only one other level—local centers.

What roles did these other centers play? In general, the answer is that they played a very small role. In all of the different aspects of curriculum decision making, these subsystems had no formal role in the majority of the systems. The actual percentage ranged from 55 to 77 percent for different types of decisions. When they did have a role, it was primarily in an advisory capacity. The only exceptions were in the setting of school-specific goals and in determining course offerings. In both cases the subsystem had final authority in these two areas in about 20 percent of the cases. These were activities that typically occurred at the school level.

The Role of Schools, Departments, and Individual Teachers

What role did schools, departments, and individual teachers play in curriculum decision making? That role differed among these three types of decision makers.

THE ROLE OF SCHOOLS Schools mostly had no formal role in determining curricular goals except in setting school-specific goals, as Table 4.3 suggests. Even for those decisions, the school had final authority in only about one-third of the systems.

Table 4.3. Percent of Educational Systems with Specific Roles Taken by the Individual School for Each Decision Area.

	No Formal Role (0)	Advice and Recommendations (1)	Constrain, Veto, or Modify Recommendations (2)	Final Authority or Approval (3)	Total
Goals					
Overall for system completion	71	14	8	7	100
Intermediate-stage specific	64	13	11	12	100
Program-type specific	60	14	10	16	100
Grade-level specific	61	17	10	12	100
School-specific	44	16	4	36	100
Content of Instruction					
Course offerings	52	15	10	23	100
Course assignment roles	55	9	6	30	100
Syllabi for courses	64	13	8	15	100
Content outside syllabi	49	8	8	35	100
Textbook selection	44	9	13	34	100
Methods of Instruction					
Lesson planning	57	18	10	15	100
Instructional methods	51	26	11	12	100
Examinations					
Content	60	14	13	13	100
Performance standards	69	8	14	9	100

The role of schools varied in decisions about the content of instruction as reflected in course offerings, course assignments, textbook selection, and content outside the syllabus. The school had final authority in these areas in about one-third of the systems yet had no formal role at all in about half of the other systems. The one area where schools consistently had little formal role, let alone final authority, was in the specification of course syllabi. Schools also had no formal role for decisions about the methods of instruction and about examinations in most systems.

THE ROLE OF DEPARTMENTS AND TEACHER GROUPS *Departments* is used here to refer to both formally organized departments within schools and groups of teachers empowered to make decisions even when not formally organized as a department.

Departments had no major role in determining goals, methods of instruction, examinations, or the content of instruction (other than textbook selection) in most systems, as Table 4.4 makes clear. Collections of teachers had final authority over any of these four areas in less than 15 percent of the systems. For decisions in these areas, they had no formal role in most systems (50 to 80 percent).

However, in about one-fourth of the systems, departments or teacher groups had final authority over textbook selection in mathematics and science. In another fourth, they had either the role of providing or modifying recommendations about textbook selections.

THE ROLE OF TEACHERS   Table 4.5 presents the corresponding results for individual teachers. They had no formal role in setting curricular goals in two-thirds or more of the educational systems surveyed. Individual teachers also had no formal role in about two-thirds or more of the systems surveyed in determining the content of instruction in the sense of course offerings, course assignments, or the content of the course syllabi. In contrast, teachers had final authority for determining content outside the syllabi to be covered and for textbook selection in about one-third of the systems. In 25 to 40 percent of the systems, individual teachers had some kind of advisory or modifying role in these areas.

Teachers had their greatest authority in decisions about methods of instruction. In about 90 percent of the systems, individual teachers had final authority in this area. The role of individual teachers varied dramatically for different aspects of decisions about examinations. Teachers had final authority for content specification in about two-thirds of the systems surveyed. However, there was a split of authority for determining

Table 4.4. Percent of Educational Systems with Specific Roles Taken by the Department/Group of Teachers for Each Decision Area.

	No Formal Role (0)	Advice and Recommendations (1)	Constrain, Veto, or Modify Recommendations (2)	Final Authority or Approval (3)	Total
Goals					
Overall for system completion	81	15	4	0	100
Intermediate-stage specific	73	19	8	0	100
Program-type specific	72	16	8	4	100
Grade-level specific	69	15	12	4	100
School-specific	67	16	13	4	100
Content of Instruction					
Course offerings	66	16	7	11	100
Course assignment roles	66	18	8	8	100
Syllabi for courses	66	22	5	7	100
Content outside syllabi	55	25	9	11	100
Textbook selection	46	17	11	26	100
Methods of Instruction					
Lesson planning	51	32	9	8	100
Instructional methods	48	33	10	9	100
Examinations					
Content	57	22	6	15	100
Performance standards	66	16	6	12	100

Table 4-5. Percent of Educational Systems with Specific Roles Taken by the Individual Teacher for Each Decision Area.

	No Formal Role (0)	Advice and Recommendations (1)	Constrain, Veto, or Modify Recommendations (2)	Final Authority or Approval (3)	Total
Goals					
Overall for system completion	77	14	8	1	100
Intermediate-stage specific	70	16	13	1	100
Program-type specific	76	14	8	2	100
Grade-level specific	67	16	11	6	100
School-specific	67	22	7	4	100
Content of Instruction					
Course offerings	70	25	1	4	100
Course assignment roles	60	21	6	13	100
Syllabi for courses	64	15	10	11	100
Content outside syllabi	42	15	10	33	100
Textbook selection	32	21	17	30	100
Methods of Instruction					
Lesson planning	9	0	5	86	100
Instructional methods	3	0	2	95	100
Examinations					
Content	19	8	5	67	99
Performance standards	54	4	2	40	100

performance standards. In over one-half of the systems, teachers had no formal role in those decisions; in nearly the rest they had final authority.

A Synthesis: Who Decides What?

We have examined our survey data on curricular decision making in terms of the various agencies and actors who played a role in those curricular decisions and in which decisions they played a role. It seems useful to make a synthesis of these results to examine the multiple roles played in each category of curricular decision making. We are interested in who the dominant player is for each decision type; that is, who primarily makes the final decision. This would be a simple matter of looking for the largest percentages were it not for joint decision making in which two separate agencies or sets of players share final authority. The amount of joint authority varied from around 10 to 45 percent across the fourteen areas of curricular decision making surveyed. The smallest percent of joint decision making was in the area of setting overall goals for system completion. The highest percentage of joint decision making was for textbook selection.

CURRICULAR GOALS The proportion of systems with joint decision making about curricular goals was 10 percent or less except for school-specific goals. The dominant decision maker for those areas was the institutional center, either national or subnational, in the small number of systems where there was no national center. Almost one-fourth of the systems had joint decision making for setting school-specific goals. This was primarily a sharing of decision making between the institutional center and individual schools. Even in this area of decision making, the sole dominant decision maker was still the institutional center in about 40 percent of the systems. It was the school itself in about 20 percent of the systems.

CONTENT OF INSTRUCTION The amount of joint decision making in decisions about the content of instruction varied from about 20 to 45 percent. About 30 percent of the decisions about course offerings were jointly made. Most of these involved the institutional center as one of the joint members. The sole dominant decision maker remained the institutional center because in about 50 percent of the systems it had the sole authority for these decisions.

About one-fourth of the systems had joint decision making regarding rules about who would be assigned to which courses. Most of this joint decision making involved the institutional center as one of the decision makers. The dominant sole authority here was still the institutional center (in about 40 percent of the systems).

About 20 percent of the systems had joint decision-making authority for decisions about the content of course syllabi. The institutional center was overwhelmingly one of the partners in this joint decision making (in about 85 percent of the cases). The institutional center was again the dominant sole authority when joint decision making was not involved (in about 60 percent of the systems).

In determining content outside course syllabi to be covered in classrooms, about one-fourth of the systems had joint decision-making authority. Here, for the first time, the institutional center was not predominantly one of the partners in these decisions. Schools and teachers were the dominant players when joint authority was involved. The dominant sole decision makers were teachers (in about 30 percent of the systems). In this case it was teachers, either alone or in joint decision making, who dominated the decisions that were made.

Almost one-half of the systems (45 percent) had joint authority in decisions about textbook selection. The most common pattern of shared authority was between the institutional center and the department within the school. However, this was not the pattern in the majority of cases. There were so many configurations of joint authority in textbook selection that no one achieved majority status. Other configurations included schools and departments, institutional centers and individual teachers, and schools and individual teachers. The institutional center (about 20 percent of the systems) was the dominant sole authority when joint decision making did not occur. Teachers were the sole authority in about 10 percent of the cases. The dominant mode of decision making for textbook selection was shared authority. This was the only area of curriculum decision making in which this was true.

METHODS OF INSTRUCTION There was relatively little joint decision making either for lesson planning or for determining methods of instruction (that is, only in about 20 percent of the systems surveyed). Most of what joint authority existed was between schools or departments within the school and individual teachers. However, the dominant sole authority for both areas when joint decision making was not present was the individual teacher (in about 75 percent of the systems). This was the only area of curriculum decision making dominated by individual teachers.

EXAMINATIONS About one-third of the systems had joint authority for decisions related to examinations. In most cases this joint authority involved the institutional center or subnational centers (regional or local) for the content of the examination and the institutional center for the examination's performance standards. When joint authority was not present, the dominant sole authority for the content of examinations was individual teachers (36 percent of the systems). Thus, the content decisions were made either jointly (37 percent of the systems) or by teachers individually (36 percent). The dominant sole authority for decisions about performance standards was the institutional center (42 percent of the systems), but joint decision making was a close second (32 percent). Decision making about examinations seems clearly to be split for performance standards and content, whether it involved joint decision making or sole authority. This area seems to have involved the most complex decision-making authority structure.

The Perception of Influence on Decisions

This section examines the perception of key players (teachers and headmasters) in educational systems as to who has influence over various curricular decisions. The previous sections of this chapter have described the formal system of curricular decision making, at least as described by national ministry officials, their representatives, or other central authorities. In this section we wish to examine the perceptions of teachers and headmasters about these same issues.

This is not an issue of whose perceptions are more accurate or even if the perceptions agree with each other. The perceptions described by country representatives (typically ministry officials) in the previous sections are described as the official policy of curricular decision making. The spheres of influence that others in the same system perceive—even if not accurate from the point of view of formal or official policy—are important because they represent how key players in the implementation of system policies perceive their role. Such perceptions are themselves important because they influence how such players will act, even if all that they are doing by some supposedly objective criterion is carrying out the formal policies. For example, teachers who believe that they have influence over curricular decisions might react differently to official policies than teachers who believe they have no such influence even though all work in the same system.

Such perceptions contribute to the stake that participants in the schooling system feel they have in its operation and success. This may reflect whether they feel a dynamic or influential part of the system rather than its pawn. It certainly may have an impact on their motivational level. This in turn may well affect the level of effort put forth in implementing policies and the degree of professionalism with which such work is pursued.

Perhaps a key to understanding some of the differences between this section and previous sections comes in considering what roles are investigated. The previous sections identified formal mechanisms of influence such as "no formal role," "developing recommendations," "constraining or limiting recommendations," "vetoing recommendations," "modifying recommendations," "giving final approval," and "having exclusive responsibility." This section deals with informal as well as formal mechanisms.

Even if teachers in a given country have no formal role in a curricular decision, they might have informal means by which they express their views and hence perceive themselves to have influence. Providing informal mechanisms or outlets by which teachers come to such perceptions (and thereby managing those perceptions) might well be one important function of successful institutional centers and could contribute to successful implementation of official policies.

This is an alternative that challenges the common notion in the United States that successful reform necessitates teachers feeling empowered to make content decisions and that top-down management of curriculum and curricular change will not work.[3] It may be more relevant whether teachers feel a part of the system and able to influence it even when the actual definition of content standards is determined by an institutional center.

Teachers' Perceptions of Their Own Influence

Teachers function on the basis of their perceptions of themselves and their role in the educational system of which they are a part. This includes their perceptions of their influence on the kinds of curricular decisions already considered.

INFLUENCE ON CONTENT TAUGHT The TIMSS data included information from twenty-two countries with a national center that provided both the national or official data on curricular decision making and teacher questionnaire data, including questions on their perceptions. The majority of the teachers indicated that they had some or a lot of influence on the content taught in fifteen of these twenty-two countries. In fact, over 75 percent of the teachers shared such a perception in eight of the twenty-two countries.[4] Five of these countries had over 50 percent of their teachers indicating that they had a lot of influence. Over all 22 countries, one-third (32 percent) of teachers indicated that they felt that they had a lot of influence on content taught. About another third (31 percent) indicated that they had some influence. Nearly 20 percent indicated that they had little influence, and only about 17 percent indicated that they had none.

These last data are particularly interesting. The countries included those with a national institutional center in which over 80 percent of their systems had final authority residing in that center for overall, intermediate, and grade-level specific decisions on curricular goals. Even so, only about 20 percent of the teachers indicated that they believed they had no influence on the subject matter to be taught. This is true even when about 70 percent of their systems had final authority for decisions regarding the content of course syllabi.

In four out of five countries with regional institutional centers, over 50 percent of teachers indicated that they perceived themselves to have either some or a lot of influence over the content taught. Ironically, in countries where control of the decisions about goals and content were closer to the level of the individual teacher, only about one-fifth of the teachers indicated that they had a lot of influence over these decisions. This compares to one-third for those with national centers ($p < .05$). For those without national centers, one-fifth indicated having a lot of influence, one-third (32 percent) indicated having some influence, one-fourth (28 percent) indicated having a little, and one-fifth indicated that they had none. Perhaps this is consistent with the data that in 86 percent of the systems in countries with regional centers (but no national centers), the center had final authority for the content of course syllabi. This contrasts with 71 percent in those countries with national centers. This is true even though only about 30 percent of the centers had final authority for intermediate and grade-level specification of goals.

The teacher perception percentages for countries with national institutional centers were not that different from those for the United States. Yet in the United States, teacher influence is commonly believed to be the norm and even ideologically defended by some. Certainly institutional centers are closer to the teachers—at the local if not the school level. In the United States, 39 percent of the teachers indicated that they had a lot of influence on the content of what is taught, 32 percent having indicated some influence, 18 percent indicated having a little, and about 11 percent indicated having none.

INFLUENCE ON TEXTBOOK SELECTION Surprisingly, teachers' perception of their influence on textbook selection in countries with national centers parallels their perceptions for decisions on the subject matter to be taught. About 24 percent indicated that they had a lot of influence; 38 percent, that they had some; 20 percent, that they had little; and 19 percent, that they had none. This is surprising because over all such systems studied, teachers had final authority or approval in 30 percent of the systems and

Table 4.6. Mathematics Teachers' Perceptions of the Amount of Their Influence on Curriculum.

Type of Institutional Center	Country	1. None Percent	S.E.*	2. Little Percent	S.E.*	3. Some Percent	S.E.*	4. A Lot Percent	S.E.*
National	Sweden	0.0	(0.0)	4.4	(1.2)	44.7	(4.6)	50.8	(4.3)
	Denmark	0.6	(0.6)	9.6	(2.3)	35.9	(2.6)	53.9	(2.7)
	Spain	2.7	(1.2)	3.4	(1.3)	32.4	(3.3)	61.4	(2.7)
	Austria	3.2	(1.1)	18.7	(2.5)	40.4	(3.2)	37.6	(3.4)
	Colombia	3.4	(1.4)	4.0	(1.4)	23.2	(2.0)	69.3	(2.4)
	Norway	3.7	(2.1)	15.0	(2.7)	47.1	(2.4)	34.3	(2.3)
	Netherlands	4.7	(1.4)	22.4	(1.7)	50.1	(2.6)	22.8	(3.1)
	Hungary	5.3	(3.1)	9.1	(4.1)	13.0	(1.9)	72.6	(2.0)
	Korea	6.7	(3.1)	9.4	(3.2)	37.4	(2.2)	46.6	(3.0)
	Israel	7.9	(3.9)	39.9	(3.0)	27.9	(2.7)	24.3	(3.4)
	New Zealand	9.9	(1.4)	23.0	(3.8)	39.5	(9.1)	27.6	(6.9)
	Portugal	13.6	(1.3)	20.9	(2.7)	45.9	(2.8)	19.5	(3.0)
	Hong Kong	14.3	(4.1)	27.5	(2.6)	37.2	(3.4)	21.0	(3.7)
	Russian Federation	14.4	(3.9)	15.9	(4.0)	42.8	(2.8)	26.9	(2.6)
	Singapore	19.9	(2.5)	23.4	(2.0)	35.4	(3.3)	21.3	(3.3)
	Slovenia	23.0	(2.9)	39.7	(3.3)	25.9	(3.5)	11.5	(3.0)
	Japan	26.3	(3.6)	26.1	(8.5)	22.5	(4.6)	25.1	(3.7)
	Romania	31.2	(2.4)	31.6	(2.8)	22.7	(4.7)	14.5	(3.6)
	Ireland	38.0	(1.5)	18.4	(1.9)	20.2	(3.6)	23.3	(3.6)
	Cyprus	40.5	(3.2)	30.7	(2.7)	20.4	(4.2)	8.4	(1.8)
	Greece	43.2	(2.6)	15.5	(3.4)	15.7	(2.7)	25.6	(2.0)

Type of Institutional Center	Country	1. None		2. Little		3. Some		4. A Lot	
		Percent	S.E.*	Percent	S.E.*	Percent	S.E.*	Percent	S.E.*
National	France	57.6	(3.6)	23.0	(3.1)	10.9	(3.3)	8.6	(3.7)
	Average (National)	*16.8*		*19.6*		*31.4*		*32.1*	
Regional	Switzerland	5.4	(1.2)	23.6	(1.4)	32.9	(3.3)	38.1	(3.7)
	Germany	11.4	(2.6)	33.2	(2.3)	31.4	(2.6)	24.0	(2.7)
	Canada	15.6	(1.9)	20.5	(4.2)	41.7	(4.2)	22.1	(1.8)
	Australia	16.6	(2.4)	29.2	(2.8)	35.4	(2.9)	18.7	(2.4)
	Belgium (Fr)	24.2	(3.5)	31.0	(3.9)	38.9	(2.0)	6.0	(2.4)
	Belgium (Fl)	49.7	(1.1)	29.9	(2.5)	9.1	(3.2)	11.3	(3.4)
	Average (Regional)	*20.5*		*27.9*		*31.6*		*20.0*	
Local	United States	11.3	(2.4)	17.7	(2.8)	32.4	(3.1)	38.6	(3.8)

* *Standard errors (S.E.) are provided for all data gathered from the sample of teachers, students, or school administrators who responded to the TIMSS surveys. For statistical purposes, standard errors provide an indication of the uncertainty due to sampling in the estimate of the statistic, given here as a percentage.*

some formal role, even if only advisory, in another 38 percent. One might have expected a higher percentage at the upper end although most did believe that they had at least a little influence in these decisions.

For countries with regional institutional centers (but no national centers), a slightly higher (but not statistically significant) percentage of teachers believed that they had some or a lot of influence. In the locally driven U.S. system, the percentage of teachers who believed that they had some influence was very similar to the other two cases.

PRINCIPALS' PERCEPTION OF TEACHER INFLUENCE Principals or headmasters were also asked to indicate their perceptions of different groups' influence over the curriculum (see the following section). This included their perceptions of teachers' influence. For countries with national centers, regional centers, and local centers (the United States), the principals' estimate of the percentage of influence that teachers had was very consistent with the teachers' own perceptions, both in import and in detail. The only exception concerned the percentage of teachers that principals believed had a lot of influence. This was somewhat lower than the percentages provided by teachers in countries with national centers and local centers. It was higher in countries with regional institutional centers.

Teachers were asked for their perceptions of their influence on specific aspects of curricular decisions such as the content of instruction and textbook selection. Principals and headmasters were asked a more general question concerning their influence on curriculum. In countries with national centers, a large percentage (almost 35 percent) of the principals believed that they had a lot of influence on curriculum. Another 31 percent felt that they had some influence. Only 15 percent believed that they had no influence.

For countries with regional but not national centers, about one-fourth felt that they had a lot of influence; about one-third, that they had some; about 30 percent, that they had little; and about 10 percent, that they had none. For the United States, about 30 percent of principals indicated that they had a lot of influence on curriculum; nearly one-half, that they had some influence; about 20 percent, that they had little; and only about 1 percent, that they had none.

It is difficult to interpret these results because one does not know of what curriculum decisions the principals were thinking when responding to the questionnaire. However, one thing is clear across all countries—the majority (no matter the nature of the institutional center) indicated that they had some or a lot of influence on curriculum. This was especially true in countries with national or local (the United States) institutional centers.

Some insight into what the principals' responses may have indicated might be gleaned from examining the formal role of the school in curriculum decision making. This assumes that this formal role would be closely tied to the principals' perceptions. In the earlier sections we noted that in about 35 percent of the systems schools (and hence principals in all likelihood) had final authority in goal specification for school-specific goals, course content outside the syllabus, and in textbook selection. They also had a formal role in determining course offerings in about one-half of the systems.

Principals' Perceptions of Others Influence

We have already discussed principals' indications of their perceptions of their own as well as teachers' influence on curriculum. They were also asked about their perceptions of the influence that other individuals or groups had over the curriculum. These included national subject matter associations, local school governing boards, parents, textbook publications, and external examinations.

NATIONAL SUBJECT MATTER ASSOCIATIONS One influence on schools and curriculum in most countries is that of the presence and work of national subject matter associations (such as the National Council of Teachers of Mathematics [NCTM] in the United States). Over all of the countries surveyed, about 40 percent of the principals indicated that national subject matter associations had some or a lot of influence on curriculum decisions. In contrast, about one-third of the principals said that they had no influence. There were no major differences across countries in these proportions for countries with different types of institutional centers.

LOCAL SCHOOL GOVERNING BOARDS Averaged over the surveyed countries with national or regional institutional centers, about one-third of the principals surveyed said that local school governing boards had no influence on curriculum decisions. A total of 65 percent said that these boards had little or no influence on curriculum decisions. Only about 12 percent said that such boards had a lot of influence. This is certainly not what would be expected in the United States, where over one half of the principals (56 percent) said that local school boards had a lot of influence on curriculum decisions. Less than 20 percent of U.S. principals surveyed indicated that local school boards had little or no influence on curriculum decisions. From these survey data, it appears that only in the United States did local school boards have much influence.

Table 4.7. Mathematics Teachers' Perceptions of the Amount of Their Influence on Textbook Selection.

Type of Institutional Center	Country	1. None		2. Little		3. Some		4. A Lot	
		Percent	S.E.	Percent	S.E.	Percent	S.E.	Percent	S.E.
National	Denmark	0.4	(2.3)	19.2	(2.5)	46.7	(3.1)	33.7	(3.7)
	Austria	2.2	(1.0)	18.5	(1.8)	49.7	(2.8)	29.7	(2.7)
	Hungary	3.4	(2.2)	46.9	(2.8)	43.4	(3.1)	6.3	(1.6)
	Sweden	3.7	(2.5)	16.8	(3.1)	45.5	(5.0)	34.0	(2.9)
	Portugal	5.1	(1.6)	7.3	(1.8)	53.1	(2.8)	34.5	(3.6)
	Colombia	6.7	(1.8)	11.8	(2.3)	36.9	(3.5)	44.6	(3.8)
	Netherlands	7.0	(2.2)	9.2	(2.1)	50.4	(3.5)	33.4	(4.1)
	Spain	7.1	(4.2)	5.8	(3.6)	37.8	(2.5)	49.3	(4.1)
	Korea	7.4	(1.1)	10.7	(3.6)	62.7	(3.4)	19.2	(2.8)
	Ireland	8.0	(1.0)	8.8	(2.7)	37.1	(4.2)	46.2	(3.8)
	Norway	8.1	(3.0)	28.6	(2.5)	55.8	(2.1)	7.5	(1.6)
	France	12.4	(2.0)	22.4	(3.1)	29.4	(4.1)	35.8	(3.7)
	Israel	12.4	(3.6)	25.2	(2.8)	47.4	(2.8)	14.9	(5.3)
	New Zealand	12.8	(4.1)	18.3	(7.0)	35.1	(8.8)	33.8	(3.2)
	Russian Federation	13.9	(2.0)	17.1	(2.6)	38.2	(2.8)	30.8	(5.1)
	Slovenia	16.3	(1.4)	31.4	(1.8)	30.6	(3.6)	21.7	(3.3)
	Hong Kong	20.0	(0.3)	35.8	(2.9)	37.4	(3.7)	6.8	(2.1)
	Singapore	30.1	(1.8)	22.8	(3.0)	37.7	(3.5)	9.5	(1.9)
	Romania	42.8	(2.3)	28.9	(2.4)	13.9	(4.4)	14.4	(2.5)
	Japan	62.9	(3.9)	21.8	(4.2)	11.6	(3.6)	3.7	(1.0)
	Greece	64.1	(3.4)	12.4	(2.4)	14.6	(2.6)	8.9	(2.2)

Type of Institutional Center	Country	1. None Percent	S.E.	2. Little Percent	S.E.	3. Some Percent	S.E.	4. A Lot Percent	S.E.
National	Cyprus	66.5	(2.9)	17.4	(2.5)	12.2	(3.9)	3.8	(1.4)
	Average (National)	*18.8*		*19.9*		*37.6*		*23.7*	
Regional	Germany	1.7	(1.0)	18.0	(2.7)	51.8	(4.2)	28.5	(2.4)
	Belgium (Fl)	5.6	(1.8)	11.0	(2.3)	36.5	(3.5)	47.0	(2.7)
	Belgium (Fr)	12.8	(2.9)	11.4	(2.5)	48.0	(3.9)	27.8	(3.5)
	Switzerland	13.2	(2.0)	42.1	(2.9)	28.9	(2.8)	15.8	(3.8)
	Australia	16.8	(2.5)	22.8	(2.0)	39.9	(2.9)	20.6	(2.5)
	Canada	20.3	(2.3)	22.4	(2.5)	31.9	(3.1)	25.4	(2.9)
	Average (Regional)	*11.7*		*21.3*		*39.5*		*27.5*	
Local	United States	25.1	(3.4)	19.1	(2.4)	32.6	(3.0)	23.1	(2.9)

Table 4.8. Principal's Perceptions of Individual Teachers' Influence on Curriculum.

Type of Institutional Center	Country	1. None		2. Little		3. Some		4. A Lot	
		Percent	S.E.	Percent	S.E.	Percent	S.E.	Percent	S.E.
National	Austria	0.0	(0.0)	6.1	(3.2)	12.9	(3.1)	81.0	(4.2)
	Sweden	1.0	(1.0)	18.4	(3.7)	36.2	(5.5)	44.4	(5.2)
	Denmark	2.0	(1.4)	8.9	(2.8)	15.7	(3.7)	73.3	(4.6)
	Hong Kong	2.6	(1.8)	50.7	(5.1)	44.1	(5.4)	2.6	(1.9)
	Russian Federation	3.0	(1.3)	12.6	(2.7)	51.5	(4.0)	32.9	(3.2)
	Netherlands	3.2	(1.9)	6.0	(2.9)	40.8	(6.3)	50.0	(6.8)
	Hungary	4.2	(1.7)	17.9	(2.6)	27.6	(3.8)	50.3	(3.9)
	Japan	7.2	(1.8)	33.2	(4.2)	46.6	(3.9)	13.0	(2.7)
	Spain	10.4	(2.9)	27.0	(3.5)	35.0	(4.2)	27.6	(3.7)
	Korea	10.9	(2.7)	23.4	(4.1)	44.7	(4.5)	21.0	(3.6)
	New Zealand	11.0	(2.8)	41.9	(4.2)	36.0	(4.3)	11.1	(2.5)
	Singapore	12.1	(2.7)	49.8	(4.9)	34.7	(4.4)	3.4	(1.6)
	Colombia	12.5	(4.7)	17.7	(3.5)	30.8	(4.5)	39.0	(4.7)
	Israel	18.0	(7.6)	48.1	(9.7)	29.9	(8.1)	3.9	(4.0)
	Slovenia	18.6	(4.4)	33.2	(5.2)	26.9	(4.6)	21.2	(4.0)
	Portugal	37.6	(4.3)	30.8	(3.9)	22.6	(3.8)	8.9	(2.8)
	Romania	44.4	(4.4)	37.8	(4.0)	11.5	(2.7)	6.4	(1.8)
	Greece	57.8	(4.3)	30.2	(4.0)	9.4	(2.3)	2.6	(0.9)
	France	60.7	(5.4)	24.0	(4.6)	6.1	(2.4)	9.2	(2.9)
	Cyprus	63.6	(0.5)	32.3	(0.5)	0.0	(0.0)	4.1	(0.1)
	Average (National)	19.0	(0.5)	27.5	(0.5)	28.2		25.3	

Type of Institutional Center	Country	1. None Percent	S.E.	2. Little Percent	S.E.	3. Some Percent	S.E.	4. A Lot Percent	S.E.
Regional	Belgium (Fl)	8.3	(2.0)	12.8	(2.3)	32.7	(4.2)	46.1	(5.0)
	Australia	8.5	(3.1)	38.5	(4.7)	40.1	(4.7)	12.9	(2.9)
	Germany	9.7	(3.7)	14.8	(4.4)	25.8	(4.6)	49.8	(6.0)
	Switzerland	11.1	(2.3)	18.7	(3.5)	18.5	(3.2)	51.7	(4.1)
	Canada	13.5	(3.1)	41.3	(3.9)	25.0	(2.8)	20.2	(3.5)
	Average (Regional)	10.2		25.2		28.4		36.1	
Local	United States	6.6	(2.4)	22.5	(3.4)	42.7	(4.1)	28.2	(4.0)

Note: *Belgium (French-speaking), Ireland, and Norway did not administer the portion of the school questionnaire from which these data are taken.*

Table 4-9. Principals' Perceptions of Their Own Influence on Curriculum.

Type of Institutional Center	Country	1. None Percent	S.E.	2. Little Percent	S.E.	3. Some Percent	S.E.	4. A Lot Percent	S.E.
National	Sweden	0.0	(0.0)	3.1	(1.8)	36.3	(4.7)	60.6	(4.6)
	Japan	0.0	(0.0)	5.9	(1.8)	35.7	(3.7)	58.5	(3.7)
	Israel	0.0	(0.0)	6.1	(4.4)	31.5	(8.0)	62.4	(9.1)
	Singapore	0.4	(0.4)	12.3	(3.0)	40.7	(4.5)	46.6	(4.6)
	Denmark	1.2	(1.2)	10.4	(2.8)	40.9	(5.2)	47.5	(4.9)
	Hong Kong	1.3	(1.3)	26.6	(5.3)	35.7	(6.0)	36.4	(5.7)
	Russian Federation	1.4	(0.9)	8.2	(1.9)	35.9	(4.2)	54.5	(4.2)
	Netherlands	2.2	(1.6)	21.6	(5.5)	36.0	(6.6)	40.1	(6.9)
	Korea	2.6	(1.3)	7.1	(2.4)	35.4	(4.1)	54.9	(4.2)
	Austria	3.6	(1.7)	19.0	(3.8)	51.1	(5.2)	26.4	(4.4)
	New Zealand	4.4	(1.7)	12.2	(2.7)	39.8	(4.0)	43.5	(3.9)
	Spain	10.2	(2.5)	45.7	(4.1)	30.4	(3.4)	13.7	(2.8)
	Columbia	10.6	(4.5)	20.5	(4.2)	25.2	(3.6)	43.7	(4.8)
	Hungary	13.1	(3.0)	23.5	(3.4)	42.7	(4.1)	20.7	(3.3)
	Portugal	19.5	(3.4)	26.2	(4.4)	29.1	(4.0)	25.2	(4.0)
	Slovenia	21.0	(4.3)	44.9	(5.7)	28.2	(4.7)	5.8	(2.4)
	Greece	53.9	(4.4)	26.0	(4.0)	8.2	(2.1)	11.9	(3.7)
	France	64.6	(4.9)	26.7	(4.8)	7.3	(2.7)	1.4	(1.1)
	Romania	71.9	(3.4)	22.0	(3.5)	3.5	(1.4)	2.6	(1.2)
	Average (National)	14.8		19.4		31.2		34.5	

Type of Institutional Center	Country	1. None		2. Little		3. Some		4. A Lot	
		Percent	S.E.	Percent	S.E.	Percent	S.E.	Percent	S.E.
Regional	Australia	3.0	(1.7)	15.7	(3.4)	35.5	(4.6)	45.7	(4.5)
	Belgium (FL)	5.1	(1.9)	29.0	(4.1)	52.9	(5.0)	13.0	(2.7)
	Germany	5.3	(2.9)	26.0	(5.4)	32.0	(5.4)	36.7	(5.8)
	Canada	9.0	(2.1)	26.9	(3.1)	45.6	(3.5)	18.6	(2.5)
	Switzerland	36.7	(3.7)	49.1	(3.9)	8.7	(1.8)	5.5	(2.1)
	Average (Regional)	11.8		29.3		34.9		23.9	
Local	United States	0.6	(0.5)	20.8	(4.0)	49.1	(4.2)	29.5	(3.5)

Note: *Belgium (French-speaking), Cyprus, Ireland, and Norway did not administer the portion of the school questionnaire from which these data are taken.*

PARENTS Averaged over the countries surveyed with regional or national institutional centers, about one-half of the principals reported that parents had no influence on curriculum decisions, and another 36 percent said that they had little influence. Thus, parents had little or no influence worldwide, at least as perceived by the principals and headmasters surveyed by TIMSS. In the United States, almost two-thirds of the principals indicated that parents had a little influence on curriculum decisions. Less than 10 percent of U.S. principals indicated that parents had no influence on curriculum decisions, which contrasts markedly with the almost one-half of principals in other surveyed countries indicating this.

TEXTBOOK PUBLICATIONS Three-fourths of the principals surveyed in countries with national and regional institutional centers indicated that textbook publications had little or no influence on curriculum decisions; in fact, over one-half said that they had no influence. By contrast, in the United States about 40 percent of the principals indicated that textbook publications had some or a lot of influence on curriculum decisions. Only about one-fourth of U.S. principals surveyed indicated that textbook publications had no influence on curriculum decisions.

EXTERNAL EXAMINATIONS In surveyed countries with national or regional institutional centers, 41 percent of the principals surveyed indicated that external examinations had no influence on curriculum decisions. In contrast, about 35 percent indicated that they had either some or a lot of influence. In the United States about 60 percent of the principals surveyed said that external examinations had a lot or some influence on curriculum decisions. Only about 10 percent of U.S. principals surveyed indicated that external examinations had no influence on curriculum decisions.

The relatively strong influence of local governing boards, parents, textbooks, and external examinations in the United States contrasts strongly with other countries, especially those with national institutional centers. This may well be a reflection of a system where curricular decisions do not have a formal institutional center and, as a result, have many players with some influence. This seems a direct reflection of dispersed decision making in the United States.

The Influence of Policy Documents on Teachers

Curriculum decisions, especially those taken by official bodies, create products. These decisions are usually reflected in various sorts of policy documents such as content standards. Although these documents may clearly reflect official intentions, the question remains as to what practical impact such documents have on the curricular decisions of teachers about what content to teach and how to teach it.

In most countries surveyed, an overwhelming majority (about 75 percent) of teachers surveyed indicated that they were somewhat or very familiar with the regional or national content standards for the subject that they taught. Teachers thus seem clearly to be aware of these policy documents. The question of the documents' actual practical influence remains an empirical question. The question here is how much influence teachers perceived these documents, however arrived at, to have over their actions—in particular, over their planning about what topics to teach, how to present them, and the homework and assessments to be used in class in instruction on these topics. This is independent of teachers' perceptions of how much influence they had on curriculum decisions and thus on the formation of these documents.

PLANNING WHAT TO TEACH What is the main source of written information that teachers indicated had affected their plans of what to teach? National and regional content standards were indicated as the main source of information for planning what to teach for around one-half of the teachers surveyed. For countries with national institutional centers for curriculum decisions, about 43 percent of the teachers indicated that they used the content standards as their main source of information in planning which topics to teach. In countries with regional institutional centers, almost one-half (49 percent) indicated that they used the standards as their main source of written information. In fact, in fourteen of twenty-six countries (the combination of both those with national and regional institutional centers), over 50 percent of the teachers in each country indicated that the content standards document was their main source of written information in deciding which topics to teach. In four countries, the percentage of teachers indicating this was over 80 percent.

From the data it is clear that national or regional content standards were the dominant resource used by teachers to help them decide which topics to teach. This was true of at least a plurality, if not a majority, of teachers. It was true in eighteen out of twenty-six countries surveyed.

Another document that played a key role in deciding what to teach was school content standards. It often was indicated as the second choice of teachers for information where the dominant choice was the national or regional standards or was indicated as itself the first choice. It was the dominant document (for a majority or plurality of teachers responding) in three countries and was the clear second choice in eight others.

The most common second source of information for planning what to teach was the textbook (either the student or teacher's edition). It was the dominant source of information in five of twenty-six countries. It was also the second most often cited source by teachers in eight countries where a majority or plurality of the teachers surveyed cited the national, regional, or school content standards.

Several of the countries in which most of the teachers chose the textbook as the major source of information on which topics to teach were countries with clearly articulated national content standards—for example, Japan and Korea. Interpreting these data is complex. For example it is probably not warranted to use these data to suggest that teachers in these countries did not follow the national content standards because the standards typically had a strong influence over the content of textbooks. However, further elucidating this point is beyond the data available in TIMSS.

PEDAGOGY, HOMEWORK, AND ASSESSMENT Teachers make other practical decisions besides what content to teach. They also decide on pedagogical strategies—on how to teach each topic they teach. They decide what in-class work and what homework to use as a part of instruction. They also decide what forms of assessment or evaluation to use. How much influence do official policy documents have on these decisions?

National and regional standards had little or no impact on how to present a topic. They were on average indicated as a source of information for these decisions by less than 10 percent of the teachers in the surveyed countries. In one country (Portugal), about 60 percent of the teachers replied that the national or regional guide was the major written source of information on how to present a topic. This response was clearly the exception. Here the textbook or some other resource book was the dominant source of information for this planning. The textbook or another resource book was also indicated as the dominant source of written information on deciding what student work to do in class and as homework.

For assessment and evaluation, the dominant source of information for teachers in most countries was indicated as other resource books. The exact meaning of what these books were is not possible to determine given the TIMSS data. One might speculate that these could be especially prepared books to aid assessment or other textbooks not used in class.

It is reasonably clear from the data that national and regional content standard documents had impact on teachers' decisions about what to teach, at least in the perception of teachers in most countries. The influence of these documents did not extend to the choice of instructional strategies or classroom activities. In the next chapter we will look across countries to characterize the content specifications that result from national and regional curriculum decisions and that, at least in teachers' minds, influence what content they teach in their classrooms.

NOTES

1. Timar, Kirp, & Kirst, 1998.

2. Timar, Kirp, & Kirst, 1998, p.36.

3. Schmidt & Prawat, 1999.

4. The TIMSS Teacher and School Questionnaires were the source of the data reported here concerning teachers' and principals' perceptions, and in subsequent chapters, for teachers' reports on what they teach. The weights that were developed for use with the TIMSS teacher and school data are all based on the number of students represented by a teacher or school, as the TIMSS sampling design was based on the number of students in a country in a particular grade. Consequently, although we refer to the percent of teachers or the percent of principals/schools, it is more accurate to interpret these in terms of students' exposure to the particular characteristics being considered. For example, the statement that "over 75 percent of the teachers shared such a perception" means that over 75 percent of students had teachers who shared such a perception.

5

CURRICULUM VARIATION

CURRICULUM GOALS and content are determined by a variety of decision makers as discussed in Chapter Four. In most cases, there was a national institutional center for such decisions. What possibilities about curriculum goals and content does this imply? One possibility is that decision makers in various countries faced with the same school discipline (science or mathematics) make similar decisions about curriculum for those disciplines. This would imply that the inherent structure of the discipline dominated national decisions enough to produce more similarities than differences among countries' school science and mathematics curricula.

This involves assuming that the content of school mathematics and science is so structured (and, in mathematics, built up so gradually) that this would cause mathematics and science curricula to cover similar content in all countries. In short, one might feel that "mathematics is mathematics" at least as regards mathematics content to be learned in school and that the same would be true for school science. This would lead one to believe that curriculum content would be similar across many countries in these subject matter areas at a particular age or grade level.

A second possibility is that especially at the national level, curricular decisions in most countries are so bound up in the situation and goals of each country that they reflect the particularities of the country more than the commonalties of the discipline. This would lead to considerable curricular variety even for curricula in the same school discipline.

Our cultural hypothesis might lead one to think that what constitutes school mathematics or school science depends on the culture in which schooling takes place. This would encompass not only what particular areas of mathematics and science to include in school curricula but also when particular content areas or parts of areas are to be covered. This would lead to differences among the school mathematics and science curricula in various countries with different cultural traditions, even for the same age or grade.

Which is truly the case with the curricula of the TIMSS countries? We believe the data clearly show that curriculum varies among countries. Why is this important other than as a description of what actually happens in countries? We want to show that curriculum matters and is related to achievement. To do this sensibly, we need to understand more clearly that curriculum does, in fact, vary and in what ways. We also need to understand the substantive meaning of this variation. For example, is it only in terms of surface features of curricula (merely quantitative, such as more pages in a textbook), or is it more structural (more qualitative, cutting to the heart of the concepts and structure of the discipline)? That is the purpose of this chapter.

School curricula vary by topic—both in science and in mathematics. That is, how a particular subject area (for example, earth sciences or geometry) is conceived, partitioned, represented for instruction, and distributed across the grades varies. How this is done for one topic differs from how it is done for another. All of this tends to point in the direction that curriculum variation is more structural and substantive rather than reflecting only surface differences.

School curricula also vary among countries. How a particular content area (for example, algebra and equations) is represented in curricula and distributed across the grades for instruction differs among different countries. Not only that, but these variations—topic and country—interact with each other. There are characteristic differences in the pattern of curriculum coverage for different countries, patterns that reflect national views of subject matter areas. This is true no matter what aspect or indicator of curriculum is examined—content standards, textbook content, or teacher content coverage. It may seem obvious that these patterns would exist, but it is important to document these patterns empirically as a context for understanding later discussions of the relationship of curriculum and achievement.

As discussed earlier, we consider four indications of curriculum. Content standards, textbook content coverage (as well as the performance expectations involved), the percentages of teachers that cover various topics, and the time that they spend on those topics reflect national goals and decisions about curriculum areas. They also reflect the textbooks that evolve nationally as potential implementations of curriculum and the impact of national priorities and agendas on the actual implementation of instruction in classrooms. They should represent enough of characteristic national choices about subject matter content to relate to student gains and attainments in those areas.

Also as discussed earlier, data were gathered on these curriculum indications through a variety of instruments (school and teacher questionnaires) and document collections (textbooks and content standards). The data were used for a variety of reasons, the most relevant of which here were to indicate what content was covered and on the differential emphasis on specific topics and content areas. To examine the relationship of curriculum to learning quantitatively requires that both curriculum and learning be measured quantitatively. There is a long tradition of measuring achievement and achievement change (as a surrogate for learning) quantitatively. No similar tradition exists for the quantitative measurement of curriculum. The methods developed to make these analyses possible were an important development.

The Structure of the Curriculum Data

To make the analytical results reported in this chapter more understandable, we offer a brief overview of these data's conceptual structure as they were organized for analysis. The basic structure for this chapter's data was conceived as a set of matrices, that is, as a set of two-dimensional arrays of data. There was one matrix for each of the four aspects of curricula. Each row of the matrix had the entries for one of the countries participating in TIMSS. Each column of the matrix represented a topic in either mathematics or science that came from the TIMSS content frameworks. Topic content was considered according to three different organizations of the TIMSS frameworks: the most finely defined (lowest) level of the framework (forty-four mathematics topics, seventy-nine science topics), the level of the teacher questionnaires (twenty-one mathematics topics, twenty-two science topics), or the level of the reporting categories, or tested topic areas, of the TIMSS assessments—there were twenty such topic areas in mathematics, which encompassed twenty-six of the forty-four most finely defined framework topics, and seventeen in science, which encompassed fifty of the seventy-nine possible framework topics. The relationships between these three topic measurements are specified in Appendix B. Thus, columns could represent the full level of detail possible (for example, forty-four topics in mathematics) or only those topic areas covered by the TIMSS achievement tests.

Within this array, entries were made based on the type of data for the specific indication of curriculum investigated. In the case of content standards, for example, entries were either a 1 (if the topic was specified as covered in a content standard document or questionnaire) or a 0 (if the topic was not specified as covered). For textbooks, the percentage of the book devoted to the topic or to the performance expectation was entered.[1] For the instructional aspect, the percentages of teachers who taught each topic and the percentage of time they indicated as devoted to each topic was entered.[2]

There were three main questions for each aspect. First, the row marginals (averaged over topics) could be examined for differences among countries (country variation). However, such row marginals did not always make sense, given the nature of the data, and as a result were not interpreted in such cases. Second, the column marginals (averaged over countries) were examined for differences among topics (topic variation). Third and finally, the individual cells (row and column combinations) were examined for interaction effects or interesting anomalies (topic-by-country variation).

In general, across all grade groupings and all four aspects of curriculum, we found that content coverage varied both by country and by topic. One way of summarizing this finding is by saying that "mathematics is not mathematics" or "science is not science"; that is, mathematics and science are *not* the same in all countries. Even with similarly named content areas covered in various countries, there were marked differences in how the countries dealt with them. The rest of the chapter is devoted to surveying this terrain, first for mathematics and then for science. In each of the two areas, we will first examine the eighth grade in detail and then provide briefer looks at the seventh grade, the sixth grade, and the first through fifth grades.[3] After working our way back through the sequence of grades for each aspect of curriculum, we will look at the correlation among topics for that school discipline (mathematics or science).

Eighth Grade Mathematics

Content Standards

We begin by examining what content standards documents from the TIMSS countries indicated about variations by topic and by country in curriculum content coverage. Official documents, of course, represent only part of the reality of the content covered in a nation's schools.

TOPIC VARIATION Table 5.1 indicates the percentage of countries that covered all of the mathematics topics, organized according to the TIMSS eighth grade mathematics test areas. The overall percentage for each of the twenty tested topic areas reflects the percentage of participating countries that indicated in content standards documents that they covered at least one of the subtopics. (Fourteen of the twenty topic areas had no subtopics.) All of the forty-four individual mathematics topics can be found in the table.

The single most widely covered topic in eighth grade[4] mathematics as reflected in content standards documents was equations and formulas. All TIMSS countries indicated that they intended to cover this topic. Following closely behind this area, 97 percent of the TIMSS countries indicated that they intended to cover the topic area of functions.

The next four most widely intended topics—from 86 to 97 percent of the TIMSS countries—were the four geometry content areas used to represent the broader area of geometry in developing the TIMSS Population 2 mathematics test. These were followed by two other topics. First, about 80 percent of the countries indicated that they intended to cover proportionality problems in eighth grade mathematics. At this level, this content is closely related to equations and formulas through coverage of proportionality equations. Second, about 80 percent of the countries (not necessarily the same countries as before) indicated that they intended to cover perimeter, area, and volume. In the TIMSS framework, this is considered a measurement content area, but it is clearly related to geometry.

Overall, this suggests that to the extent that a common core of mathematics curriculum content exists cross-nationally, the eighth grade mathematics curriculum centers primarily on algebra and geometry. Data to this effect have been noted and discussed elsewhere.[5]

This characterizes the topics most common among the TIMSS countries. At the other end of the spectrum, we might look at the topics for which content standards documents showed the smallest number of TIMSS countries intending coverage. This would emphasize some of the content differences among countries.

Clearly, Table 5.1 indicates that these included the arithmetic topics of fractions, rounding, and estimating (intended to be covered by only about one-third to one-half of the TIMSS countries). A focus on arithmetic content in eighth grade mathematics appears to be the exception rather than the rule (a feeling one would not get if one examined only U.S. data).

These same data also show what a large number of countries intended to provide in the way of educational opportunities but that the TIMSS Population 2 mathematics test did not include, as compiled in Table 5.1. This list is important as it reflects areas that could have been tested (and perhaps should have been). If the TIMSS test did cover these topics, it seems inevitable that it would have produced different orderings of countries in its rankings.

Tested Topics (26)	Coverage in Content Standards	
	Number of Countries (36)	Percent
1. Whole numbers	28	77.8
Meaning	24	66.7
Operations	25	69.4
2. Common fractions	19	52.8
3. Decimal fractions and percents	25	69.4
Decimal fractions	20	55.6
Percentages	22	61.1
4. Relations of fractions	20	55.6
5. Estimating quantity and size	13	36.1
6. Rounding	18	50.0
7. Estimating computations	17	47.2
8. Measurement units	24	66.7
9. Perimeter, area, and volume	30	83.3
10. Measurement estimations and errors	19	52.8
11. 2-D geometry	34	94.4
2-D coordinate geometry	29	80.6
2-D geometry: Basics	30	83.3
12. Polygons and circles	35	97.2
13. 3-D geometry and transformations	34	94.4
3-D geometry	31	86.1
Transformations	30	83.3
14. Congruence and similarity	31	86.1
15. Proportionality concepts	28	77.8
16. Proportionality problems	30	83.3
17. Patterns, relations, and functions	35	97.2
18. Equations and formulas	36	100.0
Equations and formulas	36	100.0
Negative numbers, integers, and their properties	28	77.8
Exponents, roots, and radicals	28	77.8
19. Data representation and analysis	27	75.0
20. Uncertainty and probability	21	58.3
Topics Not Tested (18)		
Properties of operations	21	58.3
Properties of common and decimal fractions	15	41.7
Rational numbers and their properties	28	77.8
Real numbers, their subsets and properties	25	69.4
Binary arithmetic and/or other number bases	14	38.9

(continued)

Table 5.1. (continued)

Complex numbers and their properties	8	22.2
Number theory	22	61.1
Systematic counting	12	33.3
Exponents and orders of magnitude	13	36.1
Vectors	20	55.6
Constructions w/ straightedge and compass	25	69.4
Slope and trigonometry	15	41.7
Linear interpolation and extrapolation	11	30.6
Infinite processes	7	19.4
Change	7	19.4
Validation and justification	13	36.1
Structuring and abstracting	16	44.4
Informatics	24	66.7

Note: *The numbered topics are the twenty tested areas. The eleven indented topics together with the fifteen tested areas for which there is only one framework code cover twenty-six framework topics. These twenty-six plus the eighteen topics not tested in TIMSS exhaust all forty-four topics in the TIMSS mathematics framework.*

This is a way of stressing that to some extent the total test score results from TIMSS are artifactual rather than factual. Some countries' rankings might have been higher or lower with test coverage of these topics, topics that fit those countries' intentions better than the final mix of content selected for the TIMSS tests.

What are these contents that might have been included but were not? If we examine topics for which curriculum standards documents indicated intended coverage in eighth grade mathematics by about half or more of the countries, we see many areas of more advanced school mathematics content. This includes the properties of arithmetic operations, rational numbers and their properties, real numbers, number theory (although this may be simpler arithmetic content such as greatest common divisors), vectors, constructions using straightedge and compass, and other content including informatics. Overall, the picture is that a fair number of countries might have been advantaged by a more demanding test.

A content area on a TIMSS test was often composed of several more finely defined content areas from the TIMSS content frameworks. That is, the tests' operationalization of content was less fine grained than that of the underlying design documents. This inclusion of several topics within a test area raises the interesting question of patterns of topic coverage across the topics that make up a tested area.

TIMSS earliest development efforts included creating framework documents in mathematics and in the sciences that would present an exhaustive list of topics. These frameworks are somewhat hierarchically organized so that a series of topics (or, in this context, subsumed or subtopics) collectively defined a larger topic. The TIMSS test results reported elsewhere[6] and later in this report reflect that structure, reporting results at comparatively higher, more aggregate levels of subject matter content.

The results in Table 5.1 report coverage of each topic individually (the lowest, most detailed level from the mathematics framework) as well as at the tested level. Let us examine briefly the coverage at this most detailed level, that of the subtopic within a larger tested topic area. The results discussed thus far show the percentage of countries that cover at least one of the tested subtopics that help constitute a tested topic area. Here we look a little closer.

For instance, consider the tested content area of whole numbers. Two subtopics (whole number meanings and whole number operations) constitute this area for the tests. The data show that about 80 percent of the TIMSS countries participating in the eighth grade mathematics test covered at least one of the two subtopics. What percent covered only whole number operations? Whole number meanings? Both? For this area, countries that cover at least one subtopic cover both.

This generalization holds true for virtually all the tested areas. In all cases, about two-thirds of those countries that intended coverage of a tested area intended coverage of all the subtopics that constituted that area for the tests. This makes the interpretation of the eighth grade mathematics test results more straightforward for the majority of countries. Intended coverage for a tested area generally means intended coverage for all the subtopics that constitute a tested area. If this were not true, performance might reflect which subtopics were covered and which were not. Interpretation would be considerably more difficult.

COUNTRY VARIATION We turn now to look at differences in the number of topics intended by different participating countries. Table 5.2 indicates for each country the number of topics covered as indicated in content standards documents—both relative to the total number possible and the number in the test subareas. The questionnaires used to gather data from teachers had only twenty-one topics, collapsing the forty-four. Thus, data from these sources are the number of intended covered topics relative to the forty-four or the twenty-one. There were twenty-six subareas in which test items were grouped for the TIMSS Population 2 test.

Table 5.2. Number of Mathematics Topics Included in the Curriculum (Textbooks, Content Standards, and Teachers).

Country	Content Standards	Textbook Coverage	Teacher Coverage	Topics Tested		Other Grades*		
				Standards	Textbook	1–5	6	7
Total Number of Topics	44	44	21	26	26	44	44	44
Australia	29	30	21	21	20	17	22	30
Austria	24	26	17	18	21	25	29	30
Belgium (Fl)	34	**	21	24	**	25	25	29
Belgium (Fr)	37	**	21	24	**	25	25	29
Bulgaria	15	14	21	11	10	19	21	14
Canada	35	39	21	26	26	25	28	33
Colombia	33	34	21	22	21	26	28	29
Cyprus	27	17	21	19	14	22	24	29
Czech Republic	15	32	21	12	23	21	21	17
Denmark	36	21	21	23	14	23	28	28
France	19	31	21	14	21	21	26	27
Germany	22	15	21	17	9	24	26	24
Greece	11	30	21	9	20	20	19	28
Hong Kong	39	23	21	24	20	13	11	18
Hungary	40	30	21	26	21	30	29	27
Iceland	30	27	21	23	20	24	22	23
Iran	***	22	21	***	17	17	24	17
Ireland	31	33	21	21	23	27	28	31
Israel	21	24	20	12	17	28	28	29

Japan	12	21	8	10	26	21	14
Korea	16	21	10	13	23	22	26
Latvia	39	21	25	26	18	20	16
Netherlands	20	21	14	22	15	24	25
New Zealand	44	21	26	19	21	29	29
Norway	32	21	26	22	23	25	35
Portugal	31	21	21	25	26	26	26
Romania	17	21	10	21	28	34	38
Russian Federation	12	11	9	13	20	21	16
Scotland	36	21	25	23	—	—	—
Singapore	22	20	18	19	19	20	30
Slovak Republic	15	21	12	23	20	16	14
Slovenia	20	21	16	18	23	28	36
South Africa	21	21	13	19	—	—	—
Spain	18	21	14	16	20	27	24
Sweden	29	21	22	21	16	19	21
Switzerland	40	21	26	26	38	38	38
USA	44	21	26	26	28	33	34

* Summaries are based on countries' standards collected through the GTTM process (see Chapter Three).

Scotland and South Africa did not complete the GTTM.

** No textbooks were coded for the two language systems of Belgium.

*** Iran had no official content standards.

The data also report the relative number of these subareas for which content was intended to be covered.

The range of intended coverage indicated in content standards for eighth grade and compared to all possible topics is relatively large. It goes from about ten topics (Greece, Japan, and the Russian Federation) to all forty-four possible (the United States and New Zealand). The range is also large for the number of topics intended to be covered relative to those possible on the test (twenty-six areas). This ranged also from around ten (Bulgaria, the Czech and Slovak republics, Greece, Israel, Japan, Korea, Romania, and the Russian Federation) to all twenty-six (Switzerland, Canada, Hungary, New Zealand, Norway, and the United States). Only eight of the twenty-six tested topics were in the Japanese eighth grade mathematics content standards.

Among those countries planning to cover the fewest of the tested topics, several (the Czech and Slovak republics, Japan, and Korea) were among the top seven performing countries on the eighth grade mathematics test. This ranking of performance was done on the global achievement scores. The data in Table 5.2 show that these countries intended coverage for fewer than half of the tested topics in eighth grade.

Clearly, something has happened in previous grades in the tested areas not covered in those countries during the eighth grade. This makes it clear why the curricular intentions of previous grades (first through seventh or their equivalent) are important when considering eighth grade achievement status. It seems likely that for those high-performing countries, the relevant topics were intended for coverage in earlier grades.

This is also why we focus in this report on the gains at the subtest level because we are interested in eighth grade curricular experiences and their effects. For example, in Japan we might expect small gains in eighteen of the subareas that were not emphasized in eighth grade, the grade that was tested. The overall gain score would not likely be sensitive to such effects. For other countries this might raise the question of how fair the test was if the other topics were not intended for coverage until a later grade or not to be covered at all.

Textbooks

Everything discussed so far has been at the level of what countries intend to do in covering eighth grade mathematics topics, at least as specified in their content standards. The expression of an intention in a content standard is, of course, no guarantee that this will actually be implemented in that country's classrooms. This is in part why we examine four indications of curriculum rather than merely one, such as the intentions in content standards or the percentage of teachers teaching a specific topic.

One of the common bridges between curricular intentions and classroom implementations is student textbooks. How textbooks are used in various countries differs according to cultural traditions, specifically the culture of schooling in those particular countries. In some cases the student textbook is a de facto implemented curriculum. In others, it is at best a suggestion of what is possible and, perhaps, of what is more likely than other learning opportunities to be taught. Textbooks tend by their nature to be conservative in market-driven economies in which textbooks are commercially produced and marketed (the United States being the extreme case). It is always harder to leave out a topic that is already in a textbook than to add material to textbooks to cover a topic that is not in them. At least in the United States, textbooks tend to be syncretic and build up aggregations of older content.

TOPIC VARIATION Figure 5.1 presents data on the cumulative distributions of the percentage of the textbook covering each topic for the forty-four topics in the TIMSS mathematics framework. They show how quickly or slowly the percentage of textbook space devoted to each topic builds up across the TIMSS countries. A curve that goes up faster (more to the left) indicates less variation in how many countries devote textbook space to the topic. A curve building up more slowly (to the right) indicates more variability and a larger median[*] of textbook space for the topic.[7]

The topic to which the most textbook space is given across all countries is that of equations and formulas, which on average receives almost 20 percent of the textbook space across all of the eighth grade mathematics textbooks from the participating TIMSS countries.[8] (This can be seen in Figure 5.1—although the mean itself is not listed—as the curve for this topic is the furthest to the right.) However, it also has one of the largest variances in textbook space allocated among all the topics, with a range of about 35 percent between the country allocating the least space to the country allocating the most space. The interquartile range—that is, the difference in percent of space allocated to the topic from the lowest to the highest of the middle 50 percent of countries—is almost 20 percent. Thus, this topic commonly

---

[*]The median is the middle value or midpoint in a set of ranked values or scores. If the set contains an even number of values or scores, the median is the average of the two middle scores. The median is also referred to as the fiftieth percentile which means that 50 percent of the scores are at or below it.

Figure 5.1. Percentage of Textbook Coverage for Topics (Eighth Grade Mathematics).

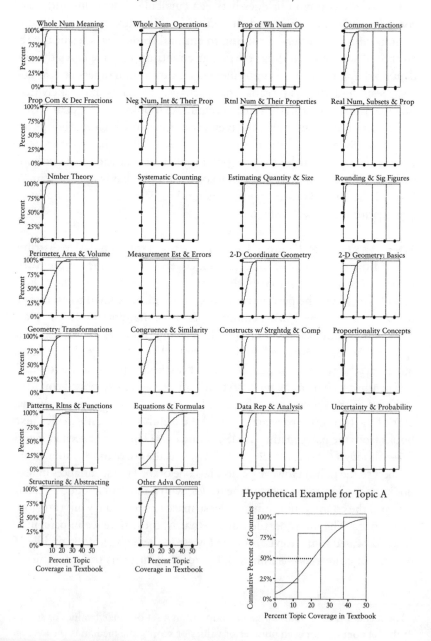

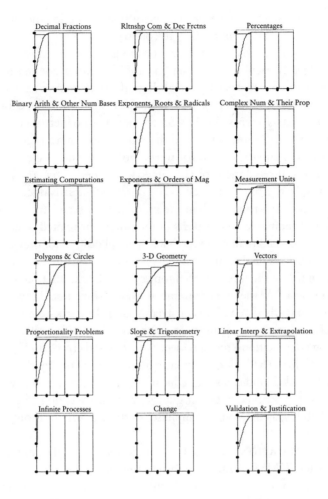

Note: *This hypothetical example illustrates that 50 percent of the countries have at most 20 percent of their textbooks devoted to Topic A. All of the graphs in this figure have the same structure as this example.*

receives a consistently higher percentage of space than do other topics, but it varies considerably from country to country.

We can use textbook space allocations to gain a sense of what a cross-national core curriculum might emphasize in eighth grade mathematics. We look at student textbooks in eighth grade mathematics as one indication of what mathematics topics make up the content with the consistently highest emphasis across the TIMSS countries. In order of emphasis in textbooks, the five topics allocated the most space on average across the countries were equations and formulas, polygons and circles, functions and relations, three-dimensional geometry, and perimeter, area, and volume. Thus, in textbooks as well as in content standards documents, the emphasized content in eighth grade mathematics seems to be primarily algebra and geometry (and aspects of measurement related to geometry).

If we restrict our attention to textbook space allocation for only those topics on the TIMSS Population 2 mathematics test, this picture does not change because all five of the most covered topics in textbooks are tested topics on the TIMSS test.[9] At the other extreme, however, some tested topics did not receive much textbook emphasis on average over the participating countries. This includes estimating quantity and size, rounding and significant figures, estimating computations, measurement estimates and errors, and uncertainty and probability. The lack of emphasis on this content in textbooks at the eighth grade likely indicates that educational opportunities to master these contents were presented in earlier grades (with the exception of uncertainty and probability, as data on the emphases of those grades bear out).

COUNTRY VARIATION Table 5.1 also indicates the number of topics covered by each TIMSS country's eighth grade mathematics textbooks. For all topics, this ranges from around fifteen framework topics (in Bulgaria, Cyprus, Germany, Japan, and Korea) to over forty (the United States and Switzerland) to all forty-four topic areas in one case (Latvia). Restricting attention to the twenty-six tested topic areas, the number of topics covered in the countries' textbooks goes from around ten (Bulgaria, Germany, Japan, Korea, and the Russian Federation) to all tested topics (the United States, Canada, Latvia, and Switzerland).

When we shift our attention to variation among countries rather than variation among topics, one adjustment needs to be considered: some topics were not covered at all in some countries. Thus, when coverage for a topic is averaged across countries, this reduces the average coverage for such a topic. This may well be appropriate in considering how coverage varies for different topics because we should take some account of countries devoting no attention to the topic. However, when averaging textbook emphasis (space allocation) over topics for a given country, it seems more informative to consider only those topics to which some textbook space was devoted. To include topics not covered by a particular country in its averages would produce a misleading picture of typical emphasis on those topics it did include.

Figure 5.2 displays the distributions of textbook emphasis (space allocation) for topics averaged only over those topics to which some space was allocated. How many topics were typically found in the eighth grade mathematics textbook of participating countries? This ranges from as low as fourteen (Bulgaria) to as many as forty-two (Switzerland).[10] For most countries the number of topics in the textbooks was in the twenties or thirties.

The medians for countries' textbook space for those topics that received some coverage ranged from a low of about 1 percent to as much as 5 percent. Clearly this number indicates something of the focus within textbooks, ranging from devoting a tiny proportion of the book (a page or so) to as many as thirteen pages of the book to a given topic. How low these proportions are generally reflects something of the syncretic nature of textbooks in many countries.

The differences in the variations in topic space allocation across countries are even more interesting. The interquartile range varies from as small as about 3 percent to as much as about 15 percent. That is, there are considerable differences in how much countries emphasize various topics in their eighth grade mathematics textbooks. The relatively larger values indicate an uneven distribution of textbook space across topics within a country. This is a pattern of peaks and valleys of emphasis rather than a flat, consistent space allocation profile across topics for each country.

This rather flat pattern of equal emphasis—or, perhaps more accurately, equal lack of emphasis—is characteristic for some countries (the United States, Austria, and Switzerland in particular). The pattern of more differentiated focus—and therefore of more marked attention to key topics—appears to hold for others (Romania, Korea, Singapore, Japan, Iceland, Bulgaria, and the Russian Federation). In Slovenia the range of emphasis is from less than 1 percent for one topic to more than 50 percent for a different topic (and the range for the middle 50 percent of topics is about 5 percent). In Japan, emphasis goes from less than 1 percent to about 40 percent for the most emphasized topic (with a range over the middle 50 percent of topics of about 10 percent). In contrast, the United States has a range of about 3 percent for the middle 50 percent of topics but ranges from less than 1 percent to about 25 percent across all topics. Australia goes from less than 1 percent to about 15 percent (with a range for the middle 50 percent of topics of 5 percent).[11]

Figure 5.2. Eighth Grade Mathematics Textbook Coverage for Countries (Including Only Topics with Some Coverage).

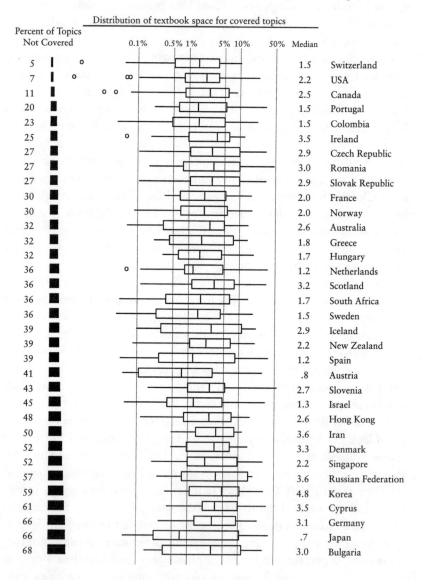

TOPIC-BY-COUNTRY VARIATION We are interested not only in the fact that textbook emphasis varies for topics (averaged over countries) and for countries (averaged over the topics they covered). We are also interested in any anomalous patterns in the combination of topics and countries. We first examine the variation in topic emphasis (as indicated by textbook space allocation) among topics averaged over the participating countries, because large variations in standard deviations seem likely to presage the potential for noteworthy interactions.

The standard deviations in textbook emphasis for topics range from less than 1 percent to more than 12 percent. The lower standard deviations indicate topics for which there is little variation across countries; the higher ones, that there is considerable variation for other topics. The range in emphasis across topics goes from around 1 percent to over 50 percent. The variation across topics within a country also differs among the participating countries, from a low of 0 to about 10 percent (Canada) to a high of 0 to over 50 percent (Slovenia). There is thus considerable variability in textbook emphasis both for topics across countries and for countries across topics.

One of the best ways to examine interactions among countries and topics to identify those that are unusual is through a technique called *median polishing*.[12] Table 5.3 presents the median polish results for the percentage of textbook space allocated to the framework topics in the participating TIMSS countries.[13] This was done with all forty-four topics in the framework. Only those residual (country-by-topic interaction) values with an absolute value greater than or equal to 10 percent are identified in the display. The topic-by-country combinations (cells) with such extreme values represent only about 5 percent of all possible country-by-topic combinations. We do this to focus on the country-by-topic interactions that are large enough to likely have practical impact. A 10 percent difference implies, on average, about a twenty- to thirty-page difference in textbook space. An asterisk in the table notes a difference of 5 percent in absolute value (a ten- to fifteen-page difference in textbook space), although we focus on those differences that are 10 percent or more.

From Table 5.3 we can see that about two-thirds of the topics have indications of some large country-by-topic interactions in textbook coverage for at least some country. (Using the 5 percent criterion shows interaction effects for at least one country in all but ten of the forty-four topic areas.) Considering only the twenty-six topics on the TIMSS Population 2 mathematics test, we see at least one large country-by-topic interaction (residual) in all but five of the topics. These are the three estimating and rounding topics plus measurement estimation and errors and

Table 5.3. Median Polish of Percentage of Mathematics Textbook Coverage for Countries and Topics (Eighth Grade).

Country	Whole Number: Meaning	Whole Number: Operations	Whole Number: Properties of Operations	Common Fractions	Decimal Fractions	Relationship of Common and Decimal Fractions	Percentages	Properties of Common and Decimal Fractions	Neg. Numbers, Integers and Their Properties	Rational Numbers and Their Properties	Real Numbers, Their Subsets and Properties	Binary Arithmetic and/or Other Number Bases	Exponents, Roots, and Radicals	Complex Numbers and Their Properties	Number Theory	Systematic Counting	Estimating Quantity and Size	Rounding and Significant Figures	Estimating Computations	Exponents and Orders of Magnitude	Measurement Units	Perimeter, Area, and Volume	Measurement Estimation and Errors
Australia																						10	
Austria																						*	
Bulgaria																						*	
Canada			*	*		*		*															
Colombia							*	*	*														
Cyprus									11				*										30
Czech Republic												12										*	*
Denmark			*	*		11	10														*		
France			*		11		*																
Germany								*															*
Greece								*												*			*
Hong Kong																							*
Hungary																							
Iceland		12	14	21		17											*				*		
Iran								*															*
Ireland	11	*	*	*	*																		
Israel																							
Japan																						*	
Korea																							
Latvia																						*	
Netherlands																						10	
New Zealand			*									*									*		
Norway		*	*	*																	*		
Portugal																		*		*			*
Romania											27						*		*				
Russian Federation																							*
Scotland	27	*	11																			31	
Singapore																						11	
Slovak Republic												12									*	*	
Slovenia																							*
South Africa						*	*																
Spain	10	*	12				*	30					*										*
Sweden	17	*		*																		15	
Switzerland		*																				*	
USA																							

Country	2-D Coordinate Geometry	2-D Geometry: Basics	2-D Geometry: Polygons and Circles	3-D Geometry	Vectors	Geometry: Transformations	Congruence and Similarity	Constructions w/ Straightedge and Compass	Proportionality Concepts	Proportionality Problems	Slope and Trigonometry	Linear Interpolation and Extrapolation	Patterns, Relations, and Functions	Equations and Formulas	Data Representation and Analysis	Uncertainty and Probability	Elementary Analysis: Infinite Processes	Elementary Analysis: Change	Validation and Justification	Structuring and Abstracting	Other Content
Australia	*																				
Austria	*	26																		21	
Bulgaria	14	15		10									*	15							*
Canada																*					*
Colombia	*							*					16	*							
Cyprus	*	18							*				*								
Czech Republic	*	*	*			*				*	*		10	16							*
Denmark		*		*									*								14
France	*													−10							
Germany	10			18	*								*								
Greece		12			*								*	*							
Hong Kong												*	16								
Hungary		*	10		18								*								
Iceland													*		10						
Iran						10							*								
Ireland		*									*										12
Israel	10	21									*			24		*					
Japan		*				22								24							
Korea	*					10				*				16		11				12	
Latvia			−11										*	−15							
Netherlands		*												21							
New Zealand		*				*							*	*						*	*
Norway																					
Portugal			*										11.5	16.5							
Romania		*	44					*					15	21						30	*
Russian Federation	13	*	*	16	14						*										
Scotland		*	−10	*					11					−10							
Singapore		*						*		11		*	*	15							
Slovak Republic	*	*	*			*				*	*		10	16							*
Slovenia	*	14	53										*								
South Africa		*						*					*	−14							
Spain			−11											22							
Sweden		*											*	−11	*						
Switzerland						*								*							*
USA		*											*	*							*

Note: *The topic "change" (related to calculus) produced strange results in the analysis. The median polish was done both with and without it, but there were no notable differences in results for other topics. The topic "change" was thus omitted from this analysis in this display.*

proportionality concepts. That is, for these five topics there was general consistency across countries, and not even one country devoted unusually high or low proportions of textbook space to the topic.

The topic area that has the greatest indication of country-by-topic interactions (the most unusually large residuals) is equations and formulas. This is also the topic that has the greatest amount of space allocated to it, averaged over countries. One-third of the countries have significant residuals for this topic. For example, Japan has a large positive estimated interaction effect, indicating that it allocates even more textbook space to this topic than would be predicted given the textbook space it allocates on average to a typical topic and given the average amount of space allocated to this topic across the countries in general. Thus, the topic usually receives a high proportion of space and especially so in Japan. Congruence and similarity is a geometric area with a similar conclusion for Japan. Polygons and circles is another topic area with a larger than usual number of big interaction effects.

Performance Expectations

Subject matter content is not the only thing that matters in characterizing curriculum. It is important also to know what students are expected to do with that content. As discussed earlier, we attempted to capture this dimension of curriculum content by specifying performance expectations—descriptions of the tasks that students were expected to be able to accomplish if they attained mastery of the content at the desired level. These descriptions of tasks were intended as much as possible to be culturally invariant, that is, to describe the tasks in terms of subject matter content and what could be accomplished with it. There was no presumption or expectation about the particular cognitive mechanisms that would underlie accomplishing those tasks. Such mechanisms would clearly be culture dependent rather than invariant.

Performance expectations were also specified in the TIMSS framework documents, and content standards and textbooks were coded with not only the content topic involved but also the performance expectations that were called for. Content standard documents were often not sufficiently specific about these performance expectations to allow consistently detailed characterization of curriculum. Textbooks were. In this section we examine what textbook space allocations as an indication of curriculum reveal about differing emphases on performance expectations.

One adjustment was made after the fact. Two major categories from the framework, investigating and problem solving and mathematical reasoning, were combined to define a more complex performance that moved beyond facts and procedures. This seems to be what has often been referred to by the term *higher-order thinking* and other similar phrases such as *more complex cognitive demands*.[14]

TOPIC VARIATION Table 5.4 displays the distributions of the percentages for a given topic requiring the level of complex performance described previously. In this display, the distributions are for each framework topic averaged across all of the countries involved.

On average, the topic with the highest percentage of its textbook coverage specifying more complex performance expectations (no matter how much textbook space, that is) is equations and formulas. Over one-third of its coverage in textbooks on average (the median was 30 percent) was associated with problem solving and mathematical reasoning. There was, however, considerable variation among countries. It has a large standard deviation (about 25 percent) and ranges from 0 percent in one country to as much as 100 percent in another country. The range for the middle 50 percent of countries was from 13 to 52 percent.

All of these statistics point to considerable intercountry variation for this topic. The implication essentially is that even if textbook coverage of equations and formulas were equal across countries (and we saw earlier that it was not), the performance that students using the eighth grade mathematics textbooks were expected to be able to accomplish would not be equal. Of course, it must be kept in mind that even when textbooks are a central part of instruction, entire textbooks are not usually covered. Nonetheless, the proportion of complex performances expected is a characteristic of those textbooks and, as such, likely indicates qualitative differences in the national experiences of students and in the nature of the curricula to which they are exposed in eighth grade mathematics.

In fact, the standard deviations and interquartile range are large for all but a very few topics (none of which are among the twenty-six tested topics). This suggests that the treatment that the topics receives varies across countries in addition to the variation in how much the topics are emphasized as described in the previous section.

COUNTRY VARIATION Table 5.5 presents the same sort of data but now summarized across all topics covered by a country to obtain an indication of characteristic emphasis and variability on this expectation of more complex performance for each country. A larger median value here would suggest a country that in general (across all topics) had textbooks that had more complex performance expectations than did the textbooks of countries with smaller values.

Table 5.4. Percentage of Complex Performance Expectations for Each Mathematics Topic (Eighth Grade).

Topic	Number of Countries Covering This	Percent of Countries with No Complex Performance	Median Percent of Complex Performance	Box Plots
Whole Num Meaning	23	26	8	
Whole Num Operations	29	28	18	
Prop of Wh Num Oper	25	28	13	
Common Fractions	31	29	13	
Decimal Fractions	28	32	12	
Rltnshp of Frac and Dec	29	45	3	
Percentages	28	18	19	
Prop of Frac and Dec	21	67	0	
Neg Num, Integers and Their	29	24	14	
Rational Numbers	29	31	14	
Real Numbers	27	33	20	
Binary Arith/Other Bases	10	30	3	
Exponents and Radicals	30	20	15	
Complex Numbers	8	50	1	
Number Theory	19	32	17	
Systematic Counting	12	42	5	
Estimating Quantity and Size	16	38	5	
Rounding and Sig Figures	20	45	3	
Estimating Computations	22	45	6	
Orders of Magnitude	14	50	1	
Measurement Units	31	26	16	
Perimeter, Area, and Volume	29	10	23	
Measurement Est and Errors	16	38	12	
2-D Coordinate Geometry	33	24	13	
2-D Geometry Basics	35	6	24	
Polygons and Circles	35	0	24	
3-D Geometry	28	14	22	
Vectors	17	41	5	
Geometry Transformations	28	11	14	
Congruence and Similarity	27	7	25	
Strghtdg and Compass	22	41	4	
Proportionality Concepts	25	28	14	
Proportionality Problems	28	4	48	
Slope and Trigonometry	19	26	18	
Linear Interp and Extrp	8	63	0	
Patterns, Rltns, and Functions	33	3	25	
Equations and Formulas	36	3	30	
Data Rep and Analysis	28	18	15	
Uncertainty and Probability	12	33	11	
Infinite Processes	6	33	6	
Change	1	0	5	
Validation and Justification	21	10	33	
Structuring and Abstracting	16	6	21	
Other Content	26	35	16	

Table 5.5. Percentage of Complex Performance Expectations in Mathematics Textbooks for Each Country (Eighth Grade).

Country	Number of Topics	Percent of Topics with No Complex Performance Expectations	Median Percent of Complex Performance Expectations	Box Plots
Australia	30	37	6	
Austria	26	42	1	
Bulgaria	14	7	24	
Canada	39	21	12	
Colombia	34	26	9	
Cyprus	17	24	17	
Czech Republic	32	9	46	
Denmark	21	57	0	
France	31	6	40	
Germany	15	0	31	
Greece	30	27	26	
Hong Kong	23	39	2	
Hungary	30	43	9	
Iceland	27	41	13	
Iran	22	18	77	
Ireland	33	15	14	
Israel	24	13	22	
Japan	15	20	13	
Korea	18	11	37	
Netherlands	28	11	22	
New Zealand	27	26	6	
Norway	31	42	6	
Portugal	35	40	19	
Romania	32	13	37	
Russian Federation	19	53	0	
Scotland	28	75	0	
Singapore	21	52	0	
Slovak Republic	32	9	46	
Slovenia	25	0	77	
South Africa	28	18	22	
Spain	27	7	50	
Sweden	28	25	10	
Switzerland	42	2	15	
USA	41	5	15	

Several countries stand out with a median of about one-half or more of content coverage, content that expected more complex performances regardless of topic involved and regardless of how much emphasis it is given. These include Iran, the Czech and Slovak republics, Spain, France, and Slovenia. The low end includes five countries for which the median was 0 implying that, for at least half of the topics, no textbook space dealt with the more complex expectations. The large ranges for most countries suggest considerable variation in complex performance expectations among the topics within each country.

TOPIC-BY-COUNTRY VARIATION A median polish of topic-by-country data was done similar to that in Table 5.3. Here the data analyzed are the percentages of complex performance expectations for each topic within each country as indicated by the proportion of textbook space allocated to content expecting those more complex performances.

There is evidence of considerable country-by-topic interactions on every topic. That is, the percentage of textbook space allocated to content that is presented in a manner that demands more complex performances varies considerably across topics within countries and across countries within topics. This is similar to what was found for content topic emphasis in eighth grade mathematics textbooks across countries and topics.

SUMMARY The implications of the data thus far are clear. Eighth grade mathematics is not the same from one country to another among the TIMSS countries (and, presumably, more generally). Even for those topics (especially the tested topics) for which coverage is intended by a high percentage of the countries (as indicated in content standards documents), how they are emphasized (as proportion of textbook space) and how they are treated (as proportion of textbook space expecting complex performances) varies markedly among the countries. Further, this variation is different for different topics.

The topic of equations and formulas is a good example. Content standards indicated that all of the countries intend coverage of this topic in eighth grade mathematics. The range of emphasis for the middle 50 percent of countries (the interquartile range) is about 20 percent in terms of the proportion of textbook space allocated. That is, even eliminating the more extremely differing countries, emphasis on this commonly intended topic still varies considerably among countries. Further, the range of emphasis for the middle 50 percent of countries is about 40 percent in terms of the percentage of the coverage of that topic associated with more complex performance expectations. Although commonly expected by all

TIMSS countries, how equations and formulas is treated in textbooks (in terms of emphasis and expecting complex performances) is very different for different countries. This reflects what we believe to be cultural influences about school mathematics content for this topic and its relative importance. Clearly the data indicate that the internal mathematical structure of the topic is not the dominant determinant of how the content is treated in school mathematics in various countries and cultures.

Teacher Coverage

We have thus far considered two indications of curriculum. We have examined content standards that reflect what nations intend to be implemented as their curriculum. We have also examined percentage of textbook space as an indication of what can be more easily implemented and how national intentions are operationalized. It yet remains to examine more direct indications of how curriculum is implemented. We do that here by looking at two further indications of curriculum. We investigate the percentage of teachers who cover various topics in eighth grade mathematics in each country. We also investigate the percentage of time that teachers indicate that they allocate to various topics in eighth grade mathematics. We take these two kinds of data, percentage of teachers and percentage of time allocated, as at least gross indicators of the nature of implemented curricula in eighth grade mathematics. We follow our usual pattern of examining topic variation, country variation, and topic-by-country interactions.

TOPIC VARIATION Figure 5.3 and Figure 5.4 display the cumulative distributions for each topic of the percentage of teachers who teach the topic and the percentage of time allocated to the topic, averaged across all TIMSS countries for eighth grade mathematics teachers (similar to Figure 5.1).

The topic covered by the highest percentage of teachers on average across countries was again equations and formulas. An average of about 90 percent of the teachers across all TIMSS countries indicated that they covered this topic. This topic also had the smallest variance across countries. It had a standard deviation of about 10 percent, varying from a low of about 60 percent of the teachers in one country to a high of 100 percent of the teachers in other countries. This accords well with the data for content standards and for textbook emphasis.

The five topics in descending order of how many teachers taught the topic were equations and formulas; two-dimensional geometry; perimeter, area, and volume; (common) fractions; and number concepts. Two-dimensional

Figure 5.3. Percentage of Teachers Teaching Each Topic in a Country (Eighth Grade Mathematics).

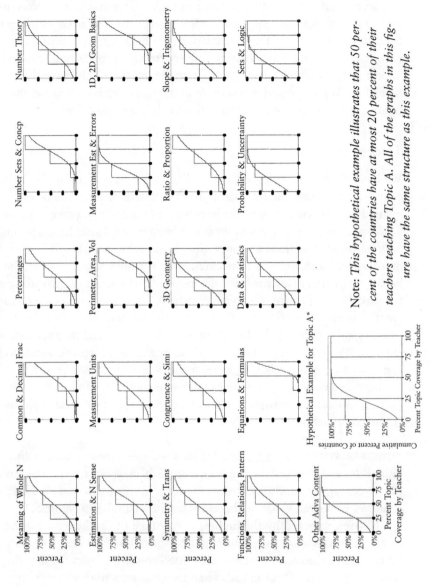

Note: *This hypothetical example illustrates that 50 percent of the countries have at most 20 percent of their teachers teaching Topic A. All of the graphs in this figure have the same structure as this example.*

Figure 5.4. Percentage of Instructional Time Spent on Teaching Each Topic in a Country (Eighth Grade Mathematics).

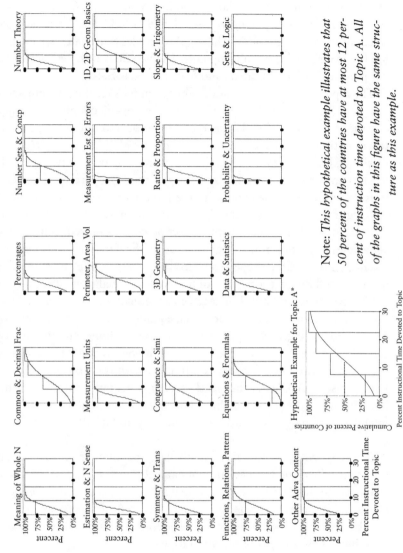

Note: This hypothetical example illustrates that 50 percent of the countries have at most 12 percent of instruction time devoted to Topic A. All of the graphs in this figure have the same structure as this example.

geometry was an aggregate label used in teacher questionnaires for several geometry topics from the framework and includes those previously indicated for textbook emphasis. The top three topics thus match well with the top five in terms of textbook emphasis. The two final arithmetic topics have not previously been indicated as so highly emphasized.

The topic receiving the most time in a country's teaching (estimated for a typical teacher in a country and averaged across all countries) was again equations and formulas. It was typically allocated about 13 percent of teaching time in a school year, averaged over all TIMSS countries. Surprisingly, however, another topic, fractions, received only slightly less teacher time over the year. It also averaged about 13 percent across countries. Fractions was the topic with the largest variance across countries, ranging from 0 percent of the time in one country to over 30 percent of the time in another country. Clearly fraction content played a differing and sometimes important role in eighth grade mathematics as implemented by teachers, a role neither expected from the intentions of content standards nor indicated by the proportion of textbook space allocated to it.

The five topics indicated by teachers as receiving the most actual classroom instructional time were, in order, equations and formulas; fractions; two-dimensional geometry; perimeter, area and volume; and number concepts. These are the same five as indicated by percentage of teachers covering the topics, but the order is different, with fractions moving from fourth to second. Clearly the eighth grade mathematics curricula actually implemented differed somewhat on average across countries from that intended nationally, as indicated by content standard documents.

COUNTRY VARIATION Table 5.2 displays the number of topics (out of twenty-one listed on teacher questionnaires for eighth grade mathematics) indicated by teachers in each country as being covered on average. In almost all countries, the countries' teachers covered all twenty-one. The only notable exception was the Russian Federation, whose teachers taught only about half (eleven) of the listed topics.

The distribution over topics of the percentage of teachers teaching a topic for each country was examined. These data do not include those topics that none of the teachers taught. The United States had the most inclusive topic coverage, with a typical topic being taught by over three-fourths of the teachers (averaged across topics that were actually taught). Israel had the least inclusive topic coverage, with a typical topic being taught by just over one-third of the teachers (again averaged over the topics that were taught by at least some of the teachers in the country). Israel, however, had considerable variation in teacher coverage, with as few as about 5 percent teaching one topic and as many as 95 percent teaching another. In the United States, the topic with the fewest teachers teaching it (of those topics taught at all) has almost 45 percent of the teachers teaching it. Certainly this is a reflection of a phenomena noted for the United States of having a curriculum that is "a mile wide and an inch deep."[15] These data indicate that U.S. teachers generally participate even in this mile-wide, inch-deep eighth grade mathematics curriculum. For whatever reason, Israel's teachers seem to differ more in how much they participate in covering topics covered within the country.

The Russian Federation (73 percent), Hungary (70), Denmark (76), Australia (69), Canada (69), Iran (66), New Zealand (73), Norway (61), and the United States had a high percentage of teachers covering each topic that was taught. Other than Israel, as already noted, most other countries had about 45 to 55 percent of the teachers covering a given topic.

It is noteworthy that even in countries with national content standards, the percentage of teachers covering a given topic was not close to 100 percent. This would seem to be the default ideal because topics not intended would not be taught by any teachers and all teachers would teach those intended for teaching. Given that topics not taught at all are eliminated from this analysis, the result would be 100 percent coverage if this ideal held. At a minimum this implies some teachers were covering one or more topics that were not officially intended. This is addressed further in the next chapter.

TOPIC-BY-COUNTRY VARIATION There were marked differences among some topics in the percentage of teachers who covered those topics, as indicated in the topic variation section. Larger standard deviations indicate more variation. The standard deviations for teacher coverage range from less than 10 percent (equations and formulas) to more than 30 percent (data representation and analyses). This indicates differences among topics and that in some topics, such as data representation, there are particularly large differences among countries in the percentage of teachers who cover the topic. For equations and formulas, the percentage of teachers including the topic in their instruction ranges from a low of about 60 percent in one country to 100 percent in others. In contrast, data representation and analyses ranges from 0 percent to a high of about 99 percent—a considerably greater contrast among countries.

For the percentage of teacher time devoted to different topics in different countries, the standard deviations range from a low of around 1 percent (uncertainty and probability) to a high of about 8 percent (fractions).

The range also illustrates the differences among topics for different countries. For example, there is a wide range for fractions—from no time in one country to almost one-third of eighth grade mathematics teachers' time in another country. This is the range in national average percentage of teachers' time, not the range in individual teachers' time within the countries. By contrast, for probability the range is from 0 to 5 percent of teachers' time from countries devoting the least time to this topic to those devoting the most.

There is also variation across topics within a country both for the percentage of teachers presenting particular topics and for the percentage of time devoted by teachers to particular topics. The upper limit of the percentage of teachers teaching a topic within a country seems to be in the nineties for virtually all countries. However, the lower bound ranges from as low as no teachers to a much higher percentage. In one country (the United States) every topic has at least some teachers covering it, whereas in most other countries some topics have less than 10 percent of the teachers covering them, including 0 or near 0 percent of those countries' teachers. For other topics these same countries have more than 90 percent of their teachers covering those topics.

Table 5.6 and Table 5.7 present median polish data for the percent of teachers covering different topics in different countries and for the percent of time devoted by teachers to different topics in different countries. These median polish data clearly indicate the presence of large country-by-topic interactions in these teacher data. This is especially true for the percentage of teachers covering various topics (Table 5.6). For almost every topic there are numerous countries displaying interaction effects (residuals) greater than 35 percent in absolute value. This is less true for teacher time devoted to various topics. In that case, there are country-by-topic interactions (residuals) at the 5 percent or greater level for all but one topic. Focusing on the more demanding 10 percent level for residuals, there are large interaction effects for about half of the topics that teachers were questioned about. For example, it can be seen from previous data that there was a large effect in textbook emphasis for Japan in congruence and similarity. Here we can see the same sort of effect for percentage of teachers covering that topic in Japan and the percentage of time they reported devoting to it.

Commonalties Across Countries: The Notion of a World Core

In the previous sections of this chapter, we have examined some of what was typical for the TIMSS countries and for eighth grade mathematics

Table 5.6. Median Polish of Percentage of Teachers Covering Specific Topics for Different Countries and Topics (Eighth Grade Mathematics).

Country	Meaning of Whole Numbers	Common and Decimal Fractions	Percentages	Number Sets and Concepts	Number Theory	Estimation and Number Sense	Measurement Units	Perimeter, Area, and Volume	Measurement Estimation and Error	1-D and 2-D Geometry Basics	Symmetry and Transformations	Congruence and Similarity	3-D Geometry	Ratio and Proportion	Slope and Trigonometry	Functions, Relations, and Patterns	Equations and Formulas	Data and Statistics	Probability and Uncertainty	Sets and Logic	Other Advanced Content
Australia																					
Austria														-60							
Belgium (Fl)										*											
Belgium (Fr)	*			*	*					58				*							
Canada															*	-52					
Colombia																					*
Cyprus								*						*				*			
Czech Republic														*		51					
Denmark																					
France															57						
Germany																					
Greece														*	77			53			
Hong Kong														*	74						
Hungary																					*
Iceland	56	57				52	*								*						
Iran															-55						
Ireland																					*
Israel														*							64
Japan		*						*						56	*	*		51			
Korea														*							
Latvia																					
Netherland																					
New Zealand																					
Norway														*	-62	-58					
Portugal				*										*				*			
Romania														69		51					*
Russian Federation	*	-61	*	*		*		*						60	*	*					88
Singapore		-55		-55	-69	-57	*							*	*		-60		*		*
Slovak Republic														*		66	51				*
Slovenia														*	54	*					
Spain																					
Sweden	*			*		*	51							*		*					
Switzerland																*					
USA																					

Note: *The * indicates residuals at the 35 percent level. Others are indicated by their specific value.*

Table 5.7. Median Polish of Percentage of Instructional Time for Specific Topics for Different Countries and Topics (Eighth Grade Mathematics).

Country	Meaning of Whole Numbers	Common and Decimal Fractions	Percentages	Number Sets and Concepts	Number Theory	Estimation and Number Sense	Measurement Units	Perimeter, Area, and Volume	Measurement Estimation and Error	1-D & 2-D Geometry Basics	Symmetry and Transformations	Congruence and Similarity	3-D Geometry	Ratio and Proportion	Slope and Trigonometry	Functions, Relations, and Patterns	Equations and Formulas	Data and Statistics	Probability and Uncertainty	Sets and Logic	Other Advanced Content
Australia																*					
Austria									*												
Belgium (Fl)		*									*	*									
Belgium (Fr)	*	*	*									12									
Canada																		*			
Colombia	*			*	*																
Cyprus						*															
Czech Republic		*										*			13	*					
Denmark		*																*			
France		*							*												
Germany																					
Greece				11								*			*	*			*		
Hong Kong										*				*	13						
Hungary																					
Iceland	*	19	14			*			*												
Iran					*				*												
Ireland																			*		
Israel												13				12					
Japan		*								*		22				11	*				
Korea		*											*								*
Latvia		*									*	*				13					
Netherland																		*			
New Zealand																		*			
Norway		11																			
Portugal		*				*				*											
Romania		*					*								19		*	*			
Russian Federation		−11	15							13	*							*			18
Singapore		*								*	*	*						*			
Slovak Republic		*										*			*	11					
Slovenia		*										*	*	*				*			
Spain		*		*	*											*	12				
Sweden	*	21	11			*	*											*			
Switzerland	*	*																*			
USA																					

Note: *The * indicates residuals at the 5 percent level. Others are indicated by their specific value.*

topics and their interactions for each of four indicators of curriculum, which were examined separately. The question considered now is to what extent the portraits are similar for these various indications of curriculum. Do these different sources of data tell one story or different stories? Are what we learn from content standards and from textbooks the same, and how do these compare to the story told by teacher data?

Ultimately these questions must be asked at the country level to inform educational policy.[16] Here we look for commonalties across the countries, for the "world according to TIMSS," using all thirty-six countries on average to portray cross-national commonalties that would presumably hold even more generally than for the TIMSS countries.

We examined the five topics most emphasized by each of the four indications of curriculum averaged across all participating TIMSS countries providing data on eighth grade mathematics. That is, they are the five topics most often included in content standards among the TIMSS countries. They are the five given the largest proportion of space in textbooks, the five covered by the greatest national percentage of teachers averaged across the TIMSS countries, and the five to which the most teacher time was allocated averaged across countries. They are not necessarily the same five topics in each case.

With all four indicators and measurements, the universally agreed-upon topic is equations and formulas. Also in the top three by all measures is two-dimensional geometry. This is the level of aggregation of geometry content as it was used in the teacher questionnaires. It most likely includes primarily polygons and circles, which is among the top three for content standards and textbooks.

From this point there begin to be divergences among the indicators. The more intention-oriented indicators—textbooks and content standards—include functions and relations and three-dimensional geometry among their top five topics. However, neither of these topics is among the top five either in the percentage of teachers covering them on average across countries or in the typical percentage of time allocated to them. They thus rank highly for the two more intention-oriented indicators but not correspondingly highly for the two implementation-oriented indicators. There appears to be a widespread split between intention and implementation in this area.

By contrast, both teacher indicators show fractions and number theory to be among the most widely implemented topics, yet neither appears in the top five of content standards. There is again a split between policy and practice but this time in the opposite direction. Perimeter, area, and volume—a measurement topic closely related to geometry—is in the top five for both teacher indicators and for textbooks but not for content standards. Here, however, the difference is not so sharp because this topic is the sixth most emphasized in content standards. Possibly the inclusion of fractions and number theory in actual instruction, although it is not a widely planned-for topic, may indicate teacher belief that content from earlier grades not yet mastered must again be covered. This, however, is only a conjecture. Clearly the core curriculum for eighth grade mathematics is not a simple matter, considering different countries, different topics, and different indications of curriculum, either intended or practiced.

To portray more accurately what is common, we have defined two world-core eighth grade mathematics curricula from these data. Rather than consider the four indications of curriculum separately, they are combined here. The more stringent core is defined as those topics covered in the content standards and textbooks of 100 percent of the countries and taught by 75 percent or more of the teachers. We have previously discussed such a core based only on content standards and textbooks,[17] but here we add the teacher data as an additional criterion. A second, less stringent core requires 70 percent of the countries to include the topic in their content standards and textbooks.

No single topic simultaneously meets all the 100 percent criteria for all the countries. There is, however, a small set of topics that meet the 70 percent criteria for content standards, textbook coverage, and implementation in 70 percent of the countries by 75 percent or more of the teachers. These topics are perimeter, area, and volume and equations and formulas.

If the criterion for implementation is made more stringent—requiring that 80 or 85 percent of the teachers in all countries teach that topic—then only one topic makes even the less stringent (70 percent of countries for content standards and textbooks) core. That topic is equations and formulas. On the other hand, if the implementation criterion is dropped to 70 percent, two-dimensional geometry basics is added to the less stringent core along with the other two topics.

Thus, in the world according to TIMSS, the central topics of eighth grade mathematics are most consistently perimeter, area, and volume and equations and formulas. This is true regardless of the way in which curriculum is made visible for examination and is true with great consistency across the TIMSS countries. How few topics meet these criteria certainly emphasize that "mathematics is not mathematics is not mathematics" in terms of the eighth grade curriculum. On the other hand, that two topics met these demanding criteria indicates how widespread the focus on them is and with what risk they are omitted from the focus of instruction in a country at eighth grade or before.

Seventh Grade Mathematics

The focus in this book is on the relationship of curriculum (as defined by its various aspects) to learning defined as the gain from seventh to eighth grade (or their equivalents). However, in some analyses we incorporate measures of learning opportunities from earlier grades such as the seventh, sixth, or a composite of the first through fifth grades (or their equivalents in other countries). The inclusion of earlier grades also provides a context for understanding the nature of the eighth grade curriculum. For example, to understand the implications of the five most commonly covered topics at eighth grade, it is important to know what main topics were actually implemented at earlier grades. Thus, although not the central focus of this chapter, the next sections are devoted to curricula in these earlier grades. They provide information on sequence and context to help better understand eighth grade curricula.

Content Standards

Table 5.8 displays the percentages of countries that cover mathematics topics at the seventh grade or its equivalent as those topics are related to the TIMSS Population 2 mathematics test. It is a parallel to Table 5.1 for eighth grade. There is a three-way tie for the most widely covered topic at seventh grade—perimeter, area, and volume; polygons and circles; and proportionality problems. For all three, all but one country intended coverage of those topics as indicated in their content standards.

Two-dimensional geometry basics and proportionality concepts were also widely intended for coverage. They were included in the content standards of over 90 percent of the countries. Judged by content standards, eighth grade mathematics seems to have been intended to be a curriculum of geometry and algebra. In contrast, the seventh grade mathematics curriculum seems to have been one of geometry (including measurement) and prealgebra (focusing especially on proportionality). It must be noted that about 89 percent of the countries had equations and formulas in their seventh grade content standards. The line between algebra and pre-algebra is likely an artificial one, consisting mainly in differences of emphasis and sophistication of content.

Three topics stand out as being in the content standards of about two-thirds of the countries but not tested on the TIMSS Population 2 test. This includes properties of operations, number theory, and constructions with a straightedge and compass. The only topic in common between the seventh and eighth grade mathematics core topics as indicated by content

Table 5.8. Variation in Intended Topic Coverage in Seventh Grade Mathematics Content Standards.

Tested Topics (26)	Coverage in Content Standards	
	Number of Countries (35)	Percent
1. Whole numbers	23	65.7
Meaning	19	54.3
Operations	22	62.9
2. Common fractions	26	74.3
3. Decimal fractions and percents	27	77.1
Decimal fractions	25	71.4
Percentages	26	74.3
4. Relations of fractions	24	68.6
5. Estimating quantity and size	20	57.1
6. Rounding	22	62.9
7. Estimating computations	25	71.4
8. Measurement units	32	91.4
9. Perimeter, area, and volume	34	97.1
10. Measurement estimations and errors	24	68.6
11. 2-D geometry	35	100.0
2-D coordinate geometry	28	80.0
2-D geometry: Basics	33	94.3
12. Polygons and circles	34	97.1
13. 3-D geometry and transformations	31	88.6
3-D geometry	25	71.4
Transformations	27	77.1
14. Congruence and similarity	24	68.6
15. Proportionality concepts	32	91.4
16. Proportionality problems	34	97.1
17. Patterns, relations, and functions	25	71.4
18. Equations and formulas	34	97.1
Equations and formulas	31	88.6
Negative numbers, integers and their properties	27	77.1
Exponents, roots, and radicals	28	80.0
19. Data representation and analysis	25	71.4
20. Uncertainty and probability	14	40.0
Topics Not Tested		
Properties of operations	23	65.7
Properties of common and decimal fractions	22	62.9
Rational numbers and their properties	22	62.9
Real numbers, their subsets and properties	14	40.0
Binary arithmetic and/or other number bases	11	31.4
Complex numbers and their properties	0	0.0
Number theory	25	71.4

Systematic counting	8	22.9
Exponents and orders of magnitude	22	62.9
Vectors	2	5.7
Constructions w/ straightedge and compass	26	74.3
Slope and trigonometry	7	20.0
Linear interpolation and extrapolation	4	11.4
Infinite processes	1	2.9
Change	2	5.7
Validation and justification	13	37.1
Structuring and abstracting	14	40.0
Informatics	12	34.3

Note: *The numbered topics are the twenty tested areas. The eleven indented topics, together with the fifteen tested areas for which there is only one framework code, cover twenty-six framework topics. These twenty-six plus the eighteen topics not tested in TIMSS exhaust all 44 topics in the TIMSS mathematics framework.*

standards was polygons and circles. This suggests a marked shift of emphasis from seventh to eighth grade cross-nationally.

Table 5.2 indicates the number of topics in country content standards relative to the total number of possible topics. The number for seventh grade varies from fourteen (Japan, Bulgaria, and the Slovak Republic) to thirty-eight (Switzerland). Again there is an indication that the extent of focus on a few rather than many topics varies among the countries.

Textbooks were not collected for seventh grade mathematics, so this indication of curriculum is not available for analysis. Attention turns now to the teacher coverage indicators. Table 5.9 gives the means and standard deviations for each topic, both in terms of the percentage of teachers who indicated covering that topic and the national average percent of a teacher's time indicated as devoted to that topic. The topic taught by the highest percentage of teachers in a country (averaged over countries) for seventh grade mathematics was fractions and decimals, closely followed by perimeter, area, and volume. Thus, by both intention and implementation, perimeter, area, and volume was one of the most consistently covered topics in seventh grade mathematics (in contrast to equations and formulas in eighth grade). However, at eighth grade, perimeter, area, and volume was still among the top five topics.

The five most frequently covered topics were fractions and decimals; perimeter, area, and volume; whole numbers; number sets and concepts; and percentage. The seventh grade mathematics curriculum seems to focus

Table 5.9. Means and Standard Deviations by Topic of Percentage of
Teachers Covering Each Topic and Percentage of Instructional Time
Devoted to Each Topic (Seventh Grade Mathematics).

Topic	Percentage of Teacher Coverage		Percentage of Instructional Time	
	Mean	Standard Deviation	Mean	Standard Deviation
Meaning of whole numbers	80.3	18.9	9.0	4.8
Common and decimal fractions		16.7	18.0	6.8
Percentages	75.5	21.5	5.3	2.6
Number sets and concepts	78.2	14.3	8.0	4.6
Number theory	64.9	28.2	4.4	2.6
Estimation and number sense	71.5	24.0	4.2	2.1
Measurement units	74.0	23.0	5.2	2.6
Perimeter, area, and volume	86.6	13.8	7.1	2.8
Measurement estimation and error	45.1	20.5	1.8	1.0
1-D and 2-D geometry basics	73.0	16.7	6.3	3.7
Symmetry and transformations	47.8	23.3	2.6	2.0
Congruence and similarity	52.8	28.8	3.3	3.0
3-D geometry	45.3	19.1	2.4	1.7
Ratio and proportion	64.3	26.5	4.4	3.4
Slope and trigonometry	16.1	16.9	0.7	1.2
Functions, relations, and patterns	31.0	22.3	2.1	2.7
Equations and formulas	68.2	23.3	7.5	6.5
Data and statistics	42.5	27.4	2.1	1.8
Probability and uncertainty	14.4	19.0	0.4	0.5
Sets and logic	28.4	27.2	1.9	2.8
Other advanced content	27.7	12.0	1.8	1.0

heavily on arithmetic topics when analyzed in terms of what teachers report actually covering.

How much preparation is done in seventh grade for the most widely intended topics in eighth grade mathematics? The five most frequently intended eighth grade mathematics topics are given here followed by the percentage of seventh grade teachers (averaged across countries) who reported teaching those topics. They are equations and formulas (68 percent); patterns, relations, and functions (31); polygons and circles (73); congruence and similarity (53); and three-dimensional geometry (45). Clearly the most widely intended topics for eighth grade are not widely taught at seventh grade, especially patterns, relations, and functions; congruence and similarity; and three-dimensional geometry.

The topic receiving the most teacher time (averaged across countries) was fractions and decimals, which accounted for roughly 18 percent of the instructional time during the seventh grade. The topic receiving the next highest amount of teacher time, whole numbers (computation), was covered for about 9 percent of the seventh grade mathematics instructional time, only about half of that for fractions and decimals.

The topics receiving the most instructional time in seventh grade, as estimated from the data reported in teacher questionnaires, were fractions and decimals; whole numbers; number sets and concepts; equations and formulas; and perimeter, area, and volume. The parallel list for eighth grade mathematics has all but one topic in common, although the topics do not appear in the same order. That topic is whole numbers (arithmetic), which is replaced at eighth grade by two-dimensional geometry basics.

In seventh grade, both equations and formulas and fractions and decimals have large ranges, varying from less than 5 percent to as much as about 30 percent of the seventh grade mathematics time. Certainly there is variation among countries in terms of how much instructional time is devoted to different topics, even those most consistently taught.

We now compare the three lists of top topics for seventh grade mathematics. These include the five topics most consistently mentioned for seventh grade coverage in content standards (intended topics). They include the five topics taught by the largest percentages of teachers averaged across countries. They also include the five topics indicated as receiving the greatest percentage of teacher time in seventh grade mathematics. These latter two we consider as indications of the curriculum as actually implemented.

As at eighth grade, countries' intentions in the aggregate are not borne out by what teachers implement. Only perimeter, area, and volume makes all three lists. The inclusion of topics such as fractions and decimals and whole numbers may well reflect teachers' view that these must be addressed again because students did not grasp them well enough in earlier grades. This may be especially likely when one considers that a top topic in content standards is proportionality problems, which make heavy use of fractions and decimals. If so, this same sense of lack of mastery appears to persist into eighth grade because considerable time is again devoted to fractions and decimals in spite of its absence from eighth grade mathematics content standards.

As was the case at eighth grade, the United States has a high proportion of teachers teaching a given topic after those topics that are not taught by any teachers have been removed from consideration. New

Zealand has this at seventh grade but not eighth. Some countries (Japan, Latvia, Romania, and Slovenia) have a somewhat smaller proportion of their teachers teaching a topic that is covered. Most countries had between 50 and 55 percent of their teachers teaching a topic that had been covered in seventh grade. There was again variation among countries as well as among topics in terms of teacher coverage.

Most of those countries with lower mean percentages than the United States and New Zealand have larger variances across topics, with some receiving virtually no coverage (less than 5 percent of the teachers) and others receiving virtually total coverage (more than 95 percent of the teachers) in the same country. A median polish again shows numerous interaction effects. The fact that this is true at seventh as well as eighth grade for mathematics suggests even more strongly that the mathematics curriculum is largely a cultural artifact treated very differently in different countries.

Sixth Grade Mathematics

The data in this section are based on a different sort of data than that for the discussion of seventh and eighth grade mathematics curricula. The data on intentions were collected from country mathematics experts using national content standards documents and reflecting their expert judgments of what was typical for their country. This method of general topic trace methodology (GTTM) was described earlier (see Chapter Three).[18] At seventh and eighth grades, data were available both on intention (GTTM at seventh, content standards document analysis at eighth) and implementation (percent of teachers covering a topic and percent of time devoted by teachers to a topic). At eighth grade there were also textbook data. At sixth grade, only the GTTM data on intention were available.

The most highly rated single topic across the countries in sixth grade mathematics was the relationship of fractions and decimals. Closely tied to this topic were the separate topics of fractions and of decimals. The five topics receiving the most emphasis were the relationship of fractions and decimals; fractions; decimals; perimeter, area, and volume; and measurement units. Other areas receiving considerable emphasis included percentages, polygons and circles, and proportionality problems. Clearly the sixth grade mathematics curriculum seemed to be a preparatory curriculum of advanced arithmetic, measurement, and some geometric ideas.

First through Fifth Grade Mathematics

The topic receiving the most intended coverage (averaged across countries) was whole number operations.[19] The top five topics were (in order) whole number operations; measurement units; whole number meaning; properties of operations; and perimeter, area, and volume. Other areas receiving substantial intended coverage were fractions, estimating quantity and size, and estimating computations.

The view from the world of TIMSS makes it clear that mathematics curricula in first through fifth grades were mainly about whole numbers and measurement. This contrasts with the sixth grade, which was mostly about fractions and decimals (an emphasis that grew in first through fifth grades) and measurement. The seventh grade mathematics curriculum was mostly geometry (including measurement) and proportionality. Finally, eighth grade mathematics was mostly algebra and geometry.

We discussed earlier the presence of fractions and decimals as one of the top five topics implemented by teachers (either by percent covering or time allocated) at seventh grade, although it was not among the top five intended topics. We suggested that the reason for this might be because this topic was intended for coverage in earlier grades; it certainly was the most widely intended topic for sixth grade mathematics. It still remains only conjecture that its place in seventh grade and even eighth grade results from teachers returning to or reviewing content previously focused on but not considered widely mastered.

The Correlation of Coverage Among Topics

This section examines the relationship of curriculum (learning opportunities) across topics. Using any of the four indications of curriculum, is coverage of one topic related to coverage of another? For example, do they tend to be taught together? Does the inclusion of one topic imply that another is likely to be included also? Is the amount of textbook space given to two topics related? If we find strong indicators of these sorts of relationships across the thirty-six countries within a grade level, this may well imply that topics may be clustered in ways that make the whole (cluster) greater than the sum of its parts (individual topics). That is, the cumulative effect of a set of clustered topics that interact in their opportunities for learning may be more than simply additive of the effects of the topics considered separately.

Consider first the percentage of teachers covering a topic (Table 5.10). At the country level, the percentage of teachers teaching whole numbers at the eighth grade is highly related to the percentage of teachers teaching number theory (correlation—r equal to .80),[*] measurement units (.74), and fractions (.74). This cluster of content topics is not surprising because many would think of them as basic skills in arithmetic. There is also a relationship between the percentage of teachers teaching fractions and percentages (correlation equal to .80), of fractions and measurement units (.67), and of percentages and measurement units (.74). This again suggests a clustering of arithmetic content, perhaps along with simple measurement. Most of the same patterns emerge for the percentage of instructional time, another indication of curriculum implementation, again suggesting a basic arithmetic cluster.

Such strong patterns of relationship do not arise for the geometry topics or for the proportionality and algebra topics. There are some modestly strong relationships within these clusters, for example, between the coverage of functions and of equations and formulas (a correlation of .46). There is also a modest correlation between coverage of slope and of equations and formulas (.42), suggesting a more weakly linked algebra cluster. Nothing of even this strength is revealed for geometry topics.

Some interesting relationships exist between clusters. For instance, there are mostly small relationships between arithmetic and geometry or algebra topics. However, the strong relationships that exist between arithmetic and algebra topics are negative, indicating that a larger percentage of teachers teaching arithmetic topics is associated with a smaller percentage of that country's teachers teaching algebra topics. This is even truer for the percentage of instructional time devoted to various topics. The correlations are larger between arithmetic and algebra, but also more of them are negative. They are larger for the relationship between arithmetic and geometry topics as well.

The general conclusion would seem to be that an arithmetic cluster of topics (whole numbers, fractions, percentages, and perhaps measurement units) tends to be taught together at the eighth grade and is negatively related to the coverage of geometry and algebra topics. The presence of an arithmetic cluster seems to imply that at eighth grade, basic topics seem to cluster together. This is not true for algebra or geometry.

---

[*]The correlation coefficient is a measure of the linear relationship between two variables. That is, it is a measure of the degree to which they vary together. The value of the coefficient ranges from -1 through 0 to $+1$. While values of zero indicate the absence of a relationship, the magnitude of the coefficient indicates the strength of the linear relationship. The sign of the coefficient indicates whether the relationship is a direct one (positive) or an indirect one (negative).

Table 5.11 displays the correlations among topics for content standards in eighth grade mathematics. Because of the higher number of topics available (forty-four compared with twenty-one for the teacher questionnaires), these displays give a summary of the correlations. There are almost a thousand correlations of topic pairs for content standards (and for textbooks). The entries in each cell of the display give the median correlation values. For display purposes, the correlations are aggregated to a higher level, the topics used in the teacher questionnaires, so that this exhibit is comparable to Table 5.10.

The same general patterns that held for the teacher indications of the implemented curriculum also hold for content standard correlations. There appears to be a basic arithmetic component involving whole number computations, fractions and decimals, as well as basic measurement. As with the two indications of implemented curriculum, the correlations for content standards indicate that when these intentions concentrate on basic arithmetic, they do not concentrate on geometry, proportionality, and function topics. These correlations suggest that learning opportunity variables in mathematics are grouped into larger aggregations such as basic arithmetic, geometry, proportionality, equations and functions, and statistics and probability.

For textbook data, the correlational patterns are for the most part similar. However, the correlations among arithmetic topics in terms of the percent of textbook space are smaller, suggesting that the eighth grade books may vary more in the arithmetic content they include. The correlations across the aggregate areas are largely negative. This suggests that more textbook space on basic arithmetic is associated with less space with geometry and algebra (and more for statistics and data analysis).

Eighth Grade Science

We have now completed our investigation of how curricula in school mathematics vary by topic, country, and the interaction of the two for the four aspects of curriculum. We have sketched a portrait of how mathematical topics are treated in the eighth grade and somewhat in prior grades among the TIMSS countries. In this section we do the same for eighth grade school science.

Content Standards

We begin with an analysis of content standard documents for eighth grade science. We look first at variations for topics in eighth grade school science and then variations among countries.

Table 5.10. Correlations Among Topics for the Percentage of Teachers Covering a Topic (Eighth Grade Mathematics).

Topic	Whole Numbers	Common and Decimal Fractions	Percentages	Number Sets and Concepts	Number Theory	Estimation and Number Sense	Measurement Units	Perimeter, Area, and Volume
Whole numbers	1.00							
Common and decimal fractions	.74	1.00						
Percentages	.55	.80	1.00					
Number sets and concepts	.33	.40	.21	1.00				
Number theory	.80	.55	.30	.45	1.00			
Estimation and number sense	.68	.57	.55	.22	.54	1.00		
Measurement units	.74	.67	.74	.07	.51	.81	1.00	
Perimeter, area, and volume	.33	.46	.71	.15	.22	.38	.63	1.00
Measurement estimation and error	.52	.29	.41	.11	.44	.70	.66	.38
1-D and 2-D geometry basics	−.27	−.07	.10	.32	−.07	.06	−.03	.29
Symmetry and transformations	.18	.24	.10	.53	.26	.11	.02	.19
Congruence and similarity	−.34	−.38	−.27	−.02	−.05	−.40	−.41	−.18
3-D geometry	.21	.09	.15	−.07	.20	.13	.38	.41
Ratio and proportion	.04	.28	.21	.05	.16	.06	.13	.32
Slope and trigonometry	−.51	−.37	−.22	−.15	−.34	−.27	−.34	.05
Functions, relations, and patterns	−.36	−.51	−.35	−.23	−.13	−.28	−.19	−.08
Equations and formulas	−.50	−.41	−.43	.13	−.17	−.54	−.55	−.25
Data and statistics	.19	.31	.44	.26	.25	.28	.26	.46
Probability and uncertainty	.50	.44	.45	.39	.62	.39	.48	.33
Sets and logic	.24	.06	−.02	.04	.39	−.13	.07	−.07
Other advanced content	.02	−.35	−.28	.14	.15	.14	−.01	−.12

	Measurement Estimation and Error	1-D & 2-D Geometry Basics	Symmetry and Transformations	Congruence and Similarity	3-D Geometry	Ratio and Proportion	Slope and Trigonometry	Functions, Relations, and Patterns	Equations and Formulas	Data and Statistics	Probability and Uncertainty	Sets and Logic	Other Advanced Content
	1.00												
	.24	1.00											
	−.00	.40	1.00										
	−.10	.36	.22	1.00									
	.27	.11	.04	−.05	1.00								
	−.01	.45	.52	.19	.25	1.00							
	−.14	.36	.14	.26	−.02	.34	1.00						
	.01	.16	−.19	.28	.48	−.05	.29	1.00					
	−.30	.42	.24	.48	.19	.29	.42	.46	1.00				
	.25	.47	.39	−.01	−.01	.30	.25	.02	−.08	1.00			
	.62	.28	.33	.16	.37	.27	−.18	.19	.02	.33	1.00		
	.14	−.07	.16	.29	.34	.02	−.12	.23	.12	−.07	.52	1.00	
	.44	.16	.19	.37	.19	−.00	.21	.26	.35	−.14	.25	.11	1.00

Table 5.11. Median Correlations Among Topics in Content Standards (Eighth Grade Mathematics).

Topic	Whole Numbers	Common and Decimal Fractions	Percentages	Number Sets and Concepts	Number Theory	Estimation and Number Sense	Measurement Units	Perimeter, Area, and Volume
Meaning of whole numbers	.60							
Common and decimal fractions	.62	.65						
Percentages	.58	.55						
Number sets and concepts	.20	.28	.40	.29				
Number theory	.37	.44	.37	.36	.44			
Estimation and number sense	.30	.43	.50	.26	.26	.68		
Measurement units	.38	.58	.40	.18	.33	.48		
Perimeter, area, and volume	.23	.35	.25	.15	.21	.23	.63	
Measurement estimation and error	.34	.41	.27	.16	.35	.32	.75	.47
1-D and 2-D geometry basics	.19	.19	.33	.26	.32	.27	.10	−.03
Symmetry and transformations	.19	.21	.25	-.06	.05	.29	.16	.00
Congruence and similarity	−.28	.03	.01	.16	.06	.07	.06	.04
3-D geometry	.31	.43	.46	.18	.24	.35	.55	.35
Ratio and proportion	.27	.32	.40	.12	.32	.29	.47	.25
Slope and trigonometry	.05	.11	.14	.08	.02	−.08	.05	.19
Functions, relations, and patterns	−.12	−.00	−.13	.00	.17	.14	.24	−.08
Equations and formulas	*	*	*	*	*	*	*	*
Data and statistics	.55	.43	.59	.16	.23	.43	.27	−.09
Probability and uncertainty	.17	.41	.37	.27	.42	.37	.48	.08
Sets and logic	−.04	.21	−.10	.21	.35	.00	.16	−.01
Other advanced content	.27	.32	.16	.09	.32	.28	.25	.16

Measurement Estimation and Error	1-D & 2-D Geometry Basics	Symmetry and Transformations	Congruence and Similarity	3-D Geometry	Ratio and Proportion	Slope and Trigonometry	Functions, Relations, and Patterns	Equations and Formulas	Data and Statistics	Probability and Uncertainty	Sets and Logic	Other Advanced Content
.24	.34											
.17	−.08											
.10	.04	−.18										
.42	.19	.35	.13	.29								
.44	.14	.16	.10	.41	.48							
.14	−.18	.19	−.03	.14	.07	.30						
.18	−.03	−.08	.42	.19	.12	−.23						
*	*	*	*	*	*	*	*					
.22	.20	.26	−.05	.17	.12	.18	−.10	*				
.44	.15	.08	.31	.15	.45	.12	.20	*	.42			
.15	.15	−.16	.25	.06	−.01	.08	.14	*	−.05	.06	.61	
.18	.08	.22	.20	.20	.22	.01	.08	*	.27	.27	.13	.35

* Because all countries intended coverage of equations and formulas in their content standards, correlations could not be computed.

TOPIC VARIATION Table 5.12 displays the percentage of countries that covered each topic but organized as they were related to the topic areas of the TIMSS Population 2 science test. The overall percentage for each of the seventeen tested topics indicates the percentage that covers at least one of the topics represented on the test.

The most covered topics as indicated by countries' content standards are energy capture, storage and transformation (including photosynthesis and respiration) and energy types, sources, and conversions, the latter being a physics topic. Each of these topics was in the content standards of about 92 percent of the participating countries (all but three countries). Three other topics were in the content standards of all but four countries (89 percent). These were human biology, electricity, and the conservation of land, air, and sea resources.

Other topics that were included in the content standards of at least 80 percent of the countries included the biology topics of organs and tissues, sensing and responding, and reproduction. No earth sciences topics were this commonly intended for coverage. There were two environmental science topics—interdependence of life and pollution and conservation. There were several topics at this level from physics and chemistry: classification of matter; physical and chemical properties of matter; atoms, ions, and molecules; heat and temperature; light; and chemical changes.

The area of physics and chemistry had the most topics represented cross-nationally at eighth grade, but environmental science and biology were also well represented. The only area not represented was, in fact, earth science. Thus, in the world according to TIMSS, the core curriculum, at least as intended, was about aspects of physics, chemistry, environmental science, and some of the more advanced topics of biology such as sensing and responding and energy handling. In contrast, the tested topics intended by the smallest numbers of countries all came from earth science. These included atmosphere, building and breaking, and beyond the solar system.

A number of topics were widely intended but were not among the topics in the TIMSS Population 2 science test. The most widely covered of these was world pollution, which was in 81 percent of the countries' content standards but not on the TIMSS test. There were four other topics not tested but included in over 75 percent of the countries' content standards. These were plants and fungi, biomes and ecosystems, food production and storage, and the nature of scientific knowledge. Ten of the topics not tested were in the content standards of 50 percent or less of the countries.

Table 5.12. Variation in Intended Topic Coverage in Countries' Eighth Grade Science Content Standards.

Tested Topics (48)	Coverage in Content Standards	
	Number of Countries (36)	Percent
1. Earth features (12)	27	75.0
Landforms	20	55.6
Bodies of water	22	61.1
Atmosphere	15	41.7
Rocks, soil	21	58.3
2. Earth processes (8)	28	77.8
Weather and climate	26	72.2
Physical cycles	20	55.6
Building and breaking	16	44.4
Earth's history	20	55.6
3. Earth in the universe (5)	20	55.6
Earth in the solar system	20	55.6
Beyond the solar system	16	44.4
4. Diversity and structure of living things (16)	33	91.7
Animals	27	75.0
Other organisms	25	69.4
Organs, tissues	30	83.3
Cells	25	69.4
5. Life processes and functions (16)	34	94.4
Energy handling	33	91.7
Sensing and responding	30	83.3
6. Life cycles and genetics (5)	33	91.7
Life cycles	26	72.2
Reproduction	29	80.6
Variation and inheritance	19	52.8
Evolution, speculation, and diversity	27	75.0
7. Interactions of living things (4)	32	88.9
Interdependence of life	29	80.6
Animal behavior	25	69.4
8. Human biology and health (16)	32	88.9
Human biology	32	88.9
Nutrition	21	58.3
Disease	24	66.7
9. Properties and classification of matter (11)	35	97.2
Classification of matter	31	86.1
Physical properties	30	83.3
Chemical properties	30	83.3
10. Structure of matter (5)	30	83.3
Atoms, ions, and molecules	30	83.3

(continued)

Table 5.12. *(continued)*

Tested Topics (48)	Coverage in Content Standards	
	Number of Countries (36)	Percent
11. Energy and physical processes (27)	35	**97.2**
Energy types, sources, and conversions	33	91.7
Heat and temperature	29	80.6
Wave phenomena	20	55.6
Sound and vibration	22	61.1
Light	30	83.3
Electricity	32	88.9
Magnetism	26	72.2
12. Physical changes (4)	27	**75.0**
Physical changes	24	66.7
Explanations of physical changes	19	52.8
13. Chemical changes (12)	29	**80.6**
Chemical changes	29	80.6
Energy and chemical change	22	61.1
14. Forces and motion (6)	28	**77.8**
Types of forces	24	66.7
Time, space, and motion	24	66.7
Dynamics of motion	20	55.6
Fluid behavior	11	30.6
15. Science, technology, and society (3)	27	**75.0**
Influence of science and technology on society	27	75.0
16. Environmental and resource issues (7)	33	**91.7**
Pollution	29	80.6
Conservation of land, water, and sea resources	32	88.9
Conservation of material and energy resources	29	80.6
17. Scientific Processes (8)	28	**77.8**
No content		
Topics Not Tested (31)		
Composition	16	44.4
Ice forms	12	33.3
Planets in the solar system	19	52.8
Evolution of the universe	14	38.9
Plants and fungi	27	75.0
Biochemical processes in cells	22	61.1
Biochemistry of genetics	11	30.6
Biomes and ecosystems	27	75.0
Habitats and niches	25	69.4
Macromolecules and crystals	20	55.6
Subatomic particles	24	66.7
Kinetic theory	13	36.1

Quantum theory and fundamental particles	9	25.0
Explanations of chemical changes	19	52.8
Rate of change and equilibria	16	44.4
Organic and biochemical changes	18	50.0
Nuclear chemistry	19	52.8
Electrochemistry	19	52.8
Relativity theory	9	25.0
Nature or conceptions of technology	25	69.4
Influence of math, technology in science	19	52.8
Applications of science in math and technology	28	77.8
Influence of society on science and technology	23	63.9
History of science	23	63.9
World pollution	29	80.6
Food production and storage	28	77.8
Effects of natural disasters	26	72.2
Nature of scientific knowledge	27	75.0
The scientific enterprise	16	44.4
Science and mathematics	20	55.6
Science and other disciplines	23	63.9

Note: *The numbered topics are the seventeen tested areas. The forty-eight indented topics, together with the thirty-one topics not tested in TIMSS, exhaust all seventy-nine topics in the TIMSS science framework.*

Also shown in Table 5.12 are the percentages of countries that cover at least one topic of those that are relevant to a given subtest area (which may often include several TIMSS science framework topics). At least 75 percent of the countries covered at least one topic in the areas represented by the test items, with the exception of earth in the universe. Is there a pattern to coverage of topics within a test area? Does coverage of an area imply that all framework topics relevant to the area were found in the content standards (as tended to be the case for eighth grade mathematics)?

For all seventeen of the tested areas in eighth grade science, the most relevant pattern given intended coverage (inclusion in content standards) of at least one topic was intended coverage of all of the framework topics constituting that area for the TIMSS test. The percentages (eliminating those for which not even one topic was intended to be covered) ranged from around 50 to over 90 percent for this pattern of total intended coverage for all but four tested areas: earth features, life cycles and genetics, energy and physical processes, and forces and motion.

For earth features, the most common alternative to covering all relevant topics was covering all but the atmosphere. For life cycles and genetics, the most common alternative was doing all but variations and inheritance. For energy and physical processes, almost every possible pattern of topic coverage existed, with no pattern other than total coverage really dominant. For forces and motion, inclusion of all topics except fluid behavior was the most common alternative pattern of topic coverage. For most tested areas, the pattern of topic inclusion in content standards seems to imply that countries intended to cover all of the topics relevant to an area, with at most one topic omitted. The one exception to this was energy and physical processes, which seems to have involved many different patterns of intended coverage: single topics, pairs, and so on.

COUNTRY VARIATION Table 5.13 displays the number of topics included in the content standards for each country. This includes the number relative to the total number of TIMSS science framework topics (seventy-nine) and to the number of tested areas (forty-eight). The number of framework topics in content standards and thus presumably intended for coverage varied from as few as eight to as many as all seventy-nine (in New Zealand, Iran, and the United States).

Focusing only on those framework topics relevant to one of the seventeen tested areas for the Population 2 science test (forty-eight topics), a considerable range of topics was still intended for coverage. This ranged from as few as six (Korea) to all forty-eight of them (Switzerland and the United States). This, of course, does not mean that Korea did not intend coverage for closer to the total of forty-eight possible topics but rather that it did not intend them to be covered at eighth grade according to its content standards.

Textbooks

As before, we turn from examining curricular intentions using content standards as an indicator to examining what student textbooks reveal about the topics that were more easily (and, perhaps, more likely) implemented. Student textbooks tell their own story of the content of school science, and the relevance of this to either curricular intentions or implementations depends on the role that student textbooks play in the educational cultures of the countries using them.

TOPIC VARIATION Figure 5.5 displays the cumulative distributions of the percentage of the textbook covering each topic for each of the seventy-nine topics in the TIMSS science framework.

The single topic covered the most in student textbooks on average over all of the TIMSS countries was electricity. This averaged over 11 percent of the textbook across countries. This is a strong contrast to eighth grade mathematics, in which the most emphasized single topic covered almost twice as much of a textbook on average. This topic, electricity, also had the largest standard deviation and a range from 0 percent (that is, not in a country's textbook) to 98 percent (meaning that electricity was a part of virtually all of that textbook's content).

The second and third most emphasized topics came from biology—human biology (9 percent) and organs and tissues (6 percent). After the two biology topics, a group of physics and chemistry topics dominated other topics, with each appearing in around 5 percent of the textbooks averaged across countries. These included the classification and physical properties of matter; energy types, sources, and conversions; light; and the chemical properties and changes of matter.

The five topics receiving the most emphasis on average in textbooks include the three disciplines of biology, chemistry, and physics. The only discipline in the TIMSS framework not represented among the top five was earth science. The same general conclusion applies to the tested topics because all of the top five topics emphasized in textbooks were among those in areas tested in the TIMSS Population 2 science test. However, several of the tested topics did not have much textbook space associated with them on average. All three of the earth science test areas fall into this category because the topics defining them had only about 2 percent or less of textbook space. Weather and climate was the only real exception; it had about 4 percent of textbook space on average and was one of the four topics comprising earth processes, a more general earth science topic area. In addition to most earth science topics, some other topics from tested areas had only around 2 percent or less coverage in the textbooks. These included interactions of living things, physical changes, and forces and motion.

COUNTRY VARIATION Table 5.13 also indicates the number of topics covered by each country's textbooks as well as the number mentioned in content standards. Over all seventy-nine possible topics, this ranges from around ten (Denmark) to seventy-eight (Switzerland and the United States). Looking only at the forty-eight tested framework topics, there was a range from less than ten to all of them. For most countries, their textbooks covered from around thirty to around forty of the forty-eight topics. Six of the countries covered considerably fewer of the forty-eight topics.

Figure 5.6 shows the distributions for each of the countries of textbook emphasis across topics. This includes only those topics that were actually

Table 5.13. Number of Science Topics in the Curriculum for Each Country (Textbook, Content Standards, and Teachers).

	Content Standards	Textbook Coverage	Teacher Coverage	Topics Tested		Other Grades*		
				Standards	Textbook	1–5	6	7
Total Number of Topics	79	79	22	48	48	79	79	79
Australia	66	65	22	43	44	41	46	49
Austria	58	60	22	36	39	33	48	54
Belgium (Fl)	60	**	22	36	**	14	15	35
Belgium (Fr)	59	**	22	38	**	14	15	35
Bulgaria	43	57	22	28	37	33	38	47
Canada	58	74	22	38	46	55	56	57
Colombia	58	65	22	43	46	51	52	55
Cyprus	41	53	22	31	39	21	23	33
Czech Republic	33	49	22	22	30	34	40	48
Denmark	50	9	22	29	8	31	34	69
France	50	37	21	30	25	32	30	31
Germany	35	32	22	21	22	42	55	60
Greece	25	49	22	22	37	49	50	45
Hong Kong	22	37	22	17	26	15	14	24
Hungary	53	62	22	36	43	6	5	14
Iceland	56	46	22	42	30	17	24	30
Iran	***	19	22	***	16	22	30	38
Ireland	61	58	22	42	40	38	37	64
Israel	37	32	22	25	21	38	36	46
Japan	19	17	22	18	15	22	27	27

	Content Standards	Textbook Coverage	Teacher Coverage	Topics Tested		Other Grades*		
				Standards	Textbook	1–5	6	7
Korea	8	38	22	6	29	39	45	46
Latvia	70	35	22	44	24	25	17	18
Netherlands	48	67	22	32	43	17	17	32
New Zealand	79	52	22	48	37	28	28	37
Norway	69	61	22	41	40	34	34	64
Portugal	66	64	22	40	39	54	54	58
Romania	29	53	22	19	33	26	22	30
Russian Federation	62	42	16	37	28	24	30	50
Scotland	57	44	22	42	36	—	—	—
Singapore	38	27	12	27	20	23	26	46
Slovak Republic	48	49	22	29	30	47	50	55
Slovenia	69	62	22	44	41	51	51	65
South Africa	39	49	22	26	35	—	—	—
Spain	66	67	22	43	41	30	45	51
Sweden	47	49	22	34	32	32	42	40
Switzerland	69	78	22	44	48	47	54	66
USA	79	78	22	48	48	38	43	50

* Summaries are based on countries' standards collected through the GTTM process (see Chapter Three).

Scotland and South Africa did not complete the GTTM.

** No textbooks were coded for the two language systems of Belgium.

*** Iran had no official content standards.

Figure 5.5. Cumulative Distribution for Science Topic Coverage in Textbooks (Eighth Grade Science).

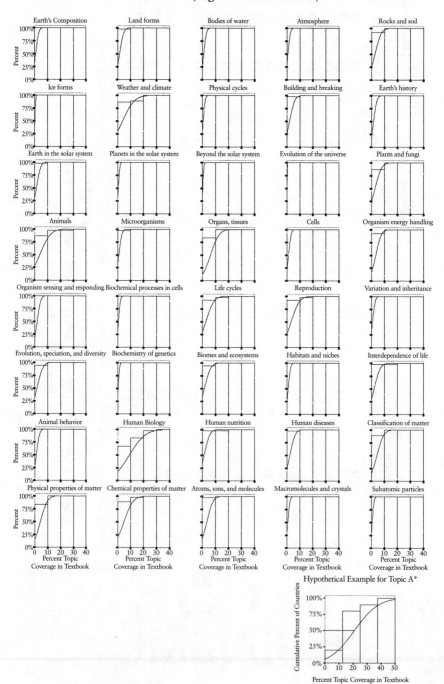

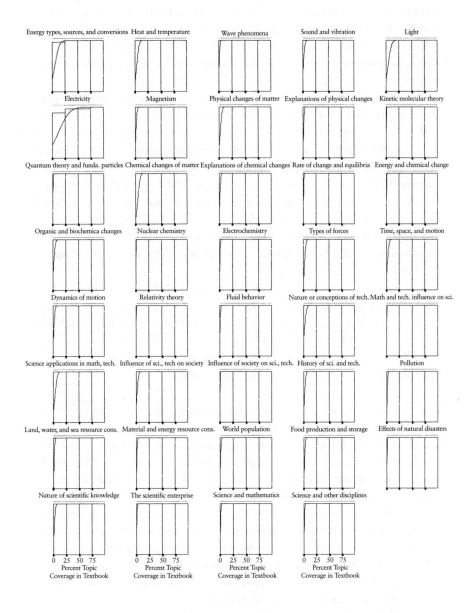

Note: *This hypothetical example illustrates that 50 percent of the countries have at most 20 percent of their textbooks devoted to Topic A. All of the graphs in this figure have the same structure as this example.*

present in textbooks for that country. The mean or median gives an estimate of the emphasis a typical topic receives in a country, and the standard deviation or range indicates how much variation there is among topics in this emphasis. This is similar to the earlier discussion about country variation in textbook emphasis in eighth grade mathematics.

The medians show a range over countries that goes from about 1 percent for a typical topic to around 5 percent (in Japan and Iran). The variability across topics within a country is important because it indicates whether topics tend to receive similar amounts of space when included or whether they tend to receive an uneven distribution of textbook space. Clearly the two extremes of these patterns would represent two very different conceptions of science. In one, science would seem to be treated as a systematic coverage of a number of relatively equally important topics. In the other, some principle must exist to determine differential emphasis—national beliefs about subject matter, topic difficulty, or something else.

The flat, even-emphasis model seems to hold for most countries. The uneven-emphasis model seems to hold for only a few countries (e.g. Denmark and the Russian Federation). The even-emphasis (perhaps -lack-of-emphasis) model seems especially characteristic of the United States. The United States, Canada, and Australia seem to have the same flat model for both eighth grade mathematics and science.

TOPIC-BY-COUNTRY VARIATION Large variances and standard deviations likely presage marked topic-by-country interactions. The standard deviations for all topics range from less than 1 to over 11 (percent of textbook space), indicating considerable variation in variability of textbook space allocation across topics. The range varies from as little as 1 percent (0 to 0.84 percent of textbook space for one virtually excluded topic) to as much as 98 percent (from 0 to 98 percent for a topic that is absent in some countries' eighth grade science textbooks and virtually omnipresent in others'). Thus on some topics—such as evolution in the universe—there is little variation (and less coverage). For other topics—such as electricity; human biology; or energy types, sources, and conversions—there is considerable variation among countries' textbook coverage.

From Figure 5.6 we can see that the variation across topics within a country also varies across countries. The ranges in country textbook space for different topics varies from around 5 percent (Spain) to almost 100 percent (Denmark). This excludes topics for which there is no textbook coverage, something that happens in every country for some topics. (This comes close to not being true for the United States, where only one topic is excluded.)

These variations in the measures of textbook emphasis for topics across countries and for countries across topics foreshadow the potential for large country-by-topic interaction effects. To examine this, we did a median polish (see the discussion surrounding Table 5.3 for eighth grade mathematics). This analysis was done with all seventy-nine topics found in the TIMSS science framework. As before, we used residuals or interactions greater than 5 percent in absolute value as an indication of marginally significant interactions but focus only on those with absolute values of 10 percent or more.

For over 40 percent of the science topics, there are indications of large country-by-topic interactions in textbook coverage. This is with the 10 percent criterion. (Using the 5 percent criterion, the number with significant interactions increases to about sixty, that is, about 75 percent of the topics.) For the forty-eight tested science topics, forty of them display large country-by-topic interactions. In fact, most of the tested topics for which there were no significant interactions shown were in earth sciences and conservation.

Like eighth grade mathematics textbooks, eighth grade science textbooks present different views of the sciences across countries.[20] This is reflected in different profiles of topic emphasis in textbooks across countries. Although speculative, this seems likely to be linked to cultural notions of the sciences and of school science in particular.

The topic areas with the most marked indication of country-by-topic interaction effects are the two most emphasized topics—electricity and human biology. Both show especially large effects in some countries and large effects in almost two-thirds of the countries. These two topics are treated very differently in how they are emphasized in textbook space in various countries, although they dominate textbook coverage across all of the countries on average. The other topic with a large number of estimated interaction effects is energy types, sources, and conversions.

Performance Expectations

We now return our attention to the second aspect of subject matter content: what students are expected to be able to do with the content that they learned. For science, more complex performances (parallel to the concept discussed for mathematics) included theorizing, analyzing, and problem solving and science investigations. The latter included, among other things, designing empirical investigations, collecting data, analyzing data, and interpreting data. This is what some would call hands-on science.

Figure 5.6. Textbook Emphasis on Topics Actually Covered (Eighth Grade Science).

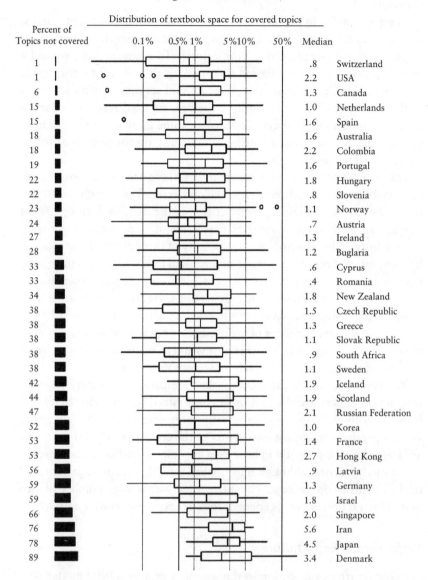

Percent of Topics not covered	Distribution of textbook space for covered topics	Median	
1		.8	Switzerland
1		2.2	USA
6		1.3	Canada
15		1.0	Netherlands
15		1.6	Spain
18		1.6	Australia
18		2.2	Colombia
19		1.6	Portugal
22		1.8	Hungary
22		.8	Slovenia
23		1.1	Norway
24		.7	Austria
27		1.3	Ireland
28		1.2	Buglaria
33		.6	Cyprus
33		.4	Romania
34		1.8	New Zealand
38		1.5	Czech Republic
38		1.3	Greece
38		1.1	Slovak Republic
38		.9	South Africa
38		1.1	Sweden
42		1.9	Iceland
44		1.9	Scotland
47		2.1	Russian Federation
52		1.0	Korea
53		1.4	France
53		2.7	Hong Kong
56		.9	Latvia
59		1.3	Germany
59		1.8	Israel
66		2.0	Singapore
76		5.6	Iran
78		4.5	Japan
89		3.4	Denmark

Distribution of Textbook Space for Covered Topics

Percent of Topics not covered	Median	Topic
32	2.5	Human diseases
11	4.0	Classification of matter
11	4.1	Physical properties of matter
16	3.6	Chemical properties of matter
16	3.6	Atoms, ions, and molecules
32	.9	Macromolecules and crystals
35	.8	Subatomic particles
14	3.3	Energy types, sources, and conversions
22	3.4	Heat and temperature
57	.6	Wave phenomena
49	1.1	Sound and vibration
19	3.3	Light
11	6.6	Electricity
38	1.5	Magnetism
19	1.8	Physical changes of matter
27	1.0	Explanations of chemical changes
54	.5	Kinetic molecular theory
76	.1	Quantum theory and fundamental particles
5	4.7	Chemical changes of matter
32	1.3	Explanations of physical changes
51	.7	Rate of change and equilibria
38	.4	Energy and chemical change
43	.8	Organic and biochemical changes
54	.5	Nuclear chemistry
27	.8	Electrochemistry
24	2.3	Types of forces
32	.9	Time, space, and motion
46	2.1	Dynamics of motion
70	.3	Relativity theory
54	.7	Fluid behavior
51	1.1	Nature or conceptions of technology
46	.3	Math and technology influence on science
19	2.4	Science applications in math and technology
24	.6	Influence of science and technology on society
62	.5	Influence of society on science and technology
24	1.1	History of science and technology
19	1.1	Pollution
27	1.3	Land, water, and sea resource conservation
24	.9	Material and energy resource conservation
35	.8	World population
30	1.3	Food production and storage
43	.9	Effects of natural disasters
41	.8	Nature of scientific knowledge
59	.2	The scientific enterprise
54	1.3	Science and mathematics
43	.3	Science and other disciplines

Scale markers: 0.1%, 0.5%, 1%, 5%, 10%, 50%

TOPIC VARIATION Table 5.14 gives the distributions for the percentage of textbook content on a topic devoted to these more complex performance expectations across countries for each topic in the TIMSS science framework. A higher mean or median implies that a greater percentage of the textbook space devoted to that topic was typically devoted to more complex performance tasks.

On average, the topic giving the largest proportion of its textbook space to more demanding, complex tasks, no matter how much space the topic received in textbooks, was physical and chemical changes. Whatever textbook space these topics received, on average more of it was devoted to complex tasks than was true for other topics. That average proportion was around 14 percent averaged across countries (the median values were 13 and 7 respectively). Other topics that also had a high average proportion of their content devoted to complex performances were physical properties, heat and temperature, magnetism and explanations of physical changes (around 11 to 13 percent on average).

All of these topics with higher proportions of demanding tasks were from physics and chemistry. Two other topics also had high proportions of textbook space for complex tasks life cycles and genetics and the nature of scientific knowledge which deals with the scientific process.

The range of values for different topics across countries was very high. For example, life cycles had none of its textbook space devoted to more complex performances in one country and all of its textbook space devoted to such in another country (a range of 100 percent). The same was true for chemical changes and magnetism.

COUNTRY VARIATION Table 5.15 displays the same sort of data but summarized across all topics for each country (among those that were actually taught in that country). Several countries stand out as having a high percentage of this complex content across topics for the topics in their textbooks. Denmark, New Zealand, and Singapore have over 20 percent of their typical textbook space per topic devoted to more complex tasks. However, these same countries also had large measures of variability for these data. This indicates that although more complex content was typical in their textbooks, this proportion was not very uniform across topics. Several countries ranged from 0 percent of textbook space devoted to a typical topic requiring more complex tasks to all (100 percent) of their textbook coverage at this more complex level (Latvia, Singapore, and New Zealand). Other countries had less than 1 percent of

Table 5.14. Distributions of Percent of Complex Performance Expectations for Countries in Science Textbooks across Topics (Eighth Grade).

Topic	Number of Countries Covering This Topic	Percent of Countries with No Complex Performance Expectations	Median Percent of Complex Performance Expectations	Box Plots
Earth's composition	25	56	0	
Land forms	21	57	0	
Bodies of water	23	61	0	
Atmosphere	24	63	0	
Rocks and soil	25	44	1	
Ice forms	18	89	0	
Weather and climate	26	42	1	
Physical cycles	24	75	0	
Building and breaking	20	65	0	
Earth's history	20	60	0	
Earth in the solar system	24	42	2	
Planets in the solar system	18	61	0	
Beyond the solar system	17	59	0	
Evolution of the universe	11	91	0	
Plants and fungi	25	48	1	
Animals	30	43	1	
Microorganisms	22	68	0	
Organs and tissues	31	23	4	
Cells	26	42	2	
Organism energy handling	32	38	4	
Organism sensing and responding	32	47	1	
Biochemical processes in cells	20	65	0	
Life cycles	25	36	2	
Reproduction	28	54	0	
Variation and inheritance	16	81	0	
Evolution, speciation, and diversity	24	67	0	
Biochemistry of genetics	9	78	0	
Biomes and ecosystems	20	65	0	
Habitats and niches	17	53	0	
Interdependence of life	24	58	0	
Animal behavior	23	61	0	
Human biology and health	29	45	0	
Human nutrition	23	52	0	
Human diseases	25	48	0	
Classification of matter	33	30	3	
Physical properties of matter	33	9	7	
Chemical properties of matter	31	19	6	
Atoms, ions, and molecules	31	48	1	
Macromolecules and crystals	25	52	0	
Subatomic particles	24	88	0	
Energy types, sources, and conversions	32	31	2	

(continued)

Table 5.14. (continued).

Topic	Number of Countries Covering This Topic	Percent of Countries with No Complex Performance Expectations	Median Percent of Complex Performance Expectations	Box Plots
Heat and temperature	29	24	7	
Wave phenomena	16	63	0	
Sound and vibration	19	47	1	
Light	30	37	2	
Electricity	33	21	4	
Magnetism	23	30	4	
Physical changes of matter	30	17	13	
Explanations of physical changes	27	41	4	
Kinetic molecular theory	17	65	0	
Quantum theory and fundamental particles	9	89	0	
Chemical changes of matter	35	20	7	
Explanations of chemical changes	25	64	0	
Rate of change and equilibria	18	39	3	
Energy and chemical change	23	48	2	
Organic and biochemical changes	21	33	4	
Nuclear chemistry	17	76	0	
Electrochemistry	27	41	4	
Types of forces	28	43	2	
Time, space, and motion	25	40	3	
Dynamics of motion	20	55	0	
Relativity theory	11	91	0	
Fluid behavior	17	71	0	
Nature or conceptions of technology	18	33	3	
Math and technology influence on science	20	75	0	
Science applications in math, technology	30	43	1	
Influence of science, technology on society	28	82	0	
Influence of society on science, technology	14	79	0	
History of science and technology	28	68	0	
Pollution	30	57	0	
Land, water, sea resource conservation	27	78	0	
Material, energy resource conservation	28	75	0	
World population	24	75	0	
Food production and storage	26	62	0	
Effects of natural disasters	21	95	0	
Nature of scientific knowledge	22	32	11	
The scientific enterprise	15	67	0	
Science and mathematics	17	47	2	
Science and other disciplines	21	76	0	

Table 5.15. Distributions of Percent of Complex Performance Expectations for Topics in Science Textbooks across Countries (Eighth Grade).

Country	Number of Topics	Percent of Topics with No Complex Performance Expectations	Median Percent of Complex Performance Expectations	Box Plots
Australia	65	35	5	
Austria	60	53	0	
Bulgaria	57	72	0	
Canada	74	12	13	
Colombia	65	100	0	
Cyprus	53	60	0	
Czech Republic	49	63	0	
Denmark	9	22	35	
France	37	30	4	
Germany	32	44	2	
Greece	49	92	0	
Hong Kong	37	43	2	
Hungary	62	52	0	
Iceland	46	85	0	
Iran	19	89	0	
Ireland	58	34	6	
Israel	32	41	2	
Japan	17	12	8	
Korea	38	55	0	
Latvia	35	57	0	
Netherlands	67	36	1	
New Zealand	52	21	25	
Norway	61	54	0	
Portugal	64	47	1	
Romania	53	77	0	
Russian Federation	42	45	1	
Scotland	44	77	0	
Singapore	27	37	20	
Slovak Republic	49	61	0	
Slovenia	62	58	0	
South Africa	49	43	3	
Spain	67	36	3	
Sweden	49	71	0	
Switzerland	78	71	0	
USA	78	3	4	

their topic coverage on average (median values of 0) devoted to complex performances.

TOPIC-BY-COUNTRY VARIATION Median polish analyses were done so that topic-by-country interactions can be investigated. There is considerable evidence of sizable country-by-topic interactions on all but three of the seventy-nine science topics. In fact, for these three topics— all from earth science—there are interactions using the 5 percent criterion.

Both Canada and New Zealand seem to have a large number of topics with significant interactions. New Zealand has some especially large positive estimated interaction effects. This suggests that they included in their science textbooks a great deal of material requiring more complex performances. One topic that stands out for them is physical changes. This does not necessarily imply a large proportion of textbook space devoted to this topic but rather that most of what coverage there was for this topic was devoted to more complex performance expectations demanding investigation, theorizing, and problem solving. Chemical properties stands out as one topic that had a large number of country interactions, indicating that this content was dealt with very differently across countries in terms of the performance complexity associated with it.

Teacher Coverage

From content standards as an indication of curriculum (especially of national intentions) and from textbook space, we turn to teacher coverage of various topics in various countries as further indications, particularly of curriculum as implemented. As with mathematics, we consider both the percentage of teachers teaching a topic (no matter how much time was devoted to it) and the national average of the percentage of teacher time devoted to the topic.

TOPIC VARIATION As with mathematics, we first discuss the percentage of teachers teaching each topic. Eighth grade science is very different from mathematics in this area. The eighth grade mathematics topic covered by the greatest percentage of teachers in a country across the countries had an average of 90 percent teaching it. That is, on average nine out of ten teachers spent some time teaching this topic. This is a high level of commonality. In science the topic taught by the greatest percentage of teachers on average was environmental and resource issues (about 60 percent). The next topics—properties and classification of matter and the structure of matter—were taught on average by about 55 to 60 percent of the teachers across counties.

It seems that 50 to 60 percent represents far less consensus and uniformity in curriculum implementation within a country than does 90 percent. However, there is a difficulty in interpreting this difference. Because of the way eighth grade science instruction was organized and how science instruction was sampled in the TIMSS countries, it is possible that different teachers sampled may well have been teaching different courses. Many countries had eighth grade science instruction organized into separate courses. The sampling may have drawn teachers from different science courses within the same country. There may well have been virtually complete consensus among physics teachers, but when this was averaged with biology teachers who didn't teach that topic, averages of around 50 percent could occur. (The sampling rules called for a maximum sample of only two teachers per sampled student.)[21] This argument could also help to explain the large standard deviations and ranges observed in the data. Caution must be exerted in placing too much emphasis on these measures for science topics.

The top five topics in order of the percentage of teachers teaching them on average were environmental and resource issues, structure of matter, human biology, properties and classification of matter, and energy and physical properties. As with mathematics, a different, smaller listing of topics (twenty-two) was used in the science teachers' questionnaires, compared with the more detailed level of topics in the science framework. However, it may well be that a topic such as environmental and resource issues was covered in different courses in countries that have multiple eighth grade science classes all for the same students.

The topic that received the most teaching time on average across countries was human biology. It received about 13 percent of the instructional time for eighth grade science. This value is consistent with the amount of time allocated to the most taught eighth grade mathematics topic— equations and formulas (also about 13 percent of instructional time).

The problem discussed previously regarding the percentage of teachers covering a topic is not the same for the percentage of instructional time devoted to a topic. Because, in countries with multiple science courses for each student, a student receives instruction in all of the science courses defined for eighth grade, an average over teachers of different disciplines is an appropriate estimate of the percentage of time devoted to that topic.[22]

The only other eighth grade science topic to receive over 10 percent of instructional time on average was energy and physical processes. This topic also had the largest variation (a standard deviation of 6.6 percent), with a range from 2 percent to about 30 percent.

The five topics that received the most actual classroom instruction were (in order) human biology, energy and physical processes, earth features, diversity and structure of living things, and properties and classification of matter. It is worth noting that one of the top five topics implemented by teachers was an earth sciences topic, although none were among the top topics intended as reflected in content standards. Given the sampling and estimation difficulties discussed earlier, it is encouraging that three of the topics on the top five lists were the same for both teaching indicators of curriculum.

COUNTRY VARIATION Table 5.13 also displays the number of topics (out of the twenty-two on the teacher questionnaires in science) that were covered on average by the teachers in each country. In almost all countries, all twenty-two were covered. The only exceptions were Singapore and the Russian Federation. This, of course, implied that instruction on all twenty-two topics were delivered to each student, not necessarily by the same teacher and without implying that every teacher covered all twenty-two topics.

The percentage of teachers teaching a topic in each country averaged across the topics that were actually taught suggests major differences between mathematics and science. In most countries, mathematics had about 50 percent or more of the teachers teaching a typical topic, but for science this percentage was much smaller. This is another instance in which one must be careful in interpreting the data.[23]

The two exceptions are the United States and Singapore. Singapore covers only twelve topics, and on average 80 percent of teachers covers each one (with a difference of 11 percent from the lowest to the highest percentage of the middle 50 percent of those topics). The United States covers more topics and has a much larger range (about 37 percent for the middle 50 percent of topics covered). This again likely reflects the mile-wide, inch-deep phenomena of U.S. science and mathematics curricula.

TOPIC-BY-COUNTRY VARIATION The standard deviations for the percent of instructional time devoted to each topic range from around 1 percent (e.g., kinetic and quantum theory, relativity theory, and biochemistry) to around 9 percent (human biology).[24] The range for different topics further illustrates the variability among those topics in different countries. Human biology shows a considerable range from no time in one country to over one-third of instructional time in another. Other topics had low variability (e.g., a range from 0 to about 3 percent for kinetic and quantum theory).

The variation across topics within a country also differs across countries, further suggesting the potential for an interaction of topic and country in instructional time. For some countries (Singapore and the Russian Federation), the range for the percent of teachers who teach a topic goes from some topics where no teachers taught it to others where all teachers taught it. For most (about two-thirds) of the countries, the lowest percent of coverage for any topic was 5 percent or less.

There were sizable country-by-topic interactions in the percent of teachers teaching a topic for all topics and for all countries as indicated by the median polish analysis. How to interpret this in light of the difficulties discussed previously is not clear.

For percent of instructional time, there were seven of twenty-two topics without any indication of a strong interaction with either the 5 or 10 percent criterion. Of these seven, three were not tested, and two others do not belong to a specific science (science, technology, and society and the nature of science). Large effects are noted for only about a third of the topics.

Commonalties Across Countries: The Notion of a World Core

In the previous sections we have examined some of what is typical for a topic across countries and some of what is different. We have done that for all four aspects of curriculum, as we did for mathematics. We now turn to the question of what is common as revealed by the different indications for curriculum.

Unlike mathematics, where there was a top topic consistent across all aspects, in science each of the four identifies a different top topic, and they are not similar at all. All five of the top topics for content standards were covered by 90 percent of the countries. Remembering this, the one topic that emerges clearly near the top of all four lists is human biology.

Although the order does not agree, in addition to human biology there is fairly good agreement across the indications for energy (electricity; energy types, sources, and conversions; and energy and physical properties) and environmental resource issues (including conservation of land, water, and sea resources). Several anomalies occur, such as the presence of chemical properties as a topic that receives considerable textbook space on average but not similar representation in content standards or teacher implementations. Earth features also scores highly in percent of instructional time although it is not widely emphasized in content standards or textbooks.

These differences do not necessarily imply inconsistencies, because they are all aggregations. However, it is interesting to note that in the world according to TIMSS, what is emphasized in eighth grade science seems to differ somewhat given the aspect of curriculum. Certainly there seem to be differences in what is emphasized among content standards as expressions of national intentions, textbooks, and teacher-based indications of curricular content actually implemented. There was much more consistency across indications in mathematics. This seems likely to reflect greater diversity in the way science is organized and delivered across the TIMSS countries, at least in comparison to mathematics.

As with mathematics, we defined core curricula in the world according to TIMSS using a 100 percent and a 70 percent criterion. When we add teacher data to our notion of a world core, the criterion here is different than that for mathematics. If we used the same criterion of more than 75 percent of the teachers covering the topic, no topics would meet that criterion. In fact, we had to adjust this criterion to 50 and 40 percent of teachers to get any common topics for teachers. This likely reflects the discussion of how science is organized into different courses in many countries as well as how sampling was done for science.

There is no single topic that satisfies the 100 percent criterion across content standards, textbooks, and teachers. For the 70 percent criterion, only environmental and resource issues related to science emerges. This means that this was the only topic that was intended (in content standards), covered in textbooks, and implemented by at least 50 percent of the teachers in at least 70 percent of the TIMSS countries providing these data. If the percent of teachers were dropped to 40 percent, the topic of matter would be added to this 70 percent world core.

Seventh Grade Science

As for mathematics, we now turn to the science curricula of earlier grades to provide context and information about prior coverage for eighth grade science.

Content Standards

Table 5.16 displays data on the percentage of countries that cover topics at the seventh grade. This parallels the display in Table 5.8.

According to content standards, the most commonly covered topic in seventh grade science is reproduction. It was intended for coverage in seventh grade in 90 percent of the participating countries. Other topics that were also high on the list included bodies of water, weather and climate,

Table 5.16. Percentage of Countries Intending Coverage of Seventh Grade Science Topics.

Tested Topics	Country Content Standards Coverage	
	Number of Countries (36)	Percent
1. Earth features	34	94.4
Landforms	30	83.3
Bodies of water	32	88.9
Atmosphere	28	77.8
Rocks and soil	24	66.7
2. Earth processes	35	97.2
Weather and climate	32	88.9
Physical cycles	30	83.3
Building and breaking	25	69.4
Earth's history	20	55.6
3. Earth in the universe	28	77.8
Earth in the solar system	28	77.8
Beyond the solar system	17	47.2
4. Diversity and structure of living things	35	97.2
Animals	32	88.9
Other organisms	29	80.6
Organs and tissues	32	88.9
Cells	24	66.7
5. Life processes and functions	29	80.6
Energy handling	28	77.8
Sensing and responding	21	58.3
6. Life cycles and genetics	35	97.2
Life cycles	30	83.3
Reproduction	33	91.7
Variation and inheritance	14	38.9
Evolution, speculation, and diversity	17	47.2
7. Interactions of living things	32	88.9
Interdependence of life	31	86.1
Animal behavior	25	69.4
8. Human biology and health	0	0.0
Human biology	0	0.0
Nutrition	28	77.8
Disease	24	66.7
9. Properties and classification of matter	31	86.1
Classification of matter	27	75.0
Physical properties	31	86.1
Chemical properties	24	66.7
10. Structure of matter	23	63.9
Atoms, ions, and molecules	23	63.9

(continued)

Table 5.16. *(continued)*

Tested Topics	Country Content Standards Coverage	
	Number of Countries (36)	Percent
11. Energy and physical processes	31	86.1
Energy types, sources, and conversions	28	77.8
Heat and temperature	27	75.0
Wave phenomena	12	33.3
Sound and vibration	21	58.3
Light	25	69.4
Electricity	25	69.4
Magnetism	19	52.8
12 Physical changes	29	80.6
Physical changes	29	80.6
Explanations of physical changes	19	52.8
13. Chemical changes	24	66.7
Chemical changes	24	66.7
Energy and chemical change	7	19.4
14. Forces and Motion	27	75.0
Types of forces	23	63.9
Time, space, and motion	24	66.7
Dynamics of motion	16	44.4
Fluid behavior	5	13.9
15. Science, technology, and society	14	38.9
Influence of science and technology on society	14	38.9
16. Environmental and resource issues	31	86.1
Pollution	29	80.6
Conservation of land, water, and sea resources	30	83.3
Conservation of material and energy resources	29	80.6
17. Scientific processes	17	47.2
Topics Not Tested		
Content description	27	75.0
Composition	15	41.7
Ice forms	27	75.0
Planets in the solar system	10	27.8
Evolution of the universe	31	86.1
Plants and fungi	10	27.8
Biochemical processes in cells	2	5.6
Biochemistry of genetics	29	80.6
Biomes and ecosystems	29	80.6
Habitats and niches	8	22.2
Macromolecules and crystals	13	36.1
Subatomic particles	6	16.7
Kinetic theory	2	5.6

Quantum theory and fundamental particles	13	36.1
Explanations of chemical changes	7	19.4
Rate of change and equilibria	7	19.4
Organic and biochemical changes	7	19.4
Nuclear chemistry	8	22.2
Electrochemistry	2	5.6
Relativity theory	17	47.2
Nature or conceptions of technology	10	27.8
Influence of math, technology in science	18	50.0
Applications of science in math and technology	12	33.3
Influence of society on science and technology	13	36.1
History of science	18	50.0
World pollution	18	50.0
Food production and storage	17	47.2
Effects of natural disasters	17	47.2
Nature of scientific knowledge	5	13.9
The scientific enterprise	15	41.7

Note: *The numbered topics are the seventeen tested areas. The forty-eight indented topics, together with the thirty-one topics not tested in TIMSS, exhaust all seventy-nine topics in the TIMSS science framework.*

animals, and organs and tissues. All of these topics were covered by around 90 percent of the countries.

The seventh grade science curriculum, at least at the level of intention, seems to have focused more on earth science and biology in the aggregate, whereas the eighth grade science curriculum was primarily one of human biology, physics, and chemistry. Not only was there an increased focus on human biology in the eighth grade, but the nature of the biology intended also changed somewhat. In seventh grade there was a greater focus on animals, organisms, and other descriptive parts of biology. At eighth grade the focus was more on biochemical aspects such as energy handling and sensing and responding.

Three topics were in the content standards of over 80 percent of the countries but were not tested in TIMSS. These include plants and fungi, biomes and ecosystems, and habitats and niches. We should remember that the design of the TIMSS achievement tests were only partly guided by preliminary curriculum data and depended also on the knowledge of test designers and those piloting test items in various countries. This suggests a strong argument for greater use of comparative curriculum data in designing cross-national comparative achievement tests.

There was considerable variation even in the number of topics that were covered as indicated by countries' content standards documents. Table 5.13

indicates these numbers relative to the total number (seventy-nine) of science framework topics. They ranged from around thirty or less (Iceland, France, Hong Kong, Hungary, Japan, Latvia, and Romania) to as many as sixty or more (Switzerland, Slovenia, Norway, Denmark, Germany, and Ireland).

Teacher Coverage

As with mathematics, textbook data were not available for seventh grade science. We turn next then to the two teacher indications of curriculum as implemented.

The topic taught by the highest aggregate percentage of teachers in a country averaged across countries was environmental and resource issues related to science (60 percent). This was also the most commonly covered topic for eighth grade science teachers as well, perhaps this is one of the topics that might be covered in an earth science, biology, or chemistry course. Given the scheme of organizing science courses and the TIMSS sampling procedure, this is a logical explanation of why this might be one of the topics covered by the higher aggregate percentages of teachers.

The top five topics in order of the aggregate percentage of teachers covering them averaged across countries were environmental and resource issues related to science; diversity, organization, and the structure of living things; human biology; earth features; and interactions of living things. This list differs from the corresponding one for eighth grade science, in which the first and third topics are included but the other three are replaced by physics topics. This is consistent with the change in focus for content standards in moving from seventh to eighth grade science.

The topic receiving the most instructional time on average across countries was human biology (15 percent). This was also true at the eighth grade. The topic receiving the next highest amount of instructional time was diversity, organization, and the structure of living things, which received an average of about 11 percent of instructional time across countries.

The top topics (averaged across countries) in terms of the actual amount of instructional time as estimated from the teacher questionnaires were as follows: human biology; diversity, organization, and the structure of living things; earth features; life processes and systems enabling life; and environmental and resource issues related to science. Notice that although environmental and resource issues related to science was taught by on average the largest aggregate percentage of teachers, it was fifth in the average percentage of instructional time devoted to it (about 6 percent). Compared to the eighth grade, the last two topics in this seventh grade list were replaced by two physics topics, a feature we have noticed before.

Human biology was the topic with the greatest range of instructional time across countries. This ranged from some countries that devoted no time to this topic to others that devoted as much as 40 percent of seventh grade instructional time. In the aggregate, what most countries intended at seventh grade coincides reasonably well with what teachers implemented. Three of the top five topics in the content standards were also found to have been implemented by a large aggregate percentage of teachers on average across countries.

Singapore had the highest aggregate percentage of teachers teaching a typical topic (averaged only over topics that were taught in that country). About 75 percent of Singapore teachers taught a typical topic. The range for the middle 50 percent of topics in Singapore was about 26 percent of teachers (from 74 to 100 percent). For the other countries with a higher average aggregate percentage of teachers teaching a typical topic, the figure was around 50 percent. For several, however, this was averaged over all twenty-two possible topics; that is, all were taught. These included the United States, Spain, Colombia, and Australia.

The median polish analysis for the aggregate percent of teachers and percent of instructional time showed sizable interaction effects for the percentage of teachers and more moderate effects for the percentage of teacher time. This was consistent with the eighth grade science teacher results and with both the seventh and eighth grade mathematics teacher results. All of this points strongly in the direction that curriculum is by its nature a reflection of national cultures and conceptions. As such, it would be reasonable to find both a large number of interaction effects and ones that were very large from a practical point of view.

Sixth Grade Science

The data used for this section are, as described for mathematics, based on weighted GTTM data collected for all of the topics in the TIMSS science framework. The same procedures used for mathematics were applied here.

The top five topics in these data averaged across countries were reproduction, weather and climate, organs and tissues, plants and fungi, and life cycles and animals, which were tied for fifth place. These were all earth and life sciences topics. Only a few physics and chemistry topics had remotely close to as high coverage—physical properties and changes of matter, heat, temperature, light, and electricity. None of the top five topics here except organs and tissues is found among the top five at eighth grade by any of the four indications of curriculum.

First through Fifth Grade Science

The data used here were based on the cumulative distribution of the GTTM data for the first five grades summed over the grades to give an aggregate measure of coverage, as was done for mathematics.

The topic receiving the most intended coverage during the first five grades was plants and fungi. The next four topics in order were animals, weather and climate, life cycles, and human nutrition. None of these intended topics were in the top five topics in content standards in eighth grade. Only one physics and chemistry topic—physical properties of matter—had a somewhat high mean for coverage. At the eighth grade, physics and chemistry topics dominated the top five topics from content standards.

The Correlation of Coverage Among Topics

This section examines the relationships among different topics using the four aspects of curriculum. Does the inclusion of one topic imply that another is likely to be included as well? Is the amount of textbook space given to two topics related? Is there evidence of the clustering of topics that might make the effect of the whole (cluster) greater than the sum of its parts (individual topics)? These ideas were discussed earlier in this chapter for mathematics.

Table 5.17 gives the correlation matrix for the percent of teachers covering a science topic in eighth grade averaged across countries. As one might expect from our previous observations about which sciences contribute to the curriculum at various grades, topics within earth science, within biology, and within physics and chemistry were moderately to strongly correlated. This would be expected if science instruction were organized into separate discipline-based courses. Teachers in the aggregate (as percentages of teachers covering a topic) would tend to cover many of the topics from one of the disciplines rather than another during the same year. This should produce clustering and high correlations among topics within a discipline for teacher coverage data.

There is some evidence that this was true, especially in biology (correlations of around .30 to .60) and in earth science (especially for earth features and earth processes, with a correlation of .89). The same holds for certain physics topics, such as matter and the structure of matter

(.91), matter and chemical changes (.70), energy processes and the structure of matter (.62), as well as physical changes and energy types (.69). In contrast, the correlations between categories of topics (different disciplines) tend to be low or negative. This supports the earlier observations about science disciplines as the major organizing principle for curricula.

In spite of this general pattern, there are noteworthy anomalies from this pattern, especially within physics. The coverage by teachers aggregated to the country level for some physics topics, for example, forces and motion, was not strongly related to the coverage of others. This might imply a subarea of physics treated differently from the rest of physics in organizing the curriculum.

The patterns for the percentages of instructional time devoted to different topics (averaged across countries) are somewhat similar to those described for the previous data but were generally smaller. The other noteworthy but understandable pattern is that the cross-discipline correlations were almost all negative and some of them were quite large (e.g., most of the correlations among biology and physics topics). This may well reflect the limits on instructional time within a school year.

The smaller correlations for instructional time compared with the percentage of teachers covering a topic can be viewed as an attenuation of the relationship among topics within a science discipline. This seems reasonable because whether teachers within a country teach a topic is more directly affected by content standards and is something on which individual teachers are less likely to exercise their independence. How much time they allocate is less directly determined by official or intended curricula as reflected by content standards. It may well reflect the judgment of individual teachers more and show less uniformity within countries and thus weaker correlations among countries.

We have used the teacher data to set out a hypothesis of how the science curriculum may be organized (in discipline-oriented clusters). We now turn to content standards—official statements of intent—and to textbooks to further explore these notions.

Table 5.18 displays the correlations among topics for content standards. Because of the larger number of topics available here compared with that for teacher data (seventy-nine compared with twenty-two), these correlation matrices give a summary of the correlations among topic pairs. There are over three thousand such correlations for each of content standards and textbooks. The cell entries in the display give the median correlation values.

The correlations reflecting official intentions are given for fourteen aggregated areas. Within these areas, the median correlations among topics were

Table 5.17. Correlations Among Topics for the Percentage of Teachers Covering a Topic (Eighth Grade Science).

Topic	Earth Features	Earth Processes	Earth in the Universe	Diversity and Structure of Living Things	Life Processes and Systems	Life Cycles and Genetics	Interactions of Living Things	Human Biology and Health
Earth features	1.00							
Earth processes	.89	1.00						
Earth in the universe	.49	.49	1.00					
Diversity and structure of living things	.56	.47	.24	1.00				
Life processes and systems	.24	.21	−.05	.62	1.00			
Life cycles and genetics	.22	.18	.13	.55	.27	1.00		
Interactions of living things	.18	.16	.22	.57	.66	.32	1.00	
Human biology and health	.13	.08	−.05	.38	.64	.32	.29	1.00
Types and properties of matter	.31	.23	.23	.31	.45	.07	.47	.51
Structure of matter	.28	.22	.25	.12	.30	.02	.30	.47
Energy types, sources, and conversions	.31	.13	.37	.09	−.14	.17	−.06	−.06
Energy processes	−.04	−.15	−.07	−.16	.13	−.28	.04	.32
Physical changes	.52	.34	.46	.22	−.08	.02	.01	−.17
Kinetic and quantum theory	−.08	−.02	−.20	−.18	.40	−.15	.38	.18
Chemical changes	.22	.19	.18	.13	.49	.04	.28	.57
Special chemical changes	.23	.13	.27	−.01	−.17	.33	−.16	.10
Forces and motion	.44	.18	.36	.48	.22	.25	.18	.20
Relativity theory	.40	.27	.42	.28	.07	.53	.20	.18
Science, technology, and society	−.08	−.03	.24	−.19	.14	−.09	.41	−.10
History of science and technology	.16	.21	.33	.14	−.18	.23	.07	−.47
Environmental and resource issues	.12	.16	.25	.08	.27	.22	.66	−.16
Nature of science	.19	.15	.49	.20	−.05	.20	.14	−.06

	Types and Properties of Matter	Structure of Matter	Energy Types, Sources, and Conversions	Energy Processes	Physical Changes	Kinetic and Quantum Theory	Chemical Changes	Special Chemical Changes	Forces and Motion	Relativity Theory	Science, Technology, and Society	History of Science and Technology	Environmental and Resource Issues	Nature of Science
Types and Properties of Matter	1.00													
Structure of Matter	.91	1.00												
Energy Types, Sources, and Conversions	.26	.33	1.00											
Energy Processes	.57	.62	.48	1.00										
Physical Changes	.38	.37	.69	.39	1.00									
Kinetic and Quantum Theory	.46	.48	−.04	.52	.04	1.00								
Chemical Changes	.70	.74	.10	.53	.16	.54	1.00							
Special Chemical Changes	.07	.23	.56	.34	.34	.01	.40	1.00						
Forces and Motion	.12	.09	.52	.13	.42	−.12	.15	.37	1.00					
Relativity Theory	.23	.27	.46	.20	.48	.06	.36	.75	.53	1.00				
Science, Technology, and Society	.40	.42	.27	.44	.25	.75	.43	.23	.05	.33	1.00			
History of Science and Technology	.03	.12	.33	−.03	.42	.10	−.09	.18	−.01	.22	.38	1.00		
Environmental and Resource Issues	.31	.23	.23	.11	.21	.51	.11	−.03	−.02	.24	.66	.37	1.00	
Nature of Science	.44	.31	.51	.18	.66	−.06	.04	.05	.15	.33	.28	.46	.33	1.00

Table 5.18. Median Correlations Among Topics in Content Standards (Eighth Grade Science).

Topic	Earth Sciences	Diversity, Organization, and Structure of Living Things	Life Processes and Systems Enabling Life Functions	Life Spirals, Genetic Continuity, and Diversity
Earth sciences	.44			
Diversity, organization, and structure of living things	.19	.45		
Life processes and systems enabling life functions	.06	.52	.40	
Life spirals, genetic continuity, and diversity	.26	.40	.32	.37
Interactions of living things	.23	.57	.51	.44
Human biology and health	.18	.32	.23	.29
Matter	.16	−.05	−.12	.13
Structure of matter	.19	.13	.05	.21
Energy and physical processes	.12	.20	.22	.16
Physical transformations	.08	.20	.17	.20
Chemical transformations	.22	−.03	−.07	.06
Forces and motion	.12	.26	.21	.27
Science and Society*	.16	.23	.19	.20
Environmental and resources issues related to science	.32	.28	.20	.26

*Includes the three teacher topic areas of science, technology, and society; history of science and technology; and nature of science.

Interactions of Living Things	Human Biology and Health	Matter	Structure of Matter	Energy and Physical Processes	Physical Transformations	Chemical Transformations	Forces and Motion	Science and Society*	Environmental and Resource Issues Related to Science
.60									
.37	.42								
.03	.16	.25							
.03	.13	.35	.50						
.19	.22	.08	.13	.34					
.20	.30	.13	.13	.19	.44				
.06	.16	.17	.12	.16	.16	.62			
.25	.31	.09	.16	.27	.41	.10	.49		
.25	.29	.08	.11	.20	.20	.27	.14	.38	
.37	.32	−.03	−.06	.27	.20	.28	.13	.41	.65

all positive and ranged from about .30 to about .60. As before, within-discipline correlations were moderate to strong. Within biology the topics in the five areas found in Table 5.18 are also correlated across the five areas as well as among the topics within each area. In physics the six areas all show moderate to strong correlation for the topics within each of those areas but not for topics across the areas. In the latter case the median correlations are close to zero, such as that between matter and energy and physical processes.

For the textbook coverage results, one again finds the same kind of attenuation of the correlation structure of official intentions in examining textbook coverage rather than content standards as was found for instructional time compared with the proportion of teachers covering a topic. A similar argument may well apply because the content standards indicate whether a topic should be covered, but textbooks represent authors' decisions of how much space is needed to implement these ideas. Textbooks in some countries also have the liberty of being more inclusive rather than deciding as stringently among topics. This would lead them to less clearly reflect the disciplinary organization of curriculum. Textbook space may also directly influence instructional time decisions, and the two attenuations may be related.

The smaller correlations across topics of the six areas of physics found in Table 5.18 may reflect that unlike biology, physics was not viewed as a whole discipline in and of itself. Rather, it may be broken into smaller segments in school science. The six segments somewhat arbitrarily created for Table 5.18 may not be these smaller segments, but it is worth noting that the topics *within* these areas do have moderate to strong correlations. Only for topics *across* the six areas are correlations very weak. This would seem to indicate a country-level intention to cover topics in one area somewhat independently of intentions to cover topics in another physics area. In short, the science curriculum appears to be partitioned by disciplines, and school physics seems to be even further partitioned in structuring curriculum.

NOTES

1. For the thirteen-year-olds who made up TIMSS's Population 2, only the eighth grade (or equivalent) textbooks were collected and analyzed in detail. Thus, these data on content coverage in textbooks exist only for the eighth grade in mathematics and in science.

2. This resulted in two matrices, one for mathematics and one for science, at each of two grades related to Population 2 for which individual teacher data were available—seventh and eighth grades.

3. One should not be misled by the fact that the data included those on the sixth and seventh grades and aggregate data on the first through fifth grades (or their equivalents). The emphasis in the present analyses is firmly on the eighth grade, for which the richest array of data is available. The data for the other grades are intended only as background and contextual information to aid in understanding patterns in the eighth grade data.

4. By this is meant the higher of the two grades in a country's school system that contains the majority of thirteen-year-olds. In most TIMSS countries, this meant that students were in their eighth year of formal schooling— hence our use of the term *eighth grade*. Countries' names for this grade varied. See Table 2 in Beaton, et al., 1996, p. 11.

5. Valverde & Schmidt, 2000; Schmidt, McKnight, & Raizen, 1997.

6. See Schmidt, McKnight, Cogan, Jakwerth, & Houang, 1999.

7. The curves in Figure 5.1 represent the cumulative distributions of textbook coverage for topics. The data include the percentage of the textbook devoted to each topic by those countries at the twenty-fifth, fiftieth, and seventy-fifth percentile.

8. This figure of 20 percent also includes textbook space that is double coded (see Chapter Three and the discussion surrounding signatures) where one of the codes indicates the topic of equations and formulas. This results in that textbook space being double-counted—here for equations but also for the other topic in the double coding—meaning that for some countries the sum across all topics might be greater than 100 percent. We take this approach in our analyses because there is no way to split the time between the two topics in a nonarbitrary fashion. Textbook space that truly covers two or more topics simultaneously would be relevant, we argue, for each of the topics. To restandardize by dividing the time by the number of topics, although appealing because the sum would be equal to 100 percent, seems arbitrary and potentially misleading. This would be to argue that a fictitious textbook that only covers two topics simultaneously over the entire book (such as content dealing with proportionality and equations) and one in which half of the book is allocated to each topic separately are the same in terms of their opportunities to learn each of the two topics. This does not seem reasonable to us. A cognitive task analysis would seem to be necessary to allocate the space nonarbitrarily. This was not done in TIMSS, so we tolerate the ambiguity of double coding in our analyses.

9. This should hardly be surprising because the test blueprints (Survey of Mathematics and Science Opportunities, 1993; McKnight, Schmidt, & Raizen, 1993) were governed to a large extent by a preliminary examination of the TIMSS curriculum analysis data. In effect, these presumed

consequences were actually planned characteristics. It is worth noting a few things about the number of items on the TIMSS Population 2 mathematics test for these and other tested topic areas. Equations and formulas had the most test items allocated to it (twenty-seven, including those pertaining to the related topics of real numbers and their properties and exponents, roots, and radicals). The other four topics of the top five were present in the test but did not have as high a proportion of items as might be expected from their emphases in content standards and textbooks. Data such as those in Figure 5.1 might be used in future studies to design cross-national tests in a more informed fashion that produces both greater relevance and fairness to participating countries. It is clear that the TIMSS Population 2 mathematics test has too great an emphasis on common fractions, decimals, and percents—a total of fifty items—compared with the emphasis on these topics in textbooks and content standards for the participating countries. This may well reflect a North American bias often alleged during the history of TIMSS, because U.S. eighth grade mathematics classrooms focused on these topics more than did those of most other TIMSS countries.

10. Switzerland has considerable diversity in eighth grade mathematics textbooks. These data represent an aggregation over textbooks from three distinct educational systems (German, French, and Italian Swiss schools), each with its own textbooks. This is thus quite different from either the data for a country with a single national textbook or for the case of the United States, in which the data are an aggregation of the most widely used textbooks nationally even though there is considerable variation among states in which books are used.

11. We have discussed this matter of focus and emphasis in greater detail elsewhere. See Schmidt, McKnight, & Raizen, 1997; Schmidt, McKnight, Cogan, Jakwerth, & Houang, 1999; Schmidt, McKnight, Valverde, Houang, & Wiley, 1997; Schmidt, Raizen, Britton, Bianchi, & Wolfe, 1997.

12. Median polishing makes use of the fact that data in a two-dimensional (row-by-column) array has an additive structure. In our case, rows indicate countries and columns indicate topics. Each cell (a specific topic for a specific country) may be thought of as the sum of numbers from four sources. First, there is an overall median of medians that is common to all topics and countries. It puts a specific cell's number into a general range of values. Second, there is a row effect, that is (for us), an additional percentage common to a country (row) across all columns (topics). It represents the contribution of the specific country's characteristic emphasis to the total emphasis of the specific topic for that country. Third, there is a column effect, that is (for us), an additional percentage common to a topic (column) across all

rows (countries). It represents the contribution of the specific topic's characteristic emphasis to the total emphasis of that topic for the specific country. Fourth and finally, there is an additional cell effect or residual that represents an adjustment of the combination of overall effect, row effect, and column effect to get the specific effect for that country and topic combination. It represents what is unique for a specific topic in a specific country. Median polishing is a technique that uses the iterative subtraction and accumulation of row and column medians to try to separate these four components. The result is a table with a median of medians (overall effect or centering of all the numbers in the table), row medians (characteristic country contributions across topics), column medians (characteristic topic contributions across countries), and the residual (what is left that is special to that topic-country combination in each cell of the array). Unusually high or low (that is, large absolute values with either positive or negative signs) residuals indicate unusually strong interaction effects of country and topic. We spot these by performing median polishes and identifying large residuals. The usual method of estimating two-way models is by row-and-column means. The advantage of using medians is twofold: (1) medians are more robust than means, and (2) residuals are not assumed to be random and can estimate row-by-column interaction effects. For further information on the median polish procedure, see Emerson & Hoaglin, 1983a.

13. The results in Table 5.3 are based on percents. For inferential reasons these values are often transformed for statistical analysis using a logarithmic or square root transformation. We did this and found a similar indication of interaction effects. Some of the particulars did change but even there the general pattern was similar. See the endnote in Chapter Six for a more detailed explanation.

14. As previously described (in Chapter Three) we broke textbook content into blocks. Coders from the country that used the textbooks identified the content topics and performance expectations involved in each block. Each textbook block was linked to one or more of the topic areas from the forty-four in the TIMSS mathematics framework (in the case of eighth grade mathematics textbooks). We then could examine all the blocks for each topic to determine what percentage of them were coded as expecting this more complex performance involving investigating, problem solving, reasoning, and the like (the percentage is conditional). The question we address here is whether the proportion of a content area involving these more complex expectations varied by topic, by country, or in ways that involved interactions of countries and topics.

15. See Schmidt, McKnight, Cogan, Jakwerth, & Houang, 1999.

16. This already has been examined for the TIMSS countries (see Table 7.1 in Schmidt, McKnight, Valverde, Houang, & Wiley, 1997, pp. 110–111; Schmidt, Raizen, Britton, Bianchi, & Wolfe, 1997, pp. 116–121) and in more detail for the U.S. (Schmidt, McKnight, Cogan, Jakwerth, & Houang, 1999).

17. See Tables 6.1 and 6.2 in Schmidt, McKnight, Valverde, Houang, & Wiley, 1997, pp. 97, 103.

18. When asked about the most detailed level of mathematics framework topics grade by grade, they responded with codes of 0 (not present), 1 (covered), or 2 (covered with some focused attention) to each topic for each grade. The latter two codes were recoded to indicate degree of emphasis, with either a 1 or 2 indicating coverage but a 2 indicating greater emphasis. We combined the eighth grade data on teacher percentage of time devoted to a topic and the data from GTTM codes of 0, 1, and 2 to estimate for each county separately what a 1 or a 2 meant in terms of percent of teacher time. We based this estimation on the means of the within-country empirical distribution of percentage of teacher time given to topics coded 1 or 2. This estimate arrived at for eighth grade data was used to recode the sixth grade data. This gave a combined measure of intention (0 versus 1 or 2) and degree of implementation (different percent values). It was intended as a measure indicative of learning opportunities provided in the sixth grade mathematics curriculum.

19. To get some indication of intent in first through fifth grade mathematics, the GTTM codes (0, 1, and 2) for those five grades (or their equivalents) were summed over the five grades to provide a cumulative distribution of topic emphasis. No calibration with respect to teacher time in eighth grade was used.

20. The structure of science courses at eighth grade differs across countries and, as a result, so do the textbooks. In some countries, the science textbook is about one area of science such as earth science, or it is a textbook that draws its topics from multiple sciences. In other countries, multiple science courses are provided simultaneously, in which case there are multiple textbooks. To make "the science textbook" comparable from one country to another, *textbook* in the latter case was defined as the union over all books defining science instruction during the eighth grade. These are the data analyzed in this section.

21. All of this gets very complex. The original conception of those of us who designed the teacher questionnaires was that all four science areas (or all two or three areas depending on how eighth grade science was organized in a particular country) would have a teacher responding. This would have

allowed for the science learning opportunities for tested children in a school to be fairly and completely represented. This turned out to imply a complex process. This was especially true when coupled with complex sampling rules that called for following the students in a mathematics class to their science classes and then sampling their teachers. This level of complexity made TIMSS scale back what it implemented. What we have then is very likely an errorful estimation of a country's implemented curriculum in science.

22. This is true as long as it is understood that the unit referred to is the percent of instructional time for the student, not for the teacher. One also must assume that the sampling rules were reasonably completely followed in each country so that such averages actually represent the range of science courses and are not biased by over- or undersampling some of the sciences. The behavior of the data seems supportive of this assumption.

23. For those countries that had two to four sciences taught simultaneously, the sampling would yield the artificial results discussed previously. However, aside from this, if there were two, three, or four science courses, then, assuming random sampling of the teachers across the different courses, the breakdown in this table should yield percentages of about 25, 33, and 50 percent, depending on the number of simultaneous science courses required of each student in the country. Within measurement and sampling error, the numbers actually estimated reflect this pattern.

24. Given the earlier discussion of the difficulties associated with the percentage of teachers covering a topic, we do not interpret the standard deviations associated with this variable.

6

THE STRUCTURE
OF CURRICULUM

THE CLEAR MESSAGE of the preceding chapter is that curriculum varies. Profiles of topic coverage—profiles that reveal differences in coverage among topics—differ across countries. When the country profiles were averaged over countries, aggregate indicators such as the percentage of textbook space allocated to a topic showed how topic coverage varied in the world according to TIMSS. When the average was taken over topics, country differences were revealed, for example, in the percentage of teacher coverage of a typical topic. Finally the profiles revealed patterns peculiar to each country (to which we have referred by its technical name, the interaction effect). This suggested country-specific exceptional coverage of certain topics.

This was all true no matter which aspect of curriculum one considered. A next logical question, before turning to the relationship of curriculum and achievement, is whether a structure underlies the different aspects of curriculum in ways important for its relationship to achievement. What exactly are the relationships among the different aspects of curriculum in school mathematics and science? That is the subject of this chapter.

The model for the relationship of curriculum to achievement gain was discussed in Chapter Two. We formulated a causal statistical model of this relationship in Chapter Three as seen in Figure 3.1. For the present we want only to consider the subset of the structural model that deals with the interrelationships among the aspects of curriculum. That simple model is given in Figure 6.1.

Each path in the model stands for a complex social relationship between the two aspects of curriculum involved. As discussed in Chapter Three, the path, for example, between content standards and textbook coverage stands for the social institutions and pressures that operate so

Figure 6.1. The Structure of Curriculum.

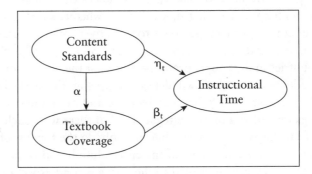

that officially articulated goals (captured in content standards) affect the shape and selection of textbooks. (See the discussion about Figure 3.1 for an explanation of the other paths in Figure 6.1.)

The complexity here is not the model but the multiple ways it can be applied to the data.[1] It is a structural model indicating how these four indications are related. Each arrow in the model indicates the presence of a relationship and has a structural coefficient (α, β, or η) to indicate the strength of the relationship among the aspects of curriculum pictured.

We can find estimates of the strength of the relationships for each of the mathematics and science topics separately over all countries. This can be done for topics at the level of either the TIMSS frameworks or the TIMSS tests. Second, we can estimate those same relationships for each participating country separately over all relevant (science or mathematics) topics (at either of the two levels).

Unfortunately, this results in a large amount of statistical information to assimilate. It would involve approximately one hundred separate regressions[a] (about thirty for countries and about twenty for topics in either science or mathematics just at the tested level, not even considering the more detailed framework level). Further, we do not wish to do analysis for its own sake. We prefer analyses that can be made relevant to educational policy. For this, it would be better to also have an overall analysis that addresses the question at a more general level.

Whether the data can be described in such a general way must be determined empirically. We begin by doing a two-way statistical analysis over topics and countries simultaneously. This will provide an umbrella analytical framework for examining the relationships among the various aspects of curriculum: three contexts in which to examine the relationship of differing opportunities for one representation of curriculum to differing opportunities for another. That is, it will show whether such a relationship exists over countries (averaged over topics), over topics (averaged over countries), or over the unique combinations of countries and topics found across countries in their topic profiles—that is, at the interaction level.

The results of this analysis will determine whether the model in Exhibit 6.1 needs to be examined separately by topic and by country or whether it can be examined at a more aggregate level. If there were such an interaction effect, this would suggest that not only do the topic profiles vary across countries for one aspect of the curriculum but also that the very way in which they vary is related to the way a second aspect of curriculum varies. If this is supported empirically it would provide further evidence of the cultural nature of curriculum.

Pairwise Relationships Among the Aspects of Curriculum

Before examining the structural model of Figure 6.1, we will first use the general two-way analysis to explore the bivariate relationships between pairs of the four curriculum indications.[2] The pairwise (bivariate) relationships are not statistically controlled for the other variables in the model. The estimated correlations reported in this section indicate the general strength of the total relationship between the two variables without attempting to understand the nature of the relationship.[b]

---

[a]Regression analysis is a statistical technique for determining the strength of the linear relationship between variables.

[b]For example, the estimated two-variable correlation between content standards and instructional time could arise because of the direct relationship of standards to instructional time (η_t in the model of Figure 6.1) or because of the indirect relationship of standards to instructional time through textbook coverage

For these analyses, topics were matched at the tested level. That is, text-book and content standard topic coverage was aggregated across all top-ics contained within a tested topic area. The regression coefficients for the independent variables (the β's)[c] provided the numerical indication of the strength of the aggregated relationship and a test for its statistical sig-nificance.[3]

MATHEMATICS For eighth grade mathematics, the focus of the pairwise relationships between the indicators of curriculum is mostly at the inter-action level. This implies that exceptional (out of the ordinary) coverage of certain topics for one aspect of curriculum was related to similar excep-tionalities for the other aspects, with this relationship being defined over all countries and all topics. At that level, content standards were signifi-cantly related to textbook space ($p < .001$).[d] Textbook space was related significantly to teacher implementation ($p < .001$) for both percent of teachers and for instructional time.[4] (There were also significant positive topic effects for these two relationships, but these are logically of no prac-tical significance given the presence of statistically significant interaction effects.)

The interaction effect for the relationship of content standards to instructional time was also significant ($p < .021$). The relationship of con-tent standards to percent of teachers implementing a topic had significant main effects at both the country level ($p < .001$) and topic level ($p < .005$). This was not true for the interaction effect ($p < .336$).

(involving both α and β_t) or both. It is even possible that the relationship exists because of a similar indirect relationship through another variable not included in the model. The later section in which the structural relationships are estimated uses statistical techniques to control for the indirect relationships in estimating the direct relationship between two variables.

[c]In the case of relationships between two variables (bivariate relationships) the regression coefficient is numerically related to the correlation coefficient.

[d]Statements of the form "$p < .001$" should be read as saying that the probability of the null form of the stated conclusion (essentially that there is no relationship) happening by chance is less than .001 (one chance in a thousand). This is statisti-cal shorthand for indicating if a conclusion is significant. For those not used to such language anything less than .05 is considered statistically significant, and anything less than .1 is considered marginally or potentially significant. Any prob-ability higher than that is usually considered as not statistically significant because there is too large a probability that it happened by chance and not because there was any systematic, likely-to-be-repeated relationship present in the data.

SCIENCE Similar patterns held for eighth grade science. There was a significant interaction effect for the relationship of textbook coverage to instructional time ($p < .001$). However, there was not a significant relationship of content standards to textbook coverage ($p < .197$) at either the interaction level or the topic level ($p < .180$). For textbook coverage's relationship to the percent of teachers covering content, the interaction, like that for mathematics, was significant ($p < .035$), as was the country effect ($p < .024$). However, the main effect for topics in this case was not significant ($p < .605$).

The interaction effect in the relationship of content standards to instructional time was only marginally significant ($p < .094$), whereas the topic effect was not significant ($p < .728$). However, for the relationship of content standards to percentage of teachers covering the content, all three effects were statistically significant (although the interaction effect was significant only at the $p < .055$ level).

SUMMARY AND DISCUSSION These findings make it clear that the pairwise relationships involving textbook space and teacher implementation (either through instructional time devoted to a topic in a country or the percentage of a country's teachers covering a topic) were significant at the interaction level. This was true both for mathematics and for science. That is, the profiles of topic coverage for these two aspects of curriculum vary across countries and they vary in a related way.

There were differences between mathematics and science in the relationship of content standards to textbook coverage. In mathematics, this relationship was interaction based and significant. However, for science, neither the interaction-based nor topic-based relationships were significant.

The pattern of relationships for content standards and teacher implementation also varied across mathematics and science. There were significant interaction-based relationships between content standards and instructional time for mathematics and between content standards and percent of teachers covering content for science. However, the relationship of content standards to instructional time in science and of content standards to teacher coverage in mathematics were not significant at the interaction level, although for science the relationship was marginally significant. For the latter two bivariate relationships, the estimated regression coefficients for the topic effects were positive but were significant only for mathematics.

In summary, the significant interaction effects led us to fit these bivariate relationships across countries for each topic separately and across topics for each country separately. This was necessary to explore the substantive meaning of the significant interaction effects. We do this in a later section of this chapter.

Examining the Structural Relationships

The results of the estimation of the structural coefficients[e] found in Figure 6.1 are shown in Figure 6.2 for eighth grade mathematics and in Figure 6.3 for eighth grade science.[5] For the relationship of content standards to textbook space and textbook space to teacher implementation, we estimated these coefficients at the interaction level.[6]

Results differed for mathematics and science in the relationship of content standards to the proportion of textbook space devoted to covering each topic. For mathematics, the estimated coefficient was statistically significant and positive, as reflected in Figure 6.2. For science, the corresponding estimated coefficient was not statistically significant and was set to 0 for Figure 6.3.[7]

The only indication of significant interaction effects for the relationship of content standards to either indication of teacher implementation in the bivariate analyses was in mathematics for instructional time and in science for the percentage of teachers covering specific content. These relationships were the same for the structural model. For mathematics when controlling for textbook space, the estimated interaction-based coefficient for the relationship of content standards to teacher coverage was not statistically significantly different from 0 ($p < .142$). However, the relationship was significant at the topic level.

For science, relating content standards to teacher coverage when controlling for textbook space showed that the estimated coefficient was positive and marginally significant ($p < .086$). For science, the same coefficient related to instructional time was 0.

For both mathematics and science the coefficient relating textbook coverage to teacher implementation was estimated to be positive, defined on the basis of the statistically significant relationships at the interaction level. Figure 6.2 and Figure 6.3 summarize the sign of the structural coefficients fitted to the model in Figure 6.1.[8]

---

[e]The structural coefficients are different from the pairwise coefficients in that they have been estimated by statistically controlling for the indirect relationships in the model.

Figure 6.2. Fitted Curriculum Model for Eighth Grade Mathematics.

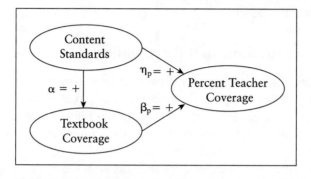

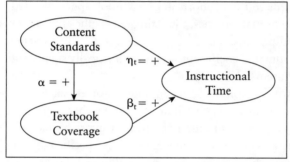

Note: + *indicates a statistically significant positive relationship between the two variables when statistically controlling for other variables in the model. 0 indicates the absence of a statistically significant relationship between the two variables, implying that the two variables are unrelated to each other when controlling for other variables in the model.*

SUMMARY Science content standards were not related significantly either to textbook space or to instructional time. However, a significant positive relationship existed between textbook coverage and instructional time. Although there was a direct relationship between content standards and proportion of teachers covering content, there was no indirect relationship between the two (content standards related to textbook space and textbook space related to proportion of teachers covering content). Textbook coverage was related positively to the proportion of teachers covering content, but there was no significant relationship between content standards and the proportion of textbook space.

Figure 6.3. Fitted Curriculum Model for Eighth Grade Science.

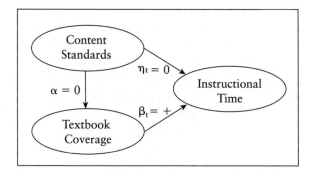

Note: *+ indicates a statistically significant positive relationship between the two variables when statistically controlling for other variables in the model. 0 indicates the absence of a statistically significant relationship between the two variables, implying that the two variables are unrelated to each other when controlling for other variables in the model.*

The situation was more complex for mathematics. There was both a direct and an indirect relationship between content standards and instructional time. That is, there was a significant relationship directly between content standards and instructional time as well as a significant indirect relationship (content standards and textbook space as well as textbook space and instructional time). This same pattern of both direct and indirect relationships was true between content standards and proportion of teachers covering content. The direct relationship of content standards to teacher coverage was based on a relationship at the topic level and thus held on average across all participating countries. The indirect relationship was interaction based, as was true for science.

The nonzero estimated structural coefficients in Figure 6.2 and Figure 6.3 were all positive, indicating a direct ("more, more") relationship among different aspects of curriculum where nonzero relationships were indicated. However, in general, these relationships were not constant across topics or across countries but rather varied across them.

What are some of the policy implications of these findings? One is that specifying content standards seems to be important as a policy instrument. Such specifications seem generally to have a positive impact on aggregate teacher implementation of topic coverage in the classroom both directly (for both mathematics and science) and indirectly (for mathematics only) through their impact on textbook space devoted to topics. The one exception, however, is that content standards do not seem to be related to instructional time in eighth grade science.

For mathematics, there is a positive, interaction-based indirect relationship between content standards and teacher implementation. This implies that the more a topic receives special coverage in a country's content standards, beyond what is average for the country and for the topic across countries, the more it is especially allocated space in that country's mathematics textbooks (beyond the average for topics in that country and the average for that topic across countries). Further, if it is in the content standards and thus receives an unusually high proportion of textbook space, the more it receives instructional time beyond the average and is taught by a greater proportion of teachers. We interpret this to mean that teacher implementation was determined to some extent by content standard coverage as it is reflected in textbook space allocations but that the specifics of those relationships can vary across countries and topics. In other words, the specific topic receiving similar exceptional coverage across the different aspects was not the same across all countries, but such exceptions defined over all topics and all countries was where the relationship across the different aspects manifested itself. However, the direct relationship between content standards and teacher implementation in eighth grade mathematics was pretty much the same across countries for teacher coverage (occurring at the topic rather than the interaction level) but varied across countries for teacher time.

For science, content standards had a direct relationship to the proportion of teachers covering content but not to instructional time for that content. However, there was no indirect relationship through textbook coverage. This direct relationship was interaction based, thus varying in detail among countries and topics. Science textbook space also had a direct relationship to teacher implementation, but this was not uniform across countries.

The interaction-based relationships involving textbooks for both mathematics and science may well reflect the lack of a uniform role for student textbooks. This likely reflects at least policy differences in the use of student textbooks if not deeper cultural differences in the nature of the textbooks as well. Are textbooks viewed as being of a different genre than ordinary books? Are there cultural conceptions of their role and how they are to function in instruction? One could imagine different answers to these questions and that these differences would be reflected in different kinds of textbooks and their use in schooling. In fact, as part of the TIMSS document analysis, the actual eighth grade science and mathematics textbooks were collected from the participating countries. Even a cursory examination of these books shows that their structure and organization varies appreciably across countries, and this, in turn, suggests that the role they play in instruction also likely varies.[9]

To put it another way, suppose one were to do a cursory examination of all the textbooks from a structural and organizational point of view (ignoring the specific content of the books), with the assumption that they all came from one country. One would be almost certain to conclude that different genres of books were represented in the collection—from free-standing narrative, to references to which instruction could refer, to collections of exercises, and so on. In short, one would almost certainly conclude that not all of these books were of the same type. This is an indication of how greatly the structural and organizational characteristics of textbooks varied among the TIMSS countries.

Further, the way in which textbooks were used in classroom instruction almost certainly varied among the countries.[10] Both this and the structural differences among textbooks are dimensions that one might hypothesize would explain the previously described differential effects of textbook emphasis on teacher time across countries. Any or all of them could be part of the explanation of why the direct effect of textbook space on teacher implementation was not consistent across the participating countries.

The results of the two-way analysis imply that there are general relationships but that the particulars are idiosyncratic to country and topic.[11] A general policy implication exists because of the positive relationships among the different aspects of curriculum. The particulars in terms of specific topics would not necessarily be the same for different countries.

If a particular topic in a given country received, for example, more textbook space than was typical for that topic (across all countries) or that country (across all topics), then one would predict that, in general, the same would likely be true for coverage by teachers. That is, teacher coverage on average would likely be more than was typical for that topic (across countries) and for that country (across topics). The relationship that permits such a prediction was established by a consideration of all topic and country combinations. For policy purposes, this suggests that it is reasonable to interpret these results as meaning that these aspects of curriculum are related—but how strongly they are related could vary by country, including the possibility of no relationship over topics within a given country. This, too, is the meaning of an interaction. As a result, to make specific policy for a particular country, one should really fit the model of Figure 6.1 separately for that country. This is done in a later section of this chapter.

The rest of this chapter is focused on exploring data and analyses that further elucidate the relationships among the various aspects of curriculum. The previous analyses among the three aspects of curriculum indicated that for the most part the relationships among these aspects are defined by the combination of country and topic. Given this, subsequent sections will examine those relationships at the topic level (that is, for each topic separately) and then across topics within a country (that is, for each country separately). Some of these further analyses will resemble those in Chapter Five in specificity. That is, some will be done for topics at the TIMSS framework level rather than the TIMSS teacher level.

Correlations Across Aspects of Curriculum

We will soon turn to the interaction effects in more detail—the topic- and country-specific results. However, first we present two other sets of analyses generalized over countries and topics that are aimed at further characterizing the general relationships among the aspects of curriculum that we use as indications of curriculum.[12]

Correlations Across Topics and Indications

First we examine the simple bivariate correlations among all pairs of topics defined by the different indications. Because the emphasis is on curriculum and not on achievement as measured by the TIMSS Population 2 tests, we use the greater detail of the TIMSS frameworks rather than the tests' topic areas. This includes the pairs both within mathematics and within science as well as the pairs across mathematics and science.

There are a large number of correlations between indications and between each topic pair. For mathematics, there are 1,936 correlations between topic pairs (at the framework level) defined by two aspects of curriculum. For science, there are 6,241. Between a mathematics and a science aspect, there are 3,476 such pairwise correlations. These are summarized in Table 6.1.

Table 6.1. Median Correlations Among the Different Aspects of Curriculum in Eighth Grade Mathematics and Science.

Curriculum Aspects	Math Textbooks	Math Content Standards	Math Instructional Time	Science Textbooks	Science Content Standards	Science Instructional Time	Number of Topics
Math textbooks	0.00						44
Math content standards	0.01	0.26					44
Math instructional time	-0.05	0.04	-0.04				21
Science textbooks	-0.02	0.07	-0.00	-0.02			79
Science content standards	0.00	0.20	0.02	0.07	0.28		79
Science instructional time	-0.01	0.01	-0.01	0.00	0.05	-0.04	22
Number of topics	44	44	21	79	79	22	

Notes: 1. For each of the diagonal values, the median is based on n(n-1)/2 different correlations, where n is the number of topics for that aspect and is given in the table. For example, the mathematics textbook median is based on 946 correlation coefficients.

2. For each off-diagonal value, the median is based on nm different correlations, where n and m are the number of topics for each of the two aspects of curriculum. For example, the median for mathematics textbook and instructional time is based on 924 correlation coefficients.

To summarize these data, for each pair of curricular indications we first calculated the correlations for each pair of topics as seen in those indications. We then found the median of those correlations (the value of the correlation for which half of the remaining correlations are larger and half are smaller than this value) over all topic pairs and used that to indicate the relationship between the two aspects. Thus, Table 6.1 displays the median correlation between any two curricular indications over all topic pairs. Teacher implementation here is represented by average instructional time spent in covering a topic. For example, the median correlation between textbook coverage and content standards for mathematics is .02.

In general the median correlations between any two curricular indications are very low. One must remember that most of the correlations that serve as the basis for these medians are between two different topics across the two indications. As such, one might not expect very high correlations, and one would be correct. Over all indications and across mathematics and science the median correlation is .01 (essentially, 0). Even within mathematics and within science, the median correlations are essentially 0.

The only real exception to this pattern is for the same indication—content standards—but between mathematics and science topics. The median correlation was .20. This suggests that countries might have coordinated coverage of topics in science and mathematics to some extent in developing content standards. When one considers that mathematics is the language of more advanced science content, this seems likely. For example, the coverage of certain topics in chemistry and physics demands an understanding of parts of algebra and geometry. Such intentional coordination among school mathematics and science topics is not the only possible explanation. The orderly but separate development of each of school science and mathematics, if somewhat parallel across countries, would produce some degree of correlation.

The diagonal elements of Table 6.1 are also interesting. These are the median correlations for all pairs of topics but within the same curricular indication (for example, within textbook coverage). These medians summarize some of the data matrices from Chapter Five. There the focus was on the individual pairs of topics, but here the focus is on the median over all topic pairs. In spite of the patterns noted in Chapter Five for particular pairs of topics, over all pairs the conclusion is similar to those across curricular indications. The median correlations are around 0, implying little or no relationship across topics within any one aspect (indication) of curriculum.

There is an exception to this pattern—topics within content standards. For both mathematics (.27) and science (.28), the correlations indicate a moderate relationship among topics. There thus appears to be a modest relationship of content standard inclusion of topics in mathematics and in science as well as across the two areas of school subject matter. Because school mathematics and school science do not really consist of isolated topics treated in complete separation, either within one of the two subject areas or across both, such a modest relationship is unsurprising.

What is perhaps surprising is the absence of such median correlations for textbook space and for instructional time. That is, the textbook space devoted to different topics within school mathematics and school science appears to be more independent than their inclusion in content standards. This is true both within disciplines and, unsurprisingly, across disciplines. The same seems true for the instructional time devoted to different topics.

We have nothing but conjecture to elucidate this relationship any further. The correlations are among amounts of space (textbook coverage) or amounts of time (instructional time). It may be that the relationship between the amount of space or time needed to cover an element of content adequately is not strongly related to the topics relative importance. Some topics may only need small amounts of coverage in textbooks or instruction even though they are important. If the inner logic of a country's development of either school mathematics or school science happens to coincide more strongly with the space or time allocated for specific topics, this could lead to the isolated instances of larger correlations noted in Chapter Five.

Certainly other plausible hypotheses could explain these relationships. The amount of textbook space (except in the United States) and, even more so, the amount of instructional time are limited and finite. Our measures of them to indicate emphasis are constrained percentages, which may have an effect on the empirical correlations. Alternatively, given these constraints, greater coverage of one topic might imply less coverage of another, whether in time or space. Over the entire topic space (of pairs), this might imply a relative balance of positive and negative correlations that would result in a median around 0. There are some data to support this latter view. The range for the middle 50 percent of topic pair correlations (interquartile range) in Table 6.1 are from $-.15$ to $+.15$ (although the absolute value in either case does not indicate even a modest relationship).

Table 6.2 addresses this latter conjecture directly. It displays the mean of the absolute values of the correlations rather than the medians (including sign). A cursory comparison of Table 6.1 and Table 6.2 supports the latter hypothesis. Although the median correlations all center around 0 with only a couple of exceptions, the mean absolute values mostly center around .20. This may not indicate a strong relationship among curricular aspects, but it certainly indicates at least a modest relationship. The fact that the mean absolute values of correlations on the main diagonal are also around .20 implies that coverage of one topic has an impact on coverage of another topic within the same aspect of curriculum. The off-diagonal correlations indicate that this even holds across curricular aspects—for example, textbook topic coverage of one topic is related to instructional time for another topic.

Another way of saying this more generally is that given that the off-diagonal correlations of about .20 refer to relationships across both topics and indications of curriculum, they indicate that there were relationships across topics even when the curricular aspects themselves were different. The diagonal and off-diagonal correlations, especially when compared to those in Table 6.1, imply relations among topics in terms of coverage and that some of these were trade-offs. Further, this indicates that these relationships cut across curricular indications.

These across-topic, across-indication correlations cannot address whether they reflect direct or indirect relationships. However, these results do provide further evidence that there are relationships among the curricular indications, that the relationships may be complex, and that they may involve trade-offs among the topics. Certainly one implication of this is that when examining the relationship from one curricular indication to another or to achievement gain, coverage or gain in a particular topic may need to be related not only to coverage in that topic but to coverage in other topics as well. We will examine the relationship of coverage across curricular indications further in this chapter. We will examine the relationship of coverage to achievement gain in Chapter Nine.

Correlations Across Indications Only

A narrower question—though still consistent with the focus of this chapter—is to what extent the different curricular indications are related to each other for specific topics. We can address this by computing medians corresponding to those in Table 6.1 but based only on those correlations between different instantiations with the topic the same. For example, this addresses to what extent coverage of a particular topic in textbooks was related to the amount of teacher coverage of that same topic. This question is narrower than the one addressed previously, to what extent indications (for example, textbook coverage to teacher coverage) were related across all pairs of topics including but not restricted to the same topics.

The expectation here is that the median correlations across pairs of indications over the same topics would not be 0. This should be true because the issues just discussed would likely only apply to pairs of

Table 6.2. **Mean Correlations Among the Different Aspects of Curriculum in Eighth Grade Mathematics and Science (Averages of Absolute Values).**

Curriculum Aspects	Math Textbooks	Math Content Standards	Math Instructional Time	Science Textbooks	Science Content Standards	Science Instructional Time	Number of Topics
Math textbooks	0.20						44
Math content standards	0.19	0.30					44
Math instructional time	0.22	0.22	0.25				21
Science textbooks	0.17	0.18	0.18	0.16			79
Science content standards	0.17	0.22	0.18	0.17	0.29		79
Science instructional time	0.16	0.17	0.17	0.17	0.16	0.19	22
Number of topics	44	44	21	79	79	22	

Notes: 1. *For each of the diagonal values, the mean is based on $n(n-1)/2$ different correlations, where n is the number of topics for that aspect and is given in the table. For example, the mathematics textbook median is based on 946 correlation coefficients.*

2. *For each off-diagonal value, the mean is based on nm different correlations, where n and m are the number of topics for each of the two aspects of curriculum. For example, the median for mathematics textbook and instructional time is based on 924 correlation coefficients.*

differing topics. For mathematics they vary between .30 and .54 (the latter for textbook coverage and instructional time). This latter large value (.54) is consistent with the estimated structural coefficients resulting from the two-way analyses and the earlier conclusion that for mathematics, textbook coverage was a strong predictor of teacher implementation. For the correlation of textbook space and instructional time, the (interquartile) range for the middle 50 percent of correlations ranged from .34 to .71. For the other two median correlations, the corresponding range varied from approximately .20 to .45.

For science, these new median correlations range from .26 to .39 (with the latter being between textbook coverage and instructional time). However, the median is smaller than the corresponding median for eighth grade mathematics. The (interquartile) range for the middle 50 percent of the correlations between textbook coverage and instructional time varied from .31 to .53.

These results indicate that for a specific topic there were moderate to strong correlations between curricular indications, although the strength of the relationship varied considerably across topics. Further, the results indicate that between different topics, the correlations were more modest in general. There were some notable exceptions to the latter finding across indications and for content standards, where there were moderately strong relationships among topics in both mathematics and science and even between the two.

For the most part, these results are consistent with those from the two-way analyses discussed earlier. However, they do suggest qualifications to the general conclusion that there were relations between curricular indications—at least adding that the strength of the relationship varied appreciably across different topics. The fact that the size of the correlations varied across topics reinforces the presence of significant interaction effects reported earlier.

Relationship of Curricular Aspects Across Topic Profiles

In fitting the structural model of Figure 6.1, the analytical focus was on the relationship of coverage in some topic and coverage as indicated by a different curricular aspect but for the same topic. This was similarly repeated for all topics, but it always centered on the relationship of a single topic to that same topic indicated by a different curricular aspect. In the immediately preceding section, the focus was the same but in terms of the relationship of a single topic to a single other topic—either the original topic or to each of the other topics.

In this section we examine the relationship across curricular aspects (indications) but in terms of the *profile* of topic coverage—that is, considering at the same time the pattern of coverage of multiple topics. For each of the indications, a coverage profile describes each of the topics according to how much emphasis or time it receives. This is essentially described by the columns of the data matrices in Chapter Five or correspondingly by the topic effect of the two-way analyses. The question here is how strongly related are the different curricular aspects when considered in terms not only of single topics or pairs but also of a whole profile of topic coverage—a pattern over all topics.

This question is reasonable given the connections of topics within mathematics or science to each other. There should be connections across topics because of the hierarchical nature of knowledge in school science or school mathematics. There might also be connections because of the deeper underlying structural features of the disciplines themselves.

Given this line of reasoning, why did we bother to examine the relationships across curricular aspects in a "bitopical" way, as we did in the previous section? The answer lies in the limits of the data. The sample consists of thirty countries and forty-four and seventy-nine topics in the mathematics and science frameworks, respectively (or twenty-one and twenty-two in the teacher questionnaires). The formal modeling of such relationships statistically is made impossible because there are more variables than countries.

The multivariate analog of the correlation coefficient is the canonical correlation that relates clusters of variables to other clusters of variables rather than a single variable to another single variable. We computed canonical correlations (the interpretations of the range of values for a canonical correlation is the same as that for the standard correlation coefficient) to correspond to the median correlations in Table 6.1. We could do this only with carefully chosen sets of topics to represent a topic profile rather than do this with a profile of all topics.[13]

Using Chapter Five's results, we chose seven topics in mathematics (out of twenty-one at the teacher questionnaire level) and eight in science (out of twenty-two) to represent the topic profiles in each aspect of curriculum. For mathematics these were fractions and decimals; number theory; perimeter, area, and volume; congruence and similarity; slope and trigonometry; functions; and statistics and data. For science these were life processes and systems; life cycles and genetics; types and properties of matter; structure of matter; energy types, sources, and conversions; energy processes; chemical changes; and forces and motion. The data suggest a strong relationship between the aspects of curriculum when considering the profiles of topics. The canonical correlations all center around .90—ranging from .86 to .94.

The fact that the canonical correlations are substantially higher than the median correlations might well reflect the fact that the conceptual or disciplinary connections among topics are translated into or captured by the topic profiles for each curricular indication. Thus, although the coverage of topic pairs is correlated to a modest degree, the strength of the relationship increases when entire profiles and their internal structure and relationships are considered. This lends credence to the argument that curriculum should not be conceptualized as a series of isolated topics but rather as a vector of topics—a content profile —which together describes the content of a curriculum. All of this has implications for Chapter Nine, in which we explore the relationship of curriculum to achievement. The primary implication is that in addition to two-way bitopical analyses, models representing curriculum as a multitopic profile (vector) need to be examined.

Country and Topic Differences in the Relationships Among Curricular Aspects

The main conclusion of the analyses examined in this chapter is that the different aspects of curriculum are related to each other. However, there is an important caveat to this conclusion: the described relationships are not the same across countries or across topics.

This section seeks to further characterize the nature of these interaction effects by examining the relationships among the curricular aspects but for each country and each topic separately. The structural coefficients for the model in Figure 6.1 are also estimated for each topic and each country separately. Taken together, these analyses portray the interactive nature of the relationships among curricular aspects.

Relationship of Textbook Coverage to Teacher Implementation

Let us first examine the relationship between textbook coverage (space allocations) and teacher implementation (either in the form of instructional time allocated or in the proportion of a nation's teachers that cover a given topic).[14] Because teacher implementation is one of the two curriculum aspects to be investigated, topics must be defined only at the level of the teacher questionnaires.

MATHEMATICS   Table 6.3 summarizes the regression analyses for each of the twenty-one teacher questionnaire–level topics in eighth grade mathematics. The percentage of textbook space for a topic is related both to the average percent of instructional time allocated to that topic and to the percentage of a country's teachers who teach that topic. The data show that the relationships were significant for one or the other or both of the teacher implementation indicators except for three of the twenty-one topics. These three were measurement estimation and error, estimation and number sense, and other content. For all other topics there was a positive relationship between textbook coverage and teacher implementation.

The strength of the relationship between textbook space and instructional time varied as can be seen from the estimated regression coefficients, which ranged from around .2 to over 1.0. That same variability can be represented by the variation in the coefficients of determination (R^2) that represent the proportion of variability in the response variable (one of the teacher implementation variables) accounted for (removable) by textbook space. (In general, the larger the value of the R^2—which may range from 0 to 1—the stronger the implied relationship.) For average instructional time across countries, these coefficients indicated that most of the models ranged from accounting for around 10 percent of the variance to accounting for around 70 percent. Less variation was displayed for the relationship of textbook space to the national proportion of teachers covering a topic, with the coefficients of determination ranging from around 10 to 40 percent.

It is interesting to note that for both of the main topics of algebra (functions, relations, and patterns and equations and formulas), only about 10 percent of the variation in average instructional time across countries was accounted for by the corresponding differences in textbook space.

Figure 6.4 displays results for some of the same relationships but analyzed over topics for most countries. These results are portrayed as a plot of the data for each country together with the fitted regression line.[15] These analyses and others not displayed address the question of whether relationships existed between the relative amount of textbook space allocated to a typical topic in a country and the average instructional time for the topic or proportion of the country's teachers covering the topic. It is a question of the within-country allocation of resources for two different aspects of curriculum and whether the two allocations were related to each other.[16]

Similar to the case for topics, the bivariate relationships between textbook space and teacher implementation in eighth grade mathematics were statistically significant for all but three of the countries—Austria, Iran, and Israel.[17] In almost all countries, the significant relationships were for both indications of teacher implementation—average instructional time and proportion of teachers covering the topic.

The variation in the coefficient of determination indices was even greater across countries than across topics. From around 20 to almost 80

Table 6.3. Relationship of Textbook Coverage to Teacher Implementation for Each Topic (Eighth Grade Mathematics).

Topic	Relation of Textbook Coverage and Instructional Time			Relation of Textbook Coverage to Teacher Implementation Coverage		
	Regression Coefficient	Standard Error	R^2	Regression Coefficient	Standard Error	R^2
Meaning of whole numbers	0.27	(0.09)**	0.24	1.91	(0.79)**	0.16
Common and decimal fractions	0.97	(0.13)**	0.65	2.19	(0.61)**	0.29
Percentages	0.83	(0.12)**	0.61	5.48	(1.25)**	0.38
Number sets and concepts	0.18	(0.09)**	0.12	0.90	(0.44)**	0.12
Number theory	1.12	(0.24)**	0.40	12.55	(2.71)**	0.41
Estimation and number sense	0.27	(0.16)*	0.09	2.66	(2.16)	0.05
Measurement units	0.32	(0.08)**	0.38	3.68	(0.95)**	0.33
Perimeter, area, and volume	0.30	(0.09)**	0.26	1.57	(0.55)**	0.21
Measurement estimation and error	0.19	(0.45)	0.01	−0.51	(10.39)	0.00
1-D and 2-D geometry basics	0.28	(0.07)**	0.32	0.56	(0.39)	0.06
Symmetry and transformations	0.38	(0.09)**	0.35	2.97	(0.84)**	0.29
Congruence and similarity	0.84	(0.14)**	0.53	3.36	(0.93)**	0.30
3-D geometry	0.26	(0.07)**	0.29	1.55	(0.45)**	0.28
Ratio and proportion	0.46	(0.13)**	0.28	4.53	(1.55)**	0.22
Slope and trigonometry	0.80	(0.09)**	0.73	5.93	(1.22)**	0.43
Functions, relations, and patterns	0.30	(0.14)**	0.12	1.46	(0.97)	0.07
Equations and formulas	0.25	(0.12)**	0.12	0.42	(0.20)**	0.12
Data and statistics	0.18	(0.16)	0.04	5.76	(1.66)**	0.28
Probability and uncertainty	0.50	(0.07)**	0.59	5.94	(2.14)**	0.20
Sets and logic	0.28	(0.09)**	0.23	3.37	(1.02)**	0.26
Other advanced content	−0.06	(0.12)	0.01	0.13	(0.75)	0.00

**Significant ($p \le .05$).
*Significant ($.05 < p \le .10$).

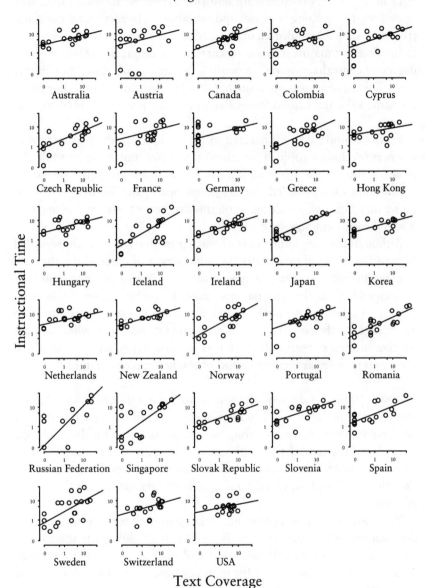

Figure 6.4. Relationship of Textbook Coverage to Instructional Time for Countries (Eighth Grade Mathematics).

percent of the variance in average instructional time across topics was accounted for by topic differences in textbook space allocation. The countries in which this relationship had the largest R^2 include Japan (the strongest), Hong Kong, Iceland, and Singapore. The fact that these countries have such a high degree of concordance between these two different indications or manifestations of curriculum might be related to their degree of centralization on curriculum matters, as discussed in Chapter Four. This issue is examined further in a later section of this chapter. In the same vein, the United States had one of the lowest levels of concordance.

From around 20 to 60 percent of the variance in the proportion of teachers teaching a topic (across topics) was accounted for by topic differences in textbook space allocation. The countries with the largest R^2 by this indication included Greece, Japan, Spain, and Sweden. It is interesting that Japan was once again on this list, but it is also interesting that it was the only country on both lists.

Although our two indications of teacher implementation are regarded as manifestations of essentially the same aspect of curriculum, they are structurally different. One focuses on coverage (yes or no), and a number is attained only in the national aggregate. The other focuses on instructional time, getting a number for each teacher that is then aggregated into an average for the country. This section presents results showing that the relative amount of textbook space within a country related differently to these two manifestations (variables) of teacher implementation.

SCIENCE Table 6.4 displays the results for science that parallel those for mathematics in Table 6.3. The relationship of textbook space to teacher implementation was not as strong for science as it was for mathematics. For eight of the twenty-two topics, textbook space was not significantly related to either indication of teacher implementation. This is far more than the number of topics without significant relationships in the case of mathematics.

Textbook space was significantly related to both teacher implementation indications for only seven of the twenty-two eighth grade science topics. This is about one-half the number of such topics for mathematics. Clearly, Table 6.4 shows that for topics at least, textbook space was not as strongly related to teacher implementation as was true for mathematics. This, of course, does not imply that some relationship was not present.

The coefficients of determination show textbook space accounting for from around 10 to 40 percent of the variance in both instructional time and proportion of teachers covering a topic. This supports the case for a

Table 6.4. Relationship of Textbook Coverage to Teacher Implementation for Each Topic (Eighth Grade Science).

Topic	Relation of Textbook Coverage and Instructional Time			Relation of Textbook Coverage and Teacher Coverage		
	Regression Coefficient	Standard Error	R^2	Regression Coefficient	Standard Error	R^2
Earth features	0.40	(0.16)**	0.17	1.15	(0.78)	0.07
Earth processes	0.09	(0.06)	0.06	0.30	(0.46)	0.01
Earth in the universe	0.41	(0.10)**	0.34	3.15	(1.02)**	0.24
Diversity and structure of living things	0.39	(0.09)**	0.39	1.59	(0.47)**	0.28
Life processes and systems	0.61	(0.15)**	0.37	3.97	(1.12)**	0.29
Life cycles and genetics	0.13	(0.06)**	0.12	1.64	(0.40)**	0.36
Interactions of living things	0.11	(0.08)	0.05	1.18	(0.70)*	0.09
Human biology and health	0.18	(0.15)	0.04	0.62	(0.68)	0.03
Types and properties of matter	0.22	(0.09)**	0.17	1.04	(0.77)	0.06
Structure of matter	0.33	(0.17)*	0.12	2.81	(1.17)**	0.16
Energy types, sources, and conversions	0.23	(0.10)**	0.15	2.33	(0.67)**	0.29
Energy processes	0.21	(0.07)**	0.20	0.35	(0.28)	0.05
Physical changes	0.21	(0.15)	0.06	2.29	(1.43)	0.08
Kinetic and quantum theory	−0.06	(0.14)	0.01	−0.48	(3.29)	0.00
Chemical changes	0.38	(0.09)**	0.37	1.77	(1.06)*	0.09
Special chemical changes	0.31	(0.07)**	0.38	3.76	(1.12)**	0.27
Forces and motion	0.35	(0.11)**	0.24	2.28	(0.78)**	0.22
Relativity theory	0.00	(0.07)	0.00	−1.25	(1.96)	0.01
Science, technology, and society	0.15	(0.05)**	0.22	1.04	(0.97)	0.04
History of science and technology	0.52	(0.22)**	0.16	4.59	(2.41)*	0.11
Environmental and resource issues	0.17	(0.13)	0.05	0.73	(1.03)	0.02
Nature of science	0.18	(0.21)	0.02	2.28	(2.30)	0.03

**Significant* $(p \le .05)$.
*Significant $(.05 < p \le .10)$.

relationship but one weaker than was true for eighth grade mathematics. It also seems that textbook space was more frequently related to instructional time than to the proportion of teachers covering a science topic. The topics for which textbook space accounted for relatively larger percentages of the variance in instructional time include diversity and structure of living things, life processes and systems, chemical changes, and special chemical changes. These topics all came from biology, chemistry, or biochemistry.

The range of coefficients was not as large for either of the implementation indications as it was for mathematics. However, there is still some relationship in most cases and also variability from topic to topic. For science, however, there were more topics for which the presumed relationship was essentially nonexistent. These data, though different from those for mathematics, were still consistent with the results of the two-way analyses.

Table 6.5 gives the science results relating textbook space to teacher implementation for each country (across topics rather than for each topic across countries, as was true in Table 6.4). There were only five of thirty-one countries for which textbook space was not significantly related to at least one of the two indications of teacher implementation. Those countries are Cyprus, Germany, Hong Kong, Hungary, and Israel, which is the one country for which this was also true in mathematics. Apparently in Israel the allocation of textbook space to a topic was unrelated to a teacher's implementation of that topic in either mathematics or science.

The coefficients of determination indicate that textbook space accounts for from around 20 to 70 percent of the variation of instructional time for science topics in the participating countries. This range is very similar to that for mathematics. This must qualify the earlier statement that the relationship of textbook space to teacher implementation was weaker in science than in mathematics. That statement was made relative to topics across countries and does not hold for countries across topics. In the latter case, the relationships are equally strong in both science and mathematics.

The countries in which the relationship of textbook space for a topic to average instructional time allocated that same topic was strongest include the Czech Republic, Iceland, and Singapore. Iceland and Singapore were also among the countries with the strongest such relationship in mathematics.

For the relationship of textbook space for a topic to the national proportion of teachers covering that same topic, the coefficients of determination varied from indicating that textbook space accounted for from around 20 to 50 percent of the proportion of teachers covering an average topic. This range is very similar to that for mathematics. The countries with higher R^2's include Iceland and Switzerland.

Relationship of Content Standard Coverage to Textbook Coverage

In this section we examine the other leg of the indirect relationship of content standards to teacher implementation—the relationsh·p of content standards coverage to textbook coverage.

This analysis could be done two ways given the nature of the variable defining content standards coverage. In the two-way analyses, the variable was defined as the percentage of topics covered where the definition of an area was in terms of the appropriate TIMSS Population 2 test. Using this approach, regression analyses were done, and these are reported in the next section dealing with the structural model. They are discussed more thoroughly there, but the general result was that they vary across topics and across countries with a broad range of values.

The specification of content standards is one of the main policy levers available to a country by which to influence teacher implementation. From our analyses, it appears that one of the ways that this relationship works is indirectly through its influence on textbook coverage. This, in turn, influences teacher implementation. Because of this, we examine the issue of the relationship of content standards to textbook coverage further.

To do this, we used a different definition of the variable defining content standards and operationalized the topics at the teacher level to gain greater flexibility. The content standards variable was dichotomized into not covered (not for any of the framework topics if more than one were involved in a teacher questionnaire content category) and covered (at least one of the framework topics was covered if more than one were involved in a teacher questionnaire content category).

For each topic (at the teacher level, twenty-one for mathematics and twenty-two for science), the dichotomy separated countries into those that called for covering the topic in their content standards and those that did not. Hence, for each group there was a distribution over countries of the percentage of textbook space allocated to that topic.

One question we addressed is to what extent the two distributions of textbook coverage were different—that is, how they differed depending on whether the topic was included in the content standards. A subquestion is whether the average percentage of textbook space allocated to a topic was greater if that topic was included in the countries' content standards.

Table 6.5. Relationship of Textbook Space to Teachers' Implementation for Each Country (Eighth Grade Science).

Country	Relation of Textbook Coverage and Instructional Time			Relation of Textbook Coverage and Teacher Coverage		
	Regression Coefficient	Standard Error	R^2	Regression Coefficient	Standard Error	R^2
Australia	0.40	(0.11)**	0.39	2.20	(0.80)**	0.28
Austria	0.34	(0.22)	0.11	0.81	(0.33)**	0.23
Canada	0.57	(0.11)**	0.56	3.28	(1.04)**	0.33
Colombia	0.21	(0.17)	0.07	1.86	(0.78)**	0.22
Cyprus	0.23	(0.17)	0.08	1.61	(0.90)*	0.14
Czech Republic	0.59	(0.08)**	0.71	2.28	(0.64)**	0.39
France	0.52	(0.11)**	0.54	1.87	(0.58)**	0.34
Germany	-0.04	(0.09)	0.01	-0.36	(0.39)	0.04
Greece	0.53	(0.12)**	0.48	2.09	(0.90)**	0.22
Hong Kong	0.06	(0.21)	0.00	0.04	(0.83)	0.00
Hungary	0.35	(0.17)**	0.18	0.43	(0.70)	0.02
Iceland	0.53	(0.08)**	0.70	2.57	(0.56)**	0.52
Iran	0.30	(0.10)**	0.30	1.95	(0.74)**	0.26
Ireland	0.46	(0.17)**	0.26	2.59	(0.84)**	0.33
Israel	0.17	(0.18)	0.05	1.26	(0.70)*	0.14
Japan	0.36	(0.12)**	0.32	2.38	(0.74)**	0.34
Korea	0.34	(0.15)**	0.21	2.01	(0.72)**	0.28
Lithuania	0.01	-(0.07)	0.08	1.92	(0.57)**	0.37
Netherlands	0.60	(0.16)**	0.42	1.60	(0.72)**	0.20

New Zealand	0.54	(0.12)**	0.53	3.82	(1.13)**	0.36
Norway	0.19	(0.08)**	0.20	1.70	(0.68)**	0.24
Portugal	0.95	(0.20)**	0.54	2.19	(0.71)**	0.32
Romania	0.39	(0.10)**	0.42	0.67	(0.40)	0.12
Russian Federation	0.29	(0.13)**	0.20	1.08	(1.01)	0.06
Singapore	0.64	(0.09)**	0.70	2.88	(1.09)**	0.26
Slovak Republic	0.69	(0.13)**	0.57	2.12	(0.65)**	0.35
Slovenia	0.33	(0.10)**	0.33	0.54	(0.72)	0.03
Spain	0.39	(0.17)**	0.21	3.19	(1.06)**	0.31
Sweden	0.34	(0.07)**	0.54	0.55	(0.46)	0.07
Switzerland	0.80	(0.15)**	0.57	3.13	(0.64)**	0.55
USA	0.33	(0.13)**	0.24	0.84	(1.27)	0.02

**Significant (p ≤ .05).

*Significant (.05 < p ≤ .10).

The answer to both questions in general was yes. The amount of text-book space was greatest on average in those countries in which the topic was in the content standards. The distributions of textbook space were also different for those countries in which the topic was in the content standards. This was true both in science and mathematics although less so for science (consistent with the nonsignificant coefficient in the two-way analyses). In general, the difference in the distributions consisted of greater variability in textbook coverage among the countries for which the topic was in the standards than among the countries for which the topic was not.[18]

For mathematics the distributions were different for all topics. This included the means of the distributions where the amount of average text-book space was greater in all cases for the countries where the topic was included in their content standards than for those in which it was not.[19]

For science, the same basic conclusions can be drawn. All but three of the twenty-two topics were testable. In only four of the nineteen testable topics were the distributions of textbook coverage the same for countries in which the topics were included in their content standards and those in which the topics were not. The topics for which there were no differences in textbook coverage between the two groups of countries were earth processes, physical changes, kinetic and quantum theory, and relativity theory. For the latter two, so little was included in the textbook in either case that the differences between being and not being included in the content standards were negligible.

Figure 6.5 displays the distributions of textbook coverage for a select set of topics in mathematics, both for those countries in which the topic was included in their content standards and for those countries in which the topic was not included. Figure 6.6 illustrates the same for a select set of science topics.

Notes: *1. The distributions are represented as box and whisker plots that indicate the typical value and spread for that aspect of curriculum. The box includes the middle 50 percent of values ranging from the twenty-fifth to seventy-fifth percentile (the interquartile range). The line in the box is the median—a measure of what is typical for the values. The whiskers indicate the middle 90 percent of values going from the fifth to the ninety-fifth percentile.*
2. The sample sizes are given in parentheses.

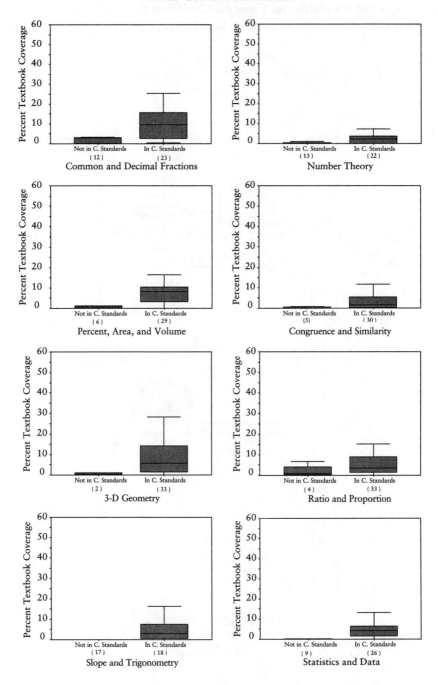

Figure 6.5. Distributions of Percent of Textbook Coverage for Selected Mathematics Topics for Countries Including the Topics in Their Content Standards and Those Not Including the Topics in Their Content Standards.

Figure 6.6. Distributions of Percent of Textbook Coverage for Selected Science Topics for Countries Including the Topics in Their Content Standards and Those Not Including the Topics in Their Content Standards.

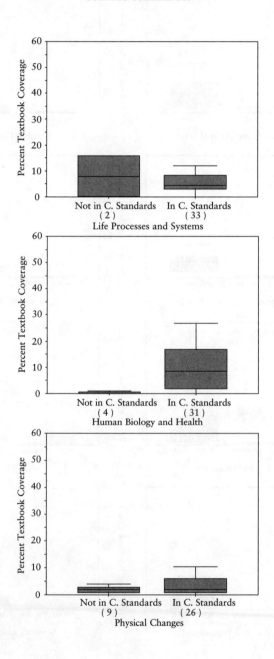

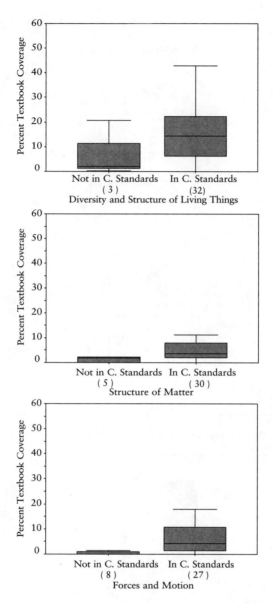

Notes: 1. *The distributions are represented as box and whisker plots that indi-*
cate the typical value and spread for that aspect of curriculum. The box
includes the middle 50 percent of values ranging from the twenty-fifth to
seventy-fifth percentile (the interquartile range). The line in the box is the
median—a measure of what is typical for the values. The whiskers indicate the
middle 90 percent of values going from the fifth to the ninety-fifth percentile.
2. *The sample sizes are given in parentheses.*

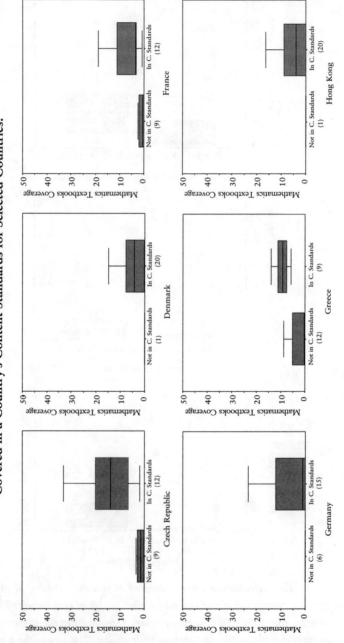

Figure 6.7. Distributions of Percent of Textbook Coverage for Mathematics Topics Covered and Not Covered in a Country's Content Standards for Selected Countries.

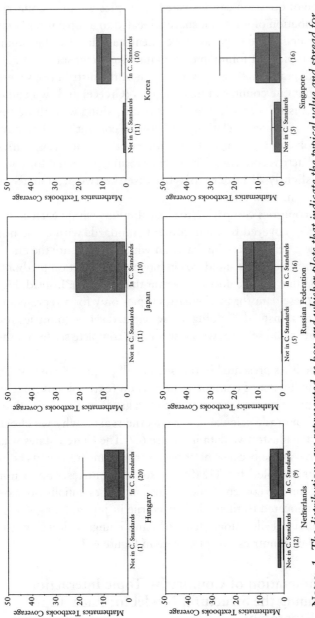

Notes: 1. The distributions are represented as box and whisker plots that indicate the typical value and spread for that aspect of curriculum. The box includes the middle 50 percent of values ranging from the twenty-fifth to seventy-fifth percentile (the interquartile range). The line in the box is the median—a measure of what is typical for the values. The whiskers indicate the middle 90 percent of values going from the fifth to the ninety-fifth percentile.

2. The sample sizes are given in parentheses.

The same type of question can be asked for topics within a country: whether the distribution of textbook space allocated to a topic is different for those topics found in the Population 2 content standards for that country and for those topics not found in that country's content standards.

For both eighth grade mathematics and science, the distributions were different for all but one country in mathematics (Greece) and two countries in science (Australia and Korea). This result, along with those for topics, once again indicates a relationship between content standard coverage and textbook coverage but that the nature of this relationship varies across topics and across countries. The science results presented for completeness are a slightly different story because the two-way analysis resulted in a nonsignificant effect.

Figures for all countries comparing the distributions within each country for those topics covered by their content standards with those not covered would be a very interesting basis on which to measure the effectiveness of a country's content standards in having an impact on textbook coverage. Space in this volume does not permit this, however. Instead, Figure 6.7 displays these data for mathematics topics only for a representative set of countries. Instead of doing a few selected set of countries for each of mathematics and science, we show a more complete set for mathematics.

The various analyses presented in this section all point to a conclusion drawn earlier: the impact of content standards on textbook coverage is larger and more pronounced for topics in eighth grade mathematics than for topics in eighth grade science. That was the reason why we chose mathematics for the illustrative data in Figure 6.7. The United States was not included in this figure because no topics were not included in its content standards as sampled for TIMSS. In some countries, topics not included in that country's content standards meant that essentially no textbook space was allocated to them. This was true in Japan, Hong Kong, Germany, the Russian Federation, Denmark, and Hungary. It was virtually true in all other countries except Greece in Figure 6.7.

A Further Examination of Country by Topic Interaction Effects: Examining the Structural Model for Each Topic and Country Separately

Figure 6.2 and Figure 6.3 presented the results of fitting the general model developed in Chapters Two and Three to the overall data. For the most part, the estimated coefficients were based on the topic-by-country interactions. To further examine the nature of these interaction-based relationships, we analyzed the same data but did so separately for each topic and each country. These results are summarized in Table 6.6, Table 6.7, Table 6.8, and Table 6.9. These give the estimates of the structural coefficients defined in Figure 6.1 for each topic and each country and for mathematics and science separately, including their associated statistical significance. In this section, the analyses were based on topics defined at the TIMSS Population 2 test level (twenty in mathematics, seventeen in science) so that they would correspond to the results of the two-way analyses relating aspects of curriculum not only to each other but also (later) to achievement gain.

MATHEMATICS Table 6.6 presents the results for each of the mathematics topics. The estimated coefficients describe the relationships among the aspects defined over countries but do so for each topic separately. For the relationship of textbook space to instructional time, β (as the structural coefficient) varies from .20 (except for the two nonsignificant negative values) to over 1, with over half of the estimates being statistically significant. For the general model described in Figure 6.2, the corresponding overall interaction-based estimate was also significant and positive. The topics for which this relationship was the strongest include several relating to fractions, geometric congruence/similarity, and proportionality.

For the coefficients relating content standards to instructional time, less than half of them were significant. The overall coefficient in Figure 6.2 was positive. The relationship of content standards to textbook coverage was significant or marginally significant for slightly less than half the topics.

Table 6.7 gives the results in mathematics for each country. Again, the interaction-based nature of the relationship is evident, although the general pattern of a significant relationship among the aspects of curriculum is consistent with the results of the overall model in that for β, most of the countries had a significant indication of a relationship. For η (the relationship of content standards to implementation), few countries had nonzero estimates. On the other hand, for α, about one-third of the countries had statistically significant estimates.[20]

The country-specific nature of how the three aspects of curriculum were related to each other can be illustrated by selecting several countries in which the patterns of such relationships were quite different. Figure 6.8 displays some examples. Diagram (a) in that exhibit shows the total pattern of relating the three aspects of curriculum as found in Figure 6.2. Diagrams (b), (c), and (d) of Figure 6.8 show the results indicated for the Czech Republic, the United States, and Japan, respectively. Arrows are indicated only if the corresponding estimate of the relational coefficient was significant or, in the case of the United States, marginally significant ($p < .06$).

Table 6.6. Estimated Structural Coefficients for the Curriculum Model for Each Topic (Eighth Grade Mathematics).

Topic	Relation of Textbook Coverage to Instructional Time		Relation of Content Standards Coverage to Instructional Time		Relation of Content Standards Coverage to Textbook Coverage	
	β_t	Standard Error	η_t	Standard Error	α	Standard Error
Whole numbers	0.25	(0.09)**	0.03	(0.01)**	0.04	(0.03)
Common fractions	1.08	(0.28)*	0.04	(0.02)*	0.04	(0.01)**
Decimal fractions and percents	0.71	(0.17)**	0.10	(0.03)**	0.08	(0.03)**
Relations of fractions	1.26	(0.58)**	0.05	(0.03)**	0.01	(0.01)
Estimating quantity and size	0.63	(1.10)	0.02	(0.01)**	0.00	(0.00)
Rounding	0.45	(0.38)	0.01	(0.01)*	0.01	(0.00)**
Estimating computations	0.22	(0.22)	0.02	(0.01)**	0.01	(0.01)
Measurement units	0.24	(0.08)**	0.02	(0.01)**	0.02	(0.02)
Perimeter, area, and volume	0.23	(0.08)**	-0.00	(0.02)	0.06	(0.04)
Measurement estimations and errors	-0.22	(0.39)	0.00	(0.00)	0.00	(0.00)*
2-D geometry	0.23	(0.14)	-0.01	(0.02)	0.01	(0.03)
Polygons and circles	0.21	(0.12)*	0.02	(0.04)	-0.09	(0.06)
3-D geometry and transformations	0.24	(0.04)**	0.01	(0.02)	-0.06	(0.10)
Congruence and similarity	0.65	(0.11)**	0.01	(0.02)	0.04	(0.03)
Proportionality concepts	1.10	(0.46)**	0.01	(0.01)	0.00	(0.00)
Proportionality problems	0.25	(0.14)*	0.01	(0.01)	0.03	(0.02)*
Patterns, relations, and functions	0.42	(0.10)**	0.01	(0.01)	0.04	(0.06)
Equations and formulas	0.18	(0.08)**	-0.02	(0.05)	-0.21	(0.11)*
Data representation and analysis	-0.05	(0.15)	0.03	(0.01)**	0.04	(0.01)**
Uncertainty and probability	0.39	(0.06)**	0.01	(0.00)**	0.01	(0.01)

**Significant ($p \leq .05$).
*Significant ($.05 < p \leq .10$).

The differences among the diagrams reflect the nature of the interaction effect. The differences illustrated by these three countries, we hypothesize, may well reflect cultural differences in schooling and the way decisions about curriculum are made. For example, the high degree of curricular centralization (see Chapter Four) found in Japan is likely reflected in the fact that there are significant direct as well as indirect effects of the content standards on teacher implementation.

Content standards are national in Japan. Further, the Japanese efforts at curricular coherence are well known.[21] Such efforts include books written for teachers that interpret the standards and give instructional examples. As a result, it is not surprising that the content standards in Japan would have had a direct as well as indirect impact on teacher implementation.

The Czech Republic reflects a system in which content standards had only an indirect relationship to teacher time through textbook coverage. That is, the content standards were related to what was in the textbooks, and the textbook coverage was related to average instructional time for topics within the country in eighth grade mathematics.

Finally, the United States has at best regional standards and a strong tradition of local control of schools. Corresponding to this, there is no strong tradition of centralized curricular control even within most states, let alone for the country as a whole. Textbooks are influenced heavily by the need for multiple adoptions and are thus large and inclusive. This weakens their relationship to even those content standards that exist. Teachers most often related to textbooks in mathematics.

SCIENCE Table 6.8 gives the results for different topics in eighth grade science. The pattern for the science topics is very similar to that for the mathematics topics. About half of the coefficients for the relationship of textbook space to teacher time are significant, but the range of values of these coefficients is smaller than for mathematics, varying from 0 to about .4. This is consistent with the results in an earlier section indicating that the effect of textbooks on average instructional time was less strong for science than for mathematics at eighth grade.

Similar results hold for the relationship of content standards to instructional time (coefficient η as set out in Figure 6.1). There are fewer topics for which significant relationships are indicated than was true for mathematics. The range of values of the coefficients indicating the strength of the relationships is smaller. For the relationship of content standards to textbook space (coefficient α in Figure 6.1), the relationships in science are on average similar to those for mathematics.

Table 6.7. Estimated Structural Coefficients for the Curriculum and Achievement Model for Each Country (Eighth Grade Mathematics).

Country	Relation of Textbook Coverage to Instructional Time		Relation of Content Standards Coverage to Instructional Time		Relation of Content Standards Coverage to Textbook Coverage	
	β_t	Standard Error	η_t^1	Standard Error	α^1	Standard Error
Australia	0.36	(0.19)*	−0.07	(0.03)*	0.00	(0.04)
Austria	0.32	(0.22)	−0.04	(0.03)	0.05	(0.04)
Belgium (Fl)	†		0.02	(0.05)	0.07	(0.05)
Belgium (Fr)	†		0.00	(0.05)	0.06	(0.06)
Canada	1.00	(0.31)**				
Colombia	0.34	(0.15)**	0.01	(0.04)	0.06	(0.05)
Cyprus	0.33	(0.14)**	0.01	(0.03)	0.08	(0.04)*
Czech Republic	0.40	(0.08)**	0.01	(0.02)	0.13	(0.05)**
Denmark	1.36	(0.34)**	−0.01	(0.03)	0.04	(0.02)
France	0.68	(0.36)*	0.01	(0.04)	0.06	(0.02)**
Germany	0.35	(0.15)**	0.02	(0.02)	0.01	(0.04)
Greece	0.21	(0.29)	0.03	(0.04)	0.08	(0.03)**
Hong Kong	0.55	(0.17)**	0.00	(0.03)	0.04	(0.04)
Hungary	0.28	(0.13)**				
Iceland	1.09	(0.20)**	−0.15	(0.06)**	0.08	(0.07)
Ireland	0.27	(0.17)	0.03	(0.02)	0.07	(0.03)**
Japan	0.51	(0.07)**	0.06	(0.02)**	0.11	(0.05)**

Korea	0.45	(0.11)**	−0.02	(0.02)	0.11	(0.03)**
Netherlands	0.12	(0.10)	−0.04	(0.02)	−0.03	(0.05)
New Zealand	0.48	(0.21)**				
Norway	0.83	(0.33)**				
Portugal	0.38	(0.07)**	−0.01	(0.02)	0.06	(0.07)
Romania	0.32	(0.04)**	0.01	(0.02)	0.23	(0.09)**
Russian Federation	0.82	(0.13)**	0.04	(0.03)	0.11	(0.04)**
Singapore	0.59	(0.09)**	0.00	(0.02)	0.05	(0.05)
Slovak Republic	0.33	(0.07)**	0.01	(0.02)	0.13	(0.05)**
Slovenia	0.19	(0.07)**	0.03	(0.02)	0.05	(0.07)
Spain	0.64	(0.12)**	−0.04	(0.03)	−0.04	(0.06)
Sweden	0.63	(0.45)	0.08	(0.09)	0.01	(0.04)
Switzerland	0.33	(0.36)				
USA	0.39	(0.19)*				

**Significant (p ≤ .05).

*Significant (.05 < p ≤ .10).

†No textbooks were coded for the two language systems of Belgium.

[1]Because content standards had no variance, some countries' coefficients were not estimable.

Table 6.8. Estimated Structural Coefficients for the Curriculum Model for Each Topic (Eighth Grade Science).

Country	Relation of Textbook Coverage to Instructional Time		Relation of Content Standards Coverage to Instructional Time		Relation of Content Standards Coverage to Textbook Coverage	
	β_t	Standard Error	η_t^1	Standard Error	α^1	Standard Error
Earth features	0.22	(0.14)	0.02	(0.02)	0.04	(0.03)
Earth processes	0.09	(0.06)	0.01	(0.01)	−0.04	(0.04)
Earth in the universe	0.35	(0.16)**	0.02	(0.01)**	0.02	(0.01)**
Diversity and structure of living things	0.24	(0.09)**	0.03	(0.02)	0.10	(0.05)**
Life processes and functions	0.41	(0.11)**	0.04	(0.02)**	0.01	(0.03)
Life cycles and genetics	0.14	(0.05)**	0.01	(0.01)	0.12	(0.04)**
Interactions of living things	0.13	(0.10)	0.03	(0.01)*	0.03	(0.03)
Human biology and health	0.29	(0.17)*	−0.07	(0.05)	0.09	(0.06)
Properties and classification of matter	0.06	(0.06)	0.03	(0.02)	0.10	(0.06)
Structure of matter	0.25	(0.12)**	0.02	(0.01)	0.01	(0.02)
Energy and physical processes	0.35	(0.10)**	0.01	(0.05)	0.02	(0.11)
Physical changes	0.03	(0.09)	0.01	(0.01)	0.03	(0.02)
Chemical changes	0.39	(0.10)**	0.00	(0.01)	0.00	(0.00)
Forces and motion	0.20	(0.10)**	0.00	(0.01)	0.06	(0.03)**
Science, technology, and society	0.05	(0.07)	0.01	(0.01)	0.00	(0.01)
Environmental and resource issues	0.11	(0.18)	0.01	(0.01)	0.01	(0.02)
Scientific processes	0.20	(0.16)	0.00	(0.01)	0.04	(0.01)**

*Significant (p ≤ .05).
*Significant (.05 < p ≤ .10).

Once again these results could be used to support the conclusion that in general, the relationships among the aspects of curriculum are stronger for mathematics than is true for science. It is tempting to draw that conclusion. However, the caution needs repeating that was first made in Chapter Five concerning the implications of the sampling design for TIMSS.[22]

Table 6.9 gives the science results for each country (across topics). Once again, the interaction-based nature of the relationships among the curricular indications is fairly obvious. The pattern over the countries is consistent with the overall results presented in Figure 6.3. Similar to the illustration in Figure 6.8 for mathematics, we chose three countries to illustrate the likely cultural impact on how curriculum operates.

As Figure 6.9 shows, the pattern for the United States is the same in eighth grade science as it was for mathematics. The pattern for Singapore in science is the same as the pattern was for Japan in mathematics, that is, a pattern of both direct and indirect influence of content standards on instructional time.

However, the pattern for Japan in science is very different from its pattern in mathematics. This might reflect differences in how science as a curriculum area is viewed in Japan as compared with mathematics. It might be an artifact of the TIMSS sampling design as was discussed earlier. It also might reflect a difference in the nature of Japanese eighth grade science textbooks compared with the corresponding eighth grade mathematics textbooks. There could be a difference in the impact on instructional time of laboratory-based textbooks from more expository based textbooks.[23]

SUMMARY This section set out to explore the nature and meaning of the interaction-based relationships found in the two-way analyses presented at the beginning of this chapter. In one sense the answer is simple—there is a general pattern of positive relationships among the aspects of curriculum. However, it differs for eighth grade mathematics and science. One relationship is constant—the direct relationship of textbook space to teacher implementation. However, there are exceptions to this general pattern, and even within it, the strength of the relationships varies across topics and countries.

In other words, there are country-specific patterns in how the curriculum aspects (indications) relate to each other. This derives from the within-country allocation of textbook space, content standards coverage, and instructional time across the topics. Differences within a country in any of these curricular aspects likely reflect cultural conceptions of school subject matter and of what is important for eighth grade.

Table 6.9. Estimated Structural Coefficients for the Curriculum Model for Each Country (Eighth Grade Science).

Country	Relation of Textbook Coverage to Instructional Time		Relation of Content Standards Coverage to Instructional Time		Relation of Content Standards Coverage to Textbook Coverage	
	β_t	Standard Error	η_t^1	Standard Error	α^1	Standard Error
Australia	0.32	(0.10)**	−0.03	(0.06)	−0.16	(0.16)
Austria	0.30	(0.20)	0.06	(0.05)	0.01	(0.06)
Belgium (Fl)	†		0.01	(0.06)	†	
Belgium (Fr)	†		0.02	(0.04)	†	
Canada	0.41	(0.08)**	−0.02	(0.02)	0.00	(0.06)
Colombia	−0.01	(0.10)	0.03	(0.04)	0.11	(0.10)
Cyprus	0.36	(0.10)**	0.06	(0.03)	0.04	(0.09)
Czech Republic	0.56	(0.06)**	0.01	(0.01)	0.07	(0.05)
France	0.33	(0.10)**	0.01	(0.02)	0.08	(0.06)
Germany	0.03	(0.14)	0.03	(0.03)	−0.12	(0.05)**
Greece	0.40	(0.14)**	0.00	(0.02)	0.07	(0.04)*
Hong Kong	0.26	(0.31)	0.09	(0.05)*	0.03	(0.04)
Hungary	0.41	(0.13)**	0.03	(0.02)	0.01	(0.04)
Iceland	0.33	(0.06)**	0.00	(0.04)	0.15	(0.14)
Ireland	0.36	(0.14)**	0.07	(0.06)	0.11	(0.11)
Japan	0.18	(0.12)	0.03	(0.03)	0.13	(0.07)*
Korea	0.21	(0.15)	−0.01	(0.03)	−0.01	(0.05)
Latvia	0.11	(0.07)	0.07	(0.08)	−0.09	(0.28)

Netherlands	0.57	(0.19)**	0.04	(0.04)	−0.05	(0.05)
New Zealand	0.41	(0.09)**				
Norway	0.08	(0.08)	0.04	(0.02)	0.06	(0.08)
Portugal	0.64	(0.14)**	0.00	(0.04)	0.09	(0.08)
Romania	0.38	(0.14)**	0.00	(0.03)	0.13	(0.05)**
Russian Federation	0.28	(0.09)**	−0.04	(0.03)	0.13	(0.08)
Singapore	0.49	(0.11)**	0.04	(0.02)*	0.09	(0.05)*
Slovak Republic	0.88	(0.09)**	−0.04	(0.03)	0.10	(0.07)
Slovenia	0.34	(0.07)**	−0.02	(0.04)	−0.07	(0.17)
Spain	0.20	(0.18)	−0.01	(0.04)	−0.02	(0.06)
Sweden	0.35	(0.09)**	0.02	(0.02)	0.01	(0.05)
Switzerland	0.76	(0.16)**	−0.03	(0.04)	0.07	(0.06)
USA	0.20	(0.09)**				

**Significant (p ≤ .05).

*Significant (.05 < p ≤ .10).

†No textbooks were coded for the two language systems of Belgium.

1Because content standards had no variance, some countries' coefficients were not estimable.

**Figure 6.8. Estimated Structural Model for Selected Countries
(Eighth Grade Mathematics).**

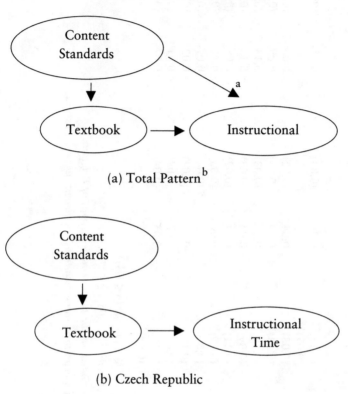

(a) Total Pattern[b]

(b) Czech Republic

One pattern worth further consideration in contrasting the topic-specific results is that there appear to be stronger within-country, across-topic relationships among the aspects than is the case across countries. This implies that relative allocations within the total available (size of the textbook or length of the school year) seem more strongly related to each other across different aspects of the curriculum than is the case across countries for a given topic.

Perhaps this is because such differences in allocations can have different meanings across countries in which cultural differences arise about schooling and school subjects. Within a country, the cultural context is typically constant for all topics, and thus the allocations across topics are directly comparable. Across countries this may not be true. For instance, textbook space could have different meanings in different countries

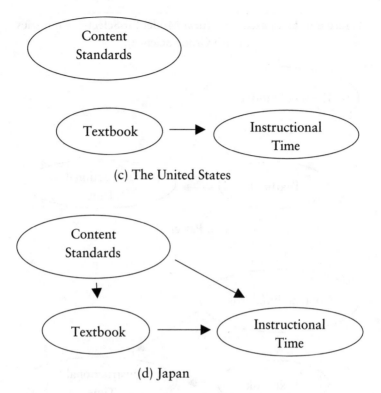

(c) The United States

(d) Japan

[a]*An arrow indicates a statistically significant relationship, and the absence of such indicates no statistically significant relationship.*
[b]*This pattern is based on the total interaction-based model (see Figure 6.2).*

because the very nature of the textbook and its use in schooling differs among countries. The cultural expectation of the role played by the textbook in instruction could vary. This may mean that establishing relationships across countries for given topics may be more difficult than establishing such relationships within a country. This does not necessarily mean that there are fewer such relationships or that such relationships are necessarily weaker. Rather it implies only that they might be more difficult to establish when the cultural context, by which variables being related are given meaning, itself varies across countries. None of these difficulties exists for within-country analyses because the cultural contexts are comparatively constant in those cases. These ideas are only a conjecture. However, they are consistent with one of the main themes of our earlier work.[24]

Figure 6.9. Estimated Structural Model for Selected Countries (Eighth Grade Science).

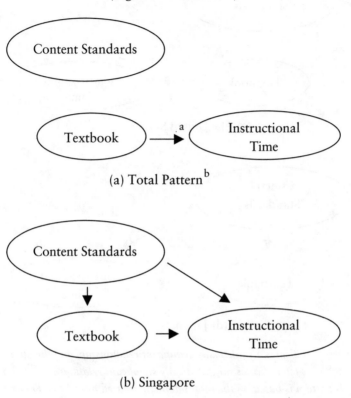

(a) Total Pattern[b]

(b) Singapore

The Concept of Opportunity to Learn

A main theme of this chapter is that the various aspects of curriculum are related to each other. This is especially true for a given topic across the different indications (aspects) of curriculum. Some of the work in this chapter suggests that such relationships also hold, although less strongly, across different topics as well. That is, the coverage of a particular topic according to one curriculum indication is not only related to the coverage of that topic in a second indication but also to the coverage of other topics in that second indication as well.

These results lead us to hypothesize a common feature of curriculum underlying these relationships of allocations for different topics in differ-

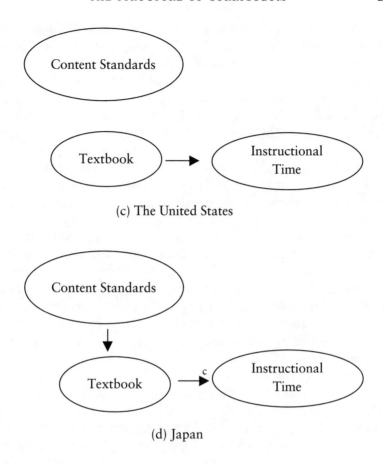

(c) The United States

(d) Japan

[a]An arrow indicates a statistically or marginally significant relationship, and the absence of such indicates no such relationship.
[b]This pattern is based on the total interaction-based model (see Figure 6.3).
[c]Significance level is p < .14.

ent aspects of curriculum. That common feature has to do with how the curriculum distributes experiences that allow the learning of particular contents. In deference to the important groundbreaking work of previous IEA (International Association for the Assessment of Educational Achievement) cross-national studies, we will call this underlying concept by the name that seems most directly related to it in those studies—opportunity to learn (OTL).[25]

The implication of the preceding sections is that the OTL concept can be conceptualized in three ways: (1) OTL in a topic area as provided by one aspect of curriculum, (2) OTL for a profile of topic opportunities as provided by a single aspect of curriculum, and (3) OTL for a topic over all aspects (indications) of curriculum considered here. The first conceptualization is the more traditional IEA way to conceive of OTL and is directly observable. This is the concept used in the previous analyses reported in this chapter and, to some extent, throughout this book.

In the third conceptualization, OTL for a topic is a latent construct. This is related to what we mean when we suggested that curriculum was invisible and could be made visible (manifest) by different indications of that invisible curriculum. We here are refining that idea to say that curriculum as a distribution of OTL is latent but observable in different indications of its presence and nature. In this way textbook space and instructional time are simply different manifestations of the same latent construct—the OTL associated with particular topics. When OTL is considered as a single underlying construct, differences among the various aspects of curriculum for a specific topic are considered to reflect measurement error, and as such the relationship among the indications is not important as a separate focus.

The second conceptualization of OTL sees it as a profile of opportunities across the topics as provided by a given aspect of curriculum. This idea is closer to the first than it is the third because the opportunities can be observed (that is, are not latent). However, it differs in that it considers the vector of coverage across all topics to represent OTL as measurable for a particular aspect. This is a much more complex notion of OTL, one that likely involves the deeper structures of the disciplines of mathematics and the sciences themselves.[26] Most of the analyses of this volume are based on the first conception of OTL. In this section (and again in Chapter Nine), we explore some results derived from the other two conceptions of OTL.

The Latent Notion of OTL

The results presented in this section are derived from fitting a structural equation model to each of the topics separately. Here OTL is defined for each topic separately, and the three aspects of curriculum associated with that topic are considered as manifestations of that underlying OTL. Teacher implementation includes measures of both instructional time and the proportion of a nation's teachers covering a particular topic. Textbook space includes both the space allocated to a topic's coverage and the performance expectations for that topic. Differences among the curricular indications are not modeled as they were in the first section of this chapter but rather are considered to reflect only errors of measurement.

For mathematics, the latent OTL model was consistent with the data for sixteen of twenty topics.[27] Only for two geometry topics (polygons and circles and three-dimensional geometry and transformations) as well as equations and formulas and data representation and analyses did the notion of a latent concept of OTL not fit with the data. This should not be taken as proof that the latent conception of OTL is the "correct" one for sixteen of the twenty topic areas in mathematics but only that this conception was consistent with the data. Other conceptions (such as that of the first OTL conceptualization discussed earlier) can also be consistent with the data.

The results of this analysis provide estimates of the reliability of each of the measures of the curriculum. The data show that which of these curricular aspects are the most reliable indicators of OTL depends on the particular topic. For example, average instructional time was the most reliable indicator for common fractions, but for estimating quantity and size, the most reliable indicator was teacher coverage—the percentage of teachers in a country who covered the topic.

For science, the results were similar. The latent conception of OTL was consistent with all but three of the science topics—human biology; science, technology, and society; and scientific processes.[28]

OTL as a Profile

The question here is, "How does the profile of OTL across topics for one curricular aspect relate to the same profile for a different aspect?" The question is very similar to the one examined in an earlier section in which we looked at the canonical correlations across profiles. However, now we are more interested in looking at such a profile as a conceptualization of OTL. Thus, we fit a more formal statistical model to similar data to examine the concept of OTL as a profile rather than OTL for a single topic. This conception does not define a latent construct, as was the case in the previous section. However, it does look at a profile (vector) rather than a single topic.

The statistical procedures do not permit testing the consistency of this conception with the data, so we only summarize information relative to the relationships among the differing curricular indications. The sample size limits the number of topics that we can include in these analyses, and as a result we chose a limited number of topics to represent the full spectrum.

In mathematics we chose five topics—common fractions; perimeter, area, and volume; congruence and similarity; functions and relations; and data representation and analyses. For science we chose six topics—life processes and functions, life cycles and genetics, properties and classification of matter, structure of matter, energy and physical processes, and chemical changes. In both cases the choices were made to best represent the profile across all topics based on the results of Chapter Five.

For mathematics, the relationships among the five aspects of curriculum (including performance expectations) characterized by a profile of topic coverage for the selected topics were all statistically significant. The median coefficients of determination (R^2's) ranged from about .3 to .6 (that is, accounting for between 30 and 60 percent of the variance). The canonical correlations were all around .8 to .9.

This suggests that OTL as a profile across topics was related for all pairs of curricular indications. It suggests, for example, that when considering the relationship of textbook space to average instructional time spent on a particular topic, not only the textbook space for that particular topic that was related to instructional time but also the textbook proportions allocated to other topics as well as those related to the instructional time for that particular topic should be examined. This has implications for Chapter Nine, where we examine the relationship of OTL to achievement. It implies that the profile of OTL may be important to consider rather than only the OTL for individual topics.

The results were very similar for science except that the relationship of content standards to the proportion of a country's teachers covering a topic was not statistically significant ($p < .10$).[29]

For mathematics, the strongest relationship was that for textbook space related to instructional time (where the median coefficient of determination was around .6). These results were consistent with those discussed earlier. They can be contrasted with the results for science for which the relationship between the same two indications was among the strongest but where the median coefficient of determination was only .4. This was also consistent with similar conclusions based on other data discussed earlier in this chapter: such a relationship of textbook space to instructional time was stronger in mathematics than it was in science.

Relationship of Curricular Centralization to Consistency Among Its Aspects

Another way to view the relationships among the curricular aspects is as a measure of the degree of consistency or coherence present in the curriculum. National curricular policy is often designed to achieve such consistency and can include not only prescriptions of topics in standards but mechanisms for determining the acceptability of textbooks in terms of those standards. National curricular policy may also include a system of inspections to ensure teacher compliance with content standards. Other related policies are found in some countries.

Even in educational systems where little such curricular policy exists (for example, in the United States), there is concern over the degree to which the various aspects of curriculum align with each other. In the United States, this is often referred to as *curricular alignment*.

Of course, it is sensible from a logical point of view for an educational system to address such consistency or coherence. Without it, the various manifestations (indications) of curriculum could work at odds to one another. In this section we examine the effect of centralization on consistency where centralization is defined in terms of curricular decision making. In Chapter Four we examined data relative to curricular decision making. The major conclusion of that chapter was that no one single notion of centralization held sway. This represents a refinement of similar findings in the literature that typically held a more monolithic notion of centralization.[30]

A system can have varying degrees of centralization with respect to different aspects of the curriculum such as setting content standards for specific grade levels or for determining textbook adoptions. Each country was classified, using the data of Chapter Four, as centralized or not based on who had the final authority in determining the content standards for each grade level. *Centralized* was the designation for an educational system if the final authority in making that decision rested with a national ministry. If not, the system was classified as noncentralized.

Centralization and the Degree of Consistency Between Content Standards and Teacher Implementation

We decided first to examine the relationship of centralization to the degree of consistency between content standards and teacher implementation. To examine this issue, we looked at instructional time and the national proportion of teacher coverage for a topic as they were related to the presence or absence of that topic in a country's content standards. The analysis examined whether the relationship was different for centralized and noncentralized countries (as described previously).[31]

The data do not suggest an effect for centralization.[32] The two-way interaction of content standards and centralization was only significant for one topic (percents). This was true both for instructional time and for teacher coverage. For half of the topics, their presence or absence in content standards was related to statistically significant differences in the average national percentage of teachers who taught them. Presence or absence in content standards was related to statistically significant differences in average instructional time for only six of the topics.

These results point in the direction that content standards did have an effect on teacher implementation and probably more so for teacher coverage than for instructional time. The presence of a topic in a country's content standards was associated with a higher percentage of that country's teachers including that topic in their instruction. This was not true for all topics. It was true for even fewer topics when examining the relationship of content standards to average instructional time.

Centralization did not have an impact on those relationships in any significant way except for one topic. It appears that whatever impact content standards had directly on teacher implementation, it was because of the content standards themselves and not because of the degree of centralization of the country having the content standards. However, as illustrated in Figure 6.2, content standards can also have an indirect impact on teacher implementation through textbooks. This raises the question of to what extent centralization affects the relationship between content standards and textbook space and between textbook space and teacher implementation. We define the strength of each of these two relationships as a country's degree of coherence or consistency between the two involved curriculum aspects.

To illustrate the concept of consistency, we examined a manifestation of it for the relationship of textbook space and instructional time. It is graphically illustrated for mathematics in Figure 6.10 and for science in Figure 6.11. The more coincidental (closer in size) the squares and the circles are for a country, the greater the degree of consistency for that country between these two aspects. The results suggest that the degree of consistency not only varies across countries but across topics as well. In general, it appears that there is more "over teaching" than there is "over textbook coverage," as indicated by the large number of cases where the circles encompass (are larger than) the squares.[33]

To examine these relationships statistically, we constructed an index of consistency between content standards and textbook space and between textbook space and teacher implementation.[34] These indices are one way to capture what is represented graphically in Figure 6.10 and 6.11. The results indicate a statistically significant relationship between content standards and textbook space ($p < .057$) and between textbook space and teacher implementation ($p < .019$ for instructional time and $p < .014$ for teacher coverage).

Figure 6.10. A Graphical Representation of the Consistency in Countries Between Instructional Time and Textbook Coverage for Mathematics.

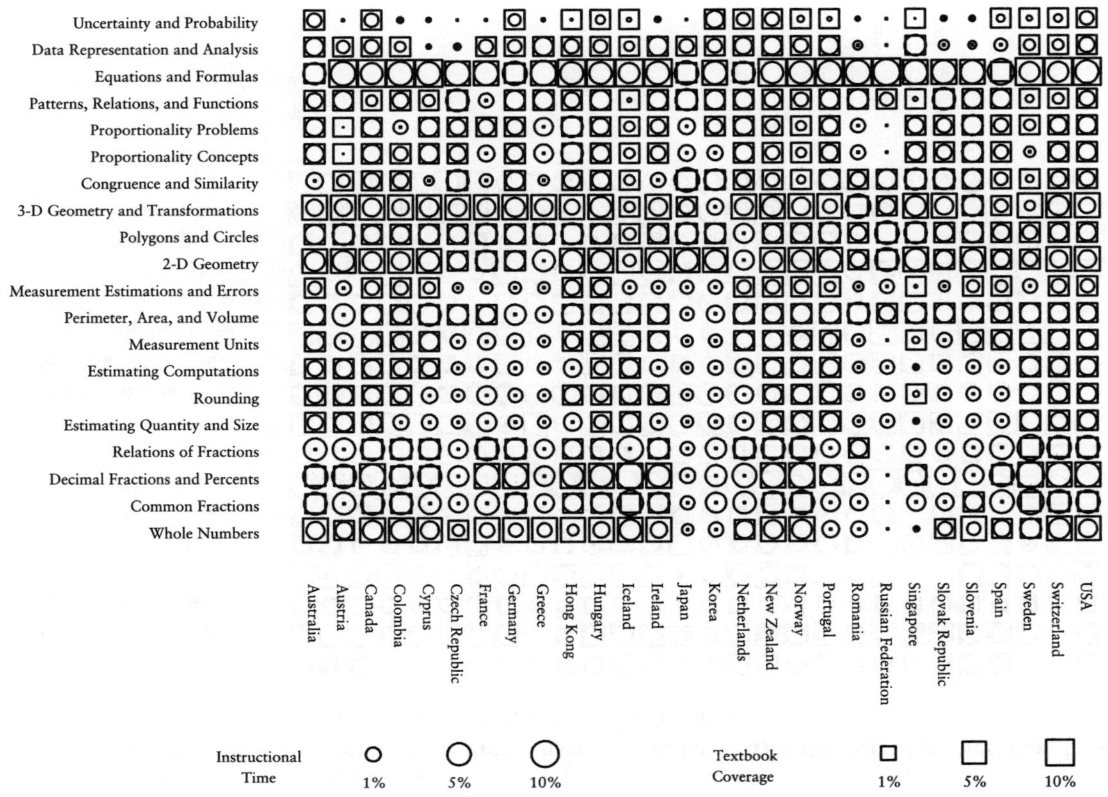

Figure 6.11. A Graphical Representation of the Consistency in Countries Between Instructional Time and Textbook Coverage for Science.

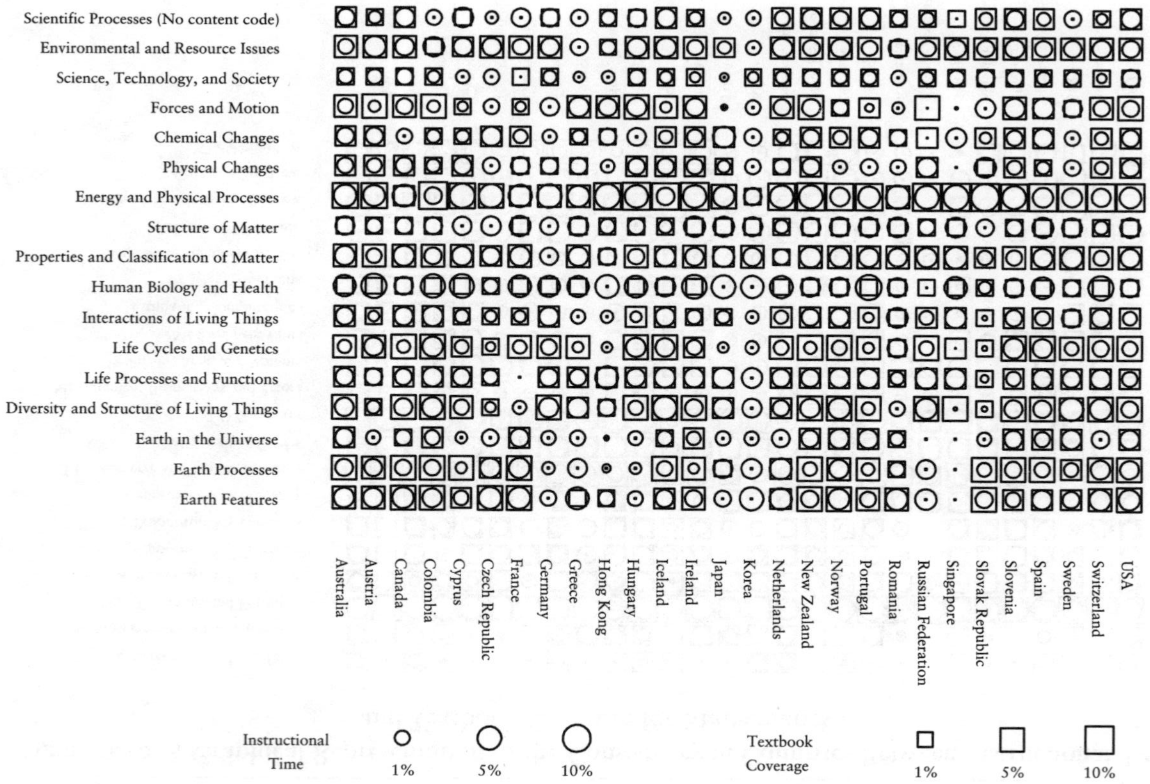

In all cases, the countries with a centralized curriculum had a higher degree of consistency. This implies that centralization was related to the coherence of the curriculum but that the effect of centralization operated on the indirect path between content standards and teacher implementation (through textbook space). Centralization did not have an impact on the direct effect of content standards on teacher implementation. Hence, the answer to the question posed at the beginning of this section is that centralization does seem to be related to the coherence of curriculum across its three aspects.

Summary

The three indications were all related to each other. However, when examining those relationships structurally (controlling for other variables), the primary path for most countries, especially in mathematics, was the indirect relationship between content standards and teacher implementation through textbook space. Although the relationships hold generally, they were interaction-based effects. This implies that these relationships varied by country.

Such relationships were likely to be described better when including the profile of opportunity across topics rather than separately topic by topic. Finally conceptualizing such relationships as indicators of coherence, we found that countries with centralized curriculum decision making related to grade by grade content standards had a higher degree of curricular coherence.

The structure of curriculum and the relationships among its indications clearly varies among countries and topics and, in particular, among the interaction of countries and topics. None of this evidence can conclusively determine the truth of our cultural hypotheses. However, it certainly accords with the impact of cultural differences on the content of school science and mathematics, on textbooks and their role, and even on the effects of content standards as they relate to what teachers actually do when teaching particular content to students.

NOTES

1. The problem in searching for structure in curriculum is the wealth of relationships that potentially exist. We have four indicators representing three aspects of curriculum. We have over forty topics in mathematics and almost eighty in science, even focusing only on the eighth grade curriculum. We have between thirty and forty countries that provided data on each of the

four indicators and for each topic. When we turn to how those aspects are related to search for underlying structure, somehow all of this must be systematically aggregated in ways that reveal rather than conceal structure.

2. The data in the two-way country-by-topic matrices described in Chapter Five were used in these analyses. There were separate matrices involved for each member of the pair investigated. That is, there was a matrix for the independent variable (for example, textbook coverage) and the dependent variable (for example, instructional time in teacher implementation of the curriculum). Dependent and independent variables were determined for each pair by the order postulated in the model in Figure 6.1. The data in each matrix were "double centered" by subtracting the row mean from each entry in a row and then the column mean from each entry in a column. The results were sets of marginals (row or column means) for countries and for topics and a set of residuals representing country by topic interactions. The cell residuals in this case resulted from removing the two means and adding in the grand mean.

The two sets of marginals for topics (each representing one of the indicators of curriculum) were related to each other using generalized least squares. Because data for different topics were measured over the same set of countries, we had to treat them as repeated measures because of the implied covariance structure. This was not true for the two sets of marginals for countries, and there we used ordinary least squares for those regressions. These regressions yielded the β's for topics aggregated across countries—the topic effects—and the β's for countries aggregated across topics—the country effects. The residuals for each pair of variables were also fitted by generalized least-squares regression models. This provided an estimate of β for the residuals—the interaction effect for the pair of indicators.

3. This implies that three values were estimated for each pairwise relationship (or structural parameter in Figure 6.1)—one each at the topic, country, and interaction level. In many ways the analysis parallels an application by Bock of MANOVA (Multivariate Analysis of Variance) to repeated measures data (Bock, 1975). However, we do assume homogeneous covariance matrices across countries but without the double symmetry assumptions. The only technical complexity involves the computation of the standard errors. For the country main effect, there was no problem in estimating the standard errors because countries are independent of each other and the analysis was over countries. For the topic and topic-by-country interaction effects, these analyses were over topics within a country where topics are not independent of each other. This produced a problem in estimating standard errors not unlike the problem encountered in repeated measures analy-

sis. Estimating these standard errors was nontrivial and relied on the block-wise diagonal nature of the variance-covariance matrix, S, but was further complicated by the double centering. A technical description of this procedure was presented earlier (Houang, Wiley, & Schmidt, 2000).

4. Probabilities are rounded either to the nearest hundredth (two digits) or the nearest thousandth (three digits). The exception is that $p < .001$ is used in place of $p < .000$ which means that the actual p-value may be considerably less than .001.

5. To accomplish this, we used generalized least squares in the two-way analysis context, estimating the coefficients for all aspects of the model simultaneously.

6. The estimated coefficients were based on the deviated cell means because estimates based on the marginal effects are biased by the presence of significant interactions such as those reflected in the bivariate analyses. This was further substantiated by the multiple regression results.

7. The actual estimated values of the structural coefficients are presented and discussed later in this chapter.

8. As indicated in Chapter Three, the aspects of curriculum used in these analyses as independent variables are all measured in the percent metric. The distributions for some of these variables as characterized in Chapter Five show a clumping of values at the low end of the distribution. This can create difficulty when fitting linear models to such data. There is a statistical literature suggesting different types of transformations that can be applied to stretch out the tails of such a distribution, making the transformed data more amenable to linear statistical inferential procedures. The question in such a case is, what is the relative advantage in using such transformations over the raw percent metric? Usually the rationale for their use is that the transformation helps identify relationships that might not be so readily visible in the raw percent metric. In our case, using the raw percent metric does not seem to mask relationships among the curriculum indicators or the relationship between curriculum and learning, at least in an appreciable way. However, some specific relationships might still be masked. In many ways the analyses using the raw percent metric seem clear enough in their impact to not warrant such transformations. Nonetheless, to be conservative, we did the transformations on the data to see if they made any substantive difference, i.e., made any difference to the conclusions based on the raw percent analyses. In general, they did not.

More specifically, we applied both a logarithmic (base-10) and square root transformation to the data. Using the transformed data, we repeated the two-way analyses to estimate both the bivariate and structural coefficients for mathematics. The substantive results for the data based on the square root transformation were identical to those for the raw percent metric. The data based on the logarithmic transformation also yielded almost identical results with only two exceptions. The relationship of instructional time to gain at the interaction level was significant (marginal in the percent metric), and the relationship of teacher coverage to gain was no longer statistically significant ($p < .28$).

We also repeated the bivariate and multiple regressions for both mathematics and science done separately for each topic and for each country—with the results summarized in this chapter and in terms of gain in both Chapters Eight and Nine. Of the almost seven hundred different estimated regression coefficients, around 85 percent were unchanged in terms of significance level. For those for which there was change, over 40 percent of them involved a single variable—content standards. Most of these differences (over 80 percent) involving content standards suggest that the corresponding coefficient was statistically significant. At most, it would appear that under the transformation there are more statistically significant relationships of content standards to gain and the other curriculum variables.

This comparison implies that the results presented in the text and based on the percent metric might be conservative for the impact of content standards. Other than that, the other changes did not follow specific patterns and do not seem to warrant using the transformed data. In no case did the analyses using the transformed data alter the basic finding that curriculum is related to learning and that the nature of the relationship is mostly interaction based.

9. This issue is explored in more detail in Valverde, Bianchi, Houang, Schmidt, & Wolfe, 2001.

10. Schmidt et al., 1996.

11. That is, the relationships were specified at the cell level after the data have been mean deviated by both country and topic marginals.

12. In the first section of this chapter, the two-way analysis results were presented. They were designed to examine the relationships between each pair of curricular aspects, with topics held constant across those aspects. That is, the definitions of the topics were the same from one indication to another. In this section we broaden the characterization of the relationship among indications to include the relationship between each pair of topics across the indications for each topic pair. We also examine the standard relationship of a given topic in two different indications. This latter relationship was the basis for the previous two-way model regressions, but in this sec-

tion we characterize the data differently using medians of correlations. We also return to examining the relationships among topic pairs within one aspect of curriculum, as we did in Chapter Five. However, here we do this again by median summarization.

13. This was to deal with the technical problem associated with the number of variables and the degrees of freedom. The representative topics for the mathematics and science profiles were selected using the results from Chapter Five.

14. To explore this relationship, we used OLS (Ordinary Least Squares) to estimate the coefficients relating the two aspects of curriculum. First (the results of which are examined in this section), the relationship between textbook coverage and teacher implementation was estimated for each topic separately. These analyses were done across countries; that is, countries were the units of analysis. There would be twenty-two such analyses for science and twenty-one for mathematics. Given the significant interaction effects found in the earlier two-way regression analyses, one would expect that these analyses would reveal estimated coefficients that are statistically significantly different from 0 for some topics and not others and that the magnitude of the coefficients would differ even among the topics for which significant relationships were found.

The second analysis type involves the relationship between textbook coverage and instructional time within each country across topics. The unit of analysis here would be the topic. This would result in a separate analysis for each country. Again, given the significant interaction effects from the earlier two-way analyses, one would expect that the fitted models would vary across countries, indicating that the relationship of textbook coverage to instructional time differs for different participating countries.

15. This display is of the fitted regression lines for the data points transformed by the logarithmic function ($\log_{10}(p + .1)$). The lines are robust regression lines. See endnote 8 concerning the transformation of the data.

16. The standard errors associated with these analyses are not entirely appropriate because the units in the analysis (in this case, topics) are correlated with each other. In general this will result in the standard errors being understated. Without moving to a hierarchical analysis of sorts for each country that uses the cross-school, within-country variation as a way to estimate country standard errors, there is no straightforward way to obtain the correct standard errors. However, the two-way analyses that provide the umbrella under which these specific country regressions are reported does correctly estimate the standard errors through weighted least-squares procedures. We use the fact that this is significant in the interaction space as

a guarded multivariate test under whose umbrella we interpret these individual country-level analyses. In other words, it is only because the two-way model indicates a statistically significant relationship between these variables at the interaction level that we interpret these results. The same holds for other tables in this chapter as well as for all tables in Chapters Eight and Nine that give regression results for individual countries.

17. The discussion that follows here is based on the fitting of a series of regression models to the raw percent data rather than the transformed data displayed in Figure 6.4.

18. To test the distributional assumptions, the overlapping points in the two distributions were first transformed using the inverse normal function. A linear model was fitted to these points estimating the slope and the intercept. The two distributions can be assumed probabilistically to have come from the same underlying distribution if the slope is equal to 1 and the intercept is equal to 0. Confidence intervals were used to determine whether these two conditions were met. In effect, the test of the intercept was a test of the equality of the means of the two distributions. The test of the slope was a test of the equality of the variances of the two distributions.

19. Several topics could not be tested in this fashion because no countries' content standards did not include the topic. This includes number sets and equations and formulas. Several others (nine) had no overlapping points, making fitting the model impossible. For these, only the means were compared statistically.

20. This was one case where transforming the data made a difference. In addition to the ten significant or marginally significant positive coefficients after transforming the data, in an additional seven countries, α was also positive and statistically significant.

21. See Stevenson & Stigler, 1992; Schmidt et al., 1996.

22. This design called for first selecting mathematics classes and then attempting to track the students (in many cases only some of the students) into their corresponding science classes. The eighth grade science curriculum in many countries involves multiple teachers, each teaching a different discipline. Data on curriculum implementation might not be available from all of them. Thus, the relationships estimated for science that involve teacher implementation might be understated. That is, the real relationships among curricular aspects might be stronger than those indicated by these data. The difficulty is that it is not possible to know from the available data whether this is true.

23. Some support for the notion that some of these results for science are artifactual is found for Japan. As noted earlier, Japan is known for its curricular consistency. The mathematics results are consistent with this notion. However, for science the two relationships involving instructional time are not significant. From what the authors know of Japan (Schmidt et al., 1996), this does not seem likely. That is, one would expect a pattern in science similar to that in mathematics. Secondly, both the nonsignificant relationships in science involve instructional (teacher) time, which is dependent on the sample of science teachers.

24. Schmidt et al., 1996.

25. Walker & Schaffarzick, 1974; Husen, 1982. For a review and summary of the role of opportunity to learn in education research and policy, see Wang, 1998.

26. This conception of OTL derives from considering the two-way structure of OTL as studied in TIMSS. That is, OTL may be considered as a two-dimensional array of topics and curricular indications (aspects). In this way OTL can be defined in terms of the (row) marginal effect (the third concept discussed previously), in terms of cell-specific effects (the first concept discussed previously), and in terms of a set of cells associated with a column (that is, across topics for a single indication of curriculum—the second concept discussed previously). We do not find a reasonable conception for a latent variable defined in terms of the instantiation marginal (cross-topic characterizations of a particular indication).

27. The results discussed in this section are derived from fitting a structural equation model to each topic separately, considering each of the four variables describing coverage of that topic as observed variables ($x = \Lambda_x \xi + e$). The model was fitted using the LISREL program. The χ^2 approximation to the likelihood ratio statistic was used to test the fit of the model to the data.

28. We did not fit a simultaneous structural model for all topics because of the limits imposed by the sample size of only thirty countries.

29. These results were based on the multivariate multiple regression model together with a canonical correlation analysis. The median coefficients of determination values (R^2's) were defined over the five or six topics separately analyzed.

30. Stevenson & Baker, 1991; Stevenson & Baker, 1996.

31. As discussed earlier, there was an inherent ambiguity in the science data. A lack of consistency could be the result of the TIMSS sampling plan and not a true indicator of coherence for a country. Because of this ambiguity, we

decided to do these analyses only for the mathematics data where such an ambiguity was not present.

32. The results summarized in this section come from doing a two-way ANOVA (Analysis of Variance) for each of the twenty topics. The first design variable was whether any of the framework topics associated with the test topic were present or not in a country's content standards. The second design variable was whether the country was centralized or not.

33. Figures 6.10 and 6.11 are constructed so that the area of the square and circle are proportional to the percent of textbook coverage and instructional time, respectively. The percents are transformed by the logarithmic function.

34. The index we used was the coefficient of determination (R^2) from the bivariate regression. An ANOVA was then done on this index with centralization as the design variable.

## 7

A FIRST LOOK AT ACHIEVEMENT

WE HAVE SPENT CONSIDERABLE SPACE discussing the variety and structure of curriculum in Chapters Five and Six. However, all of this would be beside the point of this book were we never to arrive at the relationship of curriculum to achievement. We will examine this relationship in great detail in the remaining chapters. First, however, we need to survey what TIMSS data can reveal about achievement in school science and mathematics. This chapter is that survey. It seeks to prepare the way for the later chapters relating curriculum and achievement.

The TIMSS tests—most relevantly here, the TIMSS Population 2 test for seventh and eighth grade or their equivalents—were designed based on a blueprint that was developed collaboratively involving persons from several participating countries.[1] The blueprint was based on early results from the curriculum analysis of eighth grade science and mathematics textbooks from many of the TIMSS countries. Any such blueprint or design for a cross-national achievement test must be a compromise that will fit each participating country better in some topic areas and worse in others. It is taken for granted that any such test will be fair and unfair in some ways for each country.[2]

In selecting items for the TIMSS tests, there was an inherent trade-off between breadth and depth of coverage among the topic areas of school science and mathematics. The results of textbook analyses and international consensus were only two elements that went into the design of tests that, in the end, inherently represented limited opportunities to assess student achievement because testing time had to be restricted. To maximize insight within these constraints, several areas from the TIMSS mathematics and science frameworks were designated as focal for each TIMSS test—in this case, the Population 2 tests in mathematics and in science.

More test items would be assigned to the test in focal areas to allow separate subscores for each of these areas.

These correspond essentially to the twenty areas of mathematics and seventeen areas of science (for Population 2 students) that have been reported and discussed elsewhere.[4] In this book, we have designated these as the tested areas (see Chapter Three).[5] They served as the basis for earlier country-by-topic analyses and many subsequent analyses already presented in this book.

The original reporting of the TIMMS Population 2 results was based on total scores—one for mathematics and one for science.[5] The scores were reported in terms of a statistically constructed numerical scale.[6] Using the item design as laid out in the blueprint, thirty-seven country-level subscores (twenty in mathematics and seventeen in science) were formed as described in Chapter Three.[7]

These types of scores allow us to examine topic-specific achievement. We have argued elsewhere that greater topic specificity is related to greater sensitivity to the effects of curriculum. Cross-national differences in curriculum OTL are likely to impact more specific tests than less specific ones.[8]

The design of TIMSS permits estimates at the country level of achievement gain as opposed to being able only to estimate the comparative status (rankings) of countries. This was discussed earlier in Chapter Three. The design did not provide for a true longitudinal study with sampling of the same students at two points in time (beginning and end of the school year). Instead, it provided for a quasi-longitudinal study that, by using seventh grade results as a surrogate pretest measure for eighth grade students, allowed estimation of national eighth grade gain.[9]

This estimate of gain thus serves as a measure of grade-specific learning taking place during eighth grade. This focus on gain rather than status, coupled with a focus on topic-specific rather than global scores, enables us to estimate the amount of growth taking place in each country during eighth grade in each of thirty-seven specific areas of eighth grade mathematics and science. This should provide measures in which the sensitivity to curriculum effects is maximized, given the limitations of the TIMSS study design.

This is an important feature, especially in the following chapter in which we relate curricular opportunity in the eighth grade to the learning taking place in that grade. If we were to relate curricular opportunity to achievement status rather than gain, it would be necessary to account for the curriculum for all grades up through the eighth grade.[10] Such a cumulative indication of curriculum is likely to make it more difficult to detect specific impacts of curriculum on learning.

In this chapter we summarize the nature of the achievement gains across countries and contrast this with achievement status (rankings) at both seventh and eight grades. We also seek to characterize some of the measurement properties of achievement gains in contrast to status indicators.

Achievement Gains from Seventh to Eighth Grade

Figure 7.1 presents data representing the distribution of the estimated gain in eighth grade for twenty tested topic areas in mathematics and seventeen tested areas in science. These were reported elsewhere in terms of displaying country rankings compared to U.S. performance.[11]

The measurement unit (metric) of the gain scores for the tested topic areas is the difference between the seventh and eighth grade in the average percent correct averaged over all items used to measure that tested area. The distribution is for all thirty countries for which the gain-score data could be estimated. This allows a comparison across the distributions for each of the tested topic areas. From this we can identify the tested topic areas in which students (on average nationally) are learning more and less during eighth grade.

MATHEMATICS. In mathematics, the greatest amount of learning averaged over all participating countries occurred in the following five top areas: equations and formulas; perimeter, area, and volume; polygons and circles; congruence and similarity; and three-dimensional geometry and transformations. It is interesting to contrast these top five gain areas with the five topic areas that received the most curricular emphasis as seen in the figures and tables of Chapter Five.

The topic receiving the most curricular emphasis in eighth grade mathematics as defined by all of the aspects (indications) of curriculum used to measure emphasis was equations and formulas. This, as noted previously, was the tested topic area in which the largest amount of learning (estimated national gain) took place during the eighth grade year.

Four out of five of the top gain topics were also among the top five topics emphasized as intended by the content standards of the participating countries. The only difference between the two lists was that a large number of countries intended coverage in functions, but the average gain on the TIMSS test was not as great as that for the top five gain tested areas.

Figure 7.1.　Distributions of Achievement Gains Across Countries in Eighth Grade Mathematics and Science.

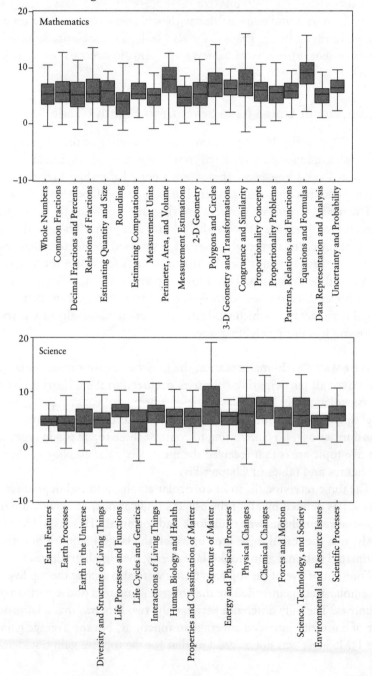

Four out of five of the top gain topics (not the same four) were also among the top five topics emphasized by percent of textbook space allocated to them. The only exception was congruence and similarity, for which large gains were not associated with comparably larger amounts of textbook space. Functions were given a larger amount of textbook space but did not show correspondingly larger achievement gains.

This indicates—at least at the rough indication of the top five topic areas—that there appears to have been a relationship averaged over countries between curriculum emphasis (as inclusion in content standards and proportion of textbook space) and estimated national gain in tested areas. There could be many reasons for the two exceptions noted previously. Some anecdotal information suggests that the items for the functions tested area might not have been difficult enough to reflect the real growth that might have taken place and instead suffered from ceiling effects that suppressed the measure of gain.[12]

There is also an assumption that the proportion of textbook space allocated for a topic is directly proportional to the importance of that topic compared with others. It assumes that textbook space allocations work with the same proportionality for other topics. This may only roughly be the case; the amount of textbook space needed to produce significant gains in the tested area of congruence and similarity might not have been as great as that required for other topics. This would at least partially explain its top five emphasis in content standards but not in textbook space compared with its top five status in estimated national achievement gain.

The same five tested topic areas that had on average the largest gains were also the ones that had the greatest variability in gains across countries. A similar conclusion was made in Chapter Five in terms of curriculum variables. This certainly suggests topics that are in the focus on average across countries and profiting from that focus by being associated with greater gains. It also suggests that such focus topics were subject to greater variability among the participating countries than were less central topics.

There was also substantial variation on some of the arithmetic topics. This reflects that even though those topics were not typically the focus of eighth grade instruction, learning was still taking place with respect to those topics. The amount of such gain, however, varied appreciably across countries, from as little as no gains to gains large enough to rival those of the top five tested areas.

SCIENCE The first generalization that seems obvious when comparing the science gains to the mathematics gains as given in Figure 7.1 is that the median gains were more uniform among the science topics than the median gains were among the mathematics topics.

For science, the tested topic areas with the largest gains were structure of matter, chemical changes, interactions of living things, life processes and functions, and physical changes. Three of these five topics were from physics and chemistry, whereas the other two were from biology. The variability in gains over countries is the largest for three of the top five gain topics—structure of matter, physical changes, and chemical changes. All three are from physics and chemistry.

Comparing the five tested topic areas with the greatest gains for eighth grade science to the topic areas that received greater opportunities to learn does not reveal the same kind of consistency as was revealed for mathematics. None of the top five gain topics were among the top five as emphasized either in content standards or textbook space allocations. There was overlap for the top five lists only for gain and national average percent of teachers covering a topic area. That overlap was only for one topic area (structure of matter).

Why is there this lack of consistency between curricular emphasis and achievement gains even at this rough indicator of top five lists? Possibly, of course, there is no relationship between curriculum and achievement gains, but that seems unlikely given the strong results for mathematics. What might be different for science? One possible explanation is that if there is less agreement across countries as to which topics to emphasize, then the stability of the means is less in science and the top five will be unstable. As a result, overlap becomes more a matter of chance. The difference may be linked to our earlier discussion of the differences in sampling for mathematics and science classes. This explanation seems inadequate, however, because the lack of relationship holds also for content standards and textbook space. The classroom sampling procedure does not affect these.

It also seems likely that this is not related to the presence of different types of science courses for eighth graders. These differences were also taken into account in the sampling of eighth grade textbooks to examine space allocation and in the gathering of content standards for the eighth grade in science.

Another possibility is that the TIMSS Population 2 test for science was not in enough depth in these areas to be sufficiently sensitive to reflect learning that was taking place in eighth grade. This is somewhat like the possibility considered for the tested area of functions in mathematics. This might be true if science were tested as isolated bits of knowledge, rather than tapping into coherent understanding of larger relationships or more complex performance knowledge. It would be especially likely to take place for topics that had been covered at least somewhat in earlier grades.

For now it seems that science must simply appear less predictable than mathematics at this gross level. This will be explored in detail, however, in the next chapter, where we will explore these relationships between gain and curriculum more fully in the context of the country-by-topic two-way analyses. This will enable us to determine if the general pattern noted above holds at the marginal (topic) level or at the interaction level (related to topic and country differences simultaneously).

Another way to examine the data for gains in tested topic areas is to look at the distributions of gains averaged over topics within a country. However, the average gain over topics for a country is essentially equivalent to the total gain for that country, which is reported elsewhere. Because the focus of this volume is on curricularly sensitive measurement, we refer interested readers to other reports that rank the countries on total gain scores and give their distributional characteristics.

Topic-by-Country Differences in Achievement Gains

How consistent are gains for different topics and for different participating countries? Does the gain for a specific topic tend to be the same across all countries? Does the gain for a specific country tend to be the same for all topics? Are the gains different within a country for different topics, and does this pattern of topic differences itself differ for different countries? We have already suggested that the latter is likely the case—that there are topic-by-country interactions among the estimated achievement gains (given high variability for some high gain topics).

Figure 7.2 gives the distributions of the cell means (mean gains) for each country and topic combination for both mathematics and science. From these data, it appears that the average gains are around 6 percent for both mathematics and science. They are also somewhat symmetrical, especially for mathematics (although science is somewhat positively skewed). This reflects the presence of some very large gains for certain topics in particular countries in science.

Figure 7.2. Distributions of Achievement Gains over All Topics and Countries for Eighth Grade Mathematics and Science.

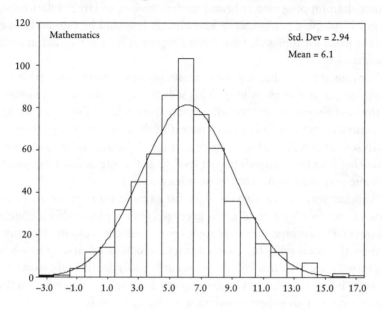

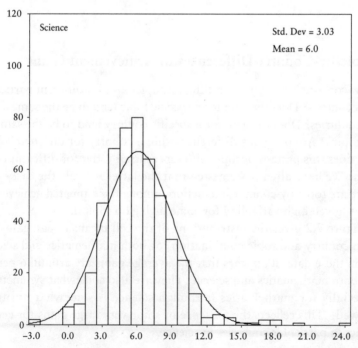

Table 7.1 and Table 7.2 present the median polish data and the values of the residuals for country-by-topic combinations that are four percent or larger in absolute value for mathematics and science respectively. This value has practical significance since the mean gain and standard deviation in both areas is six percent and three percent respectively. The marked residuals indicate gains that deviate significantly from what was typical for that topic across countries and from what was typical for that country across topics. These comparatively large estimated "residuals" or "deviations" indicate the presence of interaction effects.

In mathematics (Table 7.1), all but three topics had significant deviations in gain for at least one country: estimating quantity and size, proportionality problems, and uncertainty and probability. More than half of the countries had significant deviations for at least one topic. Some of the residual gains were particularly large—6 percent (two standard deviations) or more. These occur in seven topic areas—four geometry topics, one measurement topic, and two fraction topics. The four geometry topics represent all of the tested geometry for TIMSS Population 2. In fact, the largest number of residual gains of 4 percent or more occur for the same four geometry topics.

The topic with the largest number of residual gains exceeding 7 percent is one of the geometry topics (congruence and similarity). Three of the seven deviations for this topic were 7 percent or more. For two of the countries (Japan and the Belgian Flemish-language educational system), the large residual gains were positive, which implies that these two educational systems posted mean gains far above what would have been expected for the topic of congruence and similarity and for what would have been expected for a typical tested area in their countries. Bulgaria showed a large residual gain that was negative; that is, a gain far less than would have been expected for a typical country in congruence and similarity and far less than would have been expected for a typical tested area in Bulgaria. In fact, this was the largest negative residual gain over all countries and topics. The largest residual gain was positive (in Switzerland for two-dimensional geometry). These results imply that there was a great deal of cross-country variation in the amount of geometry that was learned in eighth grade.

Table 7.2 presents the unusually large (in absolute value) residual gains for eighth grade science. Only one physics topic did not show at least one significant residual gain—a surprising deviation from expectations. All but five countries (South Africa, the United States, Canada, New Zealand, and Germany) had significantly large residual gains for at least one topic area.

Table 7.1. Median Polish of Topic by Country Gain Data (Eighth Grade Mathematics).

Country	Whole Numbers	Common Fractions	Decimal Fractions and Percents	Relations of Fractions	Estimating Quantity and Size	Rounding	Estimating Computations	Measurement Units	Perimeter, Area, and Volume	Measurement Estimations and Errors	2-D Geometry
Australia											
Austria											
Belgium (Fl)											
Belgium (Fr)											
Bulgaria						5.0			−5.6		
Canada											
Colombia											
Cyprus									4.1		
Czech Republic											
Denmark											
France		4.0									
Germany											
Greece											
Hong Kong			5.5								
Hungary											
Iceland							4.0				
Iran								6.0			
Ireland											5.0
Japan											
Korea	−4.0										
Latvia											
Netherland											
New Zealand											4.0
Norway											
Portugal	4.5										
Romania									−4.0		
Russian Federation											
Singapore						−4.8					
Slovak Republic											
Slovenia											
South Africa											
Spain	6.0										
Sweden		4.5	6.8			5.2					
Switzerland											10.0
Scotland											
USA											

Country	Polygons and Circles	3-D Geometry and Transformations	Congruence and Similarity	Proportionality Concepts	Proportionality Problems	Patterns, Relations, and Functions	Equations and Formulas	Data Representation and Analysis	Uncertainty and Probability
Australia									
Austria			−4.5						
Belgium (Fl)		4.0	8.0						
Belgium (Fr)		5.0							
Bulgaria		4.0	−7.0	−4.0		4.0			
Canada									
Colombia									
Cyprus									
Czech Republic									
Denmark									
France			−4.0				4.4		
Germany									
Greece			4.8					5.5	
Hong Kong									
Hungary									
Iceland			−4.0						
Iran									
Ireland			4.0						
Japan		5.0	9.0						
Korea									
Latvia		9.0	4.0						
Netherland							4.4		
New Zealand									
Norway									
Portugal		−4.5							
Romania			−5.0						
Russian Federation		5.0							
Singapore			4.0						
Slovak Republic									
Slovenia									
South Africa									
Spain		−7.0	−6.0						
Sweden									
Switzerland		5.0	6.0						
Scotland									
USA									

Table 7.2. Median Polish of Topic by Country Gain Data (Eighth Grade Science).

Country	Earth Features	Earth Processes	Earth in the Universe	Diversity and Structure of Living Things	Life Processes and Functions	Life Cycles and Genetics	Interactions of Living Things	Human Biology and Health
Australia								
Austria								
Belgium (Fl)					4.0		4.0	
Belgium (Fr)								
Bulgaria							−14.0	
Canada								
Colombia								
Cyprus								
Czech Republic		7.0						
Denmark			6.0					
France							−6.0	
Germany								
Greece						−4.0		
Hong Kong	4.0							
Hungary			6.0					
Iceland								
Iran					−4.0	−4.0		
Ireland								4.0
Japan				6.0		−4.0		
Korea	4.0							
Latvia		−5.0						
Netherland		−4.0						
New Zealand								
Norway							−4.0	−5.0
Portugal	−5.0							
Romania							5.0	
Russian Federation		−4.0	−4.0					
Singapore			−4.0					5.0
Slovak Republic		5.0						
Slovenia			5.0					
South Africa								
Spain								
Sweden							−5.0	
Switzerland								
Scotland			−4.0					
USA								

	Properties and Classification of Matter	Structure of Matter	Energy and Physical Processes	Physical Changes	Chemical Changes	Forces and Motion	Science, Technology, and Society	Environmental and Resource Issues	Scientific Processes
Australia				−4.0					
Austria							4.0		
Belgium (Fl)		−4.5			5.0	−5.0			
Belgium (Fr)		−4.5			−4.0		4.0		
Bulgaria		6.5		−5.0					5.0
Canada									
Colombia		−4.5			−5.0		5.0		
Cyprus							−5.0		
Czech Republic							−4.0		
Denmark						−4.0			
France		−4.5		5.0	−4.0		4.0		
Germany									
Greece		7.5							
Hong Kong		−5.5		−4.0			4.0		
Hungary				4.0			−4.0		
Iceland		−5.5				−6.0	4.0		
Iran							4.0		
Ireland									
Japan				−4.0	7.0				
Korea				−8.0	5.0				
Latvia									
Netherland						5.0			
New Zealand									
Norway									
Portugal	5.0	5.5		4.0	6.0				
Romania									
Russian Federation		9.5				8.0	−6.0	−4.0	
Singapore	−4.0	13.5		−9.0	−4.0				5.0
Slovak Republic					4.0				
Slovenia		−6.5							
South Africa									
Spain		4.5		5.0					
Sweden		7.5							
Switzerland				−4.0					
Scotland		−5.5		−8.0					
USA									

It may be worth noting that the four countries across both mathematics and science that did not have any significant residual gains in at least one topic were British-influenced countries (Canada, the United States, New Zealand, and South Africa). Essentially, these countries produced only the expected gains appropriate to their national median gains and the median gains for each topic in either mathematics or science or both. Whether this represents the fit of the tests to the curricula of these countries or something more significant remains to be seen.

The science topics with the greatest number of significant residual gains (6 percent or more) were all physics topics: structure of matter, physical changes, chemical changes, and forces and motions. Structure of matter was the topic with the greatest number of significant residuals. There were fifteen such significant residuals out of thirty-six countries for which data were available. Science, technology, and society was the other topic reflecting an usually high number of large residual gains (although none were larger than the 6 percent absolute value criterion).

Consistent with the distribution of gains for science portrayed in Figure 7.2, there were some very large residual gains in Table 7.2. One residual gain that was large but negative was for Bulgaria on interactions of living things. Another but positive large residual was for Singapore on the structure of matter.

The results for this section all point to the presence of country differences in achievement gain. They also point to country differences that vary with the topic. That is, they were neither particularly consistent for topics or for countries. There were significant interaction effects of country and topic—as seen by unusual residual gains. This gives results for gain in eighth grade mathematics and science that are very consistent with those for curriculum discussed in Chapter Five (where significant interaction effects were also noted). The next chapter examines whether the two patterns of interaction effects (curriculum and achievement gains) are related to each other. However, it is clear at this point that learning (gains) varies both by country and by topic. This is consistent with country rankings that vary by topic.[13]

Achievement Status at the Eighth Grade

The focus of the work in this book is on the relationship of curriculum to learning. For reasons already discussed, this leads us to focus on achievement gain and not achievement status (comparative rankings among participating countries). However, in this section we provide a brief examination of eighth grade achievement status for the tested areas described in the previous section.

Figure 7.3 displays the distributions of achievement scores for each of the twenty tested areas of Population 2 mathematics and each of the seventeen tested areas of Population 2 science. This exhibit corresponds to the one for achievement gains given earlier (Figure 7.1). For mathematics, the achievement scores vary appreciably among the topics.[14] The tested areas with the highest scores were rounding and data representation and analysis.[15]

Only one of the five tested areas with the greatest achievement gains (as discussed in the last section) is among the tested areas of eighth grade mathematics with the top five achievement scores—three-dimensional geometry and transformations. This was both a high-achievement and high-gain tested area. In contrast, equations and formulas, the topic with the largest gain among the tested areas of mathematics, was among the five topics with the lowest achievement scores at eighth grade. Clearly, status and gain measures are very different aspects of achievement for mathematics.

The general conclusions for science are comparable. None of the five areas showing the greatest gains was among the five topics with the largest average achievement scores at eighth grade. In fact, structure of matter, which had the largest gain at eighth grade of any of the seventeen tested areas, had the lowest average topic achievement score. The topics with the highest average achievement—the best ranking in terms of status— were life cycles and genetics and forces and motion. Once again in science the two measures—achievement status and gain—reflect very different patterns and support different conclusions.

We did a median polish for the eighth grade average achievement scores. There were major interaction effects for both mathematics and science. For science, the topic displaying the largest number of significantly large residuals was the structure of matter. In mathematics, however, the topics with high residuals were on the whole not the same for achievement status as they were for achievement gain.

Relationships of Achievement Across Topics

The content of school mathematics and science has been divided into discrete topics to allow investigation of differing emphasis and treatment given to differing topics. However, it would be unnatural if these topics— and, as a result, achievement in them—were unrelated in student learning. In this section we examine the relationship of achievement scores in

Figure 7.3. Distributions of Achievement Scores for Tested Areas (Eighth Grade Mathematics and Science).

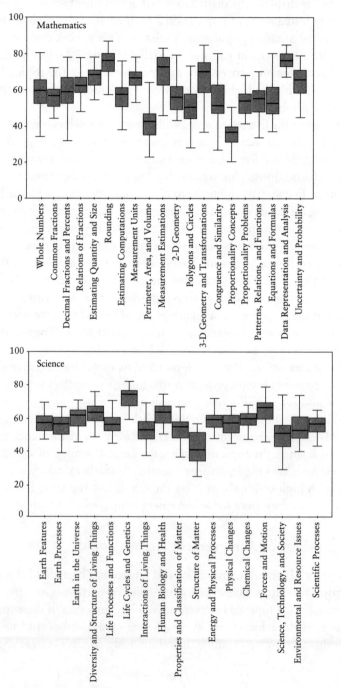

one topic to those in another. We wish to know how correlated achievement is between topics across all the participating countries.

Relationship in Achievement Gains

The correlations discussed here are among the country-level achievement scores for particular topics only (and not among individuals). Our focus here and in the next chapter is to characterize country-level relationships. Our estimations of the strength of these relationships—either between topics or between curriculum and achievement—at the country level do not represent relationships at the individual level or at the classroom level within a country.[16] Interpreting these correlations as if they applied to individuals or to classrooms would be a logical fallacy. We caution readers to think only of these as cross-country correlations of achievement. What we are attempting to understand here is not individual learning but the behavior of educational systems.

Table 7.3 displays the correlation matrices for the observed achievement gain score for topics in mathematics and science estimated for the eighth grade at the country level. In mathematics, the average correlation between topics was .46 and ranged from −.12 to .88. The range from the bottom to top of the middle 50 percent of correlations was from .32 to .61. That is, eliminating the highest and lowest 25 percent of correlations and thus the most extreme values, half of the correlations still range from just over .3 to just over .6.

For science, the average correlation was about two-thirds as large (.28), ranging from −.25 to .76. The middle half of the correlations ranged between .14 and .41. Clearly, the correlations of gain for topics on average were larger for mathematics than for science. This implies that the learning outcomes of national systems took place in eighth grade in different topic areas of mathematics in a more interrelated way than was true for science. This seems to make sense, given the more hierarchical nature of school mathematics and given that the science test ranged over four different but related science disciplines.

The preponderance of the correlations for mathematics and science topics pooled ranged between .11 and .61. This indicates that learning in one topic area as reflected by estimated achievement gain was related to learning in another topic. However, it also indicates that for many pairs of topics, the relationship was moderate at best and even very weak in other cases. This likely reflects consistency with the notion that the effects of curriculum—effects that vary across countries—are for different profiles of coverage and that these different profiles likely would create differential

Table 7.3. Correlations Between Topics for Observed Achievement Gain Across Countries (Eighth Grade Mathematics and Science).

Mathematics

Topic	Whole Numbers	Common Fractions	Decimal Fractions and Percents	Relations of Fractions	Estimating Quantity and Size	Rounding	Estimating Computations	Measurement Units	Perimeter, Area, and Volume	Measurement Estimations and Errors
Mathematics										
Whole numbers	1.00									
Common fractions	.64	1.00								
Decimal fractions and percents	.61	.50	1.00							
Relations of fractions	.61	.88	.68	1.00						
Estimating quantity and size	.58	.70	.42	.67	1.00					
Rounding	.53	.48	.75	.58	.41	1.00				
Estimating computations	.58	.65	.75	.73	.55	.78	1.00			
Measurement units	.55	.61	.59	.61	.65	.61	.79	1.00		
Perimeter, area, and volume	.60	.57	.69	.71	.65	.45	.62	.63	1.00	
Measurement estimations and errors	.54	.57	.43	.53	.76	.50	.51	.67	.50	1.00
2-D geometry	.30	.43	.20	.36	.64	.15	.37	.54	.41	.58
Polygons and circles	.06	.19	.43	.32	.19	.21	.36	.50	.47	.29
3-D geometry and transformations	.07	.26	-.12	.20	.53	-.12	-.02	.12	.25	.48
Congruence and similarity	.17	.03	.19	.03	.14	-.03	.24	.32	.25	.10
Proportionality concepts	.54	.58	.68	.75	.55	.37	.63	.59	.86	.41
Proportionality problems	.56	.51	.67	.65	.48	.27	.48	.46	.64	.31
Patterns, relations, and functions	.64	.52	.45	.52	.65	.30	.52	.58	.69	.49
Equations and formulas	.53	.70	.43	.67	.59	.25	.41	.43	.65	.61
Data representation and analysis	.56	.49	.28	.41	.71	.41	.55	.66	.48	.58
Uncertainty and probability	.50	.73	.50	.78	.58	.46	.69	.65	.63	.45
Science										
Earth features	.24	.32	.53	.42	.33	.47	.39	.35	.46	.50
Earth processes	.70	.66	.53	.59	.41	.48	.53	.37	.47	.25
Earth in the universe	.54	.35	.47	.44	.33	.48	.41	.43	.44	.51
Diversity and structure of living things	.42	.19	.19	.26	.28	.16	.24	.35	.30	.31
Life processes and functions	.04	.16	.01	.05	.19	-.01	.18	.25	.02	.24
Life cycles and genetics	.24	.24	.24	.31	.24	.14	.20	.33	.35	.36
Interactions of living things	-.16	.04	-.01	-.03	.25	-.03	.17	.23	.15	.00
Human biology and health	.11	-.13	-.16	-.18	.17	-.20	-.11	.12	.06	.27
Properties and classification of matter	.35	.22	.38	.22	.29	.42	.22	.30	.24	.41
Structure of matter	.20	.24	.07	.26	.44	.10	.22	.34	.21	.33
Energy and physical processes	.40	.21	.32	.26	.53	.16	.20	.32	.59	.49
Physical changes	.58	.43	.45	.43	.45	.62	.44	.45	.47	.59
Chemical changes	.21	.03	.13	.06	.27	.15	.13	.14	.18	.21
Forces and motion	.24	.13	.15	.21	.31	.21	.07	.23	.24	.54
Science, technology, and society	.04	.19	-.05	.02	-.04	-.01	.04	.11	-.09	.11
Environmental and resource issues	.23	.17	-.08	.03	.02	-.18	.06	.12	.01	.11
Scientific processes	.32	.13	.19	.11	.34	.14	.17	.25	.34	.36

Mathematics

Topic	2-D Geometry	Polygons and Circles	3-D Geometry and Transformations	Congruence and Similarity	Proportionality Concepts	Proportionality Problems	Patterns, Relations, and Functions	Equations and Formulas	Data Representation and Analysis	Uncertainty and Probability
Mathematics										
Whole numbers										
Common fractions										
Decimal fractions and percents										
Relations of fractions										
Estimating quantity and size										
Rounding										
Estimating computations										
Measurement units										
Perimeter, area, and volume										
Measurement estimations and errors										
2-D geometry	1.00									
Polygons and circles	.49	1.00								
3-D geometry and transformations	.64	.24	1.00							
Congruence and similarity	.42	.64	.18	1.00						
Proportionality concepts	.34	.52	.16	.30	1.00					
Proportionality problems	.21	.40	-.01	.31	.82	1.00				
Patterns, relations, and functions	.48	.29	.43	.30	.64	.57	1.00			
Equations and formulas	.48	.32	.46	.10	.54	.40	.53	1.00		
Data representation and analysis	.46	.05	.42	.14	.29	.21	.75	.43	1.00	
Uncertainty and probability	.35	.33	.26	.07	.61	.54	.67	.60	.60	1.00
Science										
Earth features	.13	.37	.11	-.06	.38	.26	.19	.37	.25	.28
Earth processes	.19	.02	.07	.11	.38	.36	.43	.47	.40	.43
Earth in the universe	.27	.22	.11	-.08	.23	.17	.39	.52	.37	.53
Diversity and structure of living things	.16	.32	.22	.36	.23	.31	.37	.16	.30	.36
Life processes and functions	.23	.20	.21	.39	-.05	-.02	.08	-.03	.19	.17
Life cycles and genetics	-.06	.07	.11	-.13	.27	.22	.24	.18	.19	.45
Interactions of living things	.39	.13	.13	.23	-.04	-.06	.28	-.07	.33	.13
Human biology and health	.19	.06	.34	.16	-.06	.03	.20	-.07	.26	.02
Properties and classification of matter	.25	.13	.24	.03	-.01	.05	.30	.32	.40	.26
Structure of matter	.24	.07	.36	.23	.07	.17	.32	.06	.53	.28
Energy and physical processes	.34	.24	.48	.27	.34	.33	.68	.40	.54	.32
Physical changes	.20	.10	.19	-.10	.20	.13	.48	.55	.55	.49
Chemical changes	.15	.22	.17	.35	.16	.32	.26	.01	.15	.09
Forces and motion	.21	-.05	.33	-.24	.06	.04	.29	.35	.42	.13
Science, technology, and society	.11	.08	.16	.04	-.20	-.20	.05	.25	.29	.19
Environmental and resource issues	.18	-.01	.09	.20	-.07	-.03	.18	.09	.32	.07
Scientific processes	.08	.02	.27	.09	.00	.03	.35	.24	.51	.32

(continued)

Table 7.3. (continued)

Topic	Earth Features	Earth Processes	Earth in the Universe	Diversity and Structure of Living Things	Life Processes and Functions	Life Cycles and Genetics	Interactions of Living Things	Human Biology and Health	Properties and Classification of Matter
Mathematics									
Whole numbers									
Common fractions									
Decimal fractions and percents									
Relations of fractions									
Estimating quantity and size									
Rounding									
Estimating computations									
Measurement units									
Perimeter, area, and volume									
Measurement estimations and errors									
2-D geometry									
Polygons and circles									
3-D geometry and transformations									
Congruence and similarity									
Proportionality concepts									
Proportionality problems									
Patterns, relations, and functions									
Equations and formulas									
Data representation and analysis									
Uncertainty and probability									
Science									
Earth features	1.00								
Earth processes	.28	1.00							
Earth in the universe	.33	.23	1.00						
Diversity and structure of living things	.14	.24	.35	1.00					
Life processes and functions	.10	.14	.01	.58	1.00				
Life cycles and genetics	.24	.18	.35	.41	.31	1.00			
Interactions of living things	−.09	.04	−.06	−.02	.41	−.02	1.00		
Human biology and health	.13	−.11	.09	.68	.50	.35	.04	1.00	
Properties and classification of matter	.16	.20	.47	.38	.27	.13	.20	.24	1.00
Structure of matter	.13	.15	.08	.63	.51	.38	.29	.60	.39
Energy and physical processes	.22	.30	.28	.48	.30	.41	.39	.38	.56
Physical changes	.23	.35	.67	.30	−.01	.28	.05	.01	.76
Chemical changes	−.09	−.03	.00	.61	.24	−.09	.06	.43	.43
Forces and motion	.46	−.01	.47	.21	−.07	.22	−.16	.41	.33
Science, technology, and society	.35	.20	.19	.21	.51	.06	.16	.26	.33
Environmental and resource issues	.22	.26	.01	.34	.50	.20	.23	.46	.18
Scientific processes	.24	.23	.36	.55	.41	.58	.22	.60	.58

Science

Topic	Structure of Matter	Energy and Physical Processes	Physical Changes	Chemical Changes	Forces and Motion	Science, Technology, and Society	Environmental and Resource Issues	Scientific Processes
Mathematics								
Whole numbers								
Common fractions								
Decimal fractions and percents								
Relations of fractions								
Estimating quantity and size								
Rounding								
Estimating computations								
Measurement units								
Perimeter, area, and volume								
Measurement estimations and errors								
2-D geometry								
Polygons and circles								
3-D geometry and transformations								
Congruence and similarity								
Proportionality concepts								
Proportionality problems								
Patterns, relations, and functions								
Equations and formulas								
Data representation and analysis								
Uncertainty and probability								
Science								
Earth features								
Earth processes								
Earth in the universe								
Diversity and structure of living things								
Life processes and functions								
Life cycles and genetics								
Interactions of living things								
Human biology and health								
Properties and classification of matter								
Structure of matter	1.00							
Energy and physical processes	.55	1.00						
Physical changes	.22	.58	1.00					
Chemical changes	.47	.45	.30	1.00				
Forces and motion	.42	.32	.33	.02	1.00			
Science, technology, and society	.18	.02	.10	−.25	.23	1.00		
Environmental and resource issues	.50	.25	−.00	−.08	.24	.64	1.00	
Scientific processes	.67	.69	.54	.32	.33	.26	.44	1.00

learning rather than uniform learning among topics. Because these profiles vary among countries, the correlation of learning in topics across countries would be weaker than if the profiles were more uniform across countries.

The presence of negative correlations (although not large and although present more between science topics than between mathematics topics) suggests that achievement gain reflects opportunity to learn and is itself, like opportunity to learn, a limited resource. Limited resources show their effects by the necessity of distributing themselves among areas, and thus receiving more in one area typically implies receiving less in another. In that sense, gains reflect allocations of limited resources. They reflect trade-offs at the national level in which emphasizing one area of learning comes at the expense of another, at least in the same year of schooling.

In general, these correlations support the conclusion in the previous section that learning varied across topics and across countries. These results are also consistent with the implications for learning that Chapter Five's results suggest. If learning (achievement gain) is related to curriculum opportunities and those opportunities varied across countries, then a correlation matrix of gain scores would likely be comprised of varied and mostly moderately sized correlations.

Table 7.3 also shows the correlations at the country level of the twenty tested mathematics topic areas and the seventeen tested science topic areas. These data can be used to explore the question of whether learning in the various topics of mathematics was related to learning in the various topics of science during eighth grade. Because mathematics serves as the language of science and is essential to some science areas, it seems likely that learning certain topics in science requires at least knowledge of some mathematics topics. As a result, one might expect at least some correlations among the science and mathematics topics across disciplinary lines.

The typical correlation of gain in a science topic with gain in a mathematics topic averaged over all 340 pairs was not very large (.22). It is interesting to note, however, that this average correlation is only slightly different from the average correlation in gain over all pairs of science topics. That is, on average at the country level, gains in eighth grade mathematics appear as strongly interrelated to gains in eighth grade science as gains appear interrelated among the tested science areas. This is consistent with the hypothesis about the relationship of school mathematics and science stated previously. However, it is also possible that these correlations simply reflect common practice of what topic areas are covered at different grade levels and what is covered in those topic areas at a particular grade. The fact that certain science contents are typically covered in the same grade with certain mathematics contents might reflect chance producing commonality of choice rather than disciplinary interconnections. However, it seems that even these less intentional connections would be affected by more indirect pedagogical concerns.

Some of the correlations were very high (.6 to .7). This may reflect important linkages between learning in mathematics and in science. An example of this is gain in functions and gain in energy and physical processes (.68), which one could imagine might reflect the necessity of that particular kind of mathematics to do that particular kind of science at the desired level. Other strong correlations might well reflect simple coincidence, such as the correlation between whole numbers and earth processes. Only a more qualitative investigation of the specific contents could reveal more detailed hypotheses.

Relationships in Eighth Grade Achievement Status

Now let us examine the same type of relationship between topics but for status (overall scores that provide rankings among countries) at the eighth grade. This will allow us to contrast these results with the similar results for estimated achievement gain at eighth grade.

We estimated two sets of results for eighth grade achievement status. One set of correlations is based on the observed (reported) scores for each country in each of the topic areas. The second set estimates the correlations among the topics for country scores as if they had no measurement error associated with them. These correlations would be truer in describing the relationship among topics over countries (these results are not presented as a display but are summarized in the following discussion). This estimation procedure is based on classical psychometrics.[17]

Table 7.4 gives the country-level correlations between all pairs of tested areas at eighth grade for the observed scores. The correlations between mathematics topics for status are appreciably higher than those for gain as found in Table 7.3. Most of the correlations reflecting status were above .80. The true score correlations are even higher (as classical psychometric theory would suggest), mostly above .90.

The same basic conclusions hold for eighth grade science, as can be seen in Table 7.5. The correlations were appreciably higher for the observed scores than for the gains but not as high as for the observed (status) scores in mathematics. Most of the correlations for status for science topics were greater than .60. The lower correlations for science again likely reflect the fact that the science test for TIMSS Population 2 was made up of content from four different science disciplines.

Table 7.4. Correlations Between Topics for Observed Achievement Scores (Eighth Grade Mathematics).

Topic	Whole Numbers	Common Fractions	Decimal Fractions and Percents	Relations of Fractions	Estimating Quantity and Size	Rounding	Estimating Computations	Measurement Units
Whole numbers	1.00							
Common fractions	.89	1.00						
Decimal fractions and percents	.91	.85	1.00					
Relations of fractions	.85	.94	.87	1.00				
Estimating quantity and size	.78	.81	.86	.91	1.00			
Rounding	.66	.70	.79	.82	.86	1.00		
Estimating computations	.78	.83	.82	.89	.92	.92	1.00	
Measurement units	.88	.84	.85	.85	.86	.74	.82	1.00
Perimeter, area, and volume	.85	.93	.83	.87	.73	.62	.76	.79
Measurement estimations and errors	.76	.74	.84	.84	.95	.85	.88	.86
2-D geometry	.82	.89	.86	.86	.80	.69	.79	.77
Polygons and circles	.77	.84	.76	.78	.59	.51	.61	.69
3-D geometry and transformations	.81	.83	.89	.86	.88	.74	.78	.83
Congruence and similarity	.77	.81	.80	.77	.62	.57	.62	.70
Proportionality concepts	.79	.92	.77	.88	.73	.67	.80	.73
Proportionality problems	.90	.95	.92	.92	.83	.73	.83	.86
Patterns, relations, and functions	.85	.89	.84	.87	.84	.75	.86	.77
Equations and formulas	.88	.92	.89	.83	.72	.63	.73	.77
Data representation and analysis	.77	.76	.80	.87	.95	.82	.85	.86
Uncertainty and probability	.71	.87	.71	.93	.88	.80	.86	.77

The previous discussion and sets of data make it clear that achievement status and gain were not the same thing for these countries and topics. The distributions in the first section of this chapter reflect this, as do the correlations among the topics. One of the arguments used against the reporting of subscores in cross-national reports is that the correlations among them—the scores for specific tested topic areas—are so high that a report of total scores is adequate and subscores for tested areas are merely redundant. Without analyzing the merits of that argument directly here, suffice it to say that these data show that this argument clearly is not as relevant when dealing with gains.

Perimeter, Area, and Volume	Measurement Estimations and Errors	2-D Geometry	Polygons and Circles	3-D Geometry and Transformations	Congruence and Similarity	Proportionality Concepts	Proportionality Problems	Patterns, Relations, and Functions	Equations and Formulas	Data Representation and Analysis	Uncertainty and Probability
1.00											
.64	1.00										
.93	.72	1.00									
.87	.54	.85	1.00								
.79	.79	.87	.76	1.00							
.89	.55	.88	.95	.79	1.00						
.95	.64	.89	.83	.72	.83	1.00					
.96	.77	.94	.87	.89	.88	.91	1.00				
.85	.77	.94	.78	.87	.79	.87	.90	1.00			
.92	.65	.93	.89	.82	.89	.86	.94	.89	1.00		
.66	.92	.73	.54	.84	.58	.68	.77	.80	.64	1.00	
.73	.81	.76	.63	.76	.59	.81	.79	.82	.70	.87	1.00

Reliability of Subscores for Tested Areas

All test measurements contain error. That is an uncontested commonplace of test theory and testing. How much measurement error is contained in a test is an important characteristic of the test and is captured in traditional psychometric estimates of the test's reliability. In this section we examine the reliability of the twenty subscores for tested areas in mathematics and the seventeen for tested areas in science.

The focus of this book for the most part (other than Chapter Ten) is on country-level portraits and analyses. The reliability of subtests for the

Table 7.5. Correlations Between Topics for Observed Achievement Scores (Eighth Grade Science).

Topic	Earth Features	Earth Processes	Earth in the Universe	Diversity and Structure of Living Things	Life Processes and Functions	Life Cycles and Genetics	Interactions of Living Things
Earth features	1.00						
Earth processes	.65	1.00					
Earth in the universe	.69	.72	1.00				
Diversity and structure of living things	.67	.55	.73	1.00			
Life processes and functions	.86	.64	.70	.81	1.00		
Life cycles and genetics	.63	.67	.74	.52	.59	1.00	
Interactions of living things	.78	.59	.68	.68	.86	.56	1.00
Human biology and health	.84	.61	.74	.77	.80	.72	.71
Properties and classification of matter	.77	.58	.75	.87	.86	.48	.83
Structure of matter	.51	−.04	.11	.34	.41	.04	.30
Energy and physical processes	.77	.71	.81	.88	.89	.63	.84
Physical changes	.73	.62	.73	.82	.81	.57	.74
Chemical changes	.71	.55	.62	.70	.75	.35	.69
Forces and motion	.80	.58	.72	.79	.78	.72	.68
Science, technology, and society	.74	.66	.70	.73	.72	.59	.78
Environmental and resource issues	.56	.77	.71	.58	.59	.48	.70
Scientific processes	.68	.59	.67	.83	.84	.46	.73

specific tested topic areas at this level is complex, being related to the number of items on a subtest but not only to this.[18] It is also related to how homogeneous the items comprising a subtest are in content.[19] The reliability of a test is very important to establishing rankings among countries on the subtest measures, as has been done in some other TIMSS reports.[20]

Table 7.6 gives estimates of the reliability coefficients for eighth grade (status) scores for each tested area as well as the reliability coefficients for the estimated eighth grade gain scores for each tested area (in science and mathematics). For mathematics, the reliabilities were all high for the achievement status scores at eighth grade. The mean reliability for mathematics achievement scores was .94 over the twenty areas. The lowest reli-

Human Biology and Health	Properties and Classification of Matter	Structure of Matter	Energy and Physical Processes	Physical Changes	Chemical Changes	Forces and Motion	Science, Technology, and Society	Environmental and Resource Issues	Scientific Processes
1.00									
.70	1.00								
.39	.33	1.00							
.78	.91	.19	1.00						
.70	.93	.12	.89	1.00					
.61	.75	.37	.73	.67	1.00				
.80	.79	.23	.84	.85	.57	1.00			
.73	.75	.13	.79	.71	.60	.69	1.00		
.57	.65	.06	.70	.55	.62	.46	.67	1.00	
.66	.82	.18	.87	.82	.74	.77	.70	.62	1.00

ability was .88. This implies that the tested area topics were defined over relatively homogeneous content domains and that these can have high and acceptable reliabilities at the country level even with relatively few items. In fact, several of the tested area topics had reliabilities of .93 at the country level with only five items. Such high reliabilities suggest that the rankings of countries done elsewhere on the basis of tested area subtest scores are reasonable, at least in terms of what is usually considered reasonable.[22]

As one would expect, the reliabilities of the estimated mathematics gain scores were lower. The average reliability was .69, with a range from .46 to .89. The gain scores correlated .77 with the eighth grade mathematics scores.

Table 7.6. Reliabilities for Eighth Gade Mathematics and Science Status and Estimated Eighth Grade Gain.

	Reliability	
	Eighth	Gain
Mathematics		
Whole numbers	.88	.62
Common fractions	.97	.89
Decimal fractions and percents	.95	.86
Relations of fractions	.95	.81
Estimating quantity and size	.95	.69
Rounding	.93	.68
Estimating computations	.95	.72
Measurement units	.91	.50
Perimeter, area, and volume	.97	.87
Measurement estimations and errors	.93	.61
2-D geometry	.92	.67
Polygons and circles	.92	.58
3-D geometry and transformations	.91	.46
Congruence and similarity	.92	.65
Proportionality concepts	.89	.62
Proportionality problems	.95	.70
Patterns, relations, and functions	.93	.59
Equations and formulas	.98	.89
Data representation and analysis	.96	.80
Uncertainty and probability	.93	.49
Science		
Earth features	.84	.34
Earth processes	.83	.40
Earth in the universe	.76	.37
Diversity and structure of living things	.89	.66
Life processes and functions	.93	.64
Life cycles and genetics	.68	.60
Interactions of living things	.72	.44
Human biology and health	.90	.76
Properties and classification of matter	.88	.58
Structure of matter	.79	.71
Energy and physical processes	.95	.79
Physical changes	.76	.61
Chemical changes	.89	.79
Forces and motion	.91	.55
Science, technology, and society	.90	.46
Environmental and resource issues	.88	.47
Scientific processes	.82	.57

The topic scores for tested areas in science at eighth grade had relatively respectable reliabilities but not as high as those for mathematics. The average reliability was .84, ranging from .68 to .95 across the seventeen tested area subtests. Again, the relationship of reliability and the number of test items appears to have been affected by content homogeneity. A test with only six items (forces and motion) had an estimated reliability higher than another test with twice as many items (earth features). The gain reliabilities were once again lower for science, with an average reliability of .57.

Some Further Results for Mathematics

As always, characterization of these scores is a battle for accurate detail versus explanatory parsimony. Mathematics had twenty tested topic subtests. Would any dimensions underlying these twenty scores allow one to represent a country fairly in eighth grade mathematics with fewer than twenty variables? If the answer is yes, then a more parsimonious explanation of the between-country variation would be possible.

We found two latent dimensions to adequately represent the cross-country variation in the estimated gain of mathematics tested area achievement at eighth grade.[22] The first dimension appears to represent a total score—such as that reported elsewhere.[23] A second interesting dimension appears to characterize a contrast between arithmetic-type topics (whole numbers, fractions, percents, rounding, and estimating computations) and topics representing algebra and geometry (the four geometry tested area topics, functions, and equations and formulas).

Applying similar techniques to the curriculum variables discussed in the previous chapter produces the same essential results. This suggests that both with respect to curricular opportunities and to learning, the countries can be divided into those for which arithmetic (including elementary measurement) dominates and those for which algebra and geometry dominate. These issues will be considered again in the next chapter. In science, although the analyses were done, the patterns were not as simply interpretable and are not pursued further.

Summary

This chapter suggests strongly that the thirty-seven tested area topic scores we constructed can be reliably measured and can provide a basis for estimating achievement gain (as an indicator of learning). Gain measures were different from status measures both in their distributions and in terms of how correlated the tested areas were to each other. Finally, gain did vary both across countries and across topics. This suggests that not only aspects of curriculum but also learning reflect interaction effects, at least as indicated by achievement gain. The question we next turn to is whether the two relate to each other and, if they do, whether the relationship also reflects a country-by-topic interaction.

NOTES

1. Survey of Mathematics and Science Opportunities, 1993.

2. What test developers strove for was a parity of the value of the test for each participating country, although the topics in which the value primarily lies may vary among countries. In spite of this, it is accepted that any such consensus test will be unfair to each country at least in some ways. The developers recognized this goal of parity in a context of inherently mixed fairness by describing themselves as trying to design tests that were "equally unfair" to all participating countries.

3. At Population 2 for both seventh and eighth grades (or their equivalents) and for both mathematics and the sciences, there were eight forms of the test. Each form had mostly different items in it. This allowed more breadth of subject matter assessment while limiting testing time. The forms were randomly assigned among the students to be tested within each school that was sampled for selection of students to be tested. This use of different forms permits the aggregation of the item responses to estimate national levels of achievement for all items. Combining the scores for the items in each area formed national estimates for subareas.

4. For example, see Schmidt, McKnight, Cogan, Jakwerth, & Houang, 1999.

5. The first cross-national reports were for Population 2 mathematics and science results. See Beaton, Mullis, Martin, Gonzalez, Kelly, & Smith, 1996, and Beaton, Martin, Mullis, Gonzalez, Smith, & Kelly, 1996. Later reports dealt with Population 1 (nine-year-olds) and Population 3 (the last year of secondary schools). See Mullis, Martin, Beaton, Gonzalez, Kelly, & Smith, 1997; Martin, Mullis, Beaton, Gonzalez, Smith, & Kelly, 1997; and Mullis, Martin, Beaton, Gonzalez, Kelly, & Smith, 1998.

6. The scale scores were derived by fitting a one-parameter logistic model using plausible values (Adams, Wu, & Macaskill, 1998).

7. Appendix C indicates the number of items combined to form each of the subarea scales. Averaging the item difficulties (p-values or estimated national percent of students correctly answering the item) formed the scale scores for each subarea over all items contained in the tested subarea.

8. See Schmidt et al., 1998.

9. A true longitudinal study would permit a less biased and a more precise measure of one grade's gain in achievement. Instead, TIMSS provided for testing (at Population 2) of eighth grade students (or their equivalents) and a matched sample of seventh grade students that would pass into the same eighth grade classrooms the next year. Thus, rather than having a true cohort of students measured at two points at time to estimate change, the study provided for a synthetic cohort by measuring two strongly related groups of students, each at one point in time. This also allowed an estimate (perhaps somewhat less accurate) of achievement gains from one grade's experiences but only by estimating this at an aggregate rather than the individual level.

10. Essentially, the effects of all prior curricular experiences are removed (statistically controlled for) by using seventh grade achievement as a surrogate premeasure of achievement prior to beginning eighth grade.

11. Schmidt, McKnight, Cogan, Jakwerth, & Houang, 1999.

12. Functions also included patterns and relations. Many of the test items for the Population 2 mathematics test in the functions tested area were items on patterns. These are less relevant to knowledge gained through instruction. They were more likely to have high scores at the seventh grade level and thus less room for gain during the eighth grade.

13. Schmidt, McKnight, Cogan, Jakwerth, & Houang, 1999.

14. The achievement score for a country and a topic here is the average percent of students nationally that got an item correct (estimated p-value) averaged over all of the items relevant for the particular tested area. These are averaged over the countries to get a score for each tested area.

15. Interpreting differences in the status scores is very risky because they reflect not only real differences in cumulative achievement but also differences in test item characteristics.

16. However, they reflect a combination of individual differences within schools, classroom/school differences within countries, and country differences. That is, the expected value of the variance-covariance matrix, Σ, defined at the country level includes components of variation and covariation at the other levels of the hierarchical design.

17. The true score correlation matrix was estimated by using the item-level data associated with each topic area. Under classical true-score theory, the true-score variance is equal to the average of the covariances among the items defining the topic area. The true-score covariance is equal to the average of the covariances across items in each of the two topic areas. Using these true

score variances and covariances, we estimated the true-score correlation matrix. One of the problems associated with such an approach is that one can obtain a non-positive-definite correlation matrix. We employed the least-squares solution in that case, using only the positive latent roots and corresponding vectors to reconstruct the estimated correlation matrix.

18. The number of items contained in the test influences the reliability of a test in part. Because of this, one of the criticisms often leveled against using subtopic scores is that for some of the subtests, only a relatively few items are available. (See Appendix C for a description of the number of items contained in each of the thirty-seven subtests of specific areas.) This is taken to imply that reporting scores for subtests would result in scores with unacceptably low estimates of reliability. The relationship of the number of the items in a test to the reliability of that test is given by the Spearman-Brown formula (Lord & Novick, 1968).

19. If we again view the data as arising from a matrix, with the columns representing the items in a subtest area and the rows representing the countries, then this homogeneity issue is one of to what degree item-by-country interactions are present in those data. Those interactions could be identified by the median polish technique we have used throughout this book. Their presence indicates that the items in a particular area do not function homogeneously—do not serve to measure the same thing—and that this contributes to measurement error and lowers reliability. Viewing reliability in the context of the generalized true-score model, the generic error of measurement includes the item-by-country interactions. If the gains, for example, are consistent across items within a subtest area, then the error component associated with this source of error variance will be negligible. This will lead to a higher reliability estimate in spite of the number of items. However, given equal item-by-country variance components, the test with the larger number of items will have a higher reliability.

20. In using subtest measures to explore the relationships between curriculum and learning, on the other hand, large measurement error (low reliability) has its greatest impact by masking relationships that actually exist at the true-score level. However, such measurement error does not create artifactual relationships. This implies that if significant relationships between curriculum and achievement are found in the data, then the reliability was good enough that the relationships were not masked. The error term in regression models using gain as the dependent variable accounts not only for equation error but also for measurement error. Because of this, the variance component related to measurement error at most suppresses the relationship of curriculum variables to gain. Measurement error cannot

suppress the combined error term and distort relationships to make significance appear to be present when it is not.

21. Schmidt, McKnight, Cogan, Jakwerth, & Houang, 1999.

22. To explore the question of whether such parsimony was possible, we did a latent root and vector resolution of the covariance matrix for gain. We found a reasonable two-factor solution for mathematics, and it is reported here. The science results were not as clearly interpretable and, as a result, are not reported here.

23. Beaton et al., 1996.

8

LEARNING AND THE
STRUCTURE OF CURRICULUM

AGAIN AND AGAIN THROUGHOUT THIS BOOK, the data have shown the presence of country-by-topic interactions. This was true for the various aspects of curriculum that we examined in Chapter Five as well as for the achievement gains that we investigated in Chapter Seven. In Chapter Six we took our first look at a structural model and found relational coefficients that also varied by country and topic.

A pressing question now emerges: Are the relationships (if any) between the aspects (the structure) of curriculum and the patterns of eighth grade achievement gains interaction based? The internal relationships among the aspects of curriculum are and among tested topic area achievement gains are. Is it also true that the relationships between curriculum and achievement gains are? This chapter focuses on this emerging question.

The main organizing principle for the first section of this chapter is the structural model first portrayed in Chapter Two, the model whose curricular aspects were examined in Chapter Five. However, before presenting these results, we examine the relationships between achievement gain paired in turn with each of the different variables representing the aspects of curriculum in school mathematics and science at eighth grade.

Two-Way Analyses: Relationships Between Achievement Gains Paired with Aspects of Curriculum

We begin, as discussed in Chapter Three and as carried out in Chapter Six, with two-way analyses of data for countries and topics. We analyze this for achievement gains paired with each of the three aspects of curriculum examined earlier. Two things are quite clear from the results of these two-way pairwise analyses of aspects of curriculum and estimated eighth grade achievement gains for both mathematics and science. First, statistically significant relationships existed between each of the curriculum aspects and learning as characterized by estimated achievement gain from seventh to eighth grade. Second, it is clear that the relationships are all interaction based ($p < .03$ for all combinations of gain and the four curriculum aspects for both mathematics and science).

The pairwise coefficients at the interaction level are all positive for both mathematics and science. This indicates that more curriculum coverage of a topic area—no matter whether manifested as emphasis in content standards, as proportion of textbook space, or as measured by either teacher implementation variable—is related to larger gains in that same topic area. We take these estimated larger gains to indicate greater learning for that topic at the country level. Remember that we are examining relationships among variables defined at the country level rather than for individuals.

The curricular priorities of a country—whether reflected by content standards, textbooks, or teacher behavior—are related to the profile of achievement gains across topics for that country. However, the nature of these general relationships is not the same for all countries. This implies that a general relationship between achievement gain and one aspect of curriculum may not even exist at all for some countries.

Two-Way Analyses: The Structural Model

There is one marked limitation of the pairwise analyses of the relationship of aspects of curriculum to estimated achievement gain: in examining the relationship of gain to that aspect of curriculum (whichever it is), it is not done in a context where the effects of the other aspects of curriculum are controlled. This limitation can be overcome by turning to the general structural model presented in Chapter Three. In estimating coefficients for that structural model, all other related aspects of curriculum are controlled while estimating the strength of the relationship between one aspect of curriculum and achievement gain.

Mathematics

Unlike the results for the pairwise relationships, the results for the structural model with statistical controls for all other relevant aspects of curriculum were different for mathematics and science. For mathematics, the relationships changed in terms of whether they were statistically signifi-cant. Moreover, they also changed in terms of whether the relationships held across all countries (the topic effect) or whether they were idiosyn-cratic to specific countries (the interaction effect). The latter was the case for the pairwise relationships.

The relationship of instructional time to learning was only marginally significant at best ($p < .126$), but it was still positive—that is, more instructional time was associated with greater gains. This was the case when statistically controlling for both textbook coverage and for content standards. The pairwise relationship between instructional time and learn-ing did not control for these other two aspects of curriculum and was sta-tistically significant ($p < .01$).

Given the way we have formulated the general structural model, the conditional analysis rather than the pairwise (uncontrolled) analysis is the correct one. However, it is possible that in our formulation of the structural model, the effects of content standards and textbooks on achievement gain should be only indirect. That is, rather than direct rela-tionships between content standards to gains and textbooks to gains, these aspects might be modeled only as related to instructional time and, through it, to achievement. Teachers should have a more direct effect than textbooks on gain because students spend more time learning from them, and we know from the other analyses that textbooks are related to what teachers teach.

If that were the case, then the two-variable result from the uncontrolled analysis would be appropriate. Then the conclusion would be that a sta-tistically significant relationship existed between instructional time and learning. It is therefore reasonable to suggest that instructional time might be related to achievement gain. This is especially true given the margin-ally significant result for the conditional (controlled) analysis.[1]

For the proportion of a country's teachers covering a topic—the other measure of teacher implementation—the relationship to gain is unchanged from that of the pairwise analysis. There was a positive relationship at the interaction level. This implies that the greater the percentage of a coun-try's eighth grade mathematics teachers who covered a topic, the greater was the learning (estimated achievement gain) that took place for the cor-responding tested area. This was true even when controlling for content standards and textbooks.

The same was true for content standards: the larger the percentage of the standards devoted to a tested topic area that were included, the greater the learning (achievement gains) in those topic areas.[2] This was the case when controlling for textbook coverage and for teacher implementation.

In contrast, the nature of the relationship between textbook coverage and achievement gain while statistically controlling for content standards and teacher implementation was very different from that implied by the pairwise analysis. There was still a positive, statistically significant relationship. However, it was no longer interaction based but rather was defined at the topic level ($p < .018$).

The implication of this result is that across topics within a country, a higher percentage of textbook space allocated to a topic relative to the other topics was associated with greater gain for that topic area. This was true averaged across countries. This implies that this relationship was essentially the same across countries. Thus, we conclude that textbook space was positively related to achievement gain.

These results can be combined with those of Chapter Six to examine the relationships both among the aspects of curriculum and between curriculum and achievement gain. These results are summarized in Figure 8.1 for both mathematics and science.

The conception proposed by and represented in the structural model is supported by the data. In general, content standards in mathematics were related to teacher implementation both directly as well as indirectly through textbook coverage. Teacher implementation was in turn related to achievement gain (although only marginally so for instructional time). Mathematics content standards had a direct relationship to learning. They also had an indirect effect through textbook coverage and teacher implementation. The relationships described previously for mathematics were primarily at the interaction level and thus were generally not uniform across countries. As described in Chapter Six, the direct effect of content standards on teacher implementation characterized the relationship in terms of differences across topics within a country. The fact that this relationship was at this level implies that it held in the same way for all countries. This was also true for the direct relationship of textbook coverage to learning (achievement gain).

Science

In science, a pattern emerged that was more complex than the one described for mathematics. Content standards were positively related to gain ($p < .016$). So was teacher implementation (both in terms of instructional time [$p < .002$] and in the percentage of teachers covering a topic [$p < .003$]). The relationships were interaction based (as was true also for mathematics). For these two variables, the conclusions were essentially the same as those presented for mathematics. The one exception is that

Figure 8.1. Estimated Structural Model.

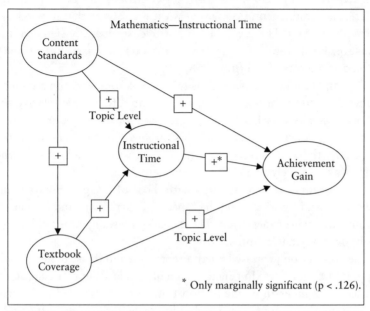

Mathematics—Instructional Time

* Only marginally significant (p < .126).

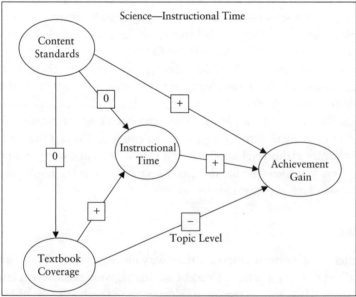

Science—Instructional Time

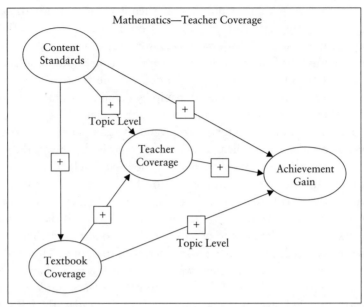

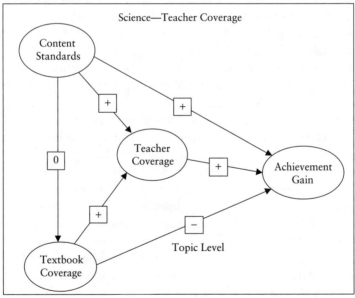

for mathematics, the relationship of instructional time to learning was only marginally significant.

Topic priorities within a country as reflected in content standards—presumably reflecting curriculum policy—were related to the profile of achievement gains. Essentially, more OTL for a topic was associated with greater amounts of learning for that topic during eighth grade. The strength of those relationships depended on the particular country involved. (The strength of the relationship by definition includes the possibility of no relationship, i.e., that δ or γ might equal 0.)

The direct relationship of textbook coverage to gain, however, was very different from that for mathematics. It was similar in that it was the same for all countries (that is, it was defined at the topic level). The difference has to do with the direction of the relationship. In science, the relationship of textbook coverage to achievement gain had an estimated coefficient that was negative ($p < .007$). This essentially means that the more a topic was covered (relative to other topics) in a country's textbooks, the smaller was the achievement gain associated with that topic. This is somewhat baffling. Why the coefficient was negative is not immediately clear.

The negative coefficient for the relationship of textbook space to achievement gain is even more puzzling when one considers the full structural model as portrayed in Figure 8.1. This figure combines the results discussed in Chapter Six with those presented here. The indirect relationship of textbook coverage to achievement gain through teacher implementation (both through teacher coverage and instructional time) was statistically significant and *positive*. The strength of this relationship also varied across countries.

Hence, textbook space seems to have had both a direct and an indirect relationship to learning (achievement gain). That in itself is not odd, and the combination of the two represents the total effect of textbook space. What is odd is for one to be negative and the other positive.[3]

Content standards also had the potential for both a direct effect and a complex array of indirect effects on learning. For teacher coverage, both direct and indirect effects existed and both were positive. Both were defined at the interaction level. That is, once again the strength of the relationship seemed to vary by country. No indirect relationships between content standards and learning were mediated by textbook space because there was no relationship between content standards and textbook space.

For instructional time, some of the relationships were different. The direct relationship of content standards to gain has already been discussed. The indirect relationship through teacher time—parallel to the indirect relationship found through teacher coverage—does not exist. There was no relationship of content standards to teacher time.

Unlike the case for teacher implementation in mathematics and for teacher coverage in science, content standards had no direct or indirect relationship to instructional time in science. That is, for science, content standards did not have the same type of relationships to teacher implementation that was true for mathematics. In mathematics, there were both direct and indirect relationships. This was the case for teacher coverage in science. All of these relationships were defined at the interaction level. Neither a direct nor an indirect relationship existed for teacher time in science. Only textbook coverage was related to instructional time in science. Interestingly, however, content standards did have a positive relationship to learning even when statistically controlling for instructional time. Combining the results for teacher coverage and instructional time in the sciences suggests that science content standards were not related to textbook coverage. Apparently, that is, the relative textbook space allocations for different topics were not affected by content standards.

The Direct Relationship of Textbook Coverage and Learning

For both mathematics and science, the direct relationship between textbook coverage and learning was defined at the topic level. In terms of gain, this was the only relationship defined at this level, which implies that the nature of the relationship was essentially the same across countries. All of the other relationships portrayed in Figure 8.1 (with the exception of content standards and teacher implementation for mathematics) were interaction based.

This makes the relationship of textbooks to learning (and content standards to teacher implementation for mathematics, as discussed in Chapter Six) unusual in terms of the total model. They are universal in the sense that the nature of the relationship generalizes across the thirty TIMSS countries on average.

For mathematics, the relationship was positive. Even when statistically controlling for teacher implementation and content standards, the relationship was statistically significant ($p < .018$). The coefficient of determination (R^2) from the analysis was .31, indicating a modestly strong relationship. This analysis included not only textbook coverage but also instructional time and content standards.

Figure 8.2 gives the scatterplot for textbook coverage and achievement gain to make understanding this relationship easier. The points represent

Figure 8.2. Scatterplots for Textbook Coverage and Achievement Gains for Topics Averaged over Countries.

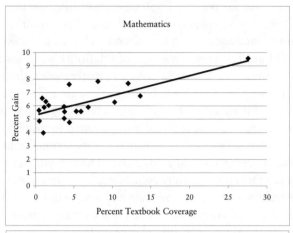

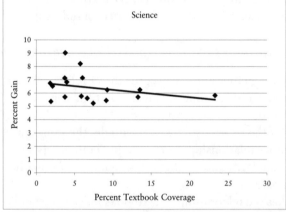

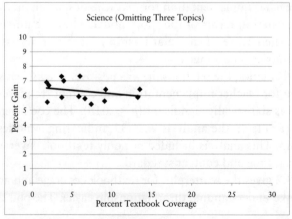

the twenty tested topic areas in mathematics averaged over countries. The data represent the pairwise relationship not controlled for instructional time and content standards.[4] It is very clear from the displayed data that there is a positive relationship between the proportion of textbook space allocated to a topic and the corresponding amount of achievement gain at the country level. This was true averaged over countries and is quite consistent with the results described in Chapters Five and Seven that listed the five topic areas with the largest gains and, separately, the five with the greatest amounts of curriculum coverage. In Chapter Seven, the large overlap of these two lists (typically four out of five topics) was discussed. For example, the point showing the largest achievement gain and the greatest relative proportion of textbook space among the various tested area topics represents the topic of equations and formulas. The estimated regression coefficient was .75 for the bivariate relationship portrayed in Figure 8.2. This is close to the value derived from the analysis including instructional time and content standards (.72).

For science, the relationship between proportion of textbook coverage and achievement gain for that topic was negative. As discussed in the previous section, the implications of this are far less clear than was the case for mathematics. The plot of the data for science is also shown in Figure 8.2. The negative relationship is obvious from the data displayed. For example, energy and physical processes was a topic that received a large proportion of textbook coverage across the countries compared with other topics. However, it was a tested area topic that showed only average achievement gain compared with other topics. On the other hand, structure of matter was a tested area topic that had a relatively small proportion compared with other topics, but it showed the largest achievement gain.

When these two topics (and chemical changes, for a reason similar to that for structure of matter) are dropped from the analysis, the relationship becomes much less negative for the remaining fourteen tested area topics. It is not significant and reflects a very weak relationship but is very different from the relationship including the three named tested area topics. This is also displayed in Figure 8.2.

Perhaps for science there was no relationship between textbook space allocations and learning once the three anomalous topics are removed. However, this does not address why the three topics are the way they were, that is, why the topic with the largest achievement gain was one of those with the lowest proportions of textbook space allocated to it (and vice versa for the structure of matter). One conjecture for explaining this centers on the nature of the TIMSS test producing floor and ceiling effects

for seventh grade achievement, effects that in turn place limits on estimated achievement gains.

A Further Analysis of the Interaction-Based Relationships

The analyses related to the structural model serve to point out that the
relationships between curriculum and achievement gain were defined
mostly at the country-by-topic interaction level. We now turn our attention to essentially examining the topic-by-country (cell) means, a long-
standing statistical tradition of exploring the nature of interactions.

This suggests exploring the interaction by doing an additional set of
regressions using the country-by-topic cell means from the two-way analyses. The cell means—600 of them in the case of mathematics—can be considered as thirty sets (each set a country) of twenty observations (each
observation a topic). They can also be considered as twenty sets (each set
a topic) of thirty observations (each observation a country).[5] This second
type of regression will be the subject of the next chapter.

Before turning to the actual cell means and the within-country regressions, we examine the cell means adjusted for country and topic effects.
We do this by looking at the doubly deviated cell means that were used
in the two-way analysis, that is, cell means from which country and topic
means have been subtracted. These residual means served as the basis for
testing the statistical significance of the interaction-based relationships
reported earlier in this chapter and under which we examine the separate
country regressions.

To illustrate this, two sets of science cell means adjusted for topic and
country effects (that is, doubly deviated) are presented as a scatterplot in
Figure 8.3. The two variables displayed are tested area topic achievement
gain and instructional time for tested area topics. Different symbols are
used in the display to represent a select number of different countries
across the topic variables. In science these 510 values are considered as
thirty sets of 17 values (tested area topics) here. They could also be considered as seventeen sets of 30 values, as will be the case in Chapter 9.

The overall regression line is represented in Figure 8.3 with a regression coefficient equal to .22. This equation is over all topics and all countries.[6] It examines instructional time on a given topic for a particular
country—beyond what was typical for the given topic over all countries
and what was typical for that country over all topics. It looks at how this
instructional time was related to gain that was similarly beyond what was
expected from the country and topic means.

Figure 8.3. Scatterplot for Instructional Time and Achievement Gains over All Tested Areas and All Countries in Eighth Grade Science.

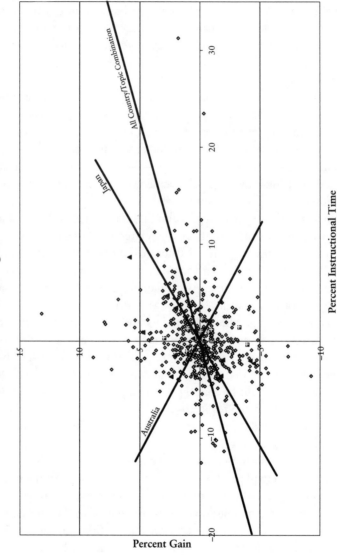

Note: *The values plotted here are cell residuals (mean deviated from the country and topic marginals) for all combinations of topic and country. Three regression lines are displayed: one for all country/topic combinations, one for Japan, and one for Australia.*

This is a single line for all 510 country-by-topic combinations. In addition, the 510 values can be partitioned into thirty country sets and a separate regression line fitted for each country. The regressions for two countries are also illustrated in Figure 8.3.[7] For example, Japan shows a strong positive relationship between instructional time and achievement gain for science. This should be interpreted as a residual regression indicating that the amount of instructional time above or below the amount expected from the country and topic averages was related for Japan to the amount of gain above or below that which was typical for the country and topic.

That is, in Japan the deviations in instructional time for a topic from that for a typical topic were positively related to the corresponding deviations in achievement gain for a topic from that for a typical topic. Where Japanese teachers allocated exceptional amounts of time (either positively or negatively)—as a national average—then Japanese eighth grade children had a national average achievement gain that was correspondingly exceptional (either high or low).

In contrast, the negative regression line for Australia does not indicate that more teacher time was inversely related to student learning (that is, to lower achievement gains). Rather, it reflects that for those topics to which Australian teachers allocated an exceptionally large (or small) amount of instructional time, Australian eighth grade students as a whole showed exceptionally weak (or strong) performance.

This relationship is difficult to understand. One must keep in mind that the definition of *exceptional* is with respect to an average over countries (with respect to a topic) and an average over topics (for a specific country) and is thus not based simply on norms for a single country. One general explanation might be that the test in a particular topic area does not reflect the nature of the topic coverage that was making such coverage exceptional. Some data point in the direction of this possibility, as was discussed in Chapter Five.

We turn to the within-country, across-topic regressions instead of continuing to try to explain the interaction-based relationships in terms of what was exceptional.[8] The previous sections of this chapter have indicated that most of the relationships were defined at the interaction level (with two exceptions mentioned in the last section). In the previous section we indicated the strength of the non-interaction-based relationships by using the marginal or average relationships.

To explore the interaction-based relationships, we fitted thirty regression analyses—one for each country—using the topic as the unit of analysis. This is still a country-level analysis because the topic variables were all defined at the country level. Given the statistically significant interaction effects we found, we would expect that the nature and strength of the various relationships of curriculum to learning in the within-country, across-topic regressions to vary across countries. That is exactly what we found.

Mathematics

Table 8.1 summarizes the pairwise relationships in eighth grade mathematics for three aspects of curriculum. Five variables are listed—emphasis in content standards, national average instructional time for a topic, proportion of a country's teachers covering a topic, proportion of textbook space devoted to a topic, and proportion of textbook space devoted to a topic but with greater complexity of student performance expected. Each of these variables was separately related to achievement gain.[9] The performance complexity variable described in Chapter Five was not used in the formal two-way analysis serving as the basis for most of Chapter Six and the first part of this chapter. This variable simply indicates for a topic area what percent of that area's coverage in a textbook had performance expectations that were more demanding.

The statistically significant pairwise relationships in Table 8.1 are noted, suggesting a fairly large number of positive significant relationships of curriculum to learning within each country. The pattern of these significant relationships is consistent with their interaction-based nature because they vary across countries. In no case were the relationships exactly the same for two countries although there were some very similar patterns. One must keep in mind that these pairwise relationships are not controlled for the other curriculum variables.[10]

The two curriculum variables related to gain for the largest number of countries were textbook coverage and instructional time. There were only six countries in which at least one of the five curriculum variables was not statistically significantly (or marginally significantly) related to gain. These six countries were Canada, Denmark, Ireland, Portugal, Romania, and Colombia.

Japan is interesting by comparison in that all five curriculum indicators were positively and statistically significantly related to achievement gain. Several countries—Canada, Hungary, New Zealand, Norway, Switzerland, and the United States—did not have indicated relationships between content standards and achievement gain because every topic area tested was 100 percent covered in terms of the test domain by the content standards in those countries. For Switzerland, this was likely the consequence

Table 8.1. Pairwise Relationship Between the Three Aspects of Curriculum (Five Variables) and Achievement Gain in Eighth Grade Mathematics.

Country	Content Standards Coverage and Gain		Textbook Coverage and Gain		Textbook's Complex Expectation Coverage and Gain		Teacher Coverage and Gain		Instructional Time and Gain	
	Coefficient (std. err.)	R^2	Coefficient (std. err.)	R^2	Coefficient (std. err.)	R^2	Coefficient (std. err.)	R^2	Coefficient (std. err.)	R^2
Australia	-0.01 (0.01)	0.06	0.11 (0.05)**	0.19	0.11 (0.07)	0.11	0.01 (0.02)	0.03	0.02 (0.06)	0.01
Austria	0.00 (0.01)	0.00	0.13 (0.08)	0.13	0.03 (0.11)	0.01	0.01 (0.02)	0.01	0.16 (0.09)*	0.16
Canada			0.15 (0.11)	0.09	0.01 (0.05)	0.00	0.01 (0.02)	0.03	0.05 (0.07)	0.03
Colombia	0.01 (0.01)	0.10	0.02 (0.04)	0.02	0.02 (0.03)	0.02	-0.02 (0.02)	0.06	-0.07 (0.05)	0.08
Cyprus	0.01 (0.01)	0.04	0.14 (0.05)**	0.34	0.05 (0.02)**	0.30	0.01 (0.02)	0.01	0.08 (0.08)	0.05
Czech Republic	0.02 (0.01)*	0.18	0.05 (0.04)	0.11	0.02 (0.02)	0.11	0.04 (0.01)**	0.30	0.17 (0.06)**	0.29
Denmark	0.01 (0.01)	0.08	0.06 (0.12)	0.02	-0.01 (0.02)	0.03	0.03 (0.02)	0.08	0.06 (0.06)	0.06
France	0.01 (0.01)	0.05	0.26 (0.10)**	0.27	0.04 (0.02)**	0.20	0.02 (0.02)	0.05	0.23 (0.06)**	0.43
Germany	0.01 (0.01)	0.02	0.16 (0.05)**	0.41	0.04 (0.03)	0.09	0.04 (0.03)	0.11	0.19 (0.07)**	0.29
Greece	0.03 (0.01)**	0.23	0.31 (0.08)**	0.45	0.02 (0.02)	0.06	0.03 (0.02)	0.13	0.18 (0.09)*	0.18
Hong Kong	0.00 (0.01)	0.00	0.07 (0.08)	0.04	0.03 (0.10)	0.00	0.03 (0.02)*	0.16	0.24 (0.08)**	0.35
Hungary			0.17 (0.06)**	0.31	0.05 (0.04)	0.08	0.06 (0.02)**	0.26	0.21 (0.11)*	0.17
Iceland	0.03 (0.02)*	0.16	0.07 (0.06)	0.07	-0.04 (0.04)	0.04	0.01 (0.02)	0.02	0.02 (0.05)	0.01
Ireland	-0.01 (0.01)	0.02	0.09 (0.09)	0.05	0.03 (0.03)	0.05	0.02 (0.03)	0.02	-0.03 (0.13)	0.00
Japan	0.04 (0.01)**	0.30	0.22 (0.06)**	0.43	0.19 (0.06)**	0.34	0.06 (0.03)**	0.27	0.38 (0.06)**	0.67
Korea	0.01 (0.01)	0.05	0.09 (0.05)	0.14	0.00 (0.02)	0.01	0.06 (0.02)**	0.39	0.12 (0.10)	0.08

Netherlands	0.00 (0.01)	0.00	0.20 (0.04)**	0.62	0.07 (0.04)*	0.16	0.00 (0.03)	0.00	0.06 (0.13)	0.01
New Zealand			0.13 (0.06)*	0.18	0.00 (0.01)	0.00	0.01 (0.02)	0.01	0.00 (0.07)	0.00
Norway	0.00 (0.01)	0.00	0.16 (0.09)*	0.16	−0.03 (0.02)	0.09	0.02 (0.01)	0.09	0.11 (0.05)*	0.18
Portugal	0.00 (0.01)	0.00	0.03 (0.04)	0.03	0.01 (0.02)	0.02	0.00 (0.02)	0.00	0.01 (0.09)	0.00
Romania	0.01 (0.01)	0.12	−0.01 (0.02)	0.02	0.01 (0.01)	0.01	0.02 (0.02)	0.07	−0.02 (0.06)	0.01
Russian Federation	0.03 (0.01)**	0.34	0.06 (0.06)	0.04	0.06 (0.02)**	0.33	0.03 (0.01)**	0.20	0.07 (0.06)	0.08
Singapore	0.01 (0.01)	0.02	0.10 (0.06)*	0.15	−0.04 (0.06)	0.02	0.02 (0.01)	0.14	0.16 (0.08)*	0.18
Slovak Republic	0.02 (0.01)	0.13	0.07 (0.04)*	0.16	0.03 (0.02)	0.14	0.05 (0.02)**	0.31	0.24 (0.08)**	0.34
Slovenia	0.02 (0.01)	0.11	0.05 (0.04)	0.06	0.02 (0.02)	0.09	0.05 (0.02)**	0.29	0.38 (0.08)**	0.54
Spain	−0.03 (0.01)**	0.21	0.18 (0.05)**	0.41	0.06 (0.02)**	0.43	0.05 (0.03)	0.13	0.16 (0.07)**	0.24
Sweden	0.01 (0.02)	0.02	0.06 (0.09)	0.02	−0.02 (0.03)	0.03	0.05 (0.01)**	0.58	0.14 (0.03)**	0.52
Switzerland			0.61 (0.16)**	0.44	0.36 (0.09)**	0.47	−0.03 (0.04)	0.03	−0.01 (0.14)	0.00
USA			0.08 (0.03)**	0.28	−0.01 (0.04)	0.01	−0.01 (0.01)	0.01	0.02 (0.04)	0.01

**Significant (p ≤ .05).

*Significant (.05 < p ≤ .10).

Note: Empty cells reflect the fact that some countries had content standards that intended coverage of all topics.

of combining curriculum variables across the three language groups in the Swiss national educational system. For the others, it was likely the result of curricula with broad coverage (see Chapter Five).

For some countries—Australia, Cyprus, the Netherlands, New Zealand, Switzerland, and the United States—the defining relationship of curriculum to learning seems to have been in terms of textbook coverage (including their performance expectations). For others—Austria, Hong Kong, Korea, Sweden, and Slovenia—the defining relationship to achievement gain was one or the other aspect of teacher implementation. For most, the relationship of curriculum to learning was through a combination of several of the five curriculum indicators.

Using coefficients of determination (R^2's) as a measure of the pairwise relationships' fit, they ranged for textbook coverage to achievement gain from around 0 to over .6. Among the fifteen countries for which the R^2 was statistically significant or marginally so ($p < .10$), the values accounted for around 15 to 60 percent of the variance in achievement gains. For instructional time, the range over the countries with statistically significant pairwise regressions was similar—from about 15 to 67 percent.

All of these relationships were based on simple pairwise relationships. Table 8.2 examines many of these same relationships but does so while statistically controlling for other curriculum variables. These analyses are based on the structural model. They estimate the structural coefficients for the relationship of curriculum to learning—δ, ξ, and γ (see Chapter Three). This analysis is similar to that presented in Chapter Six with respect to the structural coefficients relating the aspects of curriculum to each other—β, α, and η.

In ten of the countries, there was no statistically significant indication of relationship between any of the aspects of curriculum—content standards, textbook space, and instructional time—and achievement gain. The other two indicators were not included in these structural analyses but were included in Table 8.1. Among these ten countries, France and Korea did have significant pairwise relationships in Table 8.1 involving the other two curriculum variables not included in the analyses of Table 8.2. Iceland, Norway, and Singapore had marginally significant pairwise relationships (shown in Table 8.1) that, when controlling for the other curriculum variables, were no longer even marginally significant.

The anomalies between the pairwise and the model-based structural analyses warrant further comment. France and Singapore provide good examples for discussion. France showed statistically significant relationships between textbook space and achievement gain and between

Table 8.2. Estimated Structural Coefficients for the Curriculum and Achievement Model for Each Country (Eighth Grade Mathematics).

Country	R^2	Textbook Coverage to Achievement Gain (δ)	Content Standards Coverage to Achievement Gain (ξ)	Instructional Time to Achievement Gain (γ_τ)
Portugal	0.08	0.08 (0.07)	0.00 (0.01)	−0.14 (0.15)
Canada	0.09	0.16 (0.14)		−0.01 (0.09)
Korea	0.14	0.08 (0.10)	0.00 (0.01)	0.01 (0.15)
Denmark	0.14	−0.12 (0.17)	0.01 (0.01)	0.09 (0.09)
Ireland	0.15	0.18 (0.11)	−0.01 (0.02)	−0.08 (0.15)
Iceland	0.19	0.02 (0.10)	0.03 (0.02)	0.02 (0.08)
Singapore	0.19	0.03 (0.11)	0.00 (0.01)	0.12 (0.16)
Norway	0.23	0.10 (0.10)		0.07 (0.06)
New Zealand	0.23	0.16 (0.07)**		−0.07 (0.07)
Austria	0.24	0.11 (0.09)	−0.01 (0.01)	0.12 (0.09)
Romania	0.28	−0.06 (0.05)	0.02 (0.01)**	0.07 (0.14)
Colombia	0.29	0.05 (0.04)	0.01 (0.01)	−0.12 (0.06)**
USA	0.30	0.09 (0.04)**		−0.02 (0.04)
Australia	0.31	0.14 (0.06)**	−0.02 (0.01)	−0.08 (0.07)
Hungary	0.35	0.15 (0.07)**		0.10 (0.11)
Cyprus	0.36	0.16 (0.06)**	0.00 (0.01)	−0.06 (0.09)

(continued)

Table 8.2. (continued)

Country	R^2	Textbook Coverage to Achievement Gain (δ)	Content Standards Coverage to Achievement Gain (ξ)	Instructional Time to Achievement Gain (γ_τ)
Russian Federation	0.36	−0.05 (0.12)	0.04 (0.01)**	0.00 (0.12)
Slovak Republic	0.36	−0.04 (0.06)	0.01 (0.01)	0.29 (0.14)*
Czech Republic	0.39	−0.07 (0.06)	0.01 (0.01)	0.24 (0.11)**
Hong Kong	0.39	−0.09 (0.09)	0.00 (0.01)	0.30 (0.10)**
Switzerland	0.46	0.64 (0.17)**		−0.10 (0.11)
Germany	0.48	0.13 (0.05)**	0.00 (0.01)	0.13 (0.10)
France	0.49	0.16 (0.12)	−0.01 (0.01)	0.10 (0.08)
Greece	0.50	0.25 (0.10)**	0.01 (0.01)	0.09 (0.08)
Sweden	0.53	−0.04 (0.07)	0.00 (0.01)	0.15 (0.04)**
Spain	0.54	0.21 (0.08)**	−0.03 (0.01)**	−0.07 (0.10)
Slovenia	0.59	−0.05 (0.04)	0.00 (0.01)	0.45 (0.11)**
Netherlands	0.67	0.21 (0.04)**	0.01 (0.01)	−0.05 (0.09)
Japan	0.70	−0.13 (0.11)	−0.01 (0.02)	0.59 (0.18)**

**Significant (p ≤ .05).

*Significant (.05 < p ≤ .10).

Note: *Empty cells reflect the fact that some countries had content standards that intended coverage of all topics.*

instructional time and achievement gain. However, the structural model estimates suggest that neither of these relationships was statistically significant. Further, the analyses done in Chapter Six indicate a strong relationship between these two aspects of curriculum in France (Table 6.7). Because these two instantiations of curriculum were highly related to each other in France, when they were both placed in the same analysis, the procedures had difficulty in discerning which of the two was related to gain. Such situations must be carefully interpreted because to conclude that neither textbook space nor instructional time were related to learning would likely be a mistake. However, to know which of the two is related to gain when statistically controlling for the other is difficult if not impossible to determine. It is perhaps best in these circumstances to conclude that in France, instructional time and textbook space were highly related and that together they were related to achievement gain. A similar conclusion seems warranted in the cases of Singapore and Norway.[11]

Another indication of this problem can be found in Table 8.1, where there are many countries (fourteen) for which there was a significant or at least marginally significant relationship between instructional time and achievement gain. However, in Figure 8.2, when this same relationship is controlled for the other aspects of curriculum, it is no longer statistically significant in many countries. In fact there was significance in only half as many countries as for the pairwise analyses. A thoughtful comparison of the two sets of results is required in examining the specifics for any particular country.

The implication of all of these caveats is that we were unable to empirically establish a relationship between curriculum and learning for only five countries: Canada, Denmark, Ireland, Portugal, and Colombia. Romania, which had no significant pairwise relationships, had one for content standards when controlling for textbook space and instructional time. The other five countries were the same as those indicated in the discussion of Table 8.1. These individual country results can be compared to those for instructional time in Figure 8.1.

The R^2 indicators of fit in Table 8.2 have a mean of 36 percent of the variance in gain accounted for (reducible) by the three curriculum variables. They range from around 10 to 70 percent (the latter for Japan). For Japan, the pairwise relationships were all significant. For the structural model, only instructional time was significantly linked to achievement gain, which implies that the relationship of textbook space and content standards to learning were mediated through instructional time. That is, these two aspects of curriculum had only indirect effects on achievement gain. The results in Chapter Six are consistent with this because instructional time was significantly related both to textbook space and content standards.

The size of the estimated regression coefficients for the relationship of textbook space to achievement gain averaged over all countries was .09. When controlling for the other aspects of curriculum, textbook coverage indicates significant relationships for the largest number of countries when contrasted with instructional time and especially with content standards. However, for some countries, content standards defined the main relationship with achievement gain, and for others, instructional time was the dominant effect.

If one considers only the statistically significant ($p < .05$) estimates, then the average coefficient was .21. In fact, for Switzerland it was .64, which was the largest coefficient relating textbook space to gain for any country. For instructional time, the average coefficient was .07, and it was .01 for content standards. Among only those countries in which the coefficient relating instructional time to achievement gain was statistically significant, the estimated coefficient was .27. For Japan, it was .59.

Averages of the estimated coefficients can be used as values to represent δ, ξ, and γ in Figure 3.1. The substantive interpretation of these coefficients is important. For textbook coverage this implies that in general (averaged across all countries), the allocation of an additional 10 percent of textbook space within a country (for example, about 25 pages in a 250-page textbook) would predict approximately an additional 1 percent gain in achievement on that topic nationally.[12] This increase in achievement gain is slightly less than one-third of a standard deviation, assuming that both content standards and instructional time were held constant across the countries.

For instructional time, the corresponding interpretation is that if on average the teachers of a country were to allocate an additional 15 percent of their time (about a month of instruction) to a topic, then this would be associated with an additional gain in achievement of approximately 1 percent nationally related to that topic. This is more than one-third of a standard deviation, assuming that both content standards and textbook coverage were held constant across the countries.

For content standards, covering a topic area's subtopics completely as opposed to not covering the topic at all would predict a corresponding increase in achievement gain of about .25 percentage points nationally. That is, this would imply that a country's content standards going from not covering any of the two subtopics of a tested topic area to covering both would be associated with an increase of about one-fourth of a percentage point in achievement gain for that topic.

Each of the estimated effects is based on the assumption that the other aspects were held constant. Of course, this is unreasonable. The coherence of a curriculum derives from all aspects working in concert. Then what would be the predicted effect within a country of a coherent attempt to improve learning in a topic by having the country's content standards cover all aspects of that topic, allocating 10 percent coverage in the book, and having teachers on average allocate 15 percent of their mathematics periods over the whole school year (about one month) to instruction in that topic? The model (averaged over countries and based on the empirical relationships found in the data) would predict slightly more than 2 percentage points gain in achievement over all children in the country. This would translate to an increase of around two-thirds of a standard deviation in achievement gain. Given that the average gain over all topics and all countries was 6.1 percentage points, this implies that the increase predicted from the fitted model would be about one-third of that value.[13] The previous simulation was based on the average value over all countries for each of the structural coefficients. For several countries, some of the estimates of these coefficients are not statistically significantly different from 0. The problem with the average is that the effect as noted in the first part of this chapter is interaction based. This implies what we, in fact, observed—values of these coefficients differed from one country to another, including some cases where these coefficients were 0.

Suppose we eliminate those countries for which a structural coefficient is not significantly different from 0. What would be the corresponding prediction of achievement gain for a typical country in which there are statistically significant relationships? We use the same values as before—total (100 percent) coverage of the tested area in the content standards, a 10 percent increase in textbook space, and a 15 percent increase in instructional time. For textbooks, the predicted gain in achievement is 2 percentage points. For content standards and instructional time, the corresponding predictions are gains of 1 and almost 3 percentage points. Combining the effects in a coherent way implies a gain in achievement of almost 6 percentage points—a gain equal to the average gain in mathematics and representing a predicted change in gain equal to two standard deviations.

But even these predictions are inaccurate for individual countries where the particular pattern of structural coefficients would need to be taken into account. For example, in Japan, where the impact of both content standards and textbooks is indirect through their impact on instructional time, the predicted gain in achievement associated with an increase in instructional time of about one month is 9 percentage points (an increase of three standard deviations).

The Cultural Hypothesis Revisited for Mathematics

In Chapter Six we presented several examples of countries, showing how the aspects of curriculum were differently related to each other and thus how curricular structure was attained differently in those countries. We reasoned that such variations were consistent with the cultural hypothesis that suggested that curriculum, learning, and their relationship were country specific and that this also likely reflected deeper cultural differences.

In this chapter we did analyses expanding how the curricular aspects were related to learning (achievement gain) on a country-by-country basis. These results were summarized in Table 8.2. We now expand the country-specific models presented in Chapter Six to include the relationship of curriculum to achievement.

Figure 8.4 presents the specific models for several countries that illustrate several of the patterns of how curriculum—and its various aspects—were related to achievement gains. These examples are illustrative and not meant to be exhaustive. In part (a) of Figure 8.4, a schematic is presented for Japan based on the pairwise relationships among the aspects of curriculum and achievement gain for eighth grade mathematics. This is averaged over all topics. In part (b), a second schematic is presented for Japan that is based on the estimated values of the structural model.

In either case the point is clear. The Japanese educational system was very coherent, consistent, and interrelated structurally. It is interesting to note that when properly controlled, the relationship of content standards and textbooks to learning was indirect. That is, these two factors related to achievement gains only through their effects on instructional time.

Part (c) presents the structural model for the United States, where the aggregate content standards covered virtually every mathematics topic (this was also true for each of the states individually). There was essentially no variation in content standards coverage. For this reason, content standards could not be related to the other variables. Other analyses presented elsewhere showed a strong consistency between content standards and textbook coverage.[14] The model presented here, however, shows the strong role that textbooks played (both directly and indirectly) in learning mathematics in the eighth grade in the United States.

Part (d) presents the structural model for Slovenia, another country with a similar pattern of relationships among the aspects of curriculum. The structure of the estimated relationships, however, shows a different relationship of curriculum to learning. Here the relationship of textbooks to achievement gain was only indirect through its effect on instructional

Figure 8.4. Estimated Structural Model of Curriculum and Achievement for Selected Countries (Eighth Grade Mathematics).

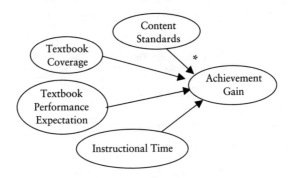

(a) Japan (pairwise relationship)

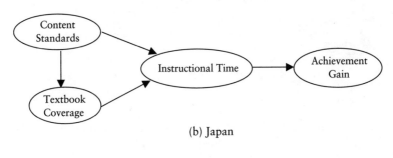

(b) Japan

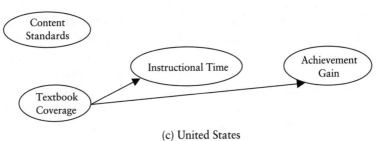

(c) United States

Arrows indicate statistically significant positive relationships; absence indicates no relationship.

Figure 8.4. (*Continued*)

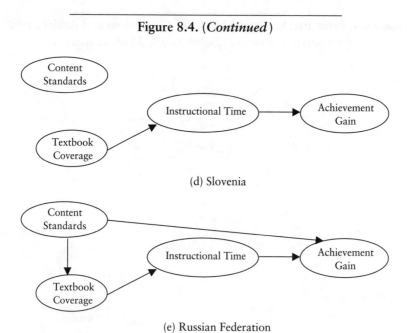

(d) Slovenia

(e) Russian Federation

time. This is in contrast to the United States, in which the relationship of textbooks to achievement gain was both direct and indirect.

Part (e) presents the structural model for Russia in eighth grade mathematics. Here the content standards bear both a direct and an indirect relationship to gain with the latter through their impact on textbook coverage, which in turn has an impact on instructional time. The other direct impact on achievement gain is instructional time, but the indirect impacts of other aspects of curriculum can clearly be seen as they operate through their effects on instructional time.[15] Other patterns of relationships were also present in the data, which illustrate the nature of the topic-by-country interaction-based relationships.

Science

Table 8.3 shows the science results that parallel those for mathematics in Table 8.1 (those for the pairwise relationships between aspects of curriculum and achievement gain but not controlled for other aspects of curriculum). At first glance it is clear that there were many fewer such pairwise relationships than there were for mathematics. For around half of the countries there were no statistically significant bivariate relationships.

Country	Content Standards Coverage and Gain		Textbook Coverage and Gain		Textbook's Complex Expectation Coverage and Gain		Teacher Coverage and Gain		Instructional Time and Gain	
	Coefficient (std. err.)	R^2	Coefficient (std. err.)	R^2	Coefficient (std. err.)	R^2	Coefficient (std. err.)	R^2	Coefficient (std. err.)	R^2
Australia	0.02 (0.05)	0.01	−0.08 (0.08)	0.06	0.04 (0.12)	0.01	0.00 (0.04)	0.00	−0.04 (0.16)	0.01
Austria	0.03 (0.01)**	0.30	0.02 (0.07)	0.01	0.21 (0.11)*	0.20	0.01 (0.06)	0.00	0.01 (0.08)	0.00
Canada	0.00 (0.01)	0.00	0.01 (0.05)	0.00	0.02 (0.04)	0.01	0.04 (0.02)**	0.23	0.09 (0.10)	0.06
Colombia	0.02 (0.02)	0.05	−0.04 (0.05)	0.06			0.00 (0.03)	0.00	0.02 (0.13)	0.00
Cyprus	0.00 (0.02)	0.00	0.01 (0.05)	0.00	0.19 (0.14)	0.12	0.01 (0.02)	0.01	0.08 (0.09)	0.05
Czech Republic	0.02 (0.02)	0.13	0.14 (0.07)*	0.22	0.13 (0.20)	0.03	0.03 (0.03)	0.06	0.16 (0.12)	0.12
France	0.02 (0.02)	0.07	0.04 (0.07)	0.02	0.19 (0.08)**	0.28	0.03 (0.03)	0.05	0.01 (0.14)	0.00
Germany	−0.01 (0.01)	0.13	−0.03 (0.04)	0.03	0.09 (0.09)	0.07	0.00 (0.03)	0.00	−0.08 (0.08)	0.06
Greece	0.02 (0.02)	0.06	−0.17 (0.13)	0.09	−5.36 (6.29)	0.05	0.05 (0.05)	0.06	0.05 (0.22)	0.00
Hong Kong	0.00 (0.01)	0.00	0.13 (0.09)	0.12	0.19 (0.12)	0.14	0.02 (0.02)	0.03	0.03 (0.07)	0.01
Hungary	−0.02 (0.01)	0.11	0.01 (0.10)	0.00	0.31 (0.37)	0.05	−0.02 (0.05)	0.01	−0.01 (0.14)	0.00
Iceland	0.03 (0.04)	0.04	0.08 (0.06)	0.09	0.02 (0.05)	0.01	0.03 (0.03)	0.07	0.07 (0.17)	0.01
Ireland	0.00 (0.02)	0.00	0.00 (0.05)	0.00	0.06 (0.08)	0.03	0.05 (0.02)**	0.39	0.17 (0.07)**	0.31
Japan	0.04 (0.02)**	0.27	0.02 (0.08)	0.00	0.03 (0.20)	0.00	0.06 (0.02)**	0.34	0.33 (0.14)**	0.27
Korea	0.01 (0.02)	0.01	0.02 (0.10)	0.00	−0.05 (0.18)	0.01	0.04 (0.03)	0.11	0.24 (0.15)	0.14
Latvia	−0.01 (0.07)	0.00	1.00 (0.06)	0.00	0.02 (0.09)	0.00	−0.02 (0.06)	0.01	−0.25 (0.20)	0.10

(continued)

Table 8.3. (continued)

Country	Content Standards Coverage and Gain		Textbook Coverage and Gain		Textbook's Complex Expectation Coverage and Gain		Teacher Coverage and Gain		Instructional Time and Gain	
	Coefficient (std. err.)	R^2	Coefficient (std. err.)	R^2	Coefficient (std. err.)	R^2	Coefficient (std. err.)	R^2	Coefficient (std. err.)	R^2
Netherlands	0.01 (0.02)	0.04	−0.03 (0.10)	0.01	0.25 (0.24)	0.07	−0.04 (0.04)	0.05	−0.12 (0.11)	0.08
New Zealand			0.02 (0.06)	0.01	0.07 (0.02)**	0.45	0.04 (0.03)	0.12	0.04 (0.12)	0.01
Norway	−0.01 (0.00)	0.01	−0.13 (0.06)**	0.26	−0.05 (0.06)	0.05	0.01 (0.03)	0.01	−0.01 (0.21)	0.00
Portugal	0.00 (0.04)	0.00	0.13 (0.12)	0.07	0.07 (0.11)	0.03	0.16 (0.05)**	0.44	0.17 (0.15)	0.08
Romania	0.01 (0.01)	0.04	−0.06 (0.06)	0.08	−0.32 (0.16)*	0.21	0.06 (0.04)	0.13	0.14 (0.10)	0.12
Russian Federation	0.05 (0.03)*	0.21	0.08 (0.09)	0.06	1.94 (0.92)**	0.23	0.00 (0.05)	0.00	0.04 (0.23)	0.00
Singapore	0.07 (0.02)**	0.34	0.09 (0.13)	0.03	0.13 (0.09)	0.12	0.05 (0.03)*	0.22	0.13 (0.19)	0.03
Slovak Republic	0.01 (0.02)	0.03	0.05 (0.05)	0.06	0.37 (0.21)*	0.18	0.00 (0.03)	0.00	0.02 (0.06)	0.01
Slovenia	−0.03 (0.04)	0.05	0.02 (0.06)	0.01	0.06 (0.08)	0.04	−0.01 (0.04)	0.01	0.09 (0.13)	0.03
Spain	−0.03 (0.03)	0.05	−0.10 (0.13)	0.04	0.40 (0.17)**	0.28	0.00 (0.03)	0.00	−1.15 (0.20)	0.00
Sweden	0.00 (0.02)	0.00	0.01 (0.10)	0.00	2.26 (0.26)	0.00	0.07 (0.06)	0.10	0.11 (0.20)	0.02
Switzerland	0.00 (0.02)	0.00	0.00 (0.07)	0.00	−0.17 (0.29)	0.02	0.01 (0.02)	0.03	0.06 (0.07)	0.05
USA			−0.11 (0.05)*	0.22	0.15 (0.08)*	0.19	0.02 (0.02)	0.09	0.02 (0.15)	0.00

**Significant ($p \le .05$).

*Significant (.05 < $p \le .10$).

Note: Empty cells reflect the fact that some countries had content standards that intended coverage of all topics. For Colombia the empty cell reflects that no complex performance expectations were found in the textbook.

The curriculum variable that was significantly related to achievement gain for the largest number of countries for eighth grade science was one not included in the two-way analyses—textbook coverage related to more demanding performance expectations. In the case of science, this not only includes analyzing and solving problems (a category similar to one used for mathematics) but also investigating the natural world. This category represents one of the major differences between science and mathematics. That is, science involves the various aspects of empirical inquiry—designing, conducting, analyzing, and interpreting data from empirical investigations. This is what many would argue is the conceptual heart of science education. Because of this, it seems very significant that this aspect of textbook coverage was related to achievement gain significantly for the largest number of countries.

In teacher implementation the percentage of teachers covering a topic and not the instructional time variable was significant in more countries. This is in clear contrast to mathematics. With some notable exceptions, the R^2 statistics were not very large for most countries and for most of the curriculum variables. In fact, the R^2 statistics averaged over countries were less than .10 for all curriculum variables except that for demanding textbook performance expectations. This is considerably smaller than the corresponding statistics for mathematics.

It is again important to bring up the caveat discussed in Chapter Six about the TIMSS sampling and questionnaire allocation designs as well as their implications for empirically examining the relationship of curriculum to learning. One of the reasons for the smaller number of statistically significant relationships in science may well be related to these design issues. We believe that this is likely, but it is also possible that curriculum and its relationship to learning could be markedly different for science.

Only one curriculum variable had an average R^2 value as large as the corresponding one for mathematics: the proportion of textbook space devoted to high-demand performance expectations, for which the average R^2 was .10. This average was .25 when averaged over the eight countries with significant or marginally significant relationships ($p < .10$) between it and achievement gain. That is, an average of 25 percent of the variance in achievement gain could be accounted for (reduced) by the proportion of textbook space that expected more demanding performances from students.

Table 8.4 gives the results for the structural relationships implied by the model for science. When controlling for the various aspects of curriculum, several relationships that were not previously evident as significant emerge.

Table 8.4. Estimated Structural Coefficients for the Curriculum and Achievement Model for Each Country (Eighth Grade Science).

Country	R^2	Textbook Coverage to Achievement Gain (δ)	Content Standards Coverage to Achievement Gain (ξ)	Instructional Time to Achievement Gain (γ_τ)
Portugal	0.08	0.08 (0.07)	0.00 (0.01)	−0.14 (0.15)
New Zealand	0.01	0.01 (0.11)		0.03 (0.20)
Sweden	0.05	−0.08 (0.16)	−0.01 (0.02)	0.26 (0.33)
Slovenia	0.07	−0.02 (0.10)	−0.03 (0.04)	0.12 (0.23)
Australia	0.09	−0.11 (0.11)	0.01 (0.05)	0.12 (0.22)
Portugal	0.09	0.08 (0.21)	−0.02 (0.04)	0.10 (0.26)
Cyprus	0.09	−0.05 (0.07)	−0.01 (0.02)	0.16 (0.14)
France	0.10	0.05 (0.10)	0.02 (0.02)	−0.11 (0.20)
Spain	0.10	−0.12 (0.15)	0.03 (0.03)	0.02 (0.21)
Hungary	0.12	−0.01 (0.13)	−0.02 (0.01)	0.07 (0.20)
Latvia	0.12	0.04 (0.07)	0.01 (0.07)	−0.31 (0.23)
Hong Kong	0.12	0.13 (0.10)	0.00 (0.02)	0.00 (0.08)
Switzerland	0.13	−0.13 (0.12)	0.00 (0.02)	0.17 (0.12)
Canada	0.14	−0.09 (0.09)	0.01 (0.01)	0.25 (0.18)
Colombia	0.14	−0.06 (0.05)	0.02 (0.02)	−0.01 (0.13)
Iceland	0.16	0.16 (0.12)	0.02 (0.04)	−0.26 (0.29)
Korea	0.16	−0.03 (0.11)	0.01 (0.02)	0.26 (0.17)

Slovak Republic	0.18	0.25 (0.16)	-0.24 (0.17)
Netherlands	0.17	0.10 (0.13)	-0.20 (0.14)
Russian Federation	0.21	0.02 (0.13)	0.01 (0.29)
Norway	0.29	-0.14 (0.06)**	0.15 (0.21)
USA	0.32	-0.15 (0.06)**	0.21 (0.15)
Germany	0.33	-0.08 (0.04)*	-0.04 (0.08)
Austria	0.34	0.03 (0.07)	-0.06 (0.08)
Greece	0.36	-0.42 (0.17)**	0.36 (0.25)
Czech Republic	0.38	0.36 (0.18)*	-0.44 (0.29)
Singapore	0.38	0.09 (0.20)	-0.28 (0.31)
Japan	0.49	-0.12 (0.07)	0.33 (0.15)**
Ireland	0.57	-0.11 (0.05)**	0.30 (0.07)**
Romania	0.75	-0.27 (0.05)**	0.39 (0.08)**

	0.00 (0.02)		
	0.02 (0.02)		
	0.05 (0.03)		
	-0.01 (0.02)		
	-0.02 (0.01)**		
	0.04 (0.01)**		
	0.04 (0.02)*		
	0.02 (0.01)		
	0.08 (0.03)**		
	0.04 (0.02)*		
	-0.02 (0.02)		
	0.03 (0.01)**		

*Significant (p ≤ .05).

*Significant (.05 < p ≤ .10).

Note: *Empty cells reflect the fact that some countries had content standards that intended coverage of all topics.*

Proportion of textbook space devoted to a topic was the aspect of curriculum that was significantly related to achievement gain in the most countries, as was true for mathematics. Unlike the case for mathematics, the average estimated regression coefficient was negative, which implies that greater proportions of science textbook space allocated to a topic were associated with smaller corresponding achievement gains. The effect for textbook space on achievement gain was not significant at the interaction level but only at the average level over countries. Also unlike the case for mathematics, two-thirds of the countries showed no significant relationships between any of the aspects of curriculum and achievement gain.

Interpreting the negative relationship for science textbook space and learning is problematic. Perhaps it, too, is reflective of the fact that science was in many countries two to four different classes and as such was represented in the analyses by composite textbooks made up from each of these classes. These composites may not have reflected instructional priorities as clearly as would a single textbook. It may have simply been that more textbook space was allocated to topics known to be more difficult and that this difficulty was reflected in smaller achievement gains.

This problematic nature of the interpretation should be taken to imply that to do a better study of the relationship of curriculum and learning in science, one might have to do that study discipline by discipline. That is, each study would not be about science but about one of the disciplines that help make up school science (for example, physics).

A further examination of the data may shed more light on the negative relationship. Two of the topics with very little textbook space allocated to them showed large achievement gains. One topic (discussed earlier in the chapter) for which considerable textbook space was allocated had only average achievement gains associated with it. Once these three topics were removed from the analyses, the relationship was close to 0 and was not statistically significant.

The substantive interpretation of these coefficients is also important. For textbook space, this implies that in general (averaged across countries) the allocation of 10 percent of textbook space to a topic within a country would be associated with an achievement gain approximately one percentage point lower. This is approximately the same magnitude (ignoring the sign) as was the case for mathematics.[16]

The corresponding interpretation for instructional time is that if teachers on average in a country had allocated 15 percent of their time (approximately one month of instruction) to a topic, this would have been associated with an additional achievement gain of about two-thirds of a percent for that topic, which is approximately one-fourth of a standard deviation. For content standards, the 100 percent coverage of a topic area's subtopics would have been associated with a corresponding increase of one percentage point in achievement gain, which is about one-third of a standard deviation.

These results are markedly different from those for mathematics, in which the largest predicted effect was for textbook space and was positive. For science, the largest predicted positive impact on learning was from content standards when controlling for the other two aspects of curriculum. Given the previous discussion, we will assume that textbook space had no significant effect in science rather than the overall negative one that appeared to be an artifact of a few topics. Instructional time was similar in both mathematics (a 1 percent increase in achievement gain) and science (.67 percent increase in achievement gain).

As discussed previously, each of the estimated effects was based on the assumption that the other two aspects of curriculum were held constant. What would have been the predicted increase in achievement gain if a country simultaneously gave 15 percent instructional time on average for a topic and included all of the relevant subtopics in its content standards? The model (averaged over countries) would predict a 1.67 percent increase in achievement gain, which translates into about three-fourths of a standard deviation and was about one-third as large as the typical gain averaged over all topics and all countries. Textbook space was left out of this estimation because its negative relationship to achievement gain was considered as likely to be artifactual.

This overall picture contrasts with that for mathematics, in which the predicted increase in achievement gain was around two percentage points. If our assumption regarding textbook space is correct, then this would imply that the same scenario of increased curriculum coverage would produce a greater impact in mathematics than it would in science. All of the caveats previously expressed must be kept in mind when interpreting this result.

Considering as we did in mathematics only the countries with statistically significant relationships and using the same values as before, we can predict achievement gains for a typical country in which there are significant relationships. For content standards and instructional time, the predictions are gains of four and five percentage points, respectively. Combining the effects implies a gain in achievement of nine percentage points, which is equal to three standard deviations. This is a predicted gain half again as large as that for mathematics under the same scenario.

The Cultural Hypothesis Revisited for Science

We now expand the country-specific models for science presented in Chapter Six to include the relationship of curriculum to achievement. We did this previously for mathematics. Because the relationships described for science were all defined at the interaction level except for the relationship of textbook space to learning (which we are assuming to be 0),

Figure 8.5. Estimated Structural Model of Curriculum and Achievement for Selected Countries (Eighth Grade Science).

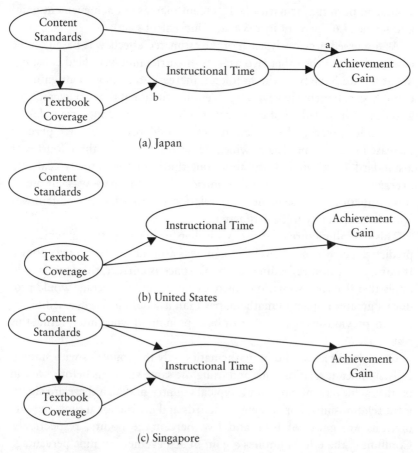

(a) Japan

(b) United States

(c) Singapore

[a]Arrows indicate statistically significant positive relationships; absence indicates no relationship.
[b]Significance: $p < .135$.

the different patterns we now present illustrate the cultural hypothesis for science education.

Part (a) of Figure 8.5 illustrates the significant relationships for Japan. This set of relationships is very different from those for mathematics. Here the content standards have a significant direct relationship with both textbook coverage and achievement gain. However, textbook coverage is apparently not related to teacher time; it should be noted that the structural coefficient for Japan relating textbook coverage to instructional time was positive but marginally significant ($p < .135$). Instructional time was significantly related to achievement gain. Once again, for Japan content standards play a significant role.

Part (b) of Figure 8.5 presents the structural relationships for the United States, which is the same set of relationships found for the United States in mathematics. This once again suggests the dominant role that textbooks play in the United States.

Part (c) of Figure 8.5 displays the structural relationships for Singapore. Here the content standards also have a prominent relationship to achievement gain, as was the case in Japan. However, in addition they influence instructional time both directly and indirectly through their effect on textbook space. Teacher time does not appear to be related to achievement gain, but teacher coverage is.

The structural relationships for these three countries' curricula illustrate that curriculum was related to learning in the sense of achievement gain. However, as was the case for mathematics, the exact set of structural relationships among aspects of curriculum and their relation to achievement gain varied by country. That was true not just for these three illustrations but for most of the countries. This is again consistent with the cultural hypothesis advanced earlier.

NOTES

1. The results from the two-way analysis on the transformed data support this even further. For the analysis based on the logarithmic transformation, the corresponding coefficient was positive and significant at $p < .058$. In the case of the square root transformation, the coefficient was also positive and significant at $p < .089$.

2. As implied by the model, the relationship of each of the two teacher implementation variables to gain must be separately controlled for the other two aspects of curriculum—content standards and textbook space. This implies that the relationship of each of these two aspects to gain could be characterized in two ways. The results are mostly parallel and lead to the same

general conclusion in both cases (with one exception, discussed in a later section). The analyses reported here for content standards and textbooks were controlled for instructional time.

3. Perhaps the negative coefficient can be explained by the overcontrol as a result of the statistical model fitted to the data in which the effect of textbook on gain is controlled for by both content standards and instructional time.

4. The fitted line shown in Figure 8.2 is not derived from the weighted least-squares procedure for the two-way model. This is just the scatterplot of the marginal data points with a simple OLS fitting of the regression line.

5. In this conception, there are two means for each cell—one each for the two variables to be related (for example, textbook coverage and achievement gain). If we use both means for each cell and select a row, that is, one of the thirty sets of twenty observations, we will have a within-country, across-topic vector of paired means. A regression using these data will correspond to what we called the country effect in the two-way analyses. If we use both means for each cell and select a column, that is, one of the twenty sets of thirty observations, we can produce within-topic, across-countries regressions. In the language of the two-way analyses, this was called the topic effect.

6. The regression line in Figure 8.3 for the full 510 data points was fitted using resistant regression methods (Haertel, Thrash, & Wiley, 1978; Emerson & Hoaglin, 1983b). As such, it was not based on the formal generalized weighted least-squares methods used to test the fit of the model. In all such potential relationships we only examine and interpret them when the formally fitted weighted least-squares regression procedures indicate the presence of a statistically significant interaction.

7. Mathematically, it can be demonstrated that the overall regression line is approximately a weighted average of the individual country regressions.

8. An additional reason for turning to these analyses is that the two-way analysis decomposes the relationship into three orthogonal components. To represent the total relationship, these components need to be combined in some way. The relationship described in Figure 8.3 examines only the residuals and hence can be interpreted only in terms of deviations. That is, it can be interpreted in terms of only one of the orthogonal spaces.

9. These are simply OLS regressions fitted for each country using tested area topics (twenty in the case of mathematics) as the unit of analysis. Given the correlated error structure resulting from the lack of independence among the topics (units), these regressions are not formally the best procedures to

use. That is why we present only these results, given the significant interaction effects from the two-way model fitting. Those results indicate that in general over all topics and over all countries, there is a positive relationship. Figure 8.3 illustrates this for science. Australia is one example of a negative relationship within the same context. As indicated previously, the overall positive relationship is a kind of composite of positive, negative, and no relationships over countries. These regressions are intended to provide the data from which to explore this issue.

10. Because these are OLS regressions, the significance level might be different if the analyses were weighted as was done in the two-way model. A different way to do this would be to do a hierarchical model within each country, using covariances defined at the school/classroom level. This would then have to be done to reflect the idiosyncrasies of the within-country sampling designs for each of the thirty countries. This was beyond the scope of what we felt we could do with given resources.

11. This is a classic illustration of the problem of multicollinearity, which occurs when variables or combinations of variables are too highly correlated for their effects to be separated statistically.

12. Technically, the coefficient that should be used here is that from the marginal regression, because it was significant ($p < .018$) and the interaction effect was not. That value, however, is .08, which is almost identical to the average (.09) and therefore would not appreciably alter the conclusions.

13. The predicted effects are made based on the estimated multiple regression model, including content standards, textbook space, and instructional time. The unstandardized estimated β's were used. The assumption made for the predictions included an average size for textbooks of 250 pages and a school year of 175 instructional periods.

14. Schmidt, McKnight, Cogan, Jakwerth, & Houang, 1999.

15. Models using the percent of teachers covering each topic as the teacher implementation variable were fitted for each country. They were not presented because of space limitations.

16. This estimated effect was based on the marginal because the significant effect was defined at the marginal level.

9

CURRICULUM AND LEARNING GAINS ACROSS COUNTRIES

HOW ARE DIFFERENCES IN LEARNING GAINS and curriculum in various topics related across countries? In Chapter Eight we were interested in questions of polity and policy in schooling and education. We believe—and the empirical data thus far is consistent with the hypothesis—that culture and the social history of individual countries structure curriculum and schooling. The polity of education—the way it is organized as a human social institution—seems to be determined by these factors, and that polity sets the arena in which the deliberate efforts at schooling must take place. Those deliberate efforts—that is, shaping learning by educational policy—require an understanding of the underlying polity to be effective.

Thus, the structure of curriculum as it is shaped in a particular country is a fundamental policy question. The structure of curriculum—at least in school mathematics and science—is related to achievement gains within a country across topics (as we found in the preceding chapter). These were country-level descriptions. However, they focused on resource allocations and priorities across topics within a country. This was necessarily a matter of *relative* gains. Scarce resources of instructional time, teacher attention, and textbook space were allocated among a range of topics in school science and mathematics. We examined how these differing priorities enacted in differing curricular structures affected achievement gains in one topic relative to another. Focused as we were within countries and across topics, we essentially had to treat the thirty or so participating countries as separate cultures or at least contexts in which we saw the effects of priorities and policy play out.

However, we are also interested in examining the absolute amount of learning that takes place in eighth grade in specific topic areas (not relative to other topic areas). That is, we are interested not just in the differences among countries but in the difference of their effectiveness in using curricular opportunities to bring about learning in a specific topic area, regardless of how they structured those opportunities relative to others.

For that purpose, this chapter focuses on cross-country differences in the allocation of curriculum resources and in their relationships to achievement gains. We are looking for the most effective allocations of resources for different mathematics and science topics. Most simply, we are interested in why some countries did better than others on the TIMSS Population 2 test and, more generally, why that would be true for other TIMSS-like tests. Why do children in some countries learn more in eighth grade than they do in other countries?

The results of the two-way analyses reported in Chapter Eight suggest that the answer to this question likely will vary by topic. Chapter Eight characterized curriculum polices and structures aimed at influencing the relative priorities among topics. This chapter seeks to characterize how those priorities—no matter how arrived at—were related to the difference in achievement gains observed across different countries. The question here is—no matter what the relative priorities were within a country— how did the resultant emphasis for a topic compare across countries? Was the resultant emphasis for a topic related to differences in achievement for that topic?

This set of questions plays to one of the strengths of cross-national comparisons of achievement when these are coupled—as in TIMSS—with empirical measures of curriculum and instruction variables. No matter how strongly the relative priorities within a country across topics are related to achievement gains, the ultimate question is how much learning is possible with different resource allocations. This is a question more in absolute than relative terms.

An oversimplified portrayal of Chapter Eight was that it centered on how curriculum policies and structures were interrelated and on the relationship of the subsequent priorities to learning. In that same sense, an oversimplified characterization of this chapter is that it focuses on the consequences of these priorities in understanding cross-national differences in achievement gains.

Country-Level Relationships Averaged Across Topics

Before turning to topic-by-topic analyses, we explore several country effects averaged over topics related to instructional time. By averaging over topics, the relationship that emerges reflects a general country-level relationship that holds on average across topics.

Because of the way in which instructional time was defined—the percent of the instructional year allocated to a topic estimated as the average for a typical teacher at the national level—the country averages over topics were constrained, conceptually, to be equal.[1] To examine the relationship of instructional time to learning on average, we transformed this variable to reflect the total amount of time (in hours) allocated to a topic within a country.[2] This was to capitalize on what variability there was in actual time amounts across countries, something that could not be done when examining relative time allocations.

Using this definition of instructional time, the two-way analyses indicate the presence of significant country effects in mathematics ($p < .015$) but not in science ($p < .899$). These analyses held constant textbook space and content standards. For mathematics the R^2 index was .24.

Figure 9.1 shows the plot of achievement gain and allocated time in hours for an average mathematics topic. (In this plot, the data points represent countries, and the other aspects of curriculum were not controlled.) In general there was a positive relationship over the twenty-seven countries whose data are displayed. The straight line represents the linear relationship (the regression line). However, the R^2 associated with the regression analysis was relatively small.

We next examined a more complex model, which is represented by the curved line in Figure 9.1.[3] This resulted in an R^2 of .12 ($p < .07$), which implies that the pairwise relationship was such that the rate of increase in gain for more time was not constant (directly proportional to time). Rather, it in fact accelerated rapidly after about nine hours per topic. Before that, the amount of time per topic did not seem to have an appreciably differential effect on gain. These simple plots do not hold constant the other aspects of curriculum as was the case with the two-way analysis.

Instructional Time for More Demanding Expectations

We are pressing analysis close to the limits of our data here, but we felt one more effort to further tease out the relationship if it exists was in order, so another measure of instructional time was constructed. Total instructional time in hours was the first measure for time used previously, but we would like to be able to focus on time devoted to instruction expecting more demanding performances from students. We did this by using textbook space devoted to more demanding student performance

Figure 9.1. Scatterplot of Achievement Gains and Instructional Time and Instructional Time Related to More Demanding Performance Expectations (Eighth Grade Mathematics).

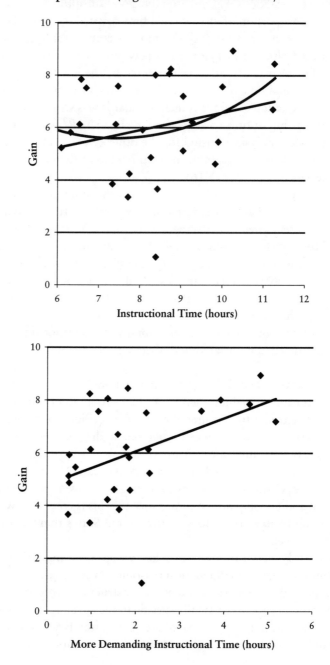

expectations as an indicator of how much instructional time was devoted to these increased expectations.[4] This involved making an assumption that the proportion of textbook space devoted to more demanding student performance expectations was a reasonably good substitute for a direct measure of the proportion of instructional time devoted to such. The data did not contain a direct measure of this more demanding instructional time.

Figure 9.1 also shows a plot of this new time variable with achievement gains. The linear relationship (represented by the line) of more demanding instructional time to achievement gain unadjusted for total textbook space given to a topic and for content standards was stronger than the general relationship of time to achievement gain. The R^2 was .20 ($p < .05$). The two-way analysis adjusted for the other two aspects of curriculum indicated a statistically significant relationship of the new time variable to achievement gain ($p < .016$).

The two plots shown in Figure 9.1 under the umbrella of the two-way analyses suggest that instructional time was related to achievement gain where both measures were averaged over topics. That is, the more time a typical topic received from teachers on average for a country, the larger the average gain was for a typical topic in that country. This relationship is defined at a marginal (country) level and not the country-by-topic interaction level (which was not statistically significant). This implies that, in general, such a relationship held for each topic. That is, those countries that allocated comparatively larger amounts of instructional time to a typical topic also had associated with them correspondingly larger achievement gains.

The positive relationship for instructional time spent on more demanding expectations to achievement gains leads to an important conjecture: more instructional time centered on topic-specific problem solving and mathematical reasoning was associated with greater learning at the country-level. Because our measure of time was a hybrid involving both instructional time and textbook coverage, we can offer this idea only as a conjecture. Certainly this seems to be an area for better curriculum measurement and investigation in future studies. This is consistent with a similar finding from a study done in the United States that focused at the classroom level.[5]

We must be very careful here. When we speak of more time spent on problem solving and mathematical reasoning averaged across topics, this is not the same as generic, content-free instruction on problem solving. The measure we used was totally specific to the coverage of specific topics even if it was averaged over several topics. It certainly was not instruction on problem solving in the absence of a specific topic.[6] At least in the

United States, some advocate problem-solving instruction that is essentially content free, focusing on the problem-solving process as its own content and with mathematical content merely incidental and subservient. This is not that, and neither does it come close to offering hard evidence about the value of content-free problem-solving instruction.

Issues of Focus and Emphasis

The previous analyses show, in effect, that the more time allocated to mathematics instruction on a typical topic in a country, the greater the associated overall or average gain. This speaks in a sense to the issue of emphasis or focus in instruction. Because these relationships were defined at the average topic level, the relationship can be simplified to that of the amount of total instructional time over the year. When considering an average over topics, allocating more time nationally is equivalent to providing greater focus or emphasis but to mathematics as a whole rather than to some topics and not others. A subtler and more important question is whether this degree of variation in emphasis through instructional time was related to achievement gain on a topic-by-topic basis. We will turn to this question in a subsequent section.

We have written on the closely related issue of focus elsewhere.[7] We have characterized the lack of focus or emphasis in U.S. curricula in school science and mathematics as being "a mile wide and an inch deep." This reflects the U.S. practice of teaching many topics but with little depth or emphasis in instruction on any of them.

The previous analyses do not directly address this use of the term *focus* because they deal with the total amount of instructional time for mathematics. This is because in those analyses, we always divided by the total number of topics when taking an average over topics. Thus, the only way in that case to obtain greater focus or emphasis for a topic would be to increase the total amount of instructional time available for mathematics over the school year. Of course, this has policy implications and might be used in arguments for increasing emphasis by increasing instructional time overall. However, this can be done only up to a point. Total available school instructional time is a scarce or at least limited resource and one that must be shared with instruction for other disciplines.

Another way to achieve greater focus—as we have argued elsewhere—is to teach fewer topics in a given school year.[8] Earlier analysis elsewhere suggested that the United States was an outlier in terms of the number of topics it included in eighth grade mathematics and eighth grade science compared with other countries. For example, U.S. eighth grade textbooks devote some space to more topics than in any other country except one, which placed them in the ninety-seventh percentile at 1.64 standard deviations above the mean. The only country with more topics was Switzerland, where the data was a composite across three distinct language-based educational subsystems. The inclusion of more topics in such a composite does not have the same meaning as that in the United States because no Swiss textbook actually included all the topics represented by the "average" textbook, whereas in the U.S. what was typical was also actual.[9]

We believe that this effect of lack of focus is a straightforward inference based on the U.S. position as an outlier in the data and on its relatively poor performance. However, this inference is specific to the United States. The question here is whether a similar inference holds in a more general way. In particular—and in contrast to the foregoing analyses—the question is whether it held without regard to the total amount of instructional time (at least within the limits found in the TIMSS data).

To answer the question of focus and use the previous findings, we returned to the textbook-based measure of the percent of a topic for which instruction focused on more demanding performance expectations. Using this measure seemed to convert total teacher time to a more sensitive measure of time—at least more sensitive with respect to learning. Using this variable as we did works with total instructional time but moves toward reflecting a qualitative difference in coverage (inferred from textbooks but presumed to carry over into classroom instruction).

To better make this measure reflect focus, we took the same average but only for those topics for which there was some textbook coverage with more demanding textbook expectations. This seemed likely to produce a more accurate measure of focus for the textbook. Given our assumption that textbook space is a good rough indicator of emphasis on more demanding performances for classroom instruction, it also becomes a more accurate measure of focus associated with instructional time.

It is, as we stated earlier, a measure of the qualitative nature of focus and not just its quantitative aspect. A large value for this measure averaged over topics would arise because only the topics receiving coverage that involved more demanding expectations would be counted in that average. We believe that this is a reasonable definition of focus because we take *focus* to mean not just more coverage but qualitatively different coverage. To be a bit trite, it's not how long you make it but how you make it long. In this measure, increased emphasis would come from including more demanding expectations rather than simply more coverage. This, we feel, makes this a better indicator of focus (albeit rough) rather than simply emphasis in the sense of increased coverage. Working with more demanding expectations likely takes more instructional time. Because instructional time is a limited resource, increased work with more demanding expectations seems likely to be linked to work with somewhat fewer topics—another sense in which we have used focus elsewhere. This does not mean that the other topics would not be covered but that that they would at best be covered in a less demanding way, perhaps as review or in a cursory introduction.

Now the question becomes, Is the amount of focus on a topic in the sense of more demanding expectations related to average achievement gain? Figure 9.2 displays a plot for mathematics. The relationship for mathematics was statistically significant ($p < .044$), was essentially linear (adding a nonlinear component did not appreciably help), and had an R^2 of .14. For science, the relationship was not statistically significant.

This provides some evidence that higher percentages of coverage of a typical topic that involved more demanding performance expectations were associated with larger-than-average achievement gains. We take this as likely to imply that coverage focused on a limited number of topics that were covered more deeply (in the sense of exploiting more demanding expectations) was related, albeit modestly, to higher average achievement gain. The number of topics covered with more demanding performance expectations was smaller than the number covered in general at eighth grade for all countries both in science and mathematics. That much of our assumption seems grounded empirically. This is consistent with our earlier discussion of emphasis on topics by increased instructional time but now is extended to the sense of focus as covering fewer topics but with more demanding performance expectations.

Topic-Specific Relationships

We now turn to analyses done for each topic separately—a course suggested by the significant interaction based relationships discussed in Chapter Eight. The analyses presented here parallel those found in that chapter's figures and tables.

Mathematics

Table 9.1 displays the pairwise relationships between each measure of curriculum and between achievement gains in eighth grade mathematics. Eight of the twenty mathematics tested area topics did not show any statistically or marginally significant relationships between any of the aspects of curriculum and achievement gain. These topics included relations of

Figure 9.2. Scatterplot for Achievement Gains and Instructional Time for More Demanding Performance Expectations Averaged over Only Topics Receiving More Demanding Coverage.

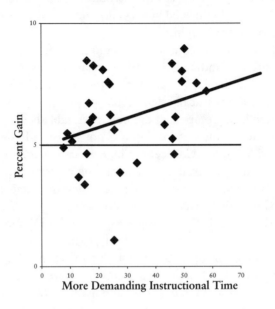

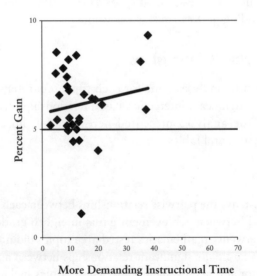

More Demanding Instructional Time

Table 9.1. Pairwise Relationships Between Aspects of Curriculum and Estimated Achievement Gains in Eighth Grade Mathematics.

Topic	Content Standards Coverage and Gain		Textbook Coverage and Gain		Textbook's Complex Expectation Coverage and Gain		Teacher Coverage and Gain		Instructional Time and Gain	
	Coefficient (std. err.)	R^2	Coefficient (std. err.)	R^2	Coefficient (std. err.)	R^2	Coefficient (std. err.)	R^2	Coefficient (std. err.)	R^2
Whole number	0.00 (0.01)	0.00	0.02 (0.09)	0.00	0.07 (0.02)**	0.28	-0.03 (0.04)	0.02	-0.16 (0.15)	0.04
Common fractions	-0.01 (0.01)	0.02	0.19 (0.14)	0.06	0.05 (0.02)**	0.16	0.01 (0.02)	0.00	0.08 (0.07)	0.04
Decimal fractions and percents	0.00 (0.01)	0.00	0.04 (0.07)	0.01	0.05 (0.03)**	0.14	0.01 (0.02)	0.01	0.05 (0.05)	0.04
Relations of fractions	-0.01 (0.01)	0.02	0.26 (0.28)	0.03	0.01 (0.03)	0.00	0.00 (0.02)	0.00	0.07 (0.08)	0.03
Estimating quantity and size	0.01 (0.01)	0.04	1.07 (1.59)	0.02	0.01 (0.02)	0.01	0.01 (0.02)	0.01	-0.02 (0.25)	0.00
Rounding	0.00 (0.01)	0.00	0.60 (0.54)	0.04	0.02 (0.04)	0.01	0.03 (0.02)*	0.10	0.59 (0.24)**	0.17
Estimating computations	0.00 (0.01)	0.01	0.54 (0.30)*	0.10	0.02 (0.02)	0.03	0.02 (0.02)	0.02	0.25 (0.25)	0.03
Measurement units	0.00 (0.01)	0.00	0.14 (0.09)	0.08	0.02 (0.02)	0.04	0.02 (0.01)	0.07	0.19 (0.16)	0.04
Perimeter, area, and volume	0.01 (0.02)	0.01	0.10 (0.07)	0.06	0.03 (0.02)	0.09	0.07 (0.03)**	0.18	0.40 (0.15)**	0.19
Measurement estimations and error	0.01 (0.01)	0.04	-2.04 (1.02)	0.12	0.01 (0.02)	0.03	0.04 (0.02)*	0.11	0.65 (0.54)	0.05
2-D geometry	-0.01 (0.02)	0.00	-0.11 (0.12)	0.03	0.01 (0.03)	0.00	0.06 (0.07)	0.03	0.02 (0.16)	0.00
Polygons and circles	0.00 (0.03)	0.00	0.14 (0.08)	0.08	0.03 (0.02)*	0.10	0.03 (0.03)	0.03	0.19 (0.13)	0.07
3-D geometry and transformations	0.02 (0.02)	0.04	0.01 (0.04)	0.00	0.03 (0.03)	0.04	0.06 (0.03)**	0.15	-0.01 (0.12)	0.00
Congruence and similarity	0.00 (0.02)	0.00	0.23 (0.09)**	0.19	0.03 (0.02)	0.05	0.05 (0.02)**	0.20	0.38 (0.09)**	0.38
Proportionality concepts	-0.01 (0.01)	0.06	-0.01 (0.41)	0.00	0.03 (0.02)	0.06	0.00 (0.01)	0.00	0.10 (0.15)	0.02
Proportionality problems	0.00 (0.01)	0.00	0.16 (0.12)	0.06	0.01 (0.02)	0.01	0.00 (0.02)	0.00	0.19 (0.16)	0.05
Patterns, relations, and functions	0.00 (0.02)	0.00	0.08 (0.06)	0.07	0.01 (0.02)	0.02	0.02 (0.01)	0.08	0.11 (0.08)	0.06
Equations and form	-0.04 (0.02)	0.09	-0.04 (0.04)	0.04	0.06 (0.02)**	0.15	0.02 (0.05)	0.01	-0.04 (0.08)	0.01
Data representations and analysis	-0.01 (0.01)	0.01	0.13 (0.12)	0.04	0.02 (0.02)	0.09	0.03 (0.01)**	0.19	0.36 (0.15)**	0.16
Probability and uncertainty	0.01 (0.01)	0.02	-0.00 (0.19)	0.00	-0.00 (0.02)	0.00	0.01 (0.02)	0.01	-0.04 (0.36)	0.00

**Significant ($p \leq .05$).
*Significant ($.05 < p \leq .10$).

fractions, estimating quantity and size, measurement units, two-dimensional geometry, proportionality (two topics), functions, and probability.

For all other topics, at least one measure of curriculum was significantly related to learning. Teacher implementation was the aspect of curriculum producing the largest number of statistically significant or marginally significant pairwise relationships with achievement gain. For the two measures of teacher implementation—instructional time and proportion of teachers covering a topic—there were relationships with achievement gain in six of the tested topic areas.

Equations and formulas was the topic covered most across all countries and in which the largest achievement gain took place. It had only one significant pairwise relationship: the measure of the proportion of textbook space covering that topic with more demanding performance expectations. The same is true at the other end of the spectrum for three of the arithmetic test area topics—whole numbers, fractions and decimals, and percents. Analysis suggests that more OTL indicated by any aspect of curriculum was not related to increased learning at the eighth grade for any of these arithmetic topics. This is not surprising because these topics were the focus of instruction for most of the countries at the elementary grades and not in lower secondary (middle) school. However, opportunity that was related to more demanding performances was related to learning in a statistically significant way. Put simply, these data support the conclusion that the quality, not quantity, of the opportunity was related to increased learning in arithmetic at eighth grade.

Table 9.2 displays the results for the structural relationships. These results are consistent with those of the bivariate analyses. Essentially the same eight topics were found to have statistically significant relationships of curriculum to learning, as was true for the pairwise analyses. There were four additional topics for which this was true in the pairwise case because those analyses included the performance expectation measure and teacher coverage that was not included in the multiple regressions.

For four of these tested topic areas—rounding; perimeter, area, and volume; congruence and similarity; and data analysis—if we examine the structural model of Chapter Three as it pertains to cross-country differences, the pattern is similar to that for within-country differences. Mainly either content standards or textbooks have an impact on instructional time, and this is in turn related directly to achievement gain. For the other four topic areas with statistically significant relationships, either content standards or textbook coverage (or both) were directly related to learning. In all four cases, a strong relationship existed between content standards and textbook coverage. Thus, the structural model used to describe

Table 9.2. Estimated Structural Coefficients for the Curriculum and Achievement Model for Each Topic (Eighth Grade Mathematics).

Topic	R^2	Textbook Coverage to Achievement Gain (δ)	Content Standards Coverage to Achievement Gain (ξ)	Instructional Time to Achievement Gain (γ_τ)
Congruence and similarity	0.42	−0.02 (0.12)	−0.02 (0.01)	0.43 (0.14)**
Data representation and analysis	0.35	0.25 (0.12)**	0.00 (0.01)**	0.51 (0.16)**
Measurement estimations and errors	0.24	−2.54 (1.04)**	0.01 (0.01)*	0.47 (0.50)
Rounding	0.20	0.36 (0.58)	0.01 (0.01)	0.66 (0.28)**
Perimeter, area, and volume	0.19	0.01 (0.09)	0.00 (0.01)	0.39 (0.19)**
Equations and formulas	0.19	−0.07 (0.04)*	−0.05 (0.02)**	−0.01 (0.09)
Estimating computations	0.17	0.59 (0.32)*	−0.01 (0.01)	0.29 (0.28)
Common fractions	0.16	0.21 (0.19)	−0.02 (0.01)*	0.08 (0.10)
Measurement units	0.12	0.11 (0.11)	−0.01 (0.01)	0.19 (0.22)
Polygons and circles	0.12	0.11 (0.09)	0.01 (0.03)	0.14 (0.14)
Proportionality concepts	0.10	−0.11 (0.45)	−0.02 (0.01)	0.18 (0.17)
Relations of fractions	0.09	0.21 (0.31)	−0.02 (0.01)	0.09 (0.09)
Proportionality problems	0.09	0.15 (0.13)	−0.01 (0.01)	0.14 (0.17)
Patterns, relations, and functions	0.08	0.05 (0.07)	−0.01 (0.02)	0.07 (0.11)
Whole numbers	0.07	0.09 (0.10)	0.00 (0.01)	−0.27 (0.19)
Estimating quantity and size	0.07	0.75 (1.70)	0.01 (0.01)	−0.23 (0.29)
Decimal fractions and percents	0.05	−0.03 (0.10)	−0.01 0.02	0.10 (0.09)
3-D geometry and transformations	0.05	0.03 (0.06)	0.02 (0.02)	−0.08 (0.17)
2-D geometry	0.04	−0.13 (0.13)	−0.01 (0.02)	0.07 (0.17)
Probability and uncertainty	0.04	0.11 (0.34)	0.01 (0.01)	−0.41 (0.69)

**Significant (p ≤ .05).
*Significant (.05 < p ≤ .10).

within-country relationships also held in general across countries for specific topic areas.

The strength of the relationships, both in terms of the pairwise and the more complex analyses, were not very strong, at least as measured by the traditional index of fit—the coefficient of determination (R^2). The average values were all relatively small (.20 or less). For the topics with significant relationships, the R^2 index ranged from around .10 to .40. For the structural model analyses, the two topics with the largest R^2 values were congruence and similarity (.42) and data analysis (.35).

It must be kept in mind that these analyses are not related to how curriculum policy played out within a country but rather are related to exploring cross-national differences. The general conclusion is similar to those of the within-country, across-topic priorities and their relationship to learning. That is, more curricular opportunity to learn a topic was related to larger achievement gains. This occurred in mathematics primarily through textbook coverage or instructional time, although content standards were related to both of these two other aspects of curriculum.

Congruence and similarity was a tested area of geometry among those with the largest achievement gains at eighth grade (see Chapter Seven). It was also a topic that was first introduced in most countries at eighth grade (see Chapter Five). Substantively, this topic is related to other geometry topics but does not build as incrementally from them or depend on them as much as many other topics do. It is essentially more insular than other geometry topics and is thus an area ripe for learning; it was not surprising to see such large achievement gains associated with it at eighth grade.

As a relatively insular topic, it could be mostly influenced by curricular opportunity provided directly to it and not as much as that provided indirectly through other areas. Both textbook space and instructional time had statistically significant relationships to achievement gain in this tested area. However, of the two, only instructional time was statistically significant when the other was controlled.

Using the 10 percent increase in textbook coverage argument utilized in Chapter Eight, this criterion would predict a 2.3 percent increase in achievement gain, considering only textbook space. How much increase does this represent? The average gain for this topic was 7.5 percentage points during eighth grade. The 2.3 percent increase would be an increase of two-thirds of a standard deviation.

Instructional time was significantly related to learning for this topic area, both in the pairwise sense and in terms of the structural relationships. The estimated effect was a predicted increase in gain of 6.5 percentage points. Even when controlling for textbook coverage, a 15 percent increase in instructional time would have been associated with an increase in achievement gains of about two standard deviations.

For data analysis, the predicted effect of instructional time (controlling for textbook coverage and content standards) was even larger—a 7.5 percent increase in achievement gain. This would represent an increase of over three standard deviations. Unlike congruence and similarity, data analysis was a topic area covered by most countries from the primary grades onward. It was neither new nor insular. However, several countries reported not covering the topic at all—literally no teachers reported teaching this topic. In many other countries, the percent of instructional time was trivially small. So across countries a strong relationship existed between opportunity and learning.

The other curricular area worth mentioning is equations, which was the topic both with the greatest OTL provided at eighth grade and the topic with the largest gains in achievement. From the pairwise analyses, the main relationship for this topic involved textbook coverage that involved more demanding performance expectations. This topic was covered to some extent across the entire curriculum from the early grades onward, and in many countries it received a large focus at seventh grade. It was also related explicitly to other parts of mathematics (especially number theory). All of this may make it more difficult to establish a relationship between curricular indicators at eighth grade and learning.

It seems reasonable to assume that at eighth grade, countries for which their textbooks (and presumably to some extent, their typical classroom instruction) focused on the more demanding aspects of problem solving and mathematical reasoning in dealing with this topic were beginning to deal with it in a way qualitatively different from their treatment of it in previous grades. Thus, it also seems reasonable that this was associated with greater achievement gains for this topic.

Science

Table 9.3 gives the science results for the pairwise relationships among aspects of curriculum and achievement gains. As was the case for the within-country analyses for science reported in Chapter Eight, there were fewer statistically significant or marginally significant relationships than there were for mathematics. Nine of the seventeen science tested area topics had at least one significant or marginally significant pairwise relationship between an aspect of curriculum and achievement gain. These were earth processes, earth in the universe, diversity and structure of living things, life processes and functions, life cycles and genetics, physical

Table 9.3. Pairwise Relationships Between Aspects of Curriculum and Estimated Achievement Gains in Eighth Grade Science.

Topic	Content Standards Coverage and Gain		Textbook Coverage and Gain		Textbook's Complex Expectation Coverage and Gain		Teacher Coverage and Gain		Instructional Time and Gain	
	Coefficient (std. err.)	R^2	Coefficient (std. err.)	R^2	Coefficient (std. err.)	R^2	Coefficient (std. err.)	R^2	Coefficient (std. err.)	R^2
Earth features	−0.03 (0.03)	0.04	0.11 (0.21)	0.01	0.02 (0.20)	0.00	−0.06 (0.06)	0.04	−0.16 (0.27)	0.01
Earth processes	−0.02 (0.03)	0.01	0.03 (0.14)	0.00	0.86 (0.48)*	0.10	0.02 (0.06)	0.01	0.22 (0.46)	0.01
Earth in the universe	−0.06 (0.03)**	0.14	−0.13 (0.70)	0.00	0.14 (0.03)	0.01	0.03 (0.08)	0.01	0.48 (0.69)	0.02
Diversity and structure of living things	−0.06 (0.03)*	0.12	−0.03 (0.12)	0.00	0.05 (0.18)	0.00	−0.05 (0.05)	0.04	−0.32 (0.22)	0.07
Life processes and functions	−0.06 (0.04)	0.06	0.12 (0.29)	0.01	0.30 (0.16)*	0.10	0.01 (0.05)	0.00	0.06 (0.39)	0.00
Life cycles and genetics	−0.02 (0.05)	0.01	−0.39 (0.16)**	0.17	0.08 (0.26)	0.00	−0.04 (0.08)	0.01	−0.42 (0.57)	0.02
Interactions of living things	−0.02 (0.04)	0.00	−0.24 (0.30)	0.02	0.21 (0.17)	0.05	−0.02 (0.06)	0.00	−0.50 (0.54)	0.03
Human biology and health	−0.02 (0.04)	0.01	−0.07 (0.13)	0.01	0.15 (0.16)	0.21	−0.02 (0.04)	0.01	−0.08 (0.14)	0.01
Properties and classification of matter	−0.06 (0.06)	0.04	−0.22 (0.16)	0.06	0.12 (0.14)	0.03	0.01 (0.06)	0.00	0.26 (0.52)	0.01
Structure of matter	0.00 (0.04)	0.00	0.57 (0.45)	0.05	−0.10 (0.18)	0.01	−0.01 (0.07)	0.00	0.22 (0.68)	0.00

Energy and physical processes	−0.06 (0.05)	0.05	0.03 (0.09)	0.00	0.16 (0.15)	0.04	0.00 (0.07)	0.00	0.11 (0.14)	0.02
Physical changes	−0.01 (0.04)	0.00	−0.70 (0.36)*	0.12	−0.03 (0.11)	0.00	−0.19 (0.08)**	0.15	−0.72 (0.79)	0.03
Chemical changes	−0.05 (0.03)*	0.11	0.37 (0.30)	0.05	0.11 (0.11)	0.03	0.12 (0.05)**	0.17	1.06 (0.43)**	0.17
Forces and motion	−0.04 (0.04)	0.04	−0.47 (0.27)*	0.10	0.06 (0.27)	0.00	−0.05 (0.08)	0.01	0.18 (0.53)	0.00
Science, technology, and society	0.06 (0.06)	0.04	0.41 (0.90)	0.01	0.71 (0.59)	0.05	0.05 (0.13)	0.01	1.52 (2.21)	0.02
Environmental and resource issues	0.03 (0.05)	0.01	0.41 (0.58)	0.02	1.53 (0.56)**	0.21	0.07 (0.08)	0.03	−0.76 (0.60)	0.05
Scientific processes (no science content code)	0.00 (0.04)	0.00	0.11 (0.51)	0.00	−0.07 (0.12)	0.01	−0.07 (0.06)	0.05	−0.44 (0.66)	0.02

**Significant ($p \leq .05$).
*Significant ($.05 < p \leq .10$).

changes, chemical changes, forces and motions, and environmental and resource issues. The R^2 index for most of these relationships was around .05 or less, indicating a very weak fit of these regression models. Even for those that were statistically significant, the R^2 index varied from around .10 to .20.

We do not believe that OTL was less relevant for understanding cross-country differences in learning in science. Rather, we feel that this reflects, at least in part, the sampling design used for the study. It also likely reflects the reality that, unlike mathematics, school science draws from four disciplines, not one. This poses serious methodological challenges that we have attempted to address as well as we could but that are inherent in the TIMSS data, given the study's design. Analyses in a later section that take into account the multidisciplinary nature of school science show much more promising results.[10] To explore more thoroughly the relationship of curriculum opportunity and learning in science, a study designed around the particular idiosyncrasies of school science around the world would need to be carried out.

The structural relationships seen in Table 9.4 are essentially consistent with those of Table 9.3. However, the significant relationships for four of the topic areas disappear when controlling for the other variables. This was true for earth processes, diversity and structure of living things, life processes and functions, and environmental and resource issues. The R^2 index varied from .13 to .32 for the significant topics.

Among the five topics with significant structural relationships, there were two distinct patterns in terms of the structural model of Chapter Three for exploring cross-national differences. Textbook coverage was related to instructional time, which was in turn positively related to learning for two topics (earth in the universe and chemical changes). Textbook coverage was directly related to learning for the other three areas (life cycles and genetics, physical changes, and forces and motion); however, the relationship was negative, which is consistent with the marginal topic effect noted in Chapter Eight.

Earth in the universe is a topic usually found in an earth science or geology course. Like congruence and similarity in mathematics, it is a somewhat more insular topic area among science topics. The R^2 index was the largest of that for any of the science topic areas (.32). Instructional time was the aspect of curriculum with the strongest relationship to learning when controlling for the other aspects of curriculum. (This is ignoring the negative relationship of content standards to learning, which seems to us counterintuitive.) Using the estimated regression coefficient, the predicted effect of just a 5 percent increase (about ten days) in instructional time

Table 9.4. Estimated Structural Coefficients for the Curriculum and Achievement Model for Each Topic (Eighth Grade Science).

Topic	R^2	Relation of Textbook Coverage to Achievement Gain (δ)	Relation of Content Standards Coverage to Achievement Gain (ξ)	Relation of Instructional Time Coverage to Achievement Gain (γ_τ)
Earth in the universe	0.32	0.02 (0.73)	-0.11 (0.03)**	1.90 (0.78)**
Chemical changes	0.27	-0.05 (0.34)	-0.05 (0.03)*	1.08 (0.53)**
Life cycles and genetics	0.19	-0.50 (0.21)**	0.03 (0.05)	0.34 (0.66)
Diversity and structure of living things	0.16	0.12 (0.14)	-0.06 (0.04)	-0.30 (0.27)
Forces and motion	0.14	-0.55 (0.31)*	-0.02 (0.04)	0.66 (0.56)
Physical changes	0.13	-0.70 (0.38)*	0.01 (0.04)	-0.60 (0.80)
Properties and classification of matter	0.13	-0.22 (0.17)	-0.06 (0.06)	0.63 (0.55)
Environmental and resource issues	0.10	0.47 (0.58)	0.04 (0.05)	-0.91 (0.62)
Life processes and functions	0.08	0.04 (0.36)	-0.07 (0.05)	0.27 (0.52)
Earth features	0.07	0.21 (0.22)	-0.04 (0.03)	-0.18 (0.28)
Energy and physical processes	0.07	-0.01 (0.11)	-0.06 (0.05)	0.13 (0.18)
Structure of matter	0.05	0.60 (0.51)	-0.01 (0.05)	-0.09 (0.77)
Science, technology, and society	0.05	0.33 (0.91)	0.06 (0.06)	1.00 (2.31)
Interactions of living things	0.04	-0.18 (0.33)	0.00 (0.05)	-0.42 (0.63)
Earth processes	0.02	-0.01 (0.15)	-0.02 (0.03)	0.24 (0.50)
Human biology and health	0.02	-0.04 (0.14)	-0.02 (0.04)	-0.08 (0.15)
Scientific processes (no science content code)	0.02	0.26 (0.62)	0.00 (0.04)	-0.52 (0.71)

*Significant ($p \leq .05$).
*Significant ($.05 < p \leq .10$).

(instead of the 15 percent used previously) would be associated with an increase of about ten percentage points (over three standard deviations) in achievement gain. The larger predicted effect is likely due to the fact that less than one-fourth of the teachers even taught this topic in almost half of the countries. Given little exposure, a small increase in instructional time at the national level likely results in comparatively large gains in achievement. The average amount of instructional time was small for this topic generally and very small in the case of many countries.

A similarly large effect was predicted for chemical changes (R^2 of .27), a topic first introduced in most countries either in seventh or eighth grade. A 5 percent increase in instructional time for a nation as a whole was predicted to result in an increase of over five percentage points (almost two standard deviations) in achievement gain in this area. Here, too, there were numerous countries in which only a small percentage of teachers taught the topic.

Other Measures and Their Relationships to Achievement Gain

There is a long-standing tradition in cross-national studies that achievement is explained to a large extent by more general background variables such as those associated with a country's economic wealth rather than by variables related to curriculum and schooling. Taken to its extreme, this has often been considered as a reason why it has been difficult to find empirical support for the effect of schooling and of curriculum specifics when more general background considerations have already been taken into account.

A large literature exists showing that achievement status is related to measures of a country's wealth or level of economic development.[11] This has in part encouraged agencies such as the World Bank to support educational development projects in economically developing countries. One question that must be answered is whether such measures of wealth or development are related to learning as reflected in measures of achievement gain at the national level rather than merely being related to measures of achievement status. A answer of yes would suggest not only that wealthier, more economically developed countries would stand higher in comparative achievement but also that the wealthy would get wealthier, as it were. It would certainly say a great deal about the playing field in deliberate efforts to help educational development in less wealthy or developed countries.

A second kind of question is whether such measures of wealth or development are so powerfully related to achievement gain that, as they appear to do for achievement status, they account for gains so completely that little room is left for differences made by curricular factors. Because this book is about the effects of schooling and not about economic development, the main question of interest here is whether the inclusion of such national economic measures in the analyses relating curriculum to learning would change any of the results discussed thus far. When measures of a country's wealth or level of development are statistically controlled for (that is, held constant), would this eliminate the relationships of curriculum to learning that we have seen so far?

In this section we examine this issue by doing the same type of regression analyses to examine the structural relationships of curriculum and their relationship to achievement gain while adjusting for measures such as the wealth of a nation. Several measures of wealth and development were explored. The choice did not seem to matter for our purposes of including such a measure only as a control rather than a substantive focus. Similar results were obtained for various measures explored. The variable we finally used most thoroughly and that will be discussed here is a country's gross national product (GNP) in U.S. dollars.

Somewhat more in line with the kinds of issues explored in this book, we also include other variables related to providing OTL or delivering curricular intentions as actual instruction. One of these is a measure of classroom instruction. The analyses presented thus far have included a measure of the proportion of textbook coverage of a topic related to more demanding performance expectations. No directly parallel questions were asked teachers about their classroom instruction.

However, teachers were asked some relevant questions that can help provide additional measures of the nature of classroom instruction as a purveyor of OTL. For example, they were asked how often their classroom instruction in mathematics had students practice basic computational skills and how often students were required to write equations to express a relationship. We believe that we can take teachers spending a great deal of time on the former as indicative of instruction focused on less demanding performance expectations. We also believe that we can take teachers spending a great deal of time on the latter as indicative of a focus on more demanding performance expectations. Unfortunately, these two questions were not asked in relation to specific topics.

For science, similar but slightly different questions were asked of teachers. We take a measure of more demanding expectations from a question asking science teachers how often they asked students to write explanations for what they observed and why. We take a measure of less demanding expectations from a question of how often teachers asked students to put simple events in order and explain why they put them in that order.

An entirely different sort of variable that might have been included in a model exploring factors other than the curriculum to explain achievement gains would be a measure of teachers' subject matter knowledge. The content of the curriculum is delivered through teachers as the structural model implies. Not only is the amount of time relevant to this delivery but also the quality of that delivery. We believe that at least two aspects related to the quality of classroom instruction might affect achievement gains: the first deals with the nature of how demanding teachers are in what they expect of students, and the second deals with how knowledgeable teachers were about the subject matter on which they were providing instruction. We attempted to get at the first aspect through the previously discussed questions that were asked of teachers about computation, ordering events, and so on. The second was not directly measured in TIMSS. At the time of TIMSS's design, some argued for the inclusion of such a measure, but as one can easily imagine, this issue was politically sensitive and fraught with complications in a design subject to the constraints of cross-national consensus.

Because no direct measure of teacher subject matter knowledge was included in the TIMSS design, we attempted a rough surrogate through a measure that reflects teachers' beliefs about the nature of subject matter. This measure does not directly reflect how knowledgeable teachers were about their subject matter. It does, however, indicate how they conceived of the subject matter and likely reflected qualitative differences in the instruction they enacted.

This approach was described in detail elsewhere.[12] Three country-level measures based on teacher beliefs about subject matter are included here. The first is the percent of teachers in a country who focused on the procedures of their discipline, that is, who believed a more algorithmic approach to their subject matter was appropriate for classroom instruction. The second was the percent of teachers in a country who were focused on the processes by which students come to understand the discipline. This is in a sense a valuing of students over subject matter in a teacher's belief about appropriate instruction. The third measure was the percent of teachers who focused on subject matter as a discipline with all of its formal aspects.

This chapter's previous analyses relating curriculum to learning examined a series of pairwise relationships involving five measures—textbook coverage, textbook coverage related to more demanding performance expectations, content standards, instructional time, and the percentage of a nation's teachers covering a topic. One thing that can be generalized from all these analyses is that different measures of curriculum were most strongly related to achievement gain for different topics. When we model the amount of learning (achievement gain) for a topic in the present section, we include only one aspect of curriculum in the analysis for each topic—the one curricular variable that the previous analyses showed had the strongest relationship to achievement gain for that topic.[13] This will be different for different topics.

We did analyses for each topic area separately. Each analysis included a measure of OTL, the one previously shown most strongly related to achievement gain for that topic. It also included a measure of GNP, one of the measures (science or mathematics) of classroom instruction taken as a surrogate for more demanding instruction and as characterizing the disciplinary focus of the country's teachers.

Mathematics

The first important generalization from these data is that GNP as a measure of a country's wealth was not strongly related to achievement gain. It was only statistically significantly or marginally significantly related to achievement gain for about half of the topic areas, including whole numbers, fractions, relations of fractions, rounding, two-dimensional geometry, polygons and circles, equations and formulas, data analysis, and probability.

More importantly from the point of view of this book, in no case did controlling for GNP eliminate any significant relationship of curriculum to learning found in Table 9.1, Table 9.2, Table 9.3, and Table 9.4. This was also true when several other measures of a country's wealth or development were used in the analyses. The conclusion is that even when controlling for a country's wealth, curriculum is still significantly related to learning.

The opportunity variables were statistically significant or marginally significant for eleven of the twenty mathematics tested topic areas. This was true when controlling for GNP and the other two measures and is essentially consistent with the results of Table 9.1, in which there was a significant bivariate relationship for twelve topics. The only difference was that for the area of decimals and fractions, the relationship between opportunity and achievement gain was no longer significant when the analysis controlled for the other variables. For the other topics, statistical significance remained even when holding constant those other variables.

Another interesting finding associated with these results centers on the classroom instruction and teacher subject matter orientation measures. The classroom instruction measure for mathematics was significantly related to gain for only five of twenty topic areas when controlling for curriculum through the opportunity measure: whole numbers, estimating quantity and size, measurement errors and estimation, proportionality concepts, and proportionality problems.

For whole numbers and the two proportionality topics, countries in which teachers spent a larger proportion of their classroom instructional time on writing equations were also those with larger achievement gains in the three topic areas. For estimating quantity and size and for the measurement topic, the relationship was negative and involved the time spent on computational skills. That is, when a larger proportion of time was spent on emphasizing computational skills for those two topics, there were correspondingly smaller achievement gains. Because it seems likely that there is a trade-off between emphasizing simpler performances such as computation and more demanding performances such as expressing relationships in equations, the results for the five topics were essentially similar. More demanding instruction was associated with greater gains for these few topic areas.

The measure of teacher subject matter orientation (taken here as a rough surrogate for teacher subject matter knowledge) was significantly or marginally significantly related to achievement gain for about half of the topic areas (eleven of twenty). This was true for the following seven arithmetic topics: whole number, fractions, relations of fractions, estimating quantity and size, rounding, estimating computations, and measurement units. It was also true for the more advanced topics of functions, equations and formulas, and the data analysis and probability topics.

Unfortunately, however, no consistent pattern to the relationship over topics would allow a nice generalization. This may well be because this variable did not reflect teacher subject matter knowledge as we had hoped. However, there was a relationship to achievement gain of teacher beliefs about subject matter averaged over a country's mathematics teachers. That relationship appears to have been very specific to individual topics.

The R^2 index for these twenty analyses ranged from .25 to .70, with most of the values around .40 to .50. This implies that for most topic areas, around half of the variation in achievement gain across countries was related to measures of a country's wealth, OTL, type of classroom instruction, and teachers' subject matter orientation. All but four of the regressions were statistically significant or marginally significant: two-dimensional geometry, three-dimensional geometry and transformations, functions, and probability.[14]

Science

The regression analyses were statistically or marginally significant for fourteen of the seventeen science tested area topics. This is in marked contrast to the scarcity of significant relationships described for science in the previous sections of this chapter. The R^2 index ranged from about .20 to .50, with most of the values around .30 to .40. This part is consistent with the other analyses in this chapter, which have shown that in general the strength of the relationships to achievement gain was greater for mathematics than for science.

The GNP variable was significantly related to achievement gain for only three of the seventeen topic areas, even fewer than was true for mathematics. Clearly, GNP was sufficient neither to account for most science achievement gains nor to contribute to understanding how they came about.

The opportunity variable was statistically or marginally significant in relation to gain for twelve of the seventeen topic areas. This includes six topics not found to have a significant pairwise relationship with gain, as seen in Table 9.3: interactions of living things; human biology and health; structure of matter; energy and physical processes; science, technology, and society; and scientific processes. It also excludes three topics that, when controlling for the other variables, were no longer significant: earth processes, diversity and structure of living things, and environmental and resource issues.

For the six topics in common, the relationship of the curriculum variable to gain was significant when controlling for the other measures in the analysis. All of these relationships were positive except that for science, technology, and society. On the surface, this pattern of relations seems to make conceptual sense.

For example, consider the area of scientific processes. This is not truly a content area but rather a measure of knowledge related to the methods of science. The opportunity measure that was positively related to learning in this area was the performance expectation variable related to this topic. For science, this variable included the use of empirical data to explore the natural world. Experience with this demanding expectation would be particularly relevant to understanding the methods of science and thus to the topic of scientific processes.

The classroom instructional measure was significant for eight topics: earth processes, earth in the universe, diversity and structure of living things, interactions of living things, human biology and health, structure of matter, energy and physical processes, and chemical changes. For seven topics the relationship of the subject matter belief variable was significantly related to gain. The relationship to gain was idiosyncratic to specific patterns for both the classroom measure and the belief measure. No general patterns were noted.

The Relationship of Opportunity in One Topic to Learning in Another

All of the analyses presented in this and the previous chapter have looked fairly narrowly at curriculum when focusing on its relationship to learning. Learning in one topic area was considered in relationship to the various aspects of curriculum for that particular tested area. Coverage of topics in areas other than that directly measured by the tested area was not considered for the relationship to gain in the tested area. The underlying conception was simple—opportunity to learn a topic was related to learning for that same topic.

A broader conception would allow for the possibility that curriculum coverage of topics not directly included in the domain of the tested area might be related to gain in that area. This would include topics that were related to the tested area conceptually from a disciplinary perspective.

This broader conception is explored in the analyses reported in this section. We also examine another related issue. In previous analyses, data for all subtopics that constituted a tested area were combined in forming the measure of curriculum opportunity. This has the implicit assumption that the subtopics were equal to each other in their impact on and relationship to achievement gain. For example, the whole numbers subtest was made up of two subtopics—whole number meaning and whole number operations.

Curriculum coverage for whole numbers was a combination of that for each of these two subtopics. Suppose instead that the real impact on learning in whole numbers came primarily through whole number operations. If the coverage across the countries were such that the proportion of the total coverage for whole numbers was the same for the two topics, then the types of analyses done would have been completely reasonable. However, if the proportion of whole numbers opportunity that related to each subtopic—for example, to whole number operations—varied among the countries, then an analysis that combined them could mask the true relationship to learning.

In this section, for some of the analyses we use the measure of curriculum defined at the lowest (narrowest) level possible. This is at the level of the TIMSS frameworks for textbooks and for content standards and is already at the lowest level possible for teacher implementation, given the teacher questionnaires. This, together with the fact that we will allow topics from the domain of one tested area to be related to learning in a different tested area, greatly expands the type of cross-country topic-specific relationships that are possible.

These two conceptual issues—across-domain impacts and nonequivalent impacts of subtopics—define two new sets of analyses. Between them, these analyses explore the relationship of curriculum to learning at the most precise topic level possible and allow for the relationship of curriculum to learning but not curriculum constrained to the domain of the tested area for which achievement gain is measured. This is a clear contrast to the sets of analyses already discussed in this chapter. The first way we examine this issue is to chose five representative topic areas in mathematics and six in science. We did the simultaneous relational analyses for these eleven areas as indicative of what might be found were the analyses done for all areas.[15]

Cross-Topic Analyses for Mathematics

In mathematics, the five topic areas were chosen to represent key areas that emerged in the analyses discussed thus far and in other chapters. These included fractions; perimeter, area, and volume; congruence and similarity; functions; and data analysis. Each of the five main mathematical areas (algebra, geometry, measurement, number, and data analysis) is represented. These were the key topics in terms of eighth grade coverage and gain.

Table 9.5 shows the results for mathematics.[16] The results indicate the kinds of area-to-topic relationships that we wished to explore. This was true for all of the aspects of curriculum. (All were significant at $p < .083$ or less.) The canonical correlations between opportunity in the five representative mathematics topic areas and gain in the same five areas were very high, ranging from around .7 to .9. The strongest correlation was for instructional time.

Thus, at least on a small set of representative topic areas, the results indicated that exploration of the relationship of curriculum to learning should not be constrained to only those topics that define the tested topic area. This suggests that opportunity with disciplinarily and conceptually related topics also has the potential to affect achievement gains for topics.

Table 9.5. Relational Analyses of Achievement Gain and
Representative Topics Other Than the Tested Topic Area
(Eighth Grade Mathematics).

Aspect of Curriculum	Multivariate F Significance	Average R^2 over Five Topics	Canonical Correlation
Textbook	0.053	0.17	0.69
Complex performance expectations	0.083	0.21	0.70
Content standards	0.065	0.21	0.75
Teacher coverage	0.001	0.28	0.81
Teacher time	0.000	0.25	0.88

Cross-Topic Analyses for Science

Table 9.6 displays the results for eighth grade science. The six topic areas chosen to represent science were based on criteria similar to that for mathematics: life processes and functions, life cycles and genetics, properties and classification of matter, structure of matter, energy and physical processes, and chemical changes.

The results were similar to those found for mathematics. However, the relationships were not significant for two of the curriculum measures—complex performance expectations and content standards. The (canonical) correlations were in the same range as for mathematics.

Relationships for Mathematics at the Most Detailed Level of Topic Specificity

Results for a series of analyses with topics defined at the most specific level possible are presented here. Achievement gain for each tested topic area was related to opportunity in a specific topic, helping to define the tested

Table 9.6. Relational Analyses of Achievement Gain and Representative
Topics Other Than the Tested Topic Area (Eighth Grade Science).

Aspect of Curriculum	Multivariate F Significance	Average R^2 over Six Topics	Canonical Correlation
Textbook	0.012	0.28	0.80
Complex performance expectations	0.185	0.21	0.80
Content standards	0.360	0.19	0.68
Teacher coverage	0.012	0.29	0.88
Teacher time	0.024	0.33	0.86

area but at the most specific level possible. These analyses included topics both directly and not directly included in defining the tested topic area. The results of the previous section encourage the inclusion of the latter. The determination of which topics and which curricular aspects to include was based on the insights gained from the empirical analyses thus far in this book as well as a conceptual analysis related to the mathematics involved.

Many of the results are consistent with those reported in Table 9.1 and Table 9.2. Those analyses revealed eight topics for which no significant relationship to opportunity could be found. Of these, only three still show no relationship to learning: relations of fractions, two-dimensional geometry, and probability. Gain in the other five topic areas can now be shown to be related to different aspects of curriculum for certain topics.

Because many of the relationships of curriculum to learning are consistent with the results reported previously, we will not discuss each of the topic areas separately. The R^2 index used as an indication of fit varied from around .1 to .4, which indicates that as much as 40 percent of the cross-national variation in learning could be accounted for by considering only the measures of curriculum opportunities. The estimated regression coefficients were all positive. This indicates that greater opportunity was associated with greater learning.

The aspects of curriculum most involved in significant relationships were textbook coverage, more demanding performance expectations, teacher coverage, and instructional time. Only the content standards measure was not involved in significant cross-national relationships to achievement gain. It is possible that the direct or indirect relationship of content standards to teacher implementation and their direct relationship to textbook coverage within countries (as described in Chapter Eight) were the primary means by which they had a relationship to learning across countries.

Several interesting relationships emerged. Gain in perimeter, area, and volume was related to not just teacher coverage in that topic area but also textbook coverage, the performance expectation measure, and teacher coverage of two- and three-dimensional geometry. This makes great conceptual sense because perimeter and area are typically defined in terms of two-dimensional geometric figures and volume in terms of three-dimensional geometric solids.

The set of relationships for the two proportionality topic areas was perhaps the most interesting to emerge from these analyses. In neither of these two areas was gain found to be significantly related to curriculum in any of the previous analyses that took into account curriculum topics directly for the tested areas. Here significance was noted primarily for curricular coverage in two other topic areas. One, congruence and similarity, was from geometry; the other, slope and trigonometry, was from algebra.[17]

The common thread between congruence and similarity and slope and trigonometry is proportionality. There is a strong conceptual relationship between similarity and proportionality, slope and proportionality, and even simple trigonometric ratios and proportionality. The curricular aspect through which a relationship between these two areas and achievement gain in the proportionality topics was significant was that of textbook coverage related to more demanding performance expectations such as problem solving and reasoning.

Perhaps in many countries the problems or applications used in such problem-solving or mathematical reasoning involved similarity, slope, or even simple trigonometric ratios. Anecdotally, the authors have been told that proportionality is not taught as a separate topic in many countries but rather appears in the curriculum only through such relationships as similarity in geometric figures and direct proportionality in functions.

There were, in fact, two other topic areas related to the tested area of proportionality problems in these analyses: functions and equations and formulas. The reciprocal relationship was at least marginally significant. That is, the relationship of gain in function was related to the performance expectation aspect of textbook coverage related to proportionality problems.

Measurement units and estimating quantity and size were two other topic areas where new significant relationships not seen in previous analyses emerged. The curriculum opportunity measures related to these two topics came from the same higher-order category of the TIMSS mathematics framework as the topics defining the tested areas for these topics. Perhaps the more interesting of the two involves the relationship of textbook coverage of exponents and orders of magnitude to achievement gain in estimating quantity and size, both of which came from the same higher-order category of the (hierarchical) mathematics framework, indicating a presumed conceptual relationship.

Putting these results together with those described earlier in this chapter seems to lead to a powerful, straightforward conclusion. Curriculum was related to learning in mathematics across countries in seventeen of the twenty tested topic areas as measured by the TIMSS Population 2 test. Further, the relationships with gain involved different aspects of the curriculum for different topics, but across the topics, all aspects of curriculum other than the content standards measure were represented.

In areas such as congruence and similarity and proportionality problems, almost half of the variance in achievement gain across countries was accounted for by curriculum measures. From a previous section we also know that instructional practices and teacher beliefs added to the strength of some relationships and that the inclusion of wealth or development measures did not dampen the relationship of curriculum coverage to national achievement gains in mathematics.

Relationships for Science at the Most Detailed Level of Topic Specificity

So far in this book, the story has gone something like this: the data for science did not indicate as strong a set of relationships as those for mathematics. There were more topic areas in science for which we were not able to establish significant relationships of curriculum to achievement gains. In this section, this is no longer true.

All of the seventeen tested areas in the sciences showed at least one significant relationship between curriculum and learning. The range of the R^2 index was from around .2 to .7. The science results displayed in Table 9.3 and Table 9.4 indicated no significant relationships for about half of the seventeen areas, which implies that the relationship of curriculum to learning was likely more complex for science than for mathematics.

For three topic areas, no significant relationship of curriculum to learning was found in any of the earlier analyses for science. There was a significant relationship for each of these three in the new analyses.[18] For structure of matter and science, technology, and society, the R^2 index indicated that half or more of the country variation in achievement gain was accounted for by curriculum.

All aspects of curriculum were involved in the significant relationships in science. However, the most prominent—as was also true for mathematics—were teacher implementation and textbook coverage. In strong contrast to mathematics, content standards played a much more prominent role in science as an aspect of curriculum that was related to achievement gain across the countries.

Several interesting relationships emerged that were cross-cutting in terms of curriculum topic coverage. For the area of diversity and structure of living things—an area that involved plants, animals, cells, organs, and tissues—the curriculum topics related to achievement gain were life cycles and genetics and the biochemistry of genetics. Study related to the genetic makeup of life seems to be what was related to learning about the diversity and structure of living things.

One would expect certain topic areas to have been related to achieve-ment gain in the tested area of earth features, and they were. However, so was coverage of types of forces (which included gravitational forces) in content standards. Textbook coverage on fluid behavior and types of forces was significantly related to achievement gain in forces and motion.

Science, technology, and society is a fairly new area to school science in many countries. It has been included in science curricula to deal with the relationship of science to the broader issues involved in an increas-ingly technologically oriented world. Two comments are worth making about learning in this area. First, textbook coverage of this topic was neg-atively related to learning. This may have been an artifact of the test or the ambiguity of the label but perhaps not. Some would argue that the curricular material in use at the time of the TIMSS test was not particu-larly helpful and might even have hindered learning in this area.[19] If true (and true on a wide enough scale), this might account for a negative rela-tionship between textbook coverage and achievement gain. Certainly this lack of helpfulness is one explanation consistent with the data.

In contrast, there was a statistically significant relationship of coverage of effects of natural disasters to achievement gain in science, technology, and society. This was a positive relationship and indicated a cross-topic impact on learning. The aspect of curriculum for which the relationship was significant was textbook coverage that focused on more demanding performance expectations—investigating the natural world and problem solving. It is possible that demanding study of the scientific aspects of nat-ural disasters produced some of the more effective learning that came under the rubric of science, technology, and society.

As for mathematics, the conclusion for science based on these most recent analyses was that curriculum was related to learning. Some of the earlier reservations for science based on limited empirical relationships seem to have been overcome in the most recent set of relationships inves-tigated. Still, these findings reinforce the suggestion that the relationship of curriculum to learning was likely more complex for science than for mathematics. This could be true for the simple reason that school science is really a study of four distinct disciplines, yet study in one discipline could be (and, given the data reported, was) related to learning in another discipline. We again repeat our suggestion that disentangling these rela-tionships would require a study designed differently than was TIMSS.

Overall, we found statistically or marginally significant relationships of curriculum to learning for thirty-four out of the thirty-seven topics in school science and mathematics combined. The only exceptions were three mathematics topics—relations of fractions, two-dimensional geometry, and probability.

Curricular Structure and Country Groupings

In Chapters Six and Eight we explored the relationship of the various aspects of curriculum to each other and to learning across topics within a country. These curricular relationships were characterized by the structural coefficients α, β, and η and were found to vary across countries. The two-way analyses found these relationships to be interaction based, which implies that they varied for different topics in different countries. The way curriculum was related to achievement gain was characterized by the structural coefficients δ, ξ, and γ, which also varied across countries.

The question addressed in this section is whether these patterns of relationship were totally idiosyncratic by country or whether there were clusters of countries with similar patterns. If such patterns were found, we would also like to know if those groupings were culturally or regionally based in whole or in part. To explore this issue, we first used the estimates of the structural coefficients α, β, and η for each country. On the basis of their values, we clustered (grouped) the countries.[20]

Mathematics

Table 9.7 presents the results of this clustering, which resulted in four groups of countries. Six countries could not be included in the grouping because their content standards covered all of the topics included in defining the twenty tested topic areas for mathematics. These included three

---

Table 9.7. Four Groups of Countries Clustered with Similar Curriculum Structures (Eighth Grade Mathematics).

Cluster 1	Cluster 2	Cluster 3	Cluster 4
Czech Republic	Denmark	Australia	Colombia
France	Iceland	Austria	Cyprus
Hong Kong	Spain	Germany	Greece
Japan		Netherlands	Ireland
Korea		Portugal	Romania
Russian Federation			Slovak Republic
Singapore			Slovenia
Sweden			

English-speaking countries—New Zealand, the United States, and Canada—as well as Switzerland, Norway, and Hungary. This inclusion of three English-speaking countries along with Norway may well constitute a cultural effect for schooling because Norway has a close tie to U.S. educational practices, and there are certainly close educational ties among the English-speaking countries.[21]

The clusters represented in Table 9.7 reflect some interesting regional if not cultural differences. Hong Kong, Japan, Korea, and Singapore—all Asian nations—belong to Group 1, as does the Russian Federation and the Czech Republic (both a part of the old Soviet Union and its satellite nations). Denmark and Iceland are also tied together by cultural traditions and found in the same group. Germany and Austria, in Group 3, share a language as well as other cultural traditions. Romania, the Slovak

---

Figure 9.3. Estimated Structural Model of Curriculum and Achievement for Each of the Four Clusters of Similar Countries (Eighth Grade Mathematics).

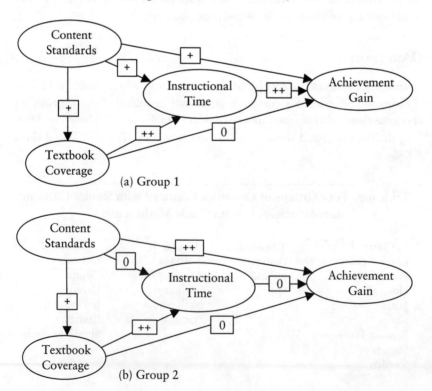

(a) Group 1

(b) Group 2

Republic, and Slovenia were once strongly related to the Soviet Union in political traditions although not by language. Greece and Cyprus (which was the only Greek-speaking part for TIMSS) share a language and a long cultural tradition.

The mean differences among the clusters for the six structural coefficients were statistically significant ($p < .001$).[22] We can use the means for the structural coefficients to describe characteristic patterns for each of the four groups.[23] These patterns are shown in Figure 9.3. A ++ indicates a relatively strong positive relationship. A + indicates a generally positive relationship but not as strong as that indicated by a ++. A 0 indicates a small or essentially nonexistent relationship between measures. A comparison of the four schematics suggests the curriculum structure for each of the four groups of countries. Each of the four clearly differs from

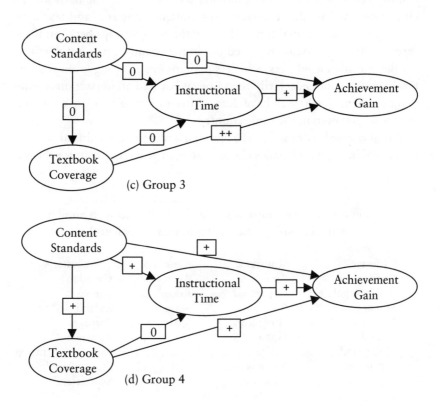

(c) Group 3

(d) Group 4

the others. In some groups (Groups 1 and 2), textbook coverage had a strong relationship to teacher implementation. In others, the influence of content standards was more pronounced. The curriculum structure in turn was related to the other three structural coefficients. Thus, the schematics also portray how the three aspects of curriculum were related to achievement gain.

Science

The clustering of countries for science also resulted in four groups. The results for these groups are shown in Table 9.8. Only two countries, New Zealand and the United States, could not be included in the analyses because 100 percent of the topics in the domains of the seventeen tested areas were covered. The same was true for both of these countries in mathematics.

The first conclusion from the science groupings is that the countries clustered together for mathematics were not clustered together for science. This suggests that the structure of curriculum was not the same within a country across school mathematics and school science. The basis for the clustering involved the relationship of content standards and textbook coverage to instructional time. The way the relationships between these three aspects of curriculum played out in the countries was not the same for the two school subjects, which is perhaps unsurprising given that the teachers were not necessarily the same. What had an impact on mathematics teachers might well have differed from what had an impact on science teachers, even in the same country.

It is also worth noting that the regional and potential cultural similarities noted in the mathematics clusters were, in general, absent for the sci-

---

Table 9.8. Four Groups of Countries Clustered with Similar Curriculum Structures (Eighth Grade Science).

Cluster 1	Cluster 2	Cluster 3	Cluster 4
Cyprus	Austria	Australia	Canada
Czech Republic	Colombia	Korea	Greece
France	Germany	Slovenia	Iceland
Hungary	Hong Kong	Spain	Portugal
Ireland	Japan		Romania
Netherlands	Latvia		Russian Federation
Singapore	Norway		Slovak Republic
	Sweden		Switzerland

ence clusters. The Asian countries were spread across three groups in science rather than all in the same group as in mathematics. Only Japan and Hong Kong were still members of the same group. A similar pattern held for central European countries and the Russian Federation. Russia, Romania, and the Slovak Republic were together as members of Group 4. Germany and Austria were still in the same group, as was the case for mathematics.

The differences in mean values of the structural coefficients across the groups of countries were significant ($p < .001$), as was true for mathematics. The mean values of these coefficients suggest the curriculum structures and relationships to achievement gain that are seen in the schematics of Figure 9.4. Once again, these schematics suggest considerable differences among the groups, both in whether content standards had a more

---

Figure 9.4. Estimated Structural Model of Curriculum and Achievement for Each of the Four Clusters of Similar Countries (Eighth Grade Science).

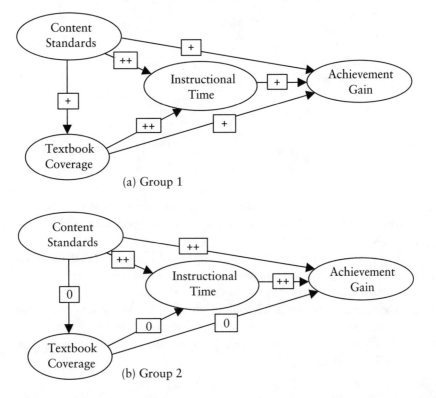

(a) Group 1

(b) Group 2

Figure 9.4. (*Continued*)

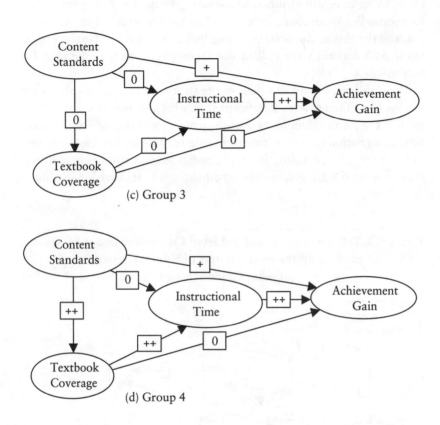

(c) Group 3

(d) Group 4

direct or a more indirect relationship (through textbook coverage) to instructional time and in how the three aspects of curriculum had impacts on achievement gains.

In the next chapter we turn to a slightly different subject. We look within countries and ask whether the cross-national patterns relating curriculum to learning for each of the topics was also found at the within-country, cross-school level. This allows us to further study the relationship of curriculum to learning by investigating whether curriculum differences across schools or classrooms were related to differences in learning in particular topic areas.

NOTES

1. The actual sum of these percents across topics within a country, however, does not equal 100 percent and, as a result, the averages across countries can vary. This has to do with the fact that the tested topic areas do not coincide with the teacher questionnaire topic categories (see Appendix C). Because the focus of the two-way analyses and those of this chapter is on the relationship of curriculum to learning, we use the tested topic area designations. For several tested topic areas, the same teacher questionnaire category is appropriate; that is, the independent variable (curriculum) is the same for more than one dependent variable (gain). In effect, the teacher content categories are at a higher level of aggregation in the curriculum frameworks for some tested topic areas. The result is that in the two-way matrices, the sum will be more than 100 percent because some teacher categories are repeated. Country differences on this variable averaged over topics would, as a result, be artifactual.

2. Using a set of questions asked in the school questionnaire relative to the allocation of time to an instructional period and the number of such periods in a year, we formed a variable—the total number of hours of mathematics (or science) in a school year. This was then averaged over schools (properly weighted) to provide a country-level indication of the total instructional time allocated to each of school science and mathematics. This was then multiplied by the average percent of teacher time for each topic to obtain an estimate of the total amount of time in hours allocated to a tested topic.

3. We fitted the simplest polynomial model—the quadratic—so that we could see whether the relationship was merely linear or whether there was evidence of a nonlinear component as well. Other models such as cubic, exponentials, and so on, might have been fitted. However, because the degrees of freedom were so few, the latter was enough to determine if a nonlinear component to the relationship existed.

4. The total time for a topic was multiplied by the country average for the textbook performance expectation variable described in Chapter Three. We recognize that this is a textbook-defined variable rather than directly and uncomplicatedly about instructional time. However, we used it at the country level as a surrogate measure for what was likely to happen in the classroom. This we view as a not unreasonable assumption, given the relationship of textbook coverage to instructional variables. This assumption can certainly be questioned, however.

5. Gamoran, Porter, Smithson, & White, 1997.

6. The measure used to convert the total time was a conditional percent of the two categories of performance expectations given the coverage of a specific topic. This measure was specific for each topic.

7. Schmidt, McKnight, & Raizen, 1997; Schmidt, McKnight, Cogan, Jakwerth, & Houang, 1999.

8. Schmidt, McKnight, Cogan, Jakwerth, & Houang, 1999.

9. To obtain representative Swiss textbooks, we took a composite of the textbooks from each system. These textbooks were quite different. In the United States, we also took a composite of widely used textbooks, but this was just an average of very similar textbooks.

10. These limitations could have their most serious impacts on teacher coverage and instructional time because not all science teachers associated with the students were sampled, as was the case in mathematics. Even for textbook coverage, there is a potential problem. Textbooks for each science discipline were analyzed and then concatenated to form a science pseudotextbook. This seems a reasonable procedure, but the measure of the percent of a book covering a topic for science is really over this pseudotextbook. If textbook space does not have the same meaning in one of the science disciplines as it does in another, then the meaning of the percent of textbook space for the pseudotextbook is less clear.

11. See Sweetland (1996) for a review of human capital theory and inquiry.

12. Schmidt, McKnight, Cogan, Jakwerth, & Houang, 1999.

13. We do this for two reasons. First, we have data for a limited number of countries and hence limited degrees of freedom for the error term in the analyses. Secondly, and perhaps more importantly, we wish to avoid the problem of collinearity. Classic evidence of collinearity was present for all measures that were included in the model here. The largest latent root of the covariance matrix was always very large, and when using measures related to the latent vectors, the condition disappeared.

14. These were all multiple regressions.

15. The ideal analyses to explore the main issue of this section would relate opportunity in all tested topic areas of science and mathematics to gain in those areas simultaneously, that is, in a multivariate multiple regression model. There are twenty tested topic areas in mathematics and seventeen in science. The TIMSS data contain the needed information for only thirty countries. This imposes methodological limitations that make it impossible to consider all of the tested topic areas simultaneously.

16. A multivariate multiple regression analysis was done for each aspect of curriculum. Wilks Λ was used to test for statistical significance. Canonical correlations were also calculated.

17. Although the category is slope and trigonometry, for most countries, coverage in this area was probably related mainly to slope, given the strong emphasis on algebra at the Population 2 level.

18. Gain in interactions of living things was not significantly related to any of the curriculum measures. However, it had a significant relationship in the analyses that were controlled for the classroom instructional measure.

19. Wang & Schmidt, 2001.

20. We did the clustering by first taking α, β, and η. Ignoring that they were themselves estimated values with standard errors, we calculated their covariance matrix over twenty-three countries in mathematics and twenty-seven countries in science. Several countries had to be eliminated because the content standards variable had no variance within those countries across topics. (Essentially these countries had 100 percent coverage for the subtopics for all the topics covered by the thirty-seven tested areas. In mathematics, the countries were Norway, Canada, New Zealand, Switzerland, the United States, and Hungary; in science, the eliminated countries were New Zealand and the United States.) The largest latent root and its associated vector were used then to cluster the countries into four groups. The principal component associated with the largest latent root accounted for approximately 50 percent of the variance for both mathematics and science.

21. Schmidt et al., 1996.

22. A multivariate test of statistical significance was done for the six estimated structural coefficients.

23. Defining the cells using estimates of α, β, and η places major constraints on their within-cell estimates.

## 10

CURRICULUM AND LEARNING
WITHIN COUNTRIES

THE MAJOR FOCUS OF THIS BOOK is on the relationship of curriculum (as opportunity to learn) and learning. So far we have dealt with this relationship defined across countries. We now stop treating countries holistically and take a look at schools and classrooms in a few selected countries. We want to characterize the variability and covariation in curriculum measures and in achievement gains across classrooms or schools within a country. We are attempting a first look, within the limits of the TIMSS data, at the policy-relevant question, Is what is taught in a country's schools related to cross-school variability in learning in that country?

This is a major change of focus in one sense. We still look at curriculum and learning but at a more microlevel than before. The issues here are not those that were explored in detail in Chapters Four through Nine, where the focus was at the national level and measures were used that were available only for data aggregated to the national level. Consequently, the analyses centered on country characteristics. Here the focus is within countries, and the analytical focus is accordingly on school or classroom characteristics.

Curriculum in this chapter is primarily curriculum in its aspect of teacher implementation. Content standards do not typically vary within a country. Textbooks were not analyzed on a classroom-by-classroom level for TIMSS but rather only at a country level. This makes it impossible to explore the effects of classroom variations in textbook coverage with the TIMSS data. Primarily, this was a result of resource limitations and not a conceptual limitation.

Logically, the presence of cross-national relationships between the aspects of curriculum and achievement gain (learning) does not imply the likely presence of such relationships across the classrooms or schools within a country. The former can exist and the latter not, especially within countries with little cross-classroom or cross-school variation in OTL. Many of the TIMSS countries had a national curriculum, one often dictated by a ministry of education (as we discussed in Chapter Four). One might expect little variation across classrooms within such a country, depending on the attendant enforcement policies. In such cases, little variation in OTL among classrooms would be expected, which would thus make it difficult to discern relationships at the classroom level between curriculum and learning if they exist.

On the other hand, one might anticipate large variations in what is taught across classrooms in some countries such as the United States, where local control or even school control of curriculum is the rule. In such cases, the policy question of the consequences of local variations in opportunity seems particularly germane.

To conduct within-country analyses for all TIMSS countries was beyond our available resources. We were forced to select a more limited set of countries to explore. The likely utility of such an analysis also seemed to vary owing to the nature of the organization of national educational systems. This should not be taken to mean that we completely ignored countries with strong institutional centers. There might be variation in curricular opportunities in spite of public policies of equal opportunities in all classrooms. In such a case, the presence of a relationship of curriculum to achievement gains could provide important information relevant to the limitations on the implementations of such a policy of equal opportunities.

Clearly, the policy questions that are addressed even for a limited set of countries are of a different nature than those examined earlier in the chapters focused on cross-national comparisons. As we move to the analyses summarized in this chapter, the distinctive nature of those analyses in terms of the policy questions addressed cannot be emphasized enough.

Selected Countries

The United States was one obvious country to choose because it relies on local control of the curriculum. Even that local control through school boards is often viewed by most as only advisory to individual schools, if not individual teachers. It would not be inaccurate to suggest that individual teachers are the final arbiters and decision makers regarding curriculum.[1] However, these decisions would be heavily influenced by the textbook used by the teacher, as suggested in the results of Chapter Eight.

Several other countries were chosen because of their strong control over curriculum. These countries include France, Hong Kong, the Czech Republic, Hungary, Japan, and Korea. Hungary describes itself as moving away from centralized control; however, at the time of the TIMSS study it was still considered to have mostly centralized decision making. Canada was also chosen both to represent countries that were between the extremes of centralization and because it was a classic example of a regionally centralized country.

The TIMSS study had particular design limitations for science, as we discussed in Chapter Five. In particular, classroom data could not be unambiguously matched to individual student data, and this was a requirement for this chapter's analyses. For that reason the focus of this chapter is only on eighth grade mathematics. Because of its unique level of decentralized decision making, the U.S. results will be discussed first and in the greatest detail.

There is also a second reason for this initial concentration on the United States. Interpreting the results of analyses such as those summarized in this chapter demands a thorough understanding of the policy context within the country analyzed. This is especially true with respect to the analyses here in contrast with those in the previous chapters because the variation characterized here is across the schools or classrooms within a country. Sensible interpretation of the analyses utilizing such variation depends on understanding the origin of such variability and the policy context that attempts either to contain, ignore, or encourage it. For this task we feel more competent to examine the U.S. results in great detail than to do so for the other countries. The results from the other countries cited previously are included as a contrast and as context. They will be interpreted on a more limited basis.

Design of the U.S. Analyses

The indicator for curriculum used for the within-country analyses was based on the instructional time variable. This is the same variable used before to indicate the percent of teacher time over the school year that was allocated to each of the topic areas. In the previous chapters, however, this variable was aggregated across teachers within a country to achieve a country-level indicator for each topic. That has not been done here.

Within the United States, the socioeconomic status (SES) background of students has been found to be related both to achievement and to curriculum opportunities that individual students receive.[2] This relationship has to be considered here to determine more accurately OTL's relationship to achievement. That is, it is necessary to examine both achievement and curricular opportunities in the context of SES in the analyses for the United States.

The relationship of SES indices to achievement has been well established in numerous studies and from multiple data sets.[3] The relationship of SES to learning opportunities is less well established, but it has been demonstrated in numerous contexts.[4] These studies show that within the United States, the practice of tracking at eighth grade (at least in mathematics) produces differences among students in their opportunities for learning. The presence of students in the various tracks is related to general ability and academic performance. This, in turn, is known to be related to SES.

This implies that in the United States at least, SES is related both to OTL and to achievement. One consequence of this is that if an analysis were to relate OTL to achievement without adjusting for SES, the magnitude of the relationship between OTL and achievement would be incorrectly estimated. This would be true because at least some of that relationship would reflect the relationship of SES to achievement rather than a pure relationship of opportunity to achievement.[5]

The U.S. practice of tracking at the middle school, especially in mathematics, is one of the major reasons for such variations in U.S. OTL. For some analyses we included this variable in addition to curriculum opportunity variables. To adequately account for SES differences among students and corresponding aggregate SES differences among classrooms, several available TIMSS variables indicative of SES were used in the analyses. These included mother's and father's education; the number of books in the home; student's age, sex, and race; several indices related to possessions found in the student's home; the educational expectations of parents for their child; the student's own educational aspirations; the size of the family; and the number of adults living in the home. These variables were included to allow statistical control for SES—to hold SES constant in examining the relationship of achievement and OTL.[6]

Several other variables describing instructional practices were used in the analyses, including some describing lesson activities—for example, the percentage of a class period that was devoted to instruction, seatwork, and homework (both to initial coverage of the homework as well as to its review and correction after it was collected). A variable characterizing additional aspects of pedagogy was also included. One question asked teachers in the TIMSS questionnaire was how often certain practices (e.g., explaining the reasoning behind an idea) were used in their classroom. An index was developed to characterize activities that could be viewed as moving beyond routine procedures to demand more complex performances from students. This index included (1) explaining the reasoning behind an idea; (2) representing and analyzing relationships using tables, graphs, and charts; and (3) working on problems for which there was no immediately obvious method of solution. (See Appendix D for a list of the variables used in the analyses presented in this chapter along with their definitions.)

The basic achievement measures used for the analyses were at the tested topic area level and for individual students. These were the same achievement areas used throughout the book; that is, the twenty tested topic areas of mathematics.[7] The focus in this chapter—as in the book as a whole—is on the learning that takes place in the eighth grade and not on achievement status. The reasons for this were discussed in Chapter Seven. Eighth grade instruction and curriculum is the central focus of the analyses. Proper control for learning that took place prior to eighth grade is essential for understanding these relationships.[8]

The appropriate analysis had to take into account the hierarchical nature of the data—classrooms that were located within schools and students who were located within classrooms. This was necessary because the SES and subtest achievement score variables were defined at the student level and the curriculum implementation (as well as other instructional variables) were defined at the classroom level.[9]

Results for the United States

Table 10.1 presents the results of the main analysis relating the curriculum opportunity variables to achievement, holding constant both SES and seventh grade prior achievement. (See Appendix D for a summary of analyses relating SES and achievement at the individual student level.) Using the seventh grade values made the analysis parallel to the achievement gain analyses used for the cross-country comparisons. This focused the analysis on learning, as has been the case throughout this book.[10]

Curriculum and Opportunity to Learn Variables

The results are for each of the twenty subtest topic areas. The general conclusion is that curriculum or OTL was significantly related to achievement in U.S. eighth grade mathematics classrooms, holding constant both SES and prior achievement. That is, differences in learning among U.S. eighth grade mathematics classrooms were related to concomitant differences in

Table 10.1. Curriculum and Achievement Change for U.S. Classrooms, Controlling for SES and Seventh Prior Achievement (Eighth Grade Mathematics).

Test Topic	R^2	Curriculum Content Topic	Regression Coefficient
Whole numbers	0.52	Equations and formulas	1.78**
		Whole numbers	−1.15**
Common fractions	0.61	Equations and formulas	3.64**
		Fractions and decimals	−1.83*
Decimal fractions and percents	0.63	Percentages	−2.57*
Relations of fractions	0.52	Integer, rational, and real numbers	1.47*
Estimating quantity and size	0.49	Integer, rational, and real numbers	2.49**
		Estimation	−6.93**
Rounding	0.38	Estimation	0.50*
		Integer, rational, and real numbers	−0.48
Estimating computations	0.57	Estimation	1.30**
Measurement units	0.47	Integer, rational, and real numbers	1.18
Perimeter, area, and volume	0.59	Units	6.83**
		2-D coordinate geometry	−1.55
Measurement estimations and errors	0.58	Perimeter, area, and volume	3.43**
		Measurement units	−4.48**
2-D geometry	0.47	Measurement estimations	3.91**
Polygons and circles	0.39	2-D coordinate geometry	2.13**
3-D geometry and transformations	0.45	2-D coordinate geometry	5.22**
Congruence and similarity	0.43	2-D coordinate geometry	1.95*
Proportionality concepts	0.42	Congruence and similarity	3.21**
Proportionality problems	0.57	Proportionality: Slope, trigonometry	7.53**
Patterns, relations, and functions	0.57	Proportionality: Slope, trigonometry	3.23**
		Patterns, relations, and functions	2.99**
Equations and formulas	0.62	Equations and formulas	6.31**
		Patterns, relations, and functions	4.86**
Data representation and analysis	0.61	Equations and formulas	−1.58
Uncertainty and probability	0.56	Data representation and analysis	−0.74*
		Fractions and decimals	−0.55
		Probability	

$**p = .05.$

$*.05 < p = .10.$

the amount of instructional time that teachers allocated to the supporting curriculum areas even when we adjusted for differences among classrooms due to SES and prior learning. This was true for all subtest areas except measurement units and data representation and analysis at either a statistically or marginally significant criterion (see Table 10.1).

The analyses were formulated to include the curriculum opportunity topic variables directly aligned with the subtest area together with the appropriate prerequisite topic areas (those that were logically related to learning in the target topic area). For example, this included the further learning of whole number arithmetic and fractions at the eighth grade. Algebra involves the manipulation of inequalities involving whole numbers as well as rational numbers (and thus fractions). Thus, algebra gave additional practice that could have led to improvements in whole number arithmetic and fractions.

Only five of the remaining eighteen tested areas were marginally significant ($.05 < p < .10$) rather than significant: decimals and percents, relations of fractions, rounding, congruence and similarity, and probability. There were statistically significant relationships of achievement to learning for thirteen of the twenty tested areas, even ignoring these five marginally significant subtest areas. (For a complete listing of coefficients for all the analyses, refer to Appendix D.)

For most of these thirteen areas, the relationship was straightforward logically. That is, more time (as a percent of total instructional time) that a teacher spent on a topic was related to a greater achievement score for that topic, given equal achievement in the topic at the seventh grade. That is, this was a measure of learning or achievement change because seventh grade achievement was also included in the model. Whole number arithmetic and fractions were exceptions; there the amount of class time spent in arithmetic was negatively related to learning. However, including linear equations (for the reasons discussed previously) gave a statistically significant positive relationship. This suggests that it is likely wasteful to allocate instructional time directly to instruction on whole number arithmetic and fractions in U.S. eighth grade mathematics classrooms.

Relations of fractions had rational and real numbers as a topic area in which opportunity to learn had a marginally significant relationship to achievement. The same was true for estimating quantity and size, rounding, and estimating computations. For perimeter, area, and volume, the corresponding opportunity variable was not significant, but time spent in one- and two-dimensional geometry was. This makes sense because these measurements are usually done for the same geometric figures that were studied in the geometry areas.

For measurement estimation and errors, the classroom coverage directly related to that topic was significant, but the relationship was negative. This suggests that the more instructional time that a U.S. teacher allocated to covering that topic, the less positive change in achievement took place. On the other hand, there was a statistically significant positive relationship between coverage of measurement units and achievement in this area.[11] Two of the marginally significant tested areas—decimals and percents and probability—also had negative effects for instructional time.

For all of the geometry, algebra, and proportionality subtest areas (nine areas if we include perimeter, area, and volume as a geometry topic), there were significant positive relationships between instructional time and achievement. This implies that cross-classroom differences in curriculum coverage of these topics was related to cross-classroom differences in achievement, even after adjusting for SES and prior achievement.[12] Note that this was true when considering U.S. eighth grade mathematics classrooms, not those of other countries (although the result might have been true there as well).

Other Instructional Variables

We also did analyses of achievement in which the instructional variables described earlier in this chapter were included with the OTL variables. They did not alter the previous conclusions concerning the effect of teacher allocations of time on learning in eighth grade mathematics. However, these other instructional variables were themselves still significantly related to learning.

The percentage of instructional time in a typical lesson allocated to activities as opposed to content was not significantly related to learning for any of the twenty subtests. How demanding the performance expectations were was also not significant for most topic areas. In fact, it was significant ($p < .05$) for only four topic areas—rounding, polygons and circles, three-dimensional geometry and transformations, and functions. The index was marginally significant ($p < .10$) for uncertainty and probability.

In all five of these cases, the coefficient relating the index of demanding performance expectations to learning was positive. This indicates that more time allocated by eighth grade mathematics teachers to activities that went beyond drill and other routine procedures was associated with higher average student scores in their classes for those five tested topic areas. This was true even after holding constant SES, prior achievement, and the amount of instructional time allocated to covering related topics.

As well, this was true not just for an arithmetic topic such as rounding but also for three geometry and algebra topics. As discussed in Chapter Five, these topics are the norm in eighth grade mathematics among top-achieving countries. The results imply that for these more advanced topics, teachers placing demands on students through the use of more complex activities had an effect on learning beyond the amount of time devoted to that instruction. This suggests that the *quality* of instruction and not just the *quantity* mattered, that how instruction was lengthened and not just that it was lengthened is what counted. This seems to have been true in U.S. eighth grade classrooms at least for functions, three-dimensional geometry, and polygons.

Size of the OTL Effect

We would like to examine further the relationship of the time teachers spent on a topic in class and the score on the appropriate achievement test, controlling for SES and prior learning, by examining the estimated regression coefficients from the analysis described previously.[13]

The estimated coefficients are given in Table 10.1. Using the logic of Chapter Eight in discussing the cross-country analyses, we ask, What would be the effect on achievement if a teacher were to increase her or his coverage of a topic by 3 percent (approximately one week of instruction)? The answer to the question is given in terms of the percent increase in the mean achievement score for the class. This gives in effect a predicted *increase* in achievement (an estimate of learning).

The predicted increases were sizable, ranging from around 3 to 24 percentage points. In other words, on average, for a classroom that spent about one week more on a topic than another classroom, where the two classrooms were similar in SES composition and in terms of prior achievement, the former would have a predicted achievement score some 3 to 24 percentage points higher than that of the other class.

The largest predicted effects for increased OTL (teacher time) were in geometry-related areas, in proportionality problems, and in equations (the latter two both a part of algebra). These are areas for which the United States in general did not provide much instructional coverage.[14] Thus, it seems unsurprising that even a small amount of additional instruction (as little as a week for each) focused on these key topics would predict large increases in learning (around 20 percentage points).

These predicted increases must be put in the context of current mathematics education in the United States. If that context was to change, then the nature of these relationships would likely change as well. These predicted increases are just that—predicted and based on empirical relationships, not causal structures, that are limited to the current U.S. milieu.[15] For example, if national content standards were adopted or if more rigorous mathematics were included in the eighth grade curriculum, especially in the areas of geometry and algebra, then these relationships would likely change.

Results from Other Countries

The same analyses were repeated with the seven other countries listed earlier in this chapter to determine if the pattern of relationships of OTL to achievement was consistent across countries. In a sense this is yet another way to examine the cultural hypothesis first discussed in Chapter One.

The prediction from the point of view of Chapter Four would be that the U.S. results would be quite different from other countries' because the U.S. educational system is based on distributed decision making and leaves instructional decisions to local districts and even to individual teachers.[16] From analyses of a similar sort conducted with the SIMS data, one might predict few such relationships at the classroom level for most other countries.[17]

This was precisely what we found: a few sporadic results for a topic area in most countries but no consistent patterns as was the case for the U.S. data. Japan and Canada were exceptions. The Czech Republic, Hungary, and Korea all had such sporadic results.

For Korea, the amount of teacher instruction in geometry was related to achievement in three-dimensional geometry when controlling for prior learning and social class. For Hungary, the OTL measure was related to achievement in estimating quantity and size and in rounding. In the Czech Republic, the percent of time that teachers spent on measurement units was significantly related to the corresponding achievement subtest.

In Japan, the related curriculum or OTL coverage was statistically significantly related to student achievement in whole number arithmetic, measurement errors and estimating, two-dimensional geometry, polygons and circles, and data representation. All of the relationships were positive, which indicated that more instructional time devoted to a topic was associated with greater learning. None of these topics were the focus—*focus* defined as one of the two topics that together accounted for over 60 percent of the textbook—of the eighth grade curriculum in Japan. As such, the coverage of these topics might well be at the discretion of the teacher and related to review, in which case such results are understandable even in a country with a tightly controlled national curriculum. However, this is only a conjecture on our part. In France and Hong Kong, there were no statistically significant relationships between achievement and the related OTL measures except for one marginal effect.

Canada was the one country that showed strikingly similar results to those of the United States. There were positive and statistically significant relationships of how much instructional time was spent and how much achievement was attained in fractions; perimeter, area, and volume; all four geometry topics; functions; equations and formulas; and data representation. This was true even when controlling for SES and prior learning.

The other instructional variables showed no strong indications of significance in the analyses with one exception: a relationship between the use of more demanding performance expectation activities by teachers and learning in Hungary. This was true for ten of the twenty tested topic areas.

Clearly the strength of the relationship of curriculum to learning within a country across schools varies with the country being studied. In the United States, there were significant relationships for thirteen of twenty topic areas (ignoring marginally significant relationships). In France, there were no significant topic areas with significant relationships. Canada was closest to the United States in results, with nine of twenty areas with significant relationships, and Japan had five.

It is also clear that the kind of analyses done in this section—an analysis that assumes that "one size fits all"—is not viable. This is why we present these brief results merely as an indication of how such analyses done more appropriately might look done in other countries. Why we do not find such relationships in other countries or only in some of them probably reflects the cultural and structural differences that exist within those countries. It seems likely that in countries with national content standards, for example, that variation in the percentage of teacher time allocated to a topic does not carry the same import as it does in a country that prides itself on local curriculum control. Some of the lack of such results may also reflect methodological issues.[18]

NOTES

1. Floden et al., 1981; Schwille et al., 1983.

2. Bond, 1981; Secada, 1992; Schmidt & Burstein, 1993; Hernstein & Murray, 1994.

3. See, for example, Anderson, Hollinger, & Conaty, 1993; Young & Fraser, 1993; Stevenson, Schiller, & Schneider, 1994.

4. McKnight et al., 1987; Burstein, 1993; Stevenson et al., 1994; Raudenbush, Fotiu, & Cheong, 1998; Schmidt, McKnight, Cogan, Jakwerth, & Houang, 1999.

5. Technically this implies that the estimated regression coefficients would be biased because of the confounding of SES and opportunity to learn.

6. That is, we wished to estimate the regression coefficient for opportunity controlled for SES. This is to ensure that the estimate of the coefficient that defines the relationship of curriculum (as OTL) to achievement gain is properly adjusted and, as a result, less biased.

7. The main goal of the analyses reported in this chapter was to identify the effects of classroom instructional variables on achievement at the subtest level. Because of the matrix-sampled design used in TIMSS, analysis of the subtests required a complete data set, including item responses at the individual student level. The procedures used for the international data file involved conditional multiple imputation (Rubin, 1987) and used Rasch scaling of the test responses to yield a total test score. In preliminary analysis trials for this research, the total imputed test score seemed to underrepresent variation at the classroom and school levels and, therefore, depressed instructional effects. To correct for this, we devised a new conditioning model that incorporated data at these levels as well as produced imputed item-level data. The U.S. test and sample design specifications for Population 2 mathematics are summarized as follows:

1. There were eight test forms distributed among the students in each class.
2. There were three mathematics classes sampled from each school (one for seventh grade, two for eighth grade).
3. Schools were sampled (pps) from regional strata.
4. The strata were geographic clusters of U.S. states.
5. Sampled classrooms could be classified into types (as regular, prealgebra, or algebra).
6. All classes in each school were identified by title and grade and then subsequently classified by type.
7. Six items (from six different content areas) were common to all eight forms.
8. There were 151 items total across all forms.

We needed to impute item responses on forms that the students did not take. The following description is for each subgroup of students that we defined. We used class type (regular, prealgebra, algebra), grade level, and student ability (as defined by the student's Rasch score) to stratify the students into groups. Therefore, there were three conditioning variables. The resulting fifteen groups were

GRADE 8   GRADE 7
   Regular   Regular
        a – Low   a – Low
        b – Middle   b – Middle
        c – High   c – High
   Prealgebra   Prealgebra
        a – Low   a – Low
        b – Middle   b – Middle
        c – High   c – High
   Algebra
        a – Low
        b – Middle
        c – High

The imputations were conducted separately in each group. Based on the six common items in each booklet, we estimated the true score distribution for each group to compute the joint distribution of (parallel) observed scores. Following Lord (1965, 1969), we assume that the true score, ξ, has a four-parameter beta distribution. We estimated the four parameters and determined the conditional distribution of observed scores on the common items, X, given ξ, and from this determined the joint distribution of two parallel six-item tests.

We further imputed individual six-item observed scores on the missing forms from the six-item observed scores on the form taken by the student using the conditional distribution of observed on observed—that is, given the original score, we drew a new score randomly using the probabilities from the conditional distribution. The steps followed include

1. Sample a person with that score on another form and select the person's item responses. This yields the imputed values for the variables available only on that form. The sampling is done in two steps: select a classroom and select a person response.
2. Select a classroom. Each classroom was selected with equal probability from all those with persons having the appropriate scores.
3. Within the selected classroom, a person was selected with equal probability from all those persons having the appropriate score. This person's scores became the imputed values for the original person.

4. After selecting an appropriately corresponding person, the imputed values were added to the original person's record.

This process was repeated for all forms and for each person.

8. However, TIMSS was not a longitudinal study (as was discussed in Chapter Three). For the country-level analyses, the seventh grade mean for the country was subtracted from the eighth grade country mean to define a measure of achievement gain. There was further statistical complexity for the analyses summarized in this chapter. There probably is no satisfactory way to do what we did at the country level in terms of defining a gain score at the individual student level. However, we implemented a parallel set of procedures to obtain appropriate adjustments at the classroom level.

Because both seventh and eighth grade classroom data were collected for each school, it was again possible to use the aggregate seventh grade score constructed at the same subtest level (at least to some extent) to account for prior achievement for each eighth grade class. The most difficult methodological issue was that one must align the appropriate seventh grade class with each eighth grade class, given tracking in U.S. schools. For example, the achievement of a seventh grade pre-algebra class could serve as the "pre" measure for an eighth grade algebra class but not for an eighth grade regular mathematics classroom. This was not a trivial problem, because only one seventh grade classroom was sampled at each school. We were forced to deal with this problem statistically.

We conducted a conditional multiple imputation to impute class means at the seventh grade for all twenty subscores. The TIMSS sample contained 184 schools with 367 classes in all for Population 2 mathematics. The classes were cross-classified by school, grade, and class type combined with stream, yielding a total of 2,944 cells (184 schools by two grades by eight class types/streams [three class types by three streams yields nine categories reduced to eight]). The grades were seventh and eighth. The class types were regular, pre-algebra, and algebra. Streams were defined using a school-determined ability ordering of specific courses. Many cells were empty because some schools had limited offerings. In particular, seventh grade algebra classes were seldom offered. A main-class ANOVA model was fitted to the class achievement means. The fitted model yielded an estimated value and a residual for every cell. Imputed values for missing classes were then calculated by using the fitted values for the cell of the missing class (school–grade–class type combination) plus a randomly selected value from the distribution of residuals. This was done for each of the twenty subscores separately.

9. TIMSS is at best only quasi-longitudinal. That is, seventh and eighth grade
   data were for parallel cohorts and therefore longitudinal only at the class
   rather than the individual level. In fact, they were only quasi-longitudinal
   even at that level. A class-level analysis of quasi-gains was possible if seventh grade class scores comparable to eighth grade class scores could be
   estimated. We accomplished this by performing a regression with the
   dependent variable as mean achievement in eighth grade classes. Independent variables consisted of (1) an SES control composite, (2) the estimate of
   a comparable seventh grade class subscore, and (3) selected class-level variables from the teacher file. The analysis was defined as follows

   1. A pooled within-class regression was performed (deviated achievement
      score regressed on deviated SES data).
   2. We calculated predicted achievement values based on the undeviated
      SES values. These were aggregated to the class level to yield the SES
      control composite.
   3. A feeder seventh grade class type was determined for the eighth grade
      class that produced the independent variable.
   4. The appropriate feeder class type actually depended on the offerings at
      the target school. The table below gives the possible pairs of seventh
      grade feeder and eighth grade classes in sampled schools. In U.S.
      schools, four combinations of class types were possible in the seventh
      grade (two by two to get four: regular alone, pre-algebra alone, both,
      and neither). Eight combinations were possible in eighth grade (two by
      two by two). Thus, in total thirty-two (four by eight) combinations
      were possible across the two grades. Only fourteen of these actually
      existed.

CONCEPTUALLY POSSIBLE MATHEMATICS CLASS TYPE COMBI-
NATIONS OF SEVENTH GRADE "FEEDER" VERSUS EIGHTH
GRADE SAMPLED CLASSES

		Eighth Grade		
		Regular	Pre-algebra	Algebra
Seventh	Regular	X	X	X
Grade	Pre-algebra		X	X

Because the class pairs resulting from the sampling often did not
include the relevant seventh grade feeder class and the seventh grade class
level imputation described elsewhere yielded imputed achievement values
for both seventh grade class types in each school, one of these values was
selected as the independent variable value. The appropriate imputed value
was selected using the following rule: a class type was eligible as a feeder if

it corresponded to an entry in the previous table. If both types were eligible, the pre-algebra imputed value was used. That is, pre-algebra, if existing, was used as a feeder for both algebra and pre-algebra.

An eighth grade class level regression analysis was performed using the SES composite, the imputed seventh grade class mean, and the instructional variables. The SES composite had been derived from the first, within-class stage described earlier.

10. The technical difference is that the gain analysis assumes the β relating seventh grade achievement to eighth grade achievement is equal to 1, whereas its inclusion as another independent variable in the current chapter allows for the unconstrained estimation of β.

11. A further fitting of models suggested that the negative estimates were not a consequence of collinearity.

12. The TIMSS data were not longitudinal as discussed earlier. Therefore, the adjustment for prior learning could be done only at the classroom level, and even this necessitated imputed data. This type of adjustment is most likely not completely adequate. The result of this could be bias, most likely an overestimation of the importance of the OTL variables. To be conservative, we ran additional analyses and found results consistent with those discussed previously for the OTL or teacher time variables. That is, the conclusions summarized earlier in general were upheld. To explore this issue methodologically, we included a dummy variable for track, a variable that was coded as 1 for algebra track and 0 for all others. This variable was then included in the second stage of the model along with the others. For all twenty tested areas, the track variable was statistically significant, which is consistent with the hypothesis that the other adjustments did not likely adequately account for all SES and prior achievement differences among classrooms.

No real differences were observed for twelve of the outcome variables. For the other eight subtest areas—those for which inclusion of track altered the conclusions relative to the OTL variables—the OTL variables that were primarily affected were integers, rational and real numbers, including exponents, roots, and radicals and complex numbers, slope and trigonometry, and equations and formulas. These moved from statistically to marginally significant or from significant to not significant. These are the main topics, along with functions, of traditional U.S. Algebra I courses. These topics are what are usually offered in the algebra track. The problem with incorporating track into the model and the reason that it was not done in the main analysis is that track membership in the United States reflects not only SES and prior achievement but also reflects real instructional differences in terms of content coverage (Cogan, Schmidt & Wiley, forthcoming). Adjusting for this as we did not only removes the SES and prior learning class differences not accounted for by the other variables in the model but also removes real instructional and curriculum differences. The fact that the variables primarily affected by this are the ones for which there are cross-track differences in terms of teacher coverage suggests that this is most likely what is happening.

13. As mentioned previously, we fitted a two-stage hierarchical model and used it as the analysis behind Table 10.1. To assure ourselves and other methodologists among the readers, we also fitted a mixed model (see Littell, Milliken, Stroup, & Wolfinger, 1996) and an HLM model (Bryk & Raudenbush, 1992). The results were remarkably close across all three estimation procedures. This was true both in terms of the estimated value of the regression coefficients and of the significance level associated with the coefficient. The differences were trivial and do not alter the general conclusions discussed here.

14. Schmidt, McKnight, Cogan, Jakwerth, & Houang, 1999.

15. They may actually be more invariant—especially when placed alongside the similar results of the cross-national analyses—but TIMSS data do not support such causal inferences.

16. See Schmidt, McKnight, Cogan, Jakwerth, & Houang, 1999, pp. 187–189.

17. Schmidt & Kifer, 1989.

18. Three methodological issues come immediately to mind. First, we did not impute the item-level data in these other countries. We only used the IRT (Item Response Theory) scale score for the within-country analyses used to produce the SES adjustment. Second, these other countries had only one seventh grade and one eighth grade class. How well the seventh grade could serve as the "pre" measure for the eight depended on school structure, stratification, and some form of ability (not content) tracking. These might be present in these countries at those particular schools, but they might not. All of this was beyond our level of knowledge. Third, if the variation across classes in a national system were small, then establishing a relationship of OTL to achievement would be difficult. This would be because we cannot estimate effects accurately with a small σ^2 across the classes on the OTL variables.

SCHOOLS MATTER

WE BEGAN THIS BOOK WITH a simple statement: schools matter. We write this book in a climate of concern about public education, a concern that seems warranted in light of how U.S. student achievement compares with that of other countries in TIMSS. However, the debate continues on how to improve the situation. Some express their belief in how much schools matter by passionately arguing about what should go into the curriculum; others argue just as strongly that they can no longer be left as a public trust but that choices about schools must be put into the hands of parents.

Grist for the mill of public debate has often been provided by cross-national comparative studies of education. This seems never to have been truer than is the case for TIMSS in the current debates about education. All sides in the debate have used TIMSS, even those that would question the value of U.S. public education.

We, the authors, have chosen to focus not on the comparative status of countries but instead on what students learn. Certainly, comparative status has implications for economic competitiveness and has prima facie political appeal. Comparative status also says something about the cumulative effect of curriculum and schooling, but it says little about learning. Learning is change and growth. Learning is not status but accumulates to result in status. If we wish to know what is effective in enhancing learning, we must go beyond looking at comparative achievement status to examine what produces changes and gains in achievement. These are our best objective indicators of student learning. Analyses that focus on comparing achievement status will almost always underestimate the importance of schooling and, in particular, curriculum because they deal only with cumulative effects that are shaped by long-term factors. It is hardly surprising that such matters as SES and parental background are the kind of long-term factors that get linked to comparative achievement status with shorter-term curricular and schooling factors swept away by the ebb and flow of the years of education.

However, the present debates are about what can be changed. One can hardly regard SES and parental background as manipulable variables to be shaped by educational policy to improve comparative achievement in school. In the abstract, surely everyone would support an educational policy such as, "Make everyone wealthier and better educated and his or her children will do better in school." Yet surely everyone would realize the futility of such a policy as a realistic recipe for educational change.

We want to understand the things that truly can be changed about schooling to produce greater achievement. In particular, schools are about learning, and we believe that schools matter because learning matters. Can we demonstrate this empirically? And if so, will it provide any useful guidance for realistic educational policies that can bring about change? We believe the answer to these questions is yes.

What did we accomplish by focusing on achievement gain rather than status? We have tried to tell some of that story in this book. One facet of this story is that schools matter because through the curriculum they provide a systematic opportunity for students to learn and master the subject matter contents and processes necessary for their successful living. As Ravitch (2000) has said, "What is it that schools and only schools can and must do? They cannot be successful as schools unless nearly all their pupils gain literacy and numeracy, as well as a good understanding of history and the sciences, literature and a foreign language."[1]

Curriculum defines for students the sequence of contents and performances necessary to acquire the knowledge of which Ravitch speaks— particularly, for us, in mathematics and the sciences. One of this book's stories is that in analysis after analysis we have clearly demonstrated that differences in curriculum exist across countries and among topics in mathematics and the sciences. We have even demonstrated that in some countries (for example, the United States), differences in curriculum exist across classrooms within the country.

The evidence presented earlier is strong. Various aspects of curriculum differ for different countries. They differ for different topics in mathematics and the sciences, at least as presented in the two grades that contain the majority of thirteen-year-olds in each country. They do not differ consistently across topics for every country in the same way. There are interactions, and the pattern of differences for different topics is not the same in each country.

Furthermore, these differences in aspects of curriculum are significantly related to achievement gains, that is, to learning in virtually all of the TIMSS countries. This may not have been true for every topic in every country, but it was true at least for some topics in almost every country. Those topics varied from country to country. The existence of a relationship between curriculum and achievement gains, however, did not vary. The topics for which it existed might differ. The aspect of curriculum related to achievement gains might differ for different topics and countries. Nonetheless, in case after case, some significant relationship was found between achievement gains and curriculum. The shift from considering achievement status to considering achievement gains allowed us to use quantitative methods for studying aspects of curriculum to empirically support the fact that curriculum was related to learning.

Variations in mathematics and science curriculum across the countries were evident in the structural relationships between various aspects of curriculum—content standards, textbook coverage, performance demands, instructional time, percent of a nation's teachers covering specific topics, and so on. These relationships vary and do so in characteristic patterns for many countries and even for groups of countries that shared similar patterns. This we find to be consistent with the cultural hypothesis laid out in Chapter One. The evidence for this was very clear in Chapters Five and Six.

There were also characteristic variations in how aspects of curriculum in school science and mathematics were related to achievement gains (learning). This was shown in the analyses presented in Chapters Eight and Nine. This empirical evidence supported the belief that curriculum mattered to learning in mathematics and the sciences. It also revealed a variety of patterns in how aspects of the curriculum brought about achievement gains. These patterns are informative for educational policy considerations. Unlike the general background factors that can be shown to be linked to achievement status, these curricular factors are manipulable and can be affected by educational policy.

How countries allocate their resources and priorities to provide learning opportunities for their children in mathematics and the sciences matters. In that sense, policy matters and these data support its importance in a way not often done by the data from cross-national comparative studies. This even extends to differences within countries such as the United States, in which the use of curriculum and resources across classrooms and schools for providing learning opportunities in mathematics and the sciences varies considerably.

We can summarize the implications of our data and our analyses from several perspectives. Let us recapitulate some of what we feel has been discovered under a few key levels.

The Political or Social Perspective

We believe that schools matter. Like others, we found evidence that economic and social factors—SES and GNP—matter to what is learned by children. However, these factors have their impacts *along with* those of curriculum and schools instead of in their place.

The Mathematics or Science Perspective

We believe that we found interesting evidence that the logic of subject matter disciplines plays an important role in school learning. This logic may not be so overpowering that "mathematics is mathematics" or "science is science" in different cultures. However, it is sufficiently important to produce commonalties as well as some important interactions. Learning a particular topic may not only be influenced by curricular experiences with that topic but also with other topics that have a structural relationship to the original topic through the logic of the sciences' or mathematics' disciplines.

The Curriculum Design Perspective

We believe that the previous assertions imply that the logic of mathematics and the sciences, particularly in the context of school, should play a strong role in designing curricular activities. Perhaps even more important, it might be that the whole structure and sequence of how topics are put together to define an overall curriculum in science and mathematics should make more use of this logic. This at least holds the promise of capitalizing on interactions in the logic of the content disciplines to develop more effective curricula.

The Teacher Perspective

We found evidence that the quantity of coverage associated with a topic is not all that contributes to the learning it produces. This is true whether the quantity of coverage is measured by how much time is typically spent on a topic or by what proportion of a country's teachers cover it. The quality of that coverage is also important, both in terms of the level of cognitive demands expected of students and in terms of the types of instructional activities the teacher uses. The data seem clearly suggestive that drill and practice does not appear to be adequate for the level of attainment sought for most students in most countries, and neither is concentrating only on absorbing knowledge and learning to perform routine processes.

The Textbook Perspective

We believe that we found powerful evidence that textbooks exert a strong influence on what teachers teach. This seems to be true in most countries despite differences in the nature and use of textbooks. Textbook coverage is important both for what topics are taught and for the levels of performances and accomplishments expected of students. Whatever should be the case, textbooks have an impact almost everywhere, and it is perilous to ignore the ways in which they at least partially shape what is taught.

The National or Regional Perspective

We also found evidence that content standards are the primary vehicle for policy impact on what teachers teach. In most countries, this impact is strongest in an indirect way, with its primary influence being on textbooks that, in turn, have a more direct impact on what is taught. However, in many cases it also has a more direct impact on what teachers do. Coverage of a topic in content standards will not ensure its coverage in classrooms. The data are telling on this point. Even countries with strong national content standards do not have absolute conformity in terms of teacher coverage. The degree of centralization of the system does seem to be related to this conformity but not enough to ensure it completely.

Decisions about setting relative priorities are made in varied ways across the countries. The most notable difference is between the United States and other countries. The setting of content standards—relative priorities—is typically a national task and represents a national vision. That is not so in the United States. However, unlike what we might have naively assumed about other countries, setting priorities at a national level is not tantamount to national control of the school system. Many other countries have regional, religious, and even local control of schools but only a national control of relative priorities involved in content standards. This is a much narrower sense of national control than most in the United States fear and one that well may be more tolerable politically.

The Systemic Perspective

A basic part of analysis is separating facets of the situation analyzed. We did that by looking at different aspects of curriculum. However, such facets are not separable in reform efforts. It is an educational system that must be changed, with all of the facets that implies. We cannot copy a single aspect of curriculum or any other part of education from another country. Those aspects are part of national systems and are interrelated to other aspects. We cannot copy an entire system, and thus we cannot import a single factor.

Other factors not in our model may affect the functioning of educational systems but could not be included because of limitations on the types and amounts of data collected. For example, out-of-school learning may be important to overall learning, as might also be teachers' subject matter knowledge, parental support, or national testing policies. Our opportunities for gathering data on these matters were severely limited by what was possible in TIMSS. We must understand what we can of the relationships among the aspects of curriculum and achievement that we could explore but also keep in mind that our model captures only part of an educational system and reveals only certain things about relationships on which to base systemic change.

The Cultural Perspective

As we have often stated in this book, the impact of culture in shaping the social institutions that affect schooling must remain a matter of conjecture and hypothesis. We believe strongly that cultural concerns give characteristic shape to national educational systems, institutions, and relationships. Nothing in the data we analyzed was inconsistent with this hypothesis. However, it still remains beyond the scope of these data to confirm this hypothesis directly. We believe that the characteristic differences we found among the educational systems and the functioning of the aspects of curriculum in different countries are indirect indications of the impact of culture, but this must remain a matter of belief and not proof.

The Statistical Indicator Perspective

We believe that the logic of using emphasis as a measure of the effort in a system where time and textbook space are limited resources is strongly upheld by these data. The measures used in the analyses here are not perfect indicators of emphasis, and neither do they function perfectly as statistical indicators. However, these measures seem clearly to reflect important aspects of education and thus to be indicators well worth attending to.

The Scientific and Methodological Perspective

In designing TIMSS as a scientific study, we began by addressing two fundamental errors common to many previous cross-national comparative studies in education. First, we decided to focus on changes in achievement rather than on comparative status in achievement. This is a fundamental reconception of the purpose of cross-national comparative studies of achievement. We consider such a study to be a laboratory, not a yardstick, being more interested in how the achievement changes in one country compared with those in another rather than in who finished first. By comparing this to different curricular priorities, uses of resources, and other schooling factors, the pool of nations becomes a laboratory. Variations in curriculum and policy are greater across nations than within one. Focus on achievement gains as an indicator of learning makes different factors relevant to producing change, factors that bear more policy significance than SES and parental background.

Second, we believe that curriculum can be measured quantitatively, in contrast to the beliefs and practices seen in many previous cross-national studies. As a distributor of OTL, it can be investigated empirically and not simply in black-box teacher responses to and ratings of achievement test items to indicate whether their students had recent opportunities in their classrooms to learn what was needed to answer those items correctly. This measure has been consistently found to be related positively to achievement. Unfortunately, OTL in this form remains a black box about which one must remain uncertain as to what is measured. Do the teachers' ratings indicate objective information about school curricula? Do they represent teachers' unarticulated assumptions about the material on which their students will do well? Are they confounded with teachers' opinions about the form in which the questions in the items are asked and to which their students would be expected to answer? Surely we can learn more about the impact of curriculum on student learning than what is provided by these teacher opinions. One of the breakthroughs behind this current book is that we were able to devise new methods for the empirical study of key aspects of curriculum—curriculum as it was intended, as it was embodied in student textbooks, and as it was implemented by teachers.

The empirical evidence presented in this book was technically demanding. It was necessary often to work on the methodological cutting edge to tease out the sorts of empirical relationships that were found between curriculum and learning. We worked within the arena of the existing TIMSS data with all the richness implied by this but also with its particular limitations and weaknesses. Not all questions have been answered, and certainly not all have been answered satisfactorily. The analyses here should provide guidance for essential qualitative studies necessary to more fully enlighten the relationships shown to exist here. Comparative studies with different designs are necessary to shed light more clearly on science education and, in particular, the role of multiple courses, multiple teachers, and differing science disciplines in many countries. Truly longitudinal studies and formal experimental studies (with randomization) are needed to refine the analysis of achievement gains and to make them possible at the individual and classroom level.

After all that has been done and in light of all that remains to be done, we must close with a sense of satisfaction in what we have accomplished. We began with the belief that schools mattered and that they mattered through their curriculum and what this implied for the learning opportunities of students. We felt that these factors were so strong that they should prove to be related to the differential achievement gains of students. However, we chose to treat these beliefs and feelings skeptically and to determine if there was an empirical basis for them in the TIMSS data on eighth grade mathematics and science education. There was.

We live in a time in which the reform of mathematics and science education in schools itself is widely felt to be in need of reform, a time in which many are skeptical that efforts at reform even matter because deliberate change seems so hard to accomplish. At the end of these investigations, we feel that we can at least answer this skepticism informedly. Ample empirical evidence points to aspects of curriculum being related to learning.

As with all science, advances are dependent upon careful observations and measurements that then allow a mathematical modeling of relationships. We set out to quantify that which has always been basically qualitative and that had not been measured before. We learned that curriculum can be measured. We also learned how to quantify its various aspects to be able to model those relationships. We learned to quantitatively assess the nature of those relationships. Through this we found what, in many ways, is obvious—that curriculum is related to learning. This is only a beginning. The measures, theory, and models need to be advanced if the scientific study of education is to advance. However, obvious though it may seem to have laboriously established that curriculum is empirically related to learning, it will have been worth the effort if any future cross-national study of education that does not take curriculum seriously or that does not include the relationship of curriculum to learning as part of its foundations will be viewed askance by those considering it.

A Final Word

We cannot tell anyone what changes they should make. We can tell anyone who cares to listen and investigate with us that changes can be made and reforms can be made effectively as long as they take seriously the complex ways in which curriculum is related to learning. In the end, schools matter, and what one proposes about school reforms should be carefully and thoughtfully crafted, for it will have effects. We believe that our culture shapes our schools and that deliberate manipulation of school policy has a place in that shaping. We know that our schools mold our national futures. Surely any reasonable individual must see that understanding these matters more fully, studying them more carefully, and using them wisely is an important priority.

NOTE

1. Ravitch, 2000, p. 465.

Appendix A

TIMSS MATHEMATICS AND SCIENCE CURRICULUM FRAMEWORKS

THE MATHEMATICS AND SCIENCE curriculum frameworks for TIMSS were designed to measure curriculum from a variety of sources: a country's content standards (curriculum guides), textbooks, teacher surveys, and achievement tests. Each framework specified three aspects of subject matter—content (subject matter topics), performance expectation (what students were expected to do with particular subject matter topics), and perspective (any overarching orientation to the subject matter and its place among the disciplines and in the everyday world). Further explanation of the frameworks and the document analysis procedures may be found in the two *Many Visions, Many Aims* volumes (Schmidt, McKnight, Valverde, Houang & Wiley, 1997; Schmidt, Raizen, Britton, Bianchi & Wolfe, 1997). First articulated only in technical reports (which is still true for the more extensive explanatory notes), the frameworks have been reproduced and documented in the monograph *Curriculum Frameworks for Mathematics and Science* (Robitaille, Schmidt, Raizen, McKnight, Britton & Nicol, 1993).

Mathematics

Content

1.1 Numbers
    1.1.1 Whole numbers
        1.1.1.1 Meaning

Performance Expectations

2.5.2 Relating representations
2.5.3 Describing/discussing
2.5.4 Critiquing

Perspectives

3.1 Attitudes toward science, mathematics, and technology
3.2 Careers involving science, mathematics, and technology
   3.2.1 Promoting careers in science, mathematics, and technology
   3.2.2 Promoting the importance of science, mathematics, and technology in nontechnical careers
3.3 Participation in science and mathematics by underrepresented groups
3.4 Science, mathematics, and technology to increase interest
3.5 Scientific and mathematical habits of mind

Science

Content

1.1 Earth sciences
   1.1.1 Earth features
      1.1.1.1 Composition
      1.1.1.2 Landforms
      1.1.1.3 Bodies of water
      1.1.1.4 Atmosphere
      1.1.1.5 Rocks, soil
      1.1.1.6 Ice forms
   1.1.2 Earth processes
      1.1.2.1 Weather and climate
      1.1.2.2 Physical cycles
      1.1.2.3 Building and breaking
      1.1.2.4 Earth's history
   1.1.3 Earth in the universe
      1.1.3.1 Earth in the solar system
      1.1.3.2 Planets in the solar system
      1.1.3.3 Beyond the solar system
      1.1.3.4 Evolution of the universe
1.2 Life sciences
   1.2.1 Diversity, organization, structure of living things
      1.2.1.1 Plants, fungi
      1.2.1.2 Animals

Performance expectations

2.1.2 Complex information

2.1.3 Thematic information

2.2 Theorizing, analyzing, and solving problems

    2.2.1 Abstracting and deducing scientific principles

    2.2.2 Applying scientific principles to solve quantitative problems

    2.2.3 Applying scientific principles to develop explanations

    2.2.4 Constructing, interpreting, and applying models

    2.2.5 Making decisions

2.3 Using tools, routine procedures, and science processes

    2.3.1 Using apparatus, equipment, and computers

    2.3.2 Conducting routine experimental operations

    2.3.3 Gathering data

    2.3.4 Organizing and representing data

    2.3.5 Interpreting data

2.4 Investigating the natural world

    2.4.1 Identifying questions to investigate

    2.4.2 Designing investigations

    2.4.3 Conducting investigations

    2.4.4 Interpreting investigational data

    2.4.5 Formulating conclusions from investigational data

2.5 Communicating

    2.5.1 Accessing and processing information

    2.5.2 Sharing information

Perspectives

3.1 Attitudes towards science, mathematics, and technology

    3.1.1 Positive attitudes toward science, mathematics, and technology

    3.1.2 Skeptical attitudes towards use of science and technology

3.2 Careers in science, mathematics, and technology

    3.2.1 Promoting careers in science, mathematics, and technology

    3.2.2 Promoting importance of science, mathematics, and technology in nontechnical careers

3.3 Participation in science and mathematics by underrepresented groups

3.4 Science, mathematics, and technology to increase interest

3.5 Safety in science performance

3.6 Scientific habits of mind

Appendix B

RELATIONSHIP BETWEEN CONTENT MEASUREMENT CATEGORIES FOR THE TIMSS FRAMEWORK, TEACHERS, AND TIMSS TEST

Mathematics

TIMSS Framework Topics		TIMSS Teacher Survey Categories		Content-Specific Subtests	
#	Label	#	Label	#	Label
1	Whole number: Meaning	1	Whole numbers	1	Whole numbers
2	Whole number: Operations	1	Whole numbers	1	Whole numbers
3	Whole number: Properties of operations	1	Whole numbers		
4	Common fractions	2	Common and decimal fractions	2	Common fractions
5	Decimal fractions	2	Common and decimal fractions	3	Decimal fractions and percents
6	Relationship of common and decimal fractions	2	Common and decimal fractions	4	Relations of fractions
7	Percentages	3	Percentages	3	Decimal fractions and percents
8	Properties of common and decimal fractions	2	Common and decimal fractions		
9	Negative numbers, integers, and their properties	4	Number sets and concepts		
10	Rational numbers and their properties	4	Number sets and concepts		
11	Real numbers, their subsets, and properties	4	Number sets and concepts	18	Equations and formulas
12	Binary arithmetic and/or other number bases	4	Number sets and concepts	18	Equations and formulas
13	Exponents, roots, and radicals	4	Number sets and concepts		
14	Complex numbers and their properties	4	Number sets and concepts		
15	Number theory	5	Number theory		
16	Counting	5	Number theory		
17	Estimating quantity and size	6	Estimation and number sense	5	Estimating quantity and size
18	Rounding and significant figures	6	Estimation and number sense	6	Rounding
19	Estimating computations	6	Estimation and number sense	7	Estimating computations
20	Exponents and orders of magnitude	6	Estimation and number sense		

TIMSS Framework Topics

#	Label
21	Measurement units
22	Perimeter, area, and volume
23	Measurement estimation and errors
24	2-D Coordinate geometry
25	2-D Geometry: Basics
26	2-D Geometry: Polygons and circles
27	3-D Geometry
28	Vectors
29	Geometry: Transformations
30	Congruence and similarity
31	Constructions w/ straightedge and compass
32	Proportionality concepts
33	Proportionality problems
34	Slope and trigonometry
35	Linear interpolation and extrapolation
36	Patterns, relations, and functions
37	Equations and formulas
38	Data representation and analysis
39	Uncertainty and probability
40	Elementary analysis: Infinite processes
41	Elementary analysis: Change
42	Validation and justification
43	Structuring and abstracting
44	Other content

TIMSS Teacher Survey Categories

#	Label
7	Measurement units and processes
8	Perimeter, area, and volume
9	Estimation and error of measurement
10	Basics of 1- and 2-D geometry
10	Basics of 1- and 2-D geometry
10	Basics of 1- and 2-D geometry
13	Constructions and 3-D geometry
13	Constructions and 3-D geometry
11	Geometric transformations and symmetry
12	Geometric congruence and similarity
13	Constructions and 3-D geometry
14	Ratio and proportion
14	Ratio and proportion
15	Ratio and proportion
15	Proportionality: Slope, trigonometry, and interpolation
16	Functions, relations, and patterns
17	Equations, inequalities, and formulas
18	Statistics and data
19	Probability and uncertainty
21	Other mathematics content
21	Other mathematics content
20	Sets and logic
20	Sets and logic
21	Other mathematics content

Content-Specific Subtests

#	Label
8	Measurement units
9	Perimeter, area and volume
10	Measurement estimations and errors
11	2-D geometry
11	2-D geometry
12	Polygons and circles
13	3-D geometry and transformations
13	3-D geometry and transformations
14	Congruence and Similarity
15	Proportionality concepts
16	Proportionality problems
17	Patterns, relations, and functions
18	Equations and formulas
19	Data representation and analysis
20	Uncertainty and probability

Science

TIMSS Framework Topics

#	Label
1	Earth's composition
2	Land forms
3	Bodies of water
4	Atmosphere
5	Rocks, soil
6	Ice forms
7	Weather and climate
8	Physical cycles
9	Building and breaking
10	Earth's history
11	Earth in the solar system
12	Planets in the solar system
13	Beyond the solar system
14	Evolution of the universe
15	Plants, fungi
16	Animals
17	Microorganisms
18	Organs, tissues
19	Cells
20	Organism energy handling
21	Organism sensing and responding
22	Biochemical processes in cells
23	Life cycles

TIMSS Teacher Survey Categories

#	Label
1	Earth features
1	Earth features
1	Earth features
1	Earth features
1	Earth features
1	Earth features
2	Earth processes
2	Earth processes
2	Earth processes
2	Earth processes
3	Earth in the universe
3	Earth in the universe
3	Earth in the universe
3	Earth in the universe
4	Diversity and structure of living things
4	Diversity and structure of living things
4	Diversity and structure of living things
4	Diversity and structure of living things
4	Diversity and structure of living things
5	Life processes and systems
5	Life processes and systems
5	Life processes and systems
6	Life cycles and genetics

Content-Specific Subtests

#	Label
1	Earth features
1	Earth features
1	Earth features
1	Earth features
1	Earth features
2	Earth processes
2	Earth processes
2	Earth processes
2	Earth processes
3	Earth in the universe
3	Earth in the universe
4	Diversity and structure of living things
4	Diversity and structure of living things
4	Diversity and structure of living things
4	Diversity and structure of living things
5	Life processes and functions
5	Life processes and functions
6	Life cycles and genetics

TIMSS Framework Topics

#	Label
24	Reproduction
25	Variation and inheritance
26	Evolution, specification, diversity
27	Biochemistry of genetics
28	Biomes and ecosystems
29	Habitats and niches
30	Interdependence of life
31	Animal behavior
32	Human biology and health
33	Human nutrition
34	Human diseases
35	Classification of matter
36	Physical properties of matter
37	Chemical properties of matter
38	Atoms, ions, molecules
39	Macromolecules, crystals
40	Subatomic particles
41	Energy types, sources, conversions
42	Heat and temperature
43	Wave phenomena
44	Sound and vibration
45	Light
46	Electricity
47	Magnetism
48	Physical changes of matter
49	Explanations of physical changes
50	Kinetic molecular theory
51	Quantum theory and fundamental particles
52	Chemical changes of matter
53	Explanations of chemical changes

TIMSS Teacher Survey Categories

#	Label
6	Life cycles and genetics
6	Life cycles and genetics
6	Life cycles and genetics
6	Life cycles and genetics
7	Interactions of living things
7	Interactions of living things
7	Interactions of living things
7	Interactions of living things
8	Human biology and health
8	Human biology and health
8	Human biology and health
9	Types and properties of matter
9	Types and properties of matter
9	Types and properties of matter
10	Structure of matter
10	Structure of matter
10	Structure of matter
11	Energy, types, sources, conversions
12	Energy processes
12	Energy processes
12	Energy processes
12	Energy processes
12	Energy processes
12	Energy processes
13	Physical changes
13	Physical changes
14	Kinetic and quantum theory
14	Kinetic and quantum theory
15	Chemical changes
15	Chemical changes

Content-Specific Subtests

#	Label
6	Life cycles and genetics
6	Life cycles and genetics
6	Life cycles and genetics
7	Interactions of living things
7	Interactions of living things
8	Human biology and health
9	Properties and classification of matter
9	Properties and classification of matter
9	Properties and classification of matter
10	Structure of matter
11	Energy and physical processes
11	Energy and physical processes
11	Energy and physical processes
11	Energy and physical processes
11	Energy and physical processes
11	Energy and physical processes
11	Energy and physical processes
12	Physical changes
12	Physical changes
13	Chemical changes

Appendix C

TIMSS FRAMEWORK CODES AND NUMBER OF ITEMS FOR EACH MATHEMATICS AND SCIENCE TEST SUBAREA

Mathematics—Population 2

	Scale Title	# of Items	TIMSS Framework Codes
1	Whole numbers	5	1111 and 1112
2	Common fractions	24	1121
3	Decimal fractions and percents	15	1122 and 1124
4	Relations of fractions	10	1123
5	Estimating quantity and size	9	1151, 1153
6	Rounding	5	1152
7	Estimating computations	7	1153
8	Measurement units	8	121
9	Perimeter, area, and volume	11	122
10	Measurement estimations and errors	7	123
11	2-D geometry	7	131, 132
12	Polygons and circles	5	133
13	3-D geometry and transformations	6	134, 141
14	Congruence and similarity	6	142
15	Proportionality concepts	7	151
16	Proportionality problems	12	152
17	Patterns, relations, and functions	8	161
18	Equations and formulas	27	162, 1133, 1142
19	Data representation and analysis	13	171
20	Uncertainty and probability	7	172

Science—Population 2

	Scale Title	# of Items	TIMSS Framework Codes
1	Earth features	12	1112–1115
2	Earth processes	8	112
3	Earth in the universe	5	1131, 1133
4	Diversity and structure of living things	16	1212–1215
5	Life processes and functions	16	1221, 1222
6	Life cycles and genetics	5	1231–1234
7	Interactions of living things	4	1243, 1244
8	Human biology and health	16	125
9	Properties and classification of matter	11	131
10	Structure of matter	5	1321
11	Energy and physical processes	27	133
12	Physical changes	4	1341, 1342
13	Chemical changes	12	1351, 1354
14	Forces and motion	6	1361, 1362, 1363, 1365
15	Science, technology, and society	3	1431
16	Environmental and resource issues	7	161, 162, 163
17	Scientific processes	8	No content

SUPPLEMENTAL MATERIAL RELATED TO THE TWO-LEVEL ANALYSIS OF MATHEMATICS ACHIEVEMENT: CHAPTER TEN

The data for the two-level analysis are from the U.S. eighth grade students and their mathematics teachers who participated in TIMSS Population 2. The two levels are students and classes (identified by teachers). The student sample consists of 6,946 students from 337 classes and 178 schools. Only 234 classes can be linked to valid teacher data. Generally, missing data points for the student-level variables were replaced by corresponding class means. Exceptions were ethnicity, highest level of parent's education, number of vehicles family owned, and number of books in home for which missing values were replaced by the class mode. Also, the class median was used to replace missing values for the number of people in home.

Classroom Level Regressions
Estimated Coefficient and Standard Error (β; SE)

	Whole Numbers	Common Fractions	Decimal Fractions and Percents	Relations of Fractions	Estimating Quantity and Size	Rounding	Estimating Computations	Measurement Units	Perimeter, Area, and Volume	Measurement Estimations and Errors
Squared multiple correlation	.5185**	.6096**	.6323**	.5154**	.4935**	.3774**	.5652**	.4716**	.5892**	.5759**
Prior achievement	.14 (.05)**	.20 (.05)**	.14 (.05)**	.20 (.04)**	.24 (.05)**	.04 (.04)	.14 (.04)**	.13 (.05)**	.28 (.05)**	.12 (.05)**
SES adjustment	5.57 (.56)**	6.88 (.60)**	9.45 (.61)**	6.21 (.51)**	10.16 (1.04)**	3.48 (.34)**	6.46 (.50)**	5.64 (.47)**	8.71 (.74)**	7.31 (.54)**
Teacher time spent on										
Whole numbers	−1.15 (.54)**									
Fractions and decimals		−1.83 (.95)*								
Percentages			−2.57 (1.42)*							
Integers, rational, and real numbers				1.47 (.85)*	2.49 (1.26)**	.50 (.29)*	1.30 (.67)*			
Estimation					−6.93 (1.98)**	−.48 (.47)				
Measurement units								1.18 (.94)		
Perimeter, area, volume									−1.55 (1.60)	3.43 (1.24)**

	Whole Numbers	Common Fractions	Decimal Fractions and Percents	Relations of Fractions	Estimating Quantity and Size	Rounding	Estimating Computations	Measurement Units	Perimeter, Area, and Volume	Measurement Estimations and Errors
Measurement estimations										
2-D coordinate geometry									6.83 (1.59)**	−4.48 (1.95)**
Congruence and similarity										
Proportionality										
Relations and functions										
Equations and formulas	1.78 (.38)**	3.64 (1.47)**								
Data representation and analysis										
Probability										
Root mean squares	.35	1.30	.80	.60	.89	.21	.48	.46	.86	.59
Model degrees of freedom	4	4	3	3	4	4	3	3	4	4
Error degrees of freedom	229	229	230	230	229	229	230	230	229	229

**$p \leq .05$

*$.05 < p \leq .10$

	2-D Geometry	Polygons and Circles	3-D Geometry and Transformations	Congruence and Similarity	Proportionality Concepts	Proportionality Problems	Patterns, Relations, and Functions	Equations and Formulas	Data Representation and Analysis	Uncertainty and Probability
Squared multiple correlation	.4666**	.3938**	.4513**	.4289**	.4158**	.5682**	.5716**	.6212**	.6135**	.5640**
Prior achievement	.21 (.05)**	.18 (.05)**	.26 (.06)**	.22 (.05)**	.33 (.06)**	.19 (.06)**	.19 (.05)**	.17 (.06)**	.17 (.04)**	.11 (.05)**
SES adjustment	8.50 (.84)**	4.71 (.58)**	5.28 (.59)**	4.83 (.46)**	6.44 (.87)**	5.80 (.49)**	8.56 (.78)**	6.93 (.57)**	6.19 (.43)**	6.97 (.56)**
Teacher time spent on										
Whole numbers										
Fractions and decimals									−.74 (.41)*	
Percentages										
Integer, rational, and real numbers										
Estimation										
Measurement units										
Perimeter, area, volume										
Measurement estimations										
2-D coordinate geometry	3.91 (.92)**	2.13 (.59)**	5.22 (1.25)**							
Congruence and similarity				1.95 (1.15)*						
Proportionality					3.21 (.96)**	7.53 (2.25)**				
Relations and functions							3.23 (1.18)**	6.31 (2.50)**		
Equations and formulas							2.99 (.65)**	4.86 (1.41)**		
Data representation and analysis									−1.58 (1.75)	
Probability										−.55 (1.49)
Root mean squares	.51	.32	.69	.47	.36	.85	.61	1.28	.82	.58
Model degrees of freedom	3	3	3	3	3	3	4	4	3	4
Error degrees of freedom	230	230	230	230	230	230	229	229	230	229

**p ≤ .05 *.05 < p ≤ .10

Student Level Regressions
Estimated Coefficients

Predictors	Whole Numbers	Common Fractions	Decimal Fractions and Percents	Relations of Fractions	Estimating Quantity and Size	Rounding	Estimating Computations	Measurement Units	Perimeter, Area, and Volume	Measurement Estimation and Errors	2-D Geometry	Polygons and Circles	3-D Geometry and Transformations	Congruence and Similarity	Proportionality Concepts	Proportionality Problems	Patterns, Relations, and Functions	Equations and Formulas	Data Representation and Analysis	Uncertainty and Probability
Age	-.016	-.134	-.051	-.088	-.072	.000	-.056	.005	-.028	-.086	.022	.017	-.010	-.048	-.043	-.082	-.034	-.154	-.100	-.003
Gender	.047	.277	.091	.199	.175	-.037	.013	.124	.228	.142	.063	-.031	.088	-.032	.071	.310	.011	.164	.058	.082
White	.135	.123	.129	.131	-.109	.063	.018	.015	.073	.096	-.023	-.103	.125	-.193	.030	.012	.259	.269	.017	.096
Black	.059	-.188	-.115	-.060	-.254	-.105	-.139	-.167	-.125	-.073	-.086	-.156	-.243	-.338	-.035	-.256	.056	-.105	-.323	-.183
Hispanic	.058	-.185	-.111	.083	-.248	-.014	-.064	-.176	-.072	-.014	-.127	-.172	-.018	-.267	-.023	.203	.217	.025	-.311	-.019
Asian	.028	.031	-.032	.186	-.138	.063	.072	-.027	-.004	.173	.115	.047	.045	-.061	-.052	-.186	.080	.360	.008	.187
Native American	.288	.270	.140	.156	.150	-.086	-.001	-.029	.294	.056	.003	-.012	.026	-.164	.066	.108	.307	.167	.032	-.166
Number of vehicles family owned	-.012	-.200	-.083	-.006	-.069	.002	-.065	-.040	-.046	-.101	.003	.012	-.018	-.017	-.027	-.049	-.024	-.164	-.066	-.073
Number of educational processions (calculator, computer, desk, dictionary, atlas, encyclopedia set)	-.006	-.007	.000	.008	-.016	.002	.042	-.002	-.019	-.002	-.002	.010	.025	.040	-.010	.011	-.028	-.019	.029	-.007
Number of recreational processions (CD player, stereo, answering machine, camcorder, video game, VCR, Walkman)	-.003	.022	-.011	-.002	-.014	-.007	-.003	-.003	.004	.007	-.012	-.021	-.030	-.007	.010	.008	.007	.033	-.042	.025
Do well in math (sum of mother's, friend's, and self)	.009	.034	.026	.002	.038	.002	-.006	.010	.014	.009	.026	.014	.021	.003	-.010	.023	.017	.027	.057	.021
Educational expectations	.091	.298	.092	.160	.058	.020	.077	.108	.144	.078	.018	.025	.059	.092	.080	.140	.078	.333	.243	.065
Number of adults in home	-.016	-.090	-.029	-.002	-.029	.011	.000	.000	-.045	-.026	-.006	-.042	-.013	-.044	-.010	-.058	-.012	-.020	-.016	-.047
Number of people in home	-.004	-.036	.012	.009	-.011	-.011	-.014	-.014	.018	-.009	.001	.008	.001	.036	.007	.024	.018	.032	.015	.001
Highest level of parent's education	.002	.072	.095	.137	-.011	.024	-.009	.025	.076	.040	.032	.032	-.034	.030	.039	.131	.077	.171	.073	-.008
Number of books in home	.012	.193	.080	.093	.102	.020	.017	-.018	.059	.087	.072	.036	.040	.038	-.032	.153	.058	.187	.116	.077
Percent time spent in educational activities	.225	-.227	-.142	-.176	-.111	-.071	.076	.153	.461	.040	-.069	.006	-.234	.028	.017	-.022	-.040	-.331	-.216	.036
Percent time spent reading	.449	1.050	.917	-.026	.220	.123	.539	.478	.354	.314	.125	.274	.044	.337	.322	1.293	.427	.858	1.143	.538
Root mean squares	.89	2.00	1.57	1.25	1.36	.68	1.17	1.19	1.28	1.20	1.09	.85	1.14	1.10	.73	1.59	1.30	1.46	1.95	1.16

Variable Definitions

Description of the Variable	Question Number on the Student Background Questionnaire	Items in the Released Database Used	Metric
Age	1 (On what date were you born?)	BSDAGE:	in years (age when TIMSS test was administered)
Gender	2a (Are you a boy or a girl?)	BSBGSEX	1–2 (1 = girl, 2 = boy)
White	2b (Which best describes you . . .)	answered A to BSBGA2B	0–1 (1 = White, 0 = otherwise)
Black	2b	answered B to BSBGA2B	0–1 (1 = Black, 0 = otherwise)
Hispanic	2b	answered C to BSBGA2B	0–1 (1 = Hispanic, 0 = otherwise)
Asian	2b	answered D to BSBGA2B	0–1 (1 = Asian/Pacific Islander, 0 = otherwise)
Native American	2b	answered E to BSBGA2B	0–1 (1 = American Indian/Alaskan Native, 0 = otherwise)
Number of vehicles family owned	12 (Do you have any of these items at your home?)	Count of yes answers to BSBGPS08, BSBGPS11	0–2
Number of educational processions (calculator, computer, desk, dictionary, atlas, encyclopedia set)	12	Count of yes answers to BSBGPS01, (BSBGPS02 or BSBGPS16), BSBGPS03, BSBGPS04, BSBGPS05, BSBGPS06	0–6
Number of recreational processions (CD player, stereo, answering machine, camcorder, video game, VCR, walkman)	12	Count of yes answers to BSBGPS07, BSBGPS09, BSBGPS10, BSBGPS12, BSBGPS13, BSBGPS14, BSBGPS15	0–7
Do well in math (sum of mother's, friend's and self)	13 (My mother thinks), 15 (Most of my friends think . . .), 16 (I think) . . . it is important for me to do well in mathematics in school.	Sum of BSBMMIP2, BSBMFIP2, BSBMSIP2	3–12 (Each item is reflected so that high score of the sum corresponds to agreement.)

Description of the Variable	Question Number on the Student Background Questionnaire	Items in the Released Database Used	Metric
Educational expectation	9 (How far in school do you expect to go?)	BSBGEDUS	1-6 (1 = primary education, 6 = college graduated)
Number of adults in home	7 (Does each of these people live at home with you most or all of the time?, mother, father, etc.)	Count of yes answers to BSBGADU1, BSBGADU2, BSBGADU5, BSBGADU6, BSBGADU7, BSBGADU8, BSBGADU9	0-7
Number of people in home	8 (Altogether, how many people live in your home? (including yourself)	BSBGHOME	2-17
Highest level of parent's education	9 (How far in school did your mother and father go?)	Highest of BSBGEDUM, BSBGEDUF	1-6 (1 = primary education, 6 = college graduated)
Number of books in home	11 (About how many books are there in your home?)	BSBGBOOK	0-1 (0 = enough to fill one or less bookcase, 1 = enough to fill two or more bookcases)
Percent time spent in educational activities	6 (On a normal school day, how much time to you spend before and after school doing each of these things? Watching TV, playing computer games, talking to friends, doing jobs at home, playing sports, reading, studying, or doing homework in mathematics, science, or other subjects)	Rescale of the sum of recorded BSBGDAY7 (studying math), BSBGDAY8 (studying science), BSBGDAY9 (studying other school subjects)	0-100% of total weekly time based on all 9 parts of question 6 (A time value is assigned to each of the 5 response categories: 0 = no time, 0.5 = less than 1 hour, 1.5 = 1-2 hours, 4 = 3.5 hours, 5 = more than 5 hours)
Percent time spent reading		Rescale of the recorded BSBGDAY6 (reading a book for enjoyment)	

REFERENCES

Achilles, C.M. (1998, April). *If not before: At least now.* Paper presented at the annual meeting of the American Educational Research Association, San Diego, CA.

Adams, R.J., Wu, M.L., & Macaskill, G. (1998). Scaling methodology and procedures for the mathematics and science scales. In M.O. Martin & D.L. Kelly (Eds.), *Third International Mathematics and Science Study Technical Report, Volume II: Implementation and Analysis—Primary and Middle School Years* (pp. 111–146). Chestnut Hill, MA: Center for the Study of Testing, Evaluation, and Educational Policy, Boston College.

Anderson, J., Hollinger, D., & Conaty, J. (1993). Re-examining the relationship between school poverty and student achievement. *ERS Spectrum, 11*(2), 21–31.

Apple, M.W. (1990). *Ideology and curriculum* (2nd ed.). New York: Routledge.

———. (1996). Power, meaning, and identity: Critical sociology of education in the United States. *British Journal of Sociology of Education, 17*(2), 125–144.

Beaton, A.E., Martin, M.O., Mullis, I., Gonzalez, E.J., Smith, T.A., & Kelly, D.L. (1996). *Science achievement in the middle school years: IEA's Third International Mathematics and Science Study.* Chestnut Hill, MA: Center for the Study of Testing, Evaluation, and Educational Policy, Boston College.

Beaton, A.E., Mullis, I., Martin, M.O., Gonzalez, E.J., Kelly, D.L., & Smith, T.A. (1996). *Mathematics achievement in the middle school years: IEA's Third International Mathematics and Science Study.* Chestnut Hill, MA: Center for the Study of Testing, Evaluation, and Educational Policy, Boston College.

Beyer, L.E., & Apple, M.W. (Eds.). (1998). *The curriculum: Problems, politics, and possibilities* (2nd ed.). Albany: State University of New York Press.

Bock, R.D. (1975). *Multivariate statistical methods in behavioral research.* New York: McGraw-Hill.

Bockarie, A. (1993). Mathematics in the Mende culture: Its general implication for mathematics teaching. *School Science and Mathematics, 93*(4), 208–211.

Bond, G.C. (1981). Social economic status and educational achievement: A review article. *Anthropology and Education Quarterly, 12*(4), 227–257.

Britton, E.D., & Raizen, S. (Eds.). (1996). *Examining the examinations: A comparison of science and mathematics examinations for college-bound students in seven countries.* Dordrecht/Boston/London: Kluwer.

Bryk, A.S., & Raudenbush, S.W. (1992). *Hierarchical linear models: Applications and data analysis methods.* Newbury Park, CA: Sage.

Burstein, L. (Ed.). (1993). *The IEA study of mathematics III: Student growth and classroom processes* (Vol. 3). Oxford, UK: Pergamon Press.

Cogan, L.S., Schmidt, W.H., & Wiley, D.E. (forthcoming article). Who takes what math and in which track? Using TIMSS to characterize learning opportunities in eighth grade.

Coleman, J.S., Campbell, E.Q., Hobson, C.J., McPartland, J., Mood, A.M., Weinfeld, F.D., & York, R.L. (1966). *Equality of educational opportunity.* Washington, DC: National Center for Educational Statistics.

Eccles, J.S., & Midgley, C. (1989). Stage-environment fit: Developmentally appropriate classrooms for young adolescents. In C. Ames & R. Ames (Eds.), *Research on motivation in education* (Vol. 3, *Goals and Cognitions,* pp. 139–186). San Diego: Academic Press.

Emerson, J.D., & Hoaglin, D.C. (1983a). Analysis of two-way tables by medians. In D.C. Hoaglin, F. Mosteller & J.W. Tukey (Eds.), *Understanding robust and exploratory data analysis* (pp. 166–210). New York: John Wiley & Sons.

———. (1983b). Resistant lines for *y* versus *x*. In D.C. Hoaglin, F. Mosteller & J.W. Tukey (Eds.), *Understanding robust and exploratory data analysis* (pp. 129–165). New York: John Wiley & Sons.

Floden, R.E., Porter, A.C., Schmidt, W.H., Freeman, D.J., & Schwille, J.R. (1981). Responses to curriculum pressures: A policy-capturing study of teacher decisions about content. *Journal of Educational Psychology, 73*(2), 129–141.

Foy, P., Rust, K., & Schleicher, A. (1996). Sample design. In M.O. Martin & D.L. Kelly (Eds.), *Third International Mathematics and Science Study technical report* (Vol. I: *Design and Development,* pp. 4–1 to 4–17). Chestnut Hill, MA: Boston College.

Foy, P., & Schleicher, A. (1994). *Sampling manual—Version 4* (ICC439/NPC117). Chestnut Hill, MA: Third International Mathematics and Science Study (TIMSS), Boston College.

Gamoran, A., Porter, A.C., Smithson, J., & White, P.A. (1997). Upgrading high school mathematics instruction: Improving learning opportunities for low-achieving, low-income youth. *Educational Evaluation and Policy Analysis, 19*(4), 325–338.

Haertel, E.H., Thrash, W.A., & Wiley, D.E. (1978). *Metric-free distributional comparisons.* Chicago: Central Educational Midwestern Regional Educational Laboratory (CEMREL), ML-GROUP for Policy Studies in Education.

Hanushek, E.A. (1997). Outcomes, incentives, and beliefs: Reflections on analysis of the economics of schools. *Educational Evaluation and Policy Analysis, 19*(4), 301–308.

Herrnstein, R.J., & Murray, C. (1994). *The bell curve: Intelligence and class structure in American life.* New York: The Free Press.

Houang, R.T., Wiley, D.E., & Schmidt, W.H. (2000, April). A two-way regression model for cross-country analyses of curriculum and achievement. In W.H. Schmidt (Chair), *Methodological issues in studying the relationship of curriculum and achievement: Illustrations from the Third International Mathematics and Science Study (TIMSS).* Symposium conducted at the annual meeting of the American Educational Researchers Association, New Orleans, LA.

Husen, T. (1982, February). *A cross-national perspective on assessing the quality of learning.* Paper presented at the meeting of the National Commission on Excellence in Education, Washington, DC.

Jackson, P.W. (1992). Conceptions of curriculum and curriculum specialists. In P.W. Jackson (Ed.), *Handbook of research on curriculum* (pp. 3–40). New York: Macmillan.

Jakwerth, P.M. (1996). Evaluating content validity in cross-national achievement tests. Unpublished Ph.D. dissertation, Michigan State University, East Lansing.

———. (1997, March). Domain definitions for curriculum-sensitive tests: Improving the content validity of cross-national assessments. In E. Owen (Chair), *Validity in cross-national assessments: Pitfalls and possibilities.* Symposium conducted at the annual meeting of the American Educational Research Association, Chicago, IL.

Jakwerth, P.M., & Wolfe, R.G. (1997, March). Evaluating test-to-curriculum match: Indices of content validity for curriculum-sensitive assessment. In E. Owen (Chair), *Validity in cross-national assessments: Pitfalls and possibilities.* Symposium conducted at the annual meeting of the American Educational Research Association, Chicago, IL.

Lave, J. (1988). *Cognition in practice: Mind, mathematics and culture in everyday life.* New York: Cambridge University Press.

———. (1990). Views of the classroom: Implications for math and science learning research. In M. Gardner, J.G. Greeno, F. Reif, A.H. Schoenfeld, A. Disessa & E. Stage (Eds.), *Toward a scientific practice of science education* (pp. 251–263). Hillsdale, NJ: Lawrence Erlbaum.

Littell, R.C., Milliken, G.A., Stroup, W.W., & Wolfinger, R.D. (1996). *SAS® system for mixed models.* Cary, NC: SAS Institute.

Lord, F.M. (1965). A strong true-score theory, with applications. *Psychometrika, 30*(3), 239–270.

———. (1969). Estimating true-score distributions in psychological testing: An empirical Bayes estimation problem. *Psychometrika, 34*(3), 259–299.

Martin, J.R. (1996). There's too much to teach: Cultural wealth in an age of scarcity. *Educational Researcher, 25*(2), 4–10.

Martin, M.O., & Kelly, D.L. (Eds.). (1996). *Technical report volume I: Design and development.* Chestnut Hill, MA: Center for the Study of Testing, Evaluation, and Educational Policy, Boston College.

———. (Eds.). (1997). *Technical report volume II: Implementation and analysis—Primary and middle school years.* Chestnut Hill, MA: Center for the Study of Testing, Evaluation, and Educational Policy, Boston College.

———. (Eds.). (1998). *Technical report volume III: Implementation and Analysis—Final Year of Secondary School.* Chestnut Hill, MA: Center for the Study of Testing, Evaluation, and Educational Policy, Boston College.

Martin, M.O., Mullis, I., Beaton, A.E., Gonzalez, E.J., Kelly, D.L., & Smith, T.A. (1997). *Science achievement in the primary school years: IEA's Third International Mathematics and Science Study.* Chestnut Hill, MA: Center for the Study of Testing, Evaluation, and Educational Policy, Boston College.

McCaslin, M., & Good, T.L. (1993). Classroom management and motivated student learning. In T.M. Tomlinson (Ed.), *Motivating students to learn: Overcoming barriers to high achievement* (pp. 245–261). Berkeley, CA: McCutchan.

McKnight, C.C., Britton, E.D., Valverde, G.A., & Schmidt, W.H. (1992). *Document analysis manual* (Survey of Mathematics and Science Opportunities Research Report Series, #42). East Lansing: Michigan State University.

McKnight, C.C., Crosswhite, F.J., Dossey, J.A., Kifer, E., Swafford, J.O., Travers, K.J., & Cooney, T.J. (1987). *The underachieving curriculum: Assessing U.S. school mathematics from an international perspective.* Champaign, IL: Stipes Publishing Company.

McKnight, C.C., Schmidt, W.H., & Raizen, S.A. (1993). *Test blueprints: A description of the TIMSS' achievement test content design* (Doc. Ref. ICC797/NRC357). Chestnut Hill, MA: TIMSS International Study Center.

Mullis, I., Martin, M.O., Beaton, A.E., Gonzalez, E.J., Kelly, D.L., & Smith, T.A. (1997). *Mathematics achievement in the primary school years: IEA's Third International Mathematics and Science Study.* Chestnut Hill, MA: Center for the Study of Testing, Evaluation, and Educational Policy, Boston College.

Mullis, I., Martin, M.O., Beaton, A.E., Gonzalez, E.J., Kelly, D.L., & Smith, T.A. (1998). *Mathematics and science achievement in the final year of secondary school: IEA's Third International Mathematics and Science Study.* Chestnut Hill, MA: Center for the Study of Testing, Evaluation, and Educational Policy, Boston College.

National Center for Education Statistics. (1996). *Pursuing excellence: A study of U.S. eighth-grade mathematics and science teaching, learning, curriculum, and achievement in international context* (NCES 97–198). Washington DC: U.S. Department of Education, National Center for Education Statistics.

Pate-Bain, H., Boyd-Zaharias, J., Cain, V.A., Word, E., & Binkley, M.E. (1997). *STAR follow-up studies, 1996–1997: The student/teacher achievement ratio (STAR) project.* Lebanon, TN: HEROS.

Porter, A.C., Archbald, D.A., & Tyree, A.K. (1991). Reforming the curriculum: Will empowerment policies replace control? In S.H. Fuhrman & B. Malen (Eds.), *The politics of curriculum and testing: The 1990 yearbook of the Politics of Education Association.* London/New York: Falmer Press.

Puma, M.J., Karweit, N., Price, C., Ricciuti, A., Thompson, W., & Vaden-Kiernan, M. (1997). *Prospects: Student outcomes. Final report.* Cambridge, MA.: Abt Associates.

Raudenbush, S.W., Fotiu, R.P., & Cheong, Y.F. (1998). Inequality of access to educational resources: A national report card for eighth-grade math. *Educational Evaluation and Policy Analysis, 20*(4), 253–267.

Ravitch, D. (1985). *The schools we deserve: Reflections on the educational crises of our times.* New York: Basic Books.

———. (Ed.). (1995a). *Debating the future of American education: Do we need national standards and assessments?* Washington, DC: Brookings Institution.

———. (1995b). *National standards in American education: A citizen's guide.* Washington, DC: Brookings Institution.

———. (2000). *Left back: A century of failed school reforms.* New York: Simon & Schuster.

Resnick, L.B., & Klopfer, L.E. (Eds.). (1989). *Toward the thinking curriculum: Current cognitive research.* Alexandria, VA: Association for Supervision and Curriculum Development.

Robitaille, D.F., Schmidt, W.H., Raizen, S., McKnight, C., Britton, E., & Nicol, C. (1993). *Curriculum frameworks for mathematics and science* (TIMSS Monograph No. 1). Vancouver, BC: Pacific Educational Press.

Rubin, D.B. (1987). *Multiple imputation for nonresponse in surveys.* New York: John Wiley & Sons.

Saxe, G.B. (1985). Effects of schooling on arithmetical understandings: Studies with Oksapmin children in Papua New Guinea. *Journal of Educational Psychology, 77*(5), 503–513.

———. (1988). The mathematics of child street vendors. *Child Development, 59,* 1415–1425.

———. (1990). The interplay between children's learning in school and out-of-school contexts. In M. Gardner, J.G. Greeno, F. Reif, A.H. Schoenfeld, A. Disessa & E. Stage (Eds.), *Toward a scientific practice of science education* (pp. 219–234). Hillsdale: Lawrence Erlbaum.

Schmidt, W.H., & Burstein, L. (1993). Concomitants of growth in mathematics achievement during the population A school year. In L. Burstein (Ed.), *The IEA study of mathematics III: Student growth and classroom processes* (Vol. 3, pp. 309–327). Oxford, UK: Pergamon Press.

Schmidt, W.H., Jakwerth, P.M., & McKnight, C.C. (1998). Curriculum-sensitive assessment: Content *does* make a difference. *International Journal of Educational Research, 29*(6), 503–527.

Schmidt, W.H., Jorde, D., Cogan, L.S., Barrier, E., Gonzalo, I., Moser, U., Shimizu, K., Sawada, T., Valverde, G., McKnight, C., Prawat, R., Wiley, D.E., Raizen, S., Britton, E.D., & Wolfe, R.G. (1996). *Characterizing pedagogical flow: An investigation of mathematics and science teaching in six countries.* Dordrecht/Boston/London: Kluwer.

Schmidt, W.H., & Kifer, E. (1989). Exploring relationships across population A systems: A search for patterns. In D.F. Robitaille & R.A. Garden (Eds.), *The IEA study of mathematics II: Contexts and outcomes of school mathematics* (Vol. 2, pp. 209–231). Oxford, UK: Pergamon Press.

Schmidt, W.H., McKnight, C., Cogan, L.S., Jakwerth, P.M., & Houang, R.T. (1999). *Facing the consequences: Using TIMSS for a closer look at U.S. mathematics and science education.* Dordrecht/Boston/London: Kluwer.

Schmidt, W.H., McKnight, C., & Raizen, S. (1997). *A splintered vision: An investigation of U.S. science and mathematics education.* Dordrecht/Boston/London: Kluwer.

Schmidt, W.H., McKnight, C., Valverde, G.A., Houang, R.T., & Wiley, D.E. (1997). *Many visions, many aims, volume I: A cross-national investigation of curricular intentions in school mathematics.* Dordrecht/Boston/London: Kluwer.

Schmidt, W.H., & Prawat, R.S. (1999). What does the Third International Mathematics and Science Study tell us about where to draw the line in the top-down versus bottom-up debate? *Educational Evaluation and Policy Analysis, 21*(1), 85–91.

Schmidt, W.H., Raizen, S.A., Britton, E.D., Bianchi, L.J., & Wolfe, R.G. (1997). *Many visions, many aims, volume II: A cross-national investigation of curricular intentions in school science.* Dordrecht/Boston/London: Kluwer.

Schweinhart, L.J., Weikart, D.P., & Larner, M.B. (1986). Consequences of three preschool curriculum models through age 15. *Early Childhood Research Quarterly, 1*(1), 15–45.

Schwille, J., Porter, A., Belli, G., Floden, R., Freeman, D., Knappen, L., Kuhs, T., & Schmidt, W. (1983). Teachers as policy brokers in the content of elementary school mathematics. In L.S. Shulman & G. Sykes (Eds.), *Handbook of teaching and policy* (pp. 370–391). New York: Longman.

Sears, J.T., with Carper, J.C. (Eds.). (1998). *Curriculum, religion, and public education: Conversations for an enlarging public square.* New York: Teachers College Press.

Secada, W.G. (1992). Race, ethnicity, social class, language, and achievement in mathematics. In D.A. Grouws (Ed.), *Handbook of research on mathematics teaching and learning* (pp. 623–660). New York: Macmillan.

Stevenson, D.L., & Baker, D.P. (1991). State control of the curriculum and classroom instruction. *Sociology of Education, 64*(1), 1–10.

———. (1996). Does state control of the curriculum matter? A response to Westbury and Hsu. *Educational Evaluation and Policy Analysis, 18*(4), 339–342.

Stevenson, D.L., Schiller, K.S., & Schneider, B. (1994). Sequences of opportunities of learning. *Sociology of Education, 67*(3), 184–198.

Stevenson, H.W., & Stigler, J.W. (1992). *The learning gap.* New York: Simon & Schuster.

Survey of Mathematics and Science Opportunities. (1991a). *Mathematics curriculum framework* (Survey of Mathematics and Science Opportunities Research Report Series, #14). East Lansing: Michigan State University.

———. (1991b). *Science curriculum framework* (Survey of Mathematics and Science Opportunities Research Report Series, #13). East Lansing: Michigan State University.

———. (1993). *A description of the TIMSS' achievement test content design: Test blueprints* (Survey of Mathematics and Science Opportunities Research Report Series, #59). East Lansing: Michigan State University.

Suter, L.E. (forthcoming). Is student achievement immutable? Evidence from international studies on schooling and student achievement. *Review of Educational Research.*

Sweetland, S.R. (1996). Human capital theory: Foundations of a field of inquiry. *Review of Educational Research, 66*(3), 341–359.

Timar, T., Kirp, D., & Kirst, M. (1998). *Institutionalizing mathematics and science reform: Do state education agencies matter?* San Francisco: WestEd.

Valverde, G.A., Bianchi, L.J., Houang, R.T., Schmidt, W.H., & Wolfe, R.G. (forthcoming). *According to the book: Using TIMSS to investigate the transition from policy to pedagogy in the world of textbooks.* Dordrecht/Boston/London: Kluwer.

Valverde, G.A., & Schmidt, W.H. (2000). Greater expectations: Learning from other nations in the quest for 'world-class standards' in US school mathematics and science. *Journal of Curriculum Studies, 32*(5), 651–687.

Walker, D.F., & Schaffarzick, J. (1974). Comparing curricula. *Review of Educational Research, 44*(1), 83–111.

Wang, H.A., & Schmidt, W.H. (2001). History, philosophy and sociology of science in science education: Results from the Third International Mathematics and Science Study. *Journal of Science & Education, 10*(1), 51–70.

Wang, J. (1998). Opportunity to learn: The impacts and policy implications. *Educational Evaluation and Policy Analysis, 20*(3), 137–156.

Wenglinsky, H. (1997). How money matters: The effect of school district spending on academic achievement. *Sociology of Education, 70*(3), 221–237.

Wiley, D.E., & Wolfe, R.G. (1992). Major survey design issues for the IEA Third International Mathematics and Science Study. *Prospects, 22*(3), 297–304.

Wolfe, R., & Wiley, D. (1992). *Sampling plan* (ICC438/NPC116). Vancouver, BC: Third International Mathematics and Science Study (TIMSS).

Young, D.J., & Fraser, B.J. (1993). Socioeconomic and gender effects on science achievement: An Australian perspective. *School Effectiveness and School Improvement, 4*(4), 265–289.

Young, M.F.D. (1998). *The curriculum of the future: from the 'New sociology of education' to a critical theory of learning.* London/Philadelphia: Falmer Press.

INDEX